TURNING POINTS
IN THE EXPANSION
OF CHRISTIANITY

TURNING POINTS

IN THE EXPANSION OF CHRISTIANITY

- - - - - - - - - - - - -

From Pentecost to the Present

ALICE T. OTT

𝕭
Baker Academic
a division of Baker Publishing Group
Grand Rapids, Michigan

Published by Baker Academic
a division of Baker Publishing Group
PO Box 6287, Grand Rapids, MI 49516-6287
www.bakeracademic.com

Printed in the United States of America

Library of Congress Cataloging-in-Publication Data
Names: Ott, Alice T., author.
Title: Turning points in the expansion of Christianity : from Pentecost to the present / Alice T. Ott.
Description: Grand Rapids : Baker Academic, a division of Baker Publishing Group, [2021] | Includes bibliographical references and index.
Identifiers: LCCN 2021023586 | ISBN 9780801099960 (paperback) | ISBN 9781540964588 (casebound) | ISBN 9781493432486 (ebook) | ISBN 9781493432493 (adobe pdf) | ISBN 9781493432509 (ebook other)
Subjects: LCSH: Missions—History. | Church history.
Classification: LCC BV2100 .O88 2021 | DDC 266—dc23
LC record available at https://lccn.loc.gov/2021023586

21 22 23 24 25 26 27   7 6 5 4 3 2 1

To Craig,
my partner in life and ministry

Contents

Sidebars

Acknowledgments

I would like to express my sincere appreciation for those who have supported or contributed to the completion of this book. This includes my students and colleagues at Trinity Evangelical Divinity School, who have challenged and stimulated my thinking on numerous aspects of the project. Dr. Harold Netland deserves special thanks for his helpful bibliography on world religions. I am also indebted to those individuals who provided feedback on all or part of the manuscript. Jim Kinney and Brandy Scritchfield on the editorial team at Baker Academic read and critiqued several early chapters of the book. They, along with my editor, Eric Salo, provided the necessary help and support to bring the project to fruition. As an outside reader, Dr. Brian Stanley went above and beyond the call of duty. He thoroughly read the whole manuscript and provided valuable feedback on how to improve the book, for which I am truly grateful. Finally, this book would not exist without the support of my husband, Dr. Craig Ott. He encouraged me to write the book and interacted with me frequently throughout the research and writing process. Many thanks to you all!

Abbreviations

General

ca. circa
d. died
r. reigned

Acronyms

ABCFM American Board of Commissioners for Foreign Missions
ABMU American Baptist Missionary Union
AMS African Missionary Society
APM American Presbyterian Mission
BEIC British East India Company
BFBS British and Foreign Bible Society
BMS Baptist Missionary Society
CES Chinese Evangelization Society
CIM China Inland Mission
CMS Church Missionary Society
DEIC Dutch East India Company
ECWA Evangelical Church of West Africa (before 2011); Evangelical Church Winning All (after 2011)
EH *Ecclesiastical History* by Venerable Bede
EMS Evangelical Missionary Society
EMSB Evangelical Missionary Society of Basel

IAC International Association of the Congo
IBEAC Imperial British East Africa Company
IMC International Missionary Council
IURD Igreja Universal do Reino Deus (Universal Church of the Kingdom of God)
JETS *Journal of the Evangelical Theological Society*
KRIM Korea Research Institute for Mission
KWMA Korean World Missions Association
LC Lausanne Covenant
LCWE Lausanne Congress on World Evangelization
LMS London Missionary Society
NEMA Nigeria Evangelical Mission Association
PCK Presbyterian Church of Korea
SC Serampore Covenant
SIM Sudan Interior Mission
SPCK Society for Promoting Christian Knowledge
UMCA Universities Mission to Central Africa
WCC World Council of Churches
WMC World Missionary Conference

Introduction

Before his ascension, Jesus commissioned his disciples to "make disciples of all nations," to baptize them in the name of the triune God, and to teach them to follow his commandments (Matt. 28:16–20). Then, in his final words, Jesus told his fearful disciples to tarry in Jerusalem until they had been endued with power from on high. The Holy Spirit would enable them to be his "witnesses in Jerusalem, and in all Judea and Samaria, and to the ends of the earth" (Acts 1:8). On the day of Pentecost, the 120 disciples huddled in the upper room were "filled with the promised Holy Spirit" (2:4). They proclaimed the "wonders of God" in unknown tongues, and three thousand believed and were baptized (2:11, 41). The church was born, and its unstoppable growth began. Repeatedly in the book of Acts, we read that the "Lord added to their number . . . those who were being saved" (2:47; cf. 6:7; 12:24; 19:20). The gospel traversed geographical boundaries, first from Jerusalem to Judea, then to Samaria and to the ends of the earth. Not only Jews believed the Messiah's saving message. Within two decades after Pentecost, gospel messengers began to cross cultural, ethnic, and religious barriers to reconcile to God "persons from every tribe and language and people and nation" (Rev. 5:9).

This is a book about the history of the expansion of Christianity across geographical, cultural, ethnic, and religious boundaries. From its cradle in Aramaic-speaking Palestine, the Christian faith spread by the second century as far west as Spain and as far east as Syria and perhaps India. In the next four centuries, the faith expanded throughout the Roman Empire and beyond, eastward into Persia, central Asia, and China, westward into Ireland and the British Isles, and southward into Egypt, Nubia, and Ethiopia. Celtic and Anglo-Saxon monks spearheaded a mission among the Germanic and Slavic peoples of Europe in the seventh and eighth centuries. The conversion of Europe was completed around 1200, and Europe became the center of Christendom. European Catholicism made hesitant steps toward global mission outreach in the thirteenth century; it was not until roughly 1500 that these efforts were dramatically expanded. The older mendicant orders (Franciscans and Dominicans) and new religious orders such as the Jesuits provided the personnel for this movement. European Protestants needed considerably longer to embrace world mission. It was not until the early eighteenth century that German Pietists first pioneered cross-cultural foreign missions. By the end of the century, however, a Protestant mission movement had been launched. In the nineteenth century, Protestant missions rivaled and soon outpaced the Roman Catholic mission enterprise. The saving message of redemption in Christ spread across the globe. Today, Christianity is the most globally dispersed of all the major world religions. It is no longer a Western phenomenon but is a diverse and multicultural religion found on every continent. Truly, the gospel has expanded to the ends of the earth.

The use of the phrase "history of the expansion of Christianity" rather than "history of Christian mission" in this book is intentional. I chose the former phrase because it better communicates that the expansion of Christianity is not just a case of the "West to the rest" of the world. In actuality, the expansion of Christianity is neither just a Western enterprise nor entirely a missionary-driven phenomenon, as the phrase "history of mission" may imply. Rather, from its inception, the church has spread by the efforts of both Western and non-Western missionaries, as well as of local lay and clerical converts. The extant documentary sources were for the most part produced by official mission personnel and organizations; hence they controlled the narrative. This means that the focus in these sources remains largely on the efforts of Western missionaries. Local evangelists and missionaries are often only superficially mentioned; at times their names are not even provided. Nevertheless, indigenous Christians were usually more effective than missionaries from the West, since they were fluent in the local language and had an insider knowledge of the culture. They were also embedded in social, occupational, and kinship networks, which provided natural and effective opportunities for sharing the gospel. The expansion of Christianity occurred through the combined efforts of Western and non-Western missionaries and through the valiant witness of local Christians. Two chapters are exclusively devoted to the role of non-Western missionaries: chapter 3 to the eastward expansion of the Christian faith by East Syrian monks and lay Christians, and chapter 12 to Majority World missionaries in the twentieth century. Elsewhere in the book, the contribution and role of indigenous converts and evangelists is also included in the narrative.

It is necessary to define what is meant by "mission" and "missions" in this book. In the last half century, the singular term "mission" has generally been used to describe *missio Dei*, God's sending activity and the church's participation in his redemptive purposes in the world. One should not maintain too sharp of a division between home and foreign mission or between mission among nominal Christians and mission among non-Christians. Nevertheless, the task of the expansion of Christianity, which is the topic of this book, concerns the advance of the Christian faith across cultural, linguistic, ethnic, and religious frontiers, into territories where there was little or no Christian presence. Therefore, in this book I draw on the definition of "mission" from James Scherer: "Mission as applied to the work of the church means the *specific intention* of bearing witness to the Gospel of salvation in Jesus Christ at the borderline between faith and unbelief. . . . The heart of mission is always making the Gospel known where it would not be known without a special and costly act of boundary-crossing witness."[1] The plural term "missions" refers to the various specific efforts that the church employed to carry out the task of world mission. In this volume, I aim to consistently maintain the distinction between "mission" and "missions" described above.

It is important to note that the meanings of words change over time. Some words that initially had neutral or nonreligious connotations developed more derogatory undertones over time. Three important terms are found repeatedly in primary-source documents dealing with the expansion of Christianity— "heathen," "pagan," and "native." The term "heathen," originally from Germanic for "heath-dweller," was for much of Christian history synonymous with Gentile and referred to all non-Christian people who did *not* adhere to the monotheistic religions of Christianity, Judaism, or Islam. Over time, it gradually developed the negative connotations of an uncivilized, irreligious, or unchristian person.[2] Due to the negative connotations that "heathen" possesses today, I will generally substitute "non-Christian" or "Gentile" for "heathen," except, of course, when that term is found in primary sources. Originally the term "pagan" referred to a rustic country-dweller, but by the nineteenth century it had developed religious connotations; in some cases, the term had become a close synonym for "Gentile" or "heathen." In other cases, however, "pagan" and "paganism" are technical terms commonly used to describe pre-Christian religious traditions, specifically "the polytheisms of the Greco-Roman world" in the classical period and late antiquity, and the

---

1. James A. Scherer, *Gospel, Church, and Kingdom: Comparative Studies in World Mission Theology* (Minneapolis: Augsburg, 1987), 37.

2. Online Etymology Dictionary, "Heathen," accessed June 3, 2021, https://www.etymonline.com/word/heathen.

amorphous "body of pagan beliefs" among the Germanic and Scandinavian peoples "beyond the old Roman *limes*" in the early Middle Ages.[3] It is in this sense that these terms are used in chapters 1 through 4. The word "native" refers to an indigenous person, someone who was not a foreigner but was born in a particular, specified location.[4] Unlike "heathen," the term "native" is not generally viewed as offensive, although it holds negative connotations for some people today. Therefore, I will generally substitute "indigenous" or "local" for "native," except in the following contexts: when the term is found in primary sources, when it refers to the place of origin of a person or group, or when it is used as a technical term to describe, for example, Native Americans (chap. 6) or the native church in Sierra Leone and elsewhere (chap. 9). Finally, there are other terms used in this book that were common during the historical period in question but that sound outdated or antiquated today because they have since been replaced with newer words. Cultural "accommodation" and "adaptation" were two terms employed by the sixteenth- and seventeenth-century Jesuits to describe what, since the 1970s, Roman Catholics call "inculturation" and Protestants call "contextualization." I will generally use the historically appropriate terms, unless they lead to misunderstanding.

This is a book about *turning points* in the historical expansion of Christianity. I was inspired by Mark Noll's *Turning Points: Decisive Moments in the History of Christianity* to adopt a similar turning-points approach to the history of the expansion of Christianity. Generally speaking, a turning point in history is a specific, decisive moment when something monumental changes. I am convinced that the use of critical turning points is an engaging way to present and organize historical material. All authors decide which material to include in their books and which to exclude. The turning-points approach means that the author makes this decision based on whether the material portrays those junctures where something changed and a new historical trend began. The turning-points approach thus provides a method not only to choose but also to organize the material around pivotal moments in the expansion of Christianity. Relevant historical context, key historical precedents, and the later development and impact of the trend are included. Furthermore, the turning-points approach helps the reader to not be overwhelmed by unfocused information and thereby miss the proverbial forest for

3. Online Etymology Dictionary, "Pagan," accessed June 3, 2021, https://www.etymonline.com/word/pagan; James Palmer, "Defining Paganism in the Carolingian World," *Early Medieval Europe* 15, no. 4 (November 2007), 404; cf. Prudence Jones and Nigel Pennick, *A History of Pagan Europe* (New York: Routledge, 1995), 1–2.

4. Online Etymology Dictionary; "Native," accessed June 3, 2021, https://www.etymonline.com/word/native.

the trees. Rather, it aims to assist the reader to understand (and remember) the most important historical trends in the expansion of Christianity.

Admittedly, my decision of which turning points are the most crucial, and therefore should be included, is somewhat subjective. Other turning points could have been chosen. For example, the Second Vatican Council and the impact of liberation theology on Roman Catholic missiology are worthy of attention. I have chosen not to include those topics in this volume for this reason: they are not directly turning points in the expansion of Christianity as I have defined it—as an expansion across cultural, linguistic, ethnic, and religious frontiers into territories where there was little or no Christian presence. Due to space limitations and the broad scope of this book from Pentecost to the present, other important issues have only been touched on briefly (Pentecostalism) or not at all (Orthodox missions). I am convinced, however, that each of the turning points contained in this volume reveals an important facet of the expansion of Christianity.

In this book, the concept of turning points has a range of meanings. In many cases, the turning point marks the beginning of a new trend in the expansion of Christianity. In other cases, however, the turning point is the climax and culmination of a trend, a key representative of a development in a new direction, or a dramatic symbol of momentous changes affecting the advance of the Christian faith. In five chapters of this book, the turning point marks the *beginning* of a new trend in history. The Jerusalem Council, described in chapter 1, was a pivotal event. It opened the door for the large-scale mission to the Gentiles in the following centuries by removing the chief hindrances to Gentile conversion (adherence to the Jewish law and circumcision). Patrick's mission to Ireland was the first example of sustained evangelization outside the boundaries of the Roman Empire (chap. 2). William Carey did more than any other single individual to turn the previously sporadic Protestant mission efforts into a growing and thriving mission movement (chap. 7). The British abolitionist crusade spawned a new geographical focus on mission in Africa. It was linked with a clear humanitarian agenda to root out all remaining vestiges of African slavery (chap. 8). Finally, the 1974 Lausanne Congress on World Evangelization was a key factor, though not the only factor, in motivating Christians in the Global South to embrace world evangelization and to launch their own mission movements (chap. 12).

But not all the turning points in this book mark the beginning of a new trend. One turning point, the East Syrian mission to China in 635, was the climax and *culmination* of widespread mission eastward into East, Central, and South Asia in the previous centuries (chap. 3). Another, the 1910 World Missionary Conference, was a turning point in a dual sense: it was a culmination of the traditional, conservative mission approach of the nineteenth century and a harbinger of newer missional trends in the twentieth (chap. 11). Three of the turning points in this book highlight a *key representative* of a developing trend, even when the representative was not the first to initiate the change. Boniface was not the first to confront Germanic pagan gods through power encounters on the European continent; Celtic missionaries had done likewise in the previous hundred years (chap. 4). But Boniface is a better example of this trend because many more reliable primary sources are available for him and because he reflected deeply on the task of converting pagans. The Moravian mission was not the first Protestant global mission; that honor is reserved for the Danish-Halle mission (chap. 6). But the Moravian mission is a better representative due to its astonishing number of missionaries, the geographic breadth of its mission outreach, and the profound impact it had on later Protestant mission efforts. Henry Venn was one of two key individuals, the other being Rufus Anderson, who virtually simultaneously developed the three-self principles for an independent, indigenous church (chap. 9). Venn, however, was the more articulate and systematic theorist, and his views were more broadly influential than Anderson's; therefore, he is chosen as the key representative of this groundbreaking mission theory.

Finally, two chapters have turning points that were *dramatic symbols* for momentous changes in the expansion of Christianity. In 1707, the emperor of China, Kangxi, mandated that only those missionaries who upheld the cultural accommodation views of the Jesuit missionary Matteo Ricci on ancestor veneration might remain in the country (chap. 5). This was not only a pivotal event but also a dramatic symbol of the ongoing Chinese Rites controversy, which lasted for over a century (ca. 1630–1742). Similarly, the Scramble for Africa serves as a dramatic symbol of the change from earlier forms of imperialism to a new and a more virulent form during the high imperialist era (chap. 10).

Each chapter begins with a "close-up" view of one critical turning point in the worldwide mission and expansion of the church. I believe that readers can more easily relate to significant historical persons and crucial concrete events (turning points) when the story is told with adequate detail to make it come alive and demonstrate its significance. I attempt to do just that for each turning point. This close-up, detailed survey of a pivotal event or person is followed by a discussion of why it is a turning point and what type of turning point it is. Then we pan out to gain a broader historical view. Key historical precedents to the turning point are discussed, as are their later or ongoing impact. Each chapter begins with a hymn and ends with a prayer from the time period and cultural context discussed.

This book seeks to make several distinct contributions. Considerable space (five out of twelve chapters) is devoted to the expansion of Christianity prior to the rise of Protestant missions. An in-depth emphasis on outreach by the early church, and by East Syrian and Roman Catholic missionaries, is often lacking in other surveys written by Protestants. Furthermore, two chapters in this book survey turning points seldom included in other volumes on the expansion of Christianity: the chapter on the role of British abolitionism on mission to Africa (chap. 8) and the detailed chapter on imperialism and mission (chap. 10). A second emphasis in the volume is the frequent use of primary sources to enliven and underpin the narrative. Primary sources are included in the body of the chapters as well as in sidebars. Finally, certain missiological, theological, and historical themes are highlighted repeatedly in the book. These include mission methods, motivation for evangelization, theology of mission, cultural accommodation, the role of indigenous converts and evangelists, and the relationship between mission and imperialism.

Embracing Ethnic Diversity

The Jerusalem Council (49)

The Lord has directed my [Jesus's] mouth by His Word. . . .

He has caused to dwell in me His deathless life; and gave me that I might speak the fruit of His peace: to convert the souls of them that are willing to come to Him; and to lead captive a good captivity for freedom. . . . And the Gentiles were gathered together who were scattered abroad. And I was unpolluted by my love for them, because they confessed me in high places . . . and they walked in my life and were saved and became my people for ever and ever. Hallelujah.[1]

The hymn quoted above is from the earliest Christian hymnbook, the *Odes of Solomon*, written in Syriac, a Semitic language, in AD 100–125. Jesus, the speaker in the hymn, affirms his love for the Gentiles, whom he has saved, gathered into his church, and made his people. This ode mirrors the successful resolution at the Council of Jerusalem (AD 49) of the most significant controversy of the church in the apostolic age—the terms of acceptance for Gentiles into the Christian community. The controversy revolved around whether non-Jews could be received into the church merely by faith in Christ and baptism, or whether they must be circumcised and adhere to aspects of

---

1. J. Rendel Harris, *The Odes and Psalms of Solomon Published from the Syriac Version* (Cambridge: Cambridge University Press, 1911), 104 (modernized).

the Jewish law—that is, whether they must first become Jewish proselytes in order to join the church. The answer to that question and its implications for mission were not immediately evident to all within the early church, hence the controversy.

The answer was not self-evident in part because Christianity had been born within the cradle of Judaism. Its earliest center was the Jewish capital, Jerusalem. The first converts to the messianic faith were Jews of one stripe or another. Some of the Jewish-background believers in the capital were converted Pharisees, who strictly followed the Torah. Others, including the majority of Jesus's disciples, interpreted the law more broadly and not always literally. Most of these, however, still kept the Jewish food laws and worshiped in the temple, at least in the first months or years after Pentecost. Finally, a sizable group of Hellenistic Jews were in the Jerusalem church—Greek-speaking diaspora Jews, who had returned to the capital to live. Hellenistic Jews had adopted some aspects of Greek culture and were in general more universalist and inclusive in their cultural and theological outlook. They were the first to engage in mission to the Gentiles.

Apostolic Christianity not only had its roots in the Jewish religion. It was also perceived by both Romans and Jews as a "sect" (Acts 24:5; 28:22) or "Way" (Acts 24:14) within the broad diversity of contemporary Judaism, and *not* as a new and separate religion. The Roman proconsul Gallio refused to listen to the charges brought against Paul by hostile Jews in Corinth, since they involved "questions about words and names and your own law" (Acts 18:12–16). Gallio clearly regarded Paul's faith as a faction or subgroup within Judaism, and therefore outside his jurisdiction. The Roman historian Suetonius likewise made no distinction between the new faith and Judaism: the *Jews* were expelled from Rome in AD 49/51 "because of *Chrestus*" or Christ.[2] Non-Christian Jews in the first decades after Pentecost also initially tolerated followers of the "Nazarene sect" in their synagogues, since they still viewed them as fellow Jews. Finally, Jewish-background Christ-followers in Jerusalem saw themselves as children of Abraham living in the prophesied eschatological age of the Spirit, which had been inaugurated by the death and resurrection of Jesus, Israel's Messiah. They were the "remnant [of Israel] chosen by grace" and the rebuilt "tabernacle of David" (Rom. 11:5; Acts 15:16 ASV)—in other words, Jews. The earliest Christian assemblies in Jerusalem were not labeled "churches" but "synagogue" meetings by James, the half brother of Jesus and a leader of the Jerusalem church (James 2:2).

---

2. Henry Bettenson and Chris Maunder, eds., *Documents of the Christian Church*, 4th ed. (Oxford: Oxford University Press, 2011), 2.

The strong Jewish character of the church in Jerusalem was retained throughout much of the first century. Therefore, it is not surprising that Jewish-born Christians struggled to comprehend the exact relationship between their messianic faith and its roots in Judaism/Israel. For example, it was not readily obvious how the Old Testament law should be interpreted and applied in light of the new covenant initiated by Jesus. They were well aware that their risen Lord had commissioned them to "make disciples" of Gentiles ("all nations"), as well as Jews (Matt. 28:16–20; Acts 1:8). But what precisely did that entail? Could Gentiles become "children of Abraham" by faith alone—in other words, *as Gentiles*—or must they first be circumcised? These issues were exposed and gradually clarified during key missional moments in the church's development until they were finally settled at the Jerusalem Council in AD 49.

In this chapter, I will first discuss the key stages in the rise and development of the Jewish-Gentile controversy in the early church. Then, in a second section, I will sketch the historical context of, the debates during, and the decree issued by the Jerusalem Council. I argue that the Jerusalem Council was a turning point in the history of the expansion of Christianity for several notable reasons. First, the apostolic decision at the council to not require circumcision of Gentiles had broad ramifications. It removed the "dividing wall" of separation and hostility between Jewish and Gentile believers (Eph. 2:14). It declared that Gentile ethnicities had equal standing with Jewishness within the Christian community. Ethnic diversity was officially embraced by the church. Second, the Jerusalem Council formally established the nature of salvation. Both Jews and Gentiles were saved by grace through faith and not by works of the law. Third, the council gave momentum to the development whereby Christianity gradually emerged from its Jewish roots. Soon it was no longer regarded as a sect within Judaism. Finally, and most importantly for this chapter, the Jerusalem Council "represents a turning point in the history of the Church" because "it prepared the way for the spread of Christianity in the Greco-Roman world" in the first three centuries.[3] It opened wide the door to full-scale mission to Gentiles of all ethnicities. The Gentile mission of Paul, the apostle to the uncircumcised, was affirmed at the Jerusalem Council. In the third section of this chapter, I examine Paul's ministry to Gentiles and that of his successors in the first century, with a special focus on the mission methods employed. In the final section, we will explore the church's Gentile mission in the second and third centuries. The church in that period

3. Vesilin Kesich, "The Apostolic Council at Jerusalem," *St. Vladimir's Seminary Quarterly* 6, no. 3 (1962): 108.

abandoned some of the first-century missional practices pioneered by Paul. Despite some significant weaknesses, the church in the pre-Constantinian era continued to expand rapidly. This chapter focuses on the westward expansion of Christianity, while chapter 3 explores its eastward expansion.

Stages in the Jewish-Gentile Controversy

The dramatic arrival of the Holy Spirit on the day of Pentecost transformed the 120 disciples of Jesus, who had been cowering in the upper room. Filled with God-given power, Peter called the "God-fearing Jews from every nation" who had gathered at the sound of the mighty wind to respond in faith, and three thousand were baptized that day. The new converts were "one in heart and mind," and the church grew rapidly (Acts 4:32; 2:42–47). But in time the first cracks in the Jerusalem church's unity appeared when Hellenistic Jews complained against the Aramaic-speaking (Hebraic) Jews that Hellenistic widows were being overlooked in the daily distribution of food (6:1). Prompt and wise action by the Twelve prevented a rift from developing between these two culturally diverse branches of Judaism. Seven Hellenistic deacons were chosen to administer the food distribution. Two of them, Stephen and Philip, preached, evangelized, and performed miracles as well (Acts 6–8).

The scattering of Jewish Christians due to persecution after the martyrdom of Stephen (Acts 8:1, 4) launched the church's mission beyond Jerusalem (1:8). Hellenistic Jewish Christians formed the spearhead of these evangelizing efforts, in part because they had fewer scruples about contact with Gentiles than Hebraic Jews. Furthermore, their Greek linguistic competency equipped them well for mission work among Gentiles and diasporic Jews. Finally, Hellenistic Jewish believers "reflected more consistently about the consequences of Jesus's death and resurrection for the Torah and the temple, and thus for Israel, than did the apostles."[4] They were quicker to realize that the believers' relationship to God was mediated by Jesus Christ alone and did not require additional Torah adherence. God's presence was no longer located in the temple, but was now in the Spirit-filled community of believers. Thus, it was not surprising that Philip, one of the Seven, initiated mission among the Samaritans, converted a prominent eunuch from Nubia, and evangelized in towns on the coastal plain with a strong Gentile presence (Acts 8). Other unnamed Hellenistic Jewish Christians carried the gospel to Phoenicia, Cyprus, and Syrian Antioch (11:19–21). In Antioch, these unnamed evangelists

4. Eckhard J. Schnabel, *Early Christian Mission* (Downers Grove, IL: InterVarsity, 2004), 1:662; cf. 653.

proclaimed the good news not only to Jews but also to Gentiles, who responded in great numbers. The apostles in Jerusalem viewed the conversion of non-Jews as a serious issue that required investigation. They sent trusted members of their circle for this purpose: the apostles Peter and John were sent to Samaria, and Barnabas to Antioch. In both cases, the Jerusalem delegates "saw what the grace of God had done" (11:23) and rejoiced that the gospel had crossed ethnic and racial boundaries. The mother church in Jerusalem presumably rejoiced as well.

The Jewish-Gentile controversy began in earnest with Cornelius's conversion through Peter's preaching (ca. AD 37). Cornelius was a Roman centurion and an uncircumcised but God-fearing Gentile who "prayed to God regularly" and gave alms (Acts 10:2). Both Cornelius and the apostle were prepared by visions for their encounter with one another. Three times Peter had a vision of a sheet filled with unclean animals. Through this vision, Peter recognized that God had not only canceled the kosher food laws but also directed him to "not call anyone impure or unclean," not even Gentiles (10:28). Therefore, when he arrived in Caesarea, Peter did not hesitate to enter Cornelius's house and accept his hospitality, something a law-abiding Jew would have been reluctant to do. Cornelius and his household believed Peter's message. The Holy Spirit descended on them as it had on the Jews at Pentecost, and they spoke in tongues, signaling the acceptance of Gentiles by God.

But when Peter returned to Jerusalem, the "circumcised believers criticized him" (Acts 11:2). Peter and his companions were, of course, also circumcised (10:45), though not a part of the ultrastrict "circumcision group" within the Jerusalem church. The circumcision group took offense at Peter's association and table fellowship with uncircumcised Gentiles, even God-fearing ones like Cornelius. Peter argued in response that God himself had orchestrated the encounter through revelatory visions. Furthermore, since "God gave them the same gift he gave us who believed in the Lord Jesus Christ, who was I to think that I could stand in God's way?" Upon hearing that, the circumcision party had no further objections. They praised God that he "has granted repentance that leads to life" even to Gentiles (11:17–18).

Then, in about AD 44, after a year of fruitful ministry in Syrian Antioch, Paul, Barnabas, and Titus brought a collection of money to Jerusalem to provide relief for Christians threatened by famine conditions (Acts 11:27–30; Gal. 2:1–10).[5] While in Jerusalem, Paul and Barnabas took the opportunity

5. For a short overview of the relationship between Acts and Galatians 1–2, see J. Julius Scott, "The Church's Progress to the Council of Jerusalem according to the Book of Acts," *Bulletin for Biblical Research* 7 (1997): 221–24. Cf. F. F. Bruce, *Paul, Apostle of the Heart Set Free* (Grand Rapids: Eerdmans, 1977), 148–59.

to consult privately with the "pillars" of the church—James, Peter, and John. Paul presented to them the gospel that he preached to the Gentiles in order to ensure that he was not "running and had not been running [his] race in vain" (Gal. 2:2). The church leaders "recognized the grace given" to Paul and extended to the two men the "right hand of fellowship" (Gal. 2:9). Paul was confirmed in his commission to preach the gospel to the Gentiles, just as Peter was the apostle to the Jews. At this point in the Jewish-Gentile controversy, circumcision as a prerequisite for acceptance into the church was not yet a major issue. After all, no pressure was exerted on Titus, a Greek Christian, to be circumcised (Gal. 2:3).

That changed after Paul and Barnabas's first missionary journey to south-central Asia Minor (today Turkey) in AD 45–47. Although they first preached to the Jews, the greatest number of converts were Gentiles. "This [missionary] effort marked the first initiative by Christians to reach large numbers of Gentiles and resulted in the beginning of a radically different racial-cultural make-up in the Christian community."[6] It was one thing when just a limited number of God-fearing Gentiles were included in the church, but quite another when droves of non-Jews responded in faith to Christ. After revisiting the various stations of their itinerant mission, Paul and Barnabas returned to Antioch, where they reported to the church how God "had opened a door of faith to the Gentiles" (Acts 14:27).

The immediate backdrop for the Jerusalem Council was a crisis that occurred in the Syrian Antioch church at about this time. Some "people came down from Judea" to Antioch without a mandate from Jerusalem (Acts 15:1, 24; Gal. 2:12), and instructed the Gentiles that circumcision and adherence to the law were essential for salvation. They also pressured Peter, who had been in the habit of eating with non-Jews, to cease from mixed table fellowship. Not surprisingly, the Gentile believers were "troubled" by this teaching, which in effect assigned them second-class status within the church. When Paul learned that Peter had complied with the demands of the circumcision party, he confronted him publicly for his hypocrisy. Paul perceived that "behind this demand . . . were not simply racial-cultural preferences or ceremonial issues, but . . . the doctrine of Christian salvation (justification by faith)."[7] He wrote to the Galatians prior to the council: "We know that a person is not justified by the works of the law, but by faith in Jesus Christ . . . because by the works of the law no one [neither Jew nor Gentile] will be justified" (Gal. 2:16). Paul and Barnabas were brought "into sharp dispute and debate" (Acts 15:2) with the circumcision party in Antioch. To resolve the issue, the two men and some companions were sent to

6. Scott, "Church's Progress," 217.
7. Scott, "Church's Progress," 224.

Jerusalem to confer with the apostles and elders. This was the first instance of a church council being called to settle a theological debate.

The Jerusalem Council (AD 49)

The church in Jerusalem had faced hard times in the 40s. King Herod Agrippa I (41–44) commenced persecution of the twelve apostles. The apostle James was executed, and Peter escaped with his life only by supernatural intervention (Acts 12:1–19). Forced to leave Jerusalem, Peter fled first to Caesarea and later to Antioch, where he was at the time of the crisis described above. After the death of Agrippa in 44, a new wave of Jewish nationalist zealotry broke out against the Roman imperial power, but also against those Jews viewed as collaborators. Furthermore, by the mid-40s, there was almost certainly an increase in the number and influence of ultraconservative Jewish believers in Jerusalem. Acts 21:20–21 reports that "many thousands of Jews" who were "zealous for the law" had accepted the messianic faith in recent times. In this highly charged atmosphere, the "influx of uncircumcised Gentile believers . . . presented the Jerusalem church with an ethical and strategic-political problem."[8] To accept Gentiles without circumcision into the Christian community went against the conviction of many local believers; it also exposed the church to hostility from Jewish Zealots.

On their arrival in Jerusalem, Paul and Barnabas were welcomed warmly by the apostles and elders of the church. The council was convened with three groups in attendance: (1) conservative Jewish Christians, including converted Pharisees, who insisted that Gentiles be circumcised; (2) Peter and James, who held a mediating position between the circumcision party and the Antioch contingent; and (3) Paul and Barnabas, representatives of the Gentile mission. The circumcision party opened the discussion with a statement of their position: "The Gentiles must be circumcised and required to keep the law of Moses" (Acts 15:5). A vigorous and lengthy debate ensued. Then Peter, the apostle to the Jews, arose and reminded the assembly how God had demonstrated in the Cornelius event that "he did not discriminate between us and them," since the Holy Spirit had been poured out upon the Gentiles (15:8–9). Despite his withdrawal from mixed table fellowship in Antioch, Peter at the council agreed with and defended Paul's theology of salvation: "We believe it is through the grace of our Lord Jesus that we [Jews] are saved, just as they are" (15:11). Paul and Barnabas then recounted the miraculous signs and wonders that God had performed among the Gentiles in Antioch and south-central Asia Minor. God

8. Schnabel, *Early Christian Mission*, 2:1010.

had supernaturally called the Gentiles to faith—this was not merely Paul's pet mission project. Finally, James, as head of the Jerusalem church, quoted Amos 9:11–12 and other passages to establish that just such an eventuality had been prophesied in the Old Testament Scriptures. Gentiles, who were "not [God's] people," would become the people of God (Hosea 2:23).

The council unanimously agreed (Acts 15:25a) to James's suggestion that no unnecessary burdens hinder Gentiles from turning to faith in Christ. Circumcision and adherence to all aspects of the law were not required. Four stipulations, however, were required to facilitate fellowship between Jewish and Gentile Christians: abstinence from food offered to idols, from sexual immorality, from the meat of strangled animals, and from blood as an ingredient in food. These stipulations were not arbitrary; they were regulations found in Leviticus 17–18 for Gentiles who lived as "foreigners" among Jews. This apostolic decree was accepted by Paul, by most Jewish Christians, and by Gentile believers in Antioch and Galatia, who were glad for the "encouraging message" of the letter from the council leadership, sent with a delegation from Jerusalem (Acts 15:24–29). Despite some minor subsequent flare-ups of the controversy (Titus 1:10), evidence from Christian writers in the second and third centuries suggests that the apostolic decree's stance regarding Gentile circumcision was consistently upheld.

After the Jerusalem Council, "conservative Judaizing Christianity became increasingly marginalized" within the church. This trend accelerated as ever more Gentiles entered the church through missionary efforts. After the destruction of the Jerusalem temple in AD 70, only vestiges of Jewish Christianity survived, largely in heretical sects, such as the Ebionites. By the end of the first century, the church had become predominately Gentile. "The most significant development of early Christianity was its ethnic expansion of including the Gentiles *as Gentiles*."[9] After the council, Christianity was no longer linked with Jewish ethnicity. The church became increasingly a transethnic entity, with a clearly articulated Pauline doctrine of salvation—by grace through faith and not by works of the law. Hindrances were removed, and the foundation was laid for a rapid expansion of Christianity among Gentiles to the very ends of the earth (Acts 1:8).

Mission among Gentiles in the First Century

The apostle Paul's mission to the Gentiles was affirmed by God and the church several times. The first affirmation took place shortly after Paul's conversion

---

9. Cornelis Bennema, "The Ethnic Conflict in Early Christianity," *JETS* 56, no. 4 (2013): 762–63.

on the Damascus Road. In a vision, the Lord told Ananias, a disciple in Damascus, that Paul was his "chosen instrument to proclaim my name to the Gentiles and their kings and to the people of Israel" (Acts 9:15). Then, during his visit to the capital to deliver the famine relief collection circa AD 44, Paul and his companions met privately with the "pillars" of the Jerusalem church. In that meeting, they recognized that Paul "had been entrusted with the task of preaching the gospel to the uncircumcised" Gentiles (Gal. 2:7). But for Paul's mission to the Gentiles to advance unhindered, the Jerusalem Council was needed. At that event, not only did the apostles, the elders, and the whole church rejoice at "everything God had done" through Paul and Barnabas for the salvation of the Gentiles. Key hindrances to Gentile conversion (circumcision and adherence to the law) were swept away by the decree promulgated at the council (Acts 15:4, 19, 22). Built on the strong foundation of the Jerusalem decree and divine and church calling, Paul's mission to the Gentiles thrived.

The apostle Paul was the missionary par excellence in the apostolic era. With the help of coworkers, he planted flourishing churches among Gentiles in the major cities of the Roman provinces of Cilicia (Tarsus), Syria (Antioch), Galatia (Lystra, Derbe, Iconium), Asia (Ephesus), Macedonia (Philippi, Thessalonica, Berea), and Achaia (Corinth, Athens). Paul's focus on district or provincial capitals was a central tenet of his mission method. Each of these urban centers were hubs of communication, commerce, and culture, and in Paul's mind, representative for the whole region. In these urban centers, Paul first preached the messianic message in synagogues to Jews and God-fearers. He only turned directly to the Gentile population after his expulsion from the synagogue or the rejection of his message by local Jews. In most instances, Jewish opposition arose rapidly, while Gentiles readily responded. Unlike some early itinerant missionaries, who hurried from one location to another, Paul stayed long enough to establish viable churches—one and a half years in Corinth and two to three in Ephesus. His role was to plant the church (1 Cor. 3:6); others would further develop and nurture it. Paul's pioneering work was accomplished when healthy urban churches were established. Therefore, he could assert that he had "fully proclaimed the gospel" in the Eastern Mediterranean "from Jerusalem all the way around to Illyricum." Since his "ambition [was] to preach the gospel where Christ was not known," he sought to move on to unreached areas, such as Spain (Rom. 15:19–20, 28). Paul's mission strategy assumed that others, normally his coworkers in the newly planted churches, would evangelize the surrounding region.[10] The conversion of rural areas,

10. Volker Rabens, "Paul's Mission Strategy in the Urban Landscape of the First-Century Roman Empire," in *The Urban World and the First Christians*, ed. Steve Walton, Paul Trebilco, and David Gill (Grand Rapids: Eerdmans, 2017), 111.

however, proved to be a slow process that was only completely accomplished in the early Middle Ages. Nevertheless, some successful regional expansion of the gospel is reflected in the New Testament. Paul rejoiced that "the Lord's message rang out" from the Thessalonians in "Macedonia [their region] and Achaia," the neighboring province (1 Thess. 1:8).

This brings us to a second key mission method of the first-century mission—the utilization of both official missionaries (Paul, other apostles, and co-workers) and the unofficial evangelistic ministry of individual believers and congregations. Both Paul and Peter were official missionaries who fulfilled their commission to preach the gospel, Paul in the Eastern Mediterranean as the apostle to the Gentiles, Peter as apostle to the Jews (Gal. 2:7–8). Peter was accompanied in his missionary travels by his wife (1 Cor. 9:5). The references to the Peter party in 1 Corinthians 1:12 and 3:22 suggest that he may have ministered in Corinth for a time. Similarly, he may have engaged in mission work in northern Asia Minor, since 1 Peter is addressed to churches in that region. Early Christian tradition claims that Peter either founded the church in Rome, had a sustained ministry there, or arrived there shortly before his martyrdom. This tradition, though early, has not been historically verified.[11] Neither has the appealing third-century tradition that the twelve apostles, while gathered together in Jerusalem, cast lots to determine which Gentile nation the Lord had assigned each of them as their mission territory. "Thomas . . . obtained by lot Parthia, Andrew Scythia, [and] John Asia."[12] That the twelve apostles engaged in mission is likely. Where the Twelve evangelized, however, is unclear. It is significant that the term "apostle" was used in this period not only for the Twelve but also for other missionaries (or emissaries), such as Barnabas (Acts 14:14). In Ephesians 4:11, "apostles" are included alongside evangelists, pastors, and teachers as gifts to the church.

Paul employed a team of coworkers as "official" missionaries to advance or further his mission initiatives. The majority of Paul's thirty-eight coworkers listed in the New Testament were fairly recent converts from the churches he planted. Some, such as Epaphroditus (Phil. 2:25), were sent to assist Paul as delegates from their home churches. Nine or ten of Paul's circle of coworkers were women—a sizable number. Two of them, Euodia and Syntyche, "con-tended at my [Paul's] side in the cause of the gospel, along with Clement and the rest of my coworkers" (4:2–3). Their ministry in Philippi was viewed as similar to that of male coworkers. Some coworkers, such as Timothy, Titus, and Silas, accompanied Paul on his itinerant missionary journeys. Others

11. Schnabel, *Early Christian Mission*, 1:528, 721.
12. Eusebius, *Ecclesiastical History*, trans. C. F. Cruse (London: Bagster and Sons, 1842), 106.

had a more localized ministry. Stephanas, Paul's first convert in Achaia, and his household witnessed to Christ on their home turf—in Corinth and its environs (1 Cor. 16:15–6). Epaphras, a native of Colossae, was present with Paul in Ephesus. He was most likely sent by Paul back to his home territory in the Lycus valley, where he planted three churches—in Colossae, Laodicea, and Hierapolis (Col. 1:3–8; 4:13).[13]

Not all evangelists or missionaries were officially appointed apostles or coworkers. Unnamed Hellenistic and Hebraic Jews witnessed to their faith when they were scattered due to persecution—with remarkable results (Acts 8:1; 11:19–21). The Pax Romana (peace of Rome) allowed great freedom of movement for the hundreds of unnamed believers who shared their faith as they traveled about the empire. These unofficial missionaries most likely contributed to the establishment of those first-century churches that were not founded by an apostle or coworker: in Syria (Tyre, Sidon, Damascus), in Asia (Miletus, Smyrna, Thyatira, Sardis, Philadelphia), in Italy (Puteoli, Pompeii, probably Rome), in Egypt (Alexandria), and in North Africa (Cyrene). Not just individual believers but local churches likewise had "an evangelistic function that appears to have developed spontaneously. . . . The strong evidence of Acts is that local congregations expanded and grew through the efforts of their members."[14] Local church worship services had evangelistic potential for unbelieving visitors (1 Cor. 14:23–25). Households and house churches "served as missional bases of operation" that provided "natural evangelistic contacts and conversation opportunities" for gospel "proclamation" and "Christian brotherly love."[15]

Expansion of Christianity in the Second and Third Centuries

The Jerusalem Council of AD 49 smoothed away key hindrances to Gentile conversion and thereby paved the way for a robust mission among diverse ethnicities in the following centuries. The church in the second and third centuries continued to grow, at times rapidly. Nevertheless, the church in the postapostolic era exhibited a number of glaring weaknesses with regard to mission that were not found in the first century. For example, in contrast to

13. Schnabel, *Early Christian Mission*, 2:1425–32, 1434, 1439–41.

14. I. Howard Marshall, "Who Were the Evangelists?," in *The Mission of the Early Church to Jews and Gentiles*, ed. Jostein Ådna and Hans Kvalbein (Tübingen: Mohr Siebeck, 2000), 262–63; Jehu J. Hanciles, *Migration and the Making of Global Christianity* (Grand Rapids: Eerdmans, 2021), 141–69.

15. Roger W. Gehring, *House Church and Mission: The Importance of Household Structures in Early Christianity* (Peabody, MA: Hendrickson, 2004), 227.

Paul's Gentile mission, missional efforts in this period lacked organization and clearly articulated methods. Mission did occur, but it came about for the most part incidentally through individual initiative. There was no longer an official church office of missionary or evangelist. By 200, the broader meaning of "apostle" as an itinerant missionary, seen occasionally in the New Testament, had all but disappeared, and the word instead referred exclusively to the Twelve. Furthermore, with only a few notable exceptions (Pantaneus, Gregory the Wonderworker), by 150 missionaries vanished from the written record, as did evidence of evangelistic preaching. Extant sermons from these

---

SIDEBAR 1.1

Irenaeus, *Against Heresies* 1.10 (AD 175–185)

The Church, though dispersed throughout the whole world, even to the ends of the earth, has received from the apostles and their disciples this [apostolic] faith. . . . She [the Church] believes these points [of doctrine] . . . and she proclaims them, and teaches them, and hands them down, with perfect harmony. . . . For the Churches which have been planted in Germany do not believe or hand down anything different, nor do those in Spain, nor those in Gaul, nor those in the East, nor those in Egypt, nor those in Libya, nor those which have been established in the central regions of the world.

Tertullian, *Apology* 37 (AD 197)

We [Christians] are but of yesterday, and we have filled every place among you—cities, islands, fortresses, towns, market-places, the very camp, tribes, companies, palace, senate, forum,—we have left nothing to you but the temples of your gods. . . . For now it is the immense number of Christians which makes your enemies so few—almost all the inhabitants of your various cities being followers of Christ.

Clement of Alexandria, *Stromata* 6.28 (AD 182–202)

But the word of our Teacher remained not in Judea alone, as philosophy did in Greece; but was diffused over the whole world, over every nation, and village, and town, bringing already over to the truth whole houses, and each individual of those who heard it by him himself, and not a few of the philosophers themselves.

Source: Francis M. DuBose, ed., *Classics of Christian Missions* (Nashville: Broadman, 1979), 278–79, 284, 282.

two centuries were almost exclusively addressed to Christians or baptismal candidates; they focused on Christian ethics, not on a call to repent and believe. One final form of mission outreach common in the first century, missional worship services, likewise became rare in this period. Due to persecution, non-Christians were seldom given access to Christian worship services.[16]

Despite these missional shortcomings in the second and third centuries, Christianity continued to spread throughout the Roman Empire and beyond. By the time of Emperor Constantine's edict of toleration (312), approximately 10 percent of the population in the empire were Christ-followers, an amazing development considering the severe but periodic state-sponsored persecutions from the 60s onward.[17] Christians were found in all social classes during the first three centuries. Pliny the Younger, governor of Bithynia, in his letter to Emperor Trajan in 112, reported that "many persons of all ages and classes and of both sexes" had become Christians.[18] Some converts were slaves (e.g., Onesimus; "those who belong to Caesar's household," Phil. 4:22; second-century martyr Blandina); others belonged to the highest echelons of society (e.g., Erastus, the city treasurer of Corinth, Rom. 16:23; noblewoman Pomponia Graecina). Furthermore, Christians were actively engaged in society and found in all occupations. Tertullian emphasized that "we [Christians] sojourn with you in the world, abjuring neither forum . . . nor workshop, nor inn, nor weekly market, nor any other places of commerce. We sail with you, and fight with you, and till the ground with you."[19] Although Christians would not participate in pagan religious festivals, they served in the military, in commercial ventures, and in the halls of government. Pliny in his letter to Trajan testified to the geographic expansion of the faith: the Christian "superstition has spread not only in the cities, but in the villages and rural districts as well."[20] Other ancient writers confirmed this rapid spread of Christianity (see sidebar 1.1). Irenaeus asserted that the apostolic faith had spread "even to the ends of the earth," specifically to Germany, Spain, Gaul, Egypt, Libya, and the East. Tertullian stressed the spread of the gospel to "every place." Clement of Alexandria noted that unlike Greek philosophy, which remained

16. Ramsey MacMullen, *Christianizing the Roman Empire AD 100–400* (New Haven: Yale University Press, 1984), 34; Reidar Hvalvik, "In Word and Deed: The Expansion of the Church in the Pre-Constantinian Era," in Ådna and Kvalbein, *Mission of the Early Church*, 267, 272, 276; Alan Kreider, "They Alone Know the Right Way to Live: The Early Church and Evangelism," in *Ancient Faith for the Church's Future*, ed. Mark Husbands and Jeffrey Greenman (Downers Grove, IL: InterVarsity, 2008), 170.

17. Rodney Stark, *The Rise of Christianity* (San Francisco: HarperCollins, 1997), 6–7.

18. Bettenson and Maunder, *Documents of the Christian Church*, 4.

19. Tertullian, *Apology* 42, quoted in Hanciles, *Migration*, 143–44.

20. Bettenson and Maunder, *Documents of the Christian Church*, 4.

in Greece, Christianity did not linger in Judea but was diffused throughout the whole world—to every nation, town, village, and household.

In the postapostolic period, Christianity continued to expand westward within the Roman Empire. Greek-speaking Christian merchants brought the gospel to Gaul (Lyons and Vienne in southern France), to Italy (Aquileia, Nola), to Croatia (Salona), and to Germany (Trier). By the end of the second century, churches had been established among the Celtic/Gallic population in southern Gaul as well. Whether the apostle Paul evangelized in Spain is unknown. The progress of the gospel there was rather slow, though by 305–306, when the council of Elvira (today Granada) convened, there were thirty-six bishoprics in Spain. The canons of the council, however, suggest that pagan influence in the church was still an ongoing problem. Tertullian reported that by 200, Christianity had "reached the haunts of the Britons."[21] Christian soldiers and merchants probably first brought the faith to the British Isles. During the empire-wide persecutions under Emperors Decius and Valerian, three named Britons (Alban and soldiers Aaron and Julius) were martyred for refusing to sacrifice to the gods. The growth of the church in Britain was further evidenced by the participation of three British bishops at the international Council of Arles in 314.

Carthage was probably the gateway in the late first century for Christianity in Roman North Africa. The first agents of evangelization were Italian immigrants who came as settlers, merchants, and soldiers. By AD 150, the church was established, and Christians were being buried in the catacombs at Hadrumetum (today Sousse, Tunisia), one hundred miles south of Carthage. Twelve Christians from the region of Scilla (west-central Tunisia) were martyred in 180. Five of the twelve had typical African (Berber) names, an indication that the gospel had crossed to the indigenous population living far inland from coastal Carthage.[22] "By the end of the third century, there was no area in the Roman Empire which had not been penetrated to some extent by the Gospel. But distribution was very uneven . . . and the village people were as yet to a large extent untouched."[23]

The most effective means of mission in the second and third centuries was the witness of ordinary lay Christians. As described above, Christian immigrants, merchants, and soldiers were the primary agents of evangelization in

21. Tertullian, *Against the Jews* 7, trans. S. Thelwall, in *Ante-Nicene Fathers*, vol. 3, *Latin Christianity: Its Founder*, ed. Alexander Roberts, James Donaldson, and A. Cleveland Coxe (Buffalo: Christian Literature, 1885), rev. and ed. Kevin Knight, http://www.newadvent.org /fathers/0308.htm.
22. Francois Decret, *Early Christianity in North Africa* (Eugene, OR: Cascade, 2009), 9–13, 30–31.
23. Stephen Neill, *A History of Christian Missions*, 2nd ed. (New York: Penguin, 1991), 35.

much of the Roman world. Some of these Christians were relocated elsewhere involuntarily: slaves when their masters moved; soldiers when assigned to other military installations; harassed believers when persecution struck. Lay merchants and tradesmen, however, voluntarily moved for their business pursuits. These lay believers "went everywhere gossiping the gospel . . . naturally, enthusiastically, and with . . . conviction," not by "formal preaching, but the informal chattering to friends and chance acquaintances, in homes and wine shops, on walks, and around market stalls."[24] Jehu Hanciles notes that "Christian *witness* was a matter of *with-ness*," which combined "intimate proximity" to non-Christians with a convincing lifestyle and gospel message.[25] Christianity spread through natural relational networks of friends, neighbors, family, and business acquaintances, but also when Christians shared the gospel with strangers. Justin Martyr was converted in 135 when an elderly Christian explained how the Old Testament prophets pointed to Christ. "Straightway a flame was kindled in my soul; and a love of the prophets, and of those men who are friends of Christ, possessed me."[26]

By 150, the office of missionary or evangelist no longer existed in the church. Nevertheless, other church officials evangelized at times. It was part of the job description of bishops to "warn and reprove the uninstructed with boldness"[27]—that is, to evangelize. We only know of a few who actually did. Polycarp, bishop of Smyrna (d. 156), did "exhort men to gain salvation" by departing from idolatrous practices.[28] Irenaeus, while bishop of Lyons (178–200), became fluent in the Celtic/Gallic language in order to evangelize the indigenous population. Cyprian, bishop of Carthage (248–258), wrote an apologetic tract to the Roman proconsul of Africa, Demetrianus, in which he defended Christians against charges that they caused wars, famines, and epidemics by abandoning the pagan gods. At the end of the tract, the bishop makes a missionary appeal, something quite unusual for apologetic writing in this era:

> Forsake the idols which human error has invented. Be turned to God. . . . Believe in Christ. . . . Pardon is granted to the man who confesses, and saving mercy is given from the divine goodness to the believer, and a passage is opened to

24. Michael Green, *Evangelism in the Early Church* (Grand Rapids: Eerdmans, 1970), 173.
25. Hanciles, *Migration*, 149–50.
26. Justin, *Dialogue with Trypho* 8.1, trans. Marcus Dods and George Reith, in *Ante-Nicene Fathers*, vol. 1, *The Apostolic Fathers with Justin Martyr and Irenaeus*, ed. Alexander Roberts, James Donaldson, and A. Cleveland Coxe (Buffalo: Christian Literature, 1885), rev. and ed. Kevin Knight, http://www.newadvent.org/fathers/01281.htm.
27. *Apostolic Constitutions* 2.2.6.
28. Hvalvik, "In Word and Deed," 272.

immortality even in death itself. This grace Christ bestows; this gift of His mercy He confers upon us by overcoming death in the trophy of the cross.[29]

Another church office, that of exorcist, was much more closely linked with evangelism than that of bishop. Originally exorcists were charismatic healers who prayed for the sick or demon-possessed in the power of Jesus. Later they became a part of the church hierarchy and performed ritual exorcisms on baptismal candidates. It was not unusual for a suffering Gentile to seek healing wherever it could be found—both from the pagan Asclepius cult and from the Christian exorcist. Successful exorcisms or healings by the Christian exorcist often led to conversions. Irenaeus reported, "Others banish demons surely and truly, and frequently those who are delivered from such, become believers and are in the Church."[30] Novation of Rome (d. 258) was baptized after Christian exorcists cast out his demons; he was ultimately healed of a grave illness. Healings and exorcisms testified to the power of the Christian God and resulted in conversions.[31]

Ironically, the persecution of Christians resulted in the growth of the church. Tertullian's famous statement, "The oftener we are mown down by you [Roman officials], the more in number we grow; *the blood of Christians is seed*," proved true. The willingness of some early Christians to be martyred to maintain their witness to Christ ("martyr" means "witness") was powerful. Executions took place in the public arena, which was thronged by all levels of society. Martyrdoms thus served to publicize the Christian faith. Trials of Christians often were attended by outsiders. Some martyrs used this opportunity to clarify aspects of their faith. The army veteran Julius declared at his trial, "It was he [Jesus] who died for our sins . . . in order to give us eternal life. This same man Christ is God and . . . whoever believes in him will have eternal life."[32] The heroism of martyrs resulted at times in sympathy for Christians, convincing some non-Christians to inquire into the faith. "At the sight of it [a martyr's suffering and death] who is not profoundly troubled, to the point of inquiring what may lie behind it all?"[33] It is impossible to

29. Cyprian, *An Address to Demetrianus* 16, 25, trans. Robert Ernest Wallis, in *Ante-Nicene Fathers*, vol. 5, *Fathers of the Third Century: Hippolytus, Cyprian, Caius, Novatian, Appendix*, ed. Alexander Roberts, James Donaldson, and A. Cleveland Coxe (Buffalo: Christian Literature, 1886), rev. and ed. Kevin Knight, http://www.newadvent.org/fathers/050705.htm.
30. Irenaeus, *Against Heresies* 2.32.4, in *The Treatise of Saint Irenaeus of Lugdunum Against the Heresies*, trans. F. R. Montgomery Hitchcock (London: SPCK, 1916), 1:77.
31. MacMullen, *Christianizing the Roman Empire*, 27–28; Eusebius, *Ecclesiastical History*, 295.
32. Tertullian, *Apology* 50, trans. S. Thelwall, in *Ante-Nicene Fathers*, vol. 3, *Latin Christianity*, http://www.newadvent.org/fathers/0301.htm; Edward L. Smither, *Mission in the Early Church: Themes and Reflections* (Eugene, OR: Cascade, 2014), 55.
33. Tertullian, *Apology* 50.15.

estimate how many might have converted after observing the martyrdom of Christians; we have only a few accounts of prison guards accepting the faith.

Finally, the lifestyle of many Christians was radically different from that of their non-Christian neighbors, and it convinced some of the truthfulness of Christianity. Minucius Felix, in his apology *Octavius* (ca. 200), claimed, "Beauty of life causes strangers to join the [Christian] ranks. . . . We do not preach great things, we live them."[34] Christians avoided the theater, the arena, and the sexual promiscuity common at the baths and taverns. They did not participate in the emperor cult or eat meat offered to idols. They upheld the sanctity of life and condemned female infanticide, incest, polygamy, and marital infidelity. Furthermore, believers practiced sacrificial love—not only toward fellow Christians but also toward those outside the faith. During the horrific epidemic that struck Alexandria around 250, most non-Christians fled the city, leaving their sick and dying relatives to fend for themselves. Christians, however, remained there and provided care for both their own and for the sick among the pagans, even though the latter had so recently persecuted them. This behavior astonished outsiders, since it often resulted in the Christians themselves becoming infected and dying. Emperor Julian the Apostate remarked that the Christian faith had been "specially advanced through the loving service rendered to strangers. . . . The godless Galileans [Christians] care not only for their own poor but for ours as well; while those who belong to us [pagans] look in vain for the help that we should render them."[35]

In conclusion, the Jerusalem Council was a turning point in the history of the expansion of Christianity. It resolved the Jewish-Gentile controversy and clarified the doctrine of salvation and the terms of acceptance for Gentiles into the church. It eliminated the key hindrances to their conversion (circumcision and adherence to the law). The council opened wide the door for Gentile conversion, ethnic diversity in the church, and mission to the ends of the earth. The outreach efforts of official and unofficial missionaries in the apostolic era brought a massive influx of Gentiles into the church. Despite some missional weaknesses in the second and third centuries, the gospel continued to spread throughout the Roman world, largely through the witness of ordinary lay Christians.

We end this chapter with the earliest Christian prayer not found in the New Testament, written by Clement, bishop of Rome, to the church in Corinth in 96. It includes the theme of mission to the Gentiles.

> May he who created everything
> keep the number of his chosen people, throughout the world,

34. Kreider, "They Alone Know," 278.
35. Neill, *History of Christian Missions*, 37–38.

up to the strength he fixed for them
through his dear Child, Jesus Christ.
Through him he called us from darkness to light,
From ignorance to knowledge
Of the glory of his name. . . .
May every nation come to know
that you alone are God,
that Jesus Christ is your Child,
that we are your people, the sheep that you pasture.[36]

36. A. Hamman, ed., *Early Christian Prayers*, trans. Walter Mitchell (London: Longmans, 1961), 25–27.

2

Pushing beyond the Boundaries of Empire

Patrick and the Conversion of Ireland (ca. 450)

> Hear ye all, lovers of God, the holy merits
> Of the man blessed in Christ: Patrick the bishop. . . .
> The Lord has chosen him to teach the barbarian tribes,
> To fish with the nets of his teaching,
> And to draw from the world unto grace the believers,
> Men who would follow the Lord to His heavenly seat.
> God's faithful servant and His distinguished ambassador,
> He gives the good an apostolic example and model,
> Preaching as he does to God's people in words as well as in deeds,
> So that him whom he converts not with words he inspires with
>   good conduct.
> God has sent him, as He sent Paul, an apostle to the gentiles,
> To offer men guidance to the kingdom of God.[1]

Saint Patrick, the fifth-century missionary to Ireland, has been the subject of many charming but fanciful legends. Muirchú's *Life of Patrick*

---

1. The Hymn of Saint Patrick is traditionally ascribed to Secundinus, one of Patrick's immediate disciples. It is more likely to have been written in the mid-seventh century by an anonymous poet. Ludwig Bieler, *The Works of St. Patrick, St. Secundinus, Hymn of St. Patrick* (New York: Newman, 1953), 61–62.

(ca. 680), written more than two centuries after Patrick's death, falsely claims that the apostle to Ireland lit an Easter fire at Tara and challenged the druids and magicians of Lóegaire, the high king of Ireland. A great harvest of souls was thereby brought into the church. Later hagiographers asserted that Patrick used the shamrock to teach the Trinity and that he drove the snakes out of Ireland.[2] Patrick's mission to Ireland did result in much evangelistic fruit. But Patrick's mission to Ireland was not only successful. It was a turning point in the expansion of Christianity for this reason: Patrick was "the first person in Christian history to take the scriptural injunctions literally; to grasp that teaching all nations meant teaching even barbarians [the Irish] who lived *beyond the frontiers of the Roman empire*."[3] The seventh-century Hymn of Saint Patrick quoted above expresses that very sentiment. Patrick "taught the barbarian tribes" by casting out his fishing net and "drawing from the world unto grace" those who became believers, thus becoming an "apostolic example and model." He earned a place in mission history as the first to initiate sustained evangelization outside the boundaries of the Roman Empire due to his literal understanding of and obedience to the apostolic commissions found in Matthew 28:16–20 and elsewhere in the New Testament, both of which were nearly unheard of in this era. Patrick also became a model for foreign missionary enterprise, which soon became a hallmark of the Irish church (see below and chap. 4).

Christians and historians today are fortunate that they do not need to rely on the embellished hagiographic accounts of the apostle to Ireland—written centuries after his death and therefore of questionable reliability. Rather, there exist two largely autobiographical works written by Patrick himself: his *Confession* and *Letter to Coroticus*. This stands in contrast to the situation for most figures from late antiquity, the transitional period from classical antiquity to the Middle Ages. The historical Patrick whom we discover in his own writings is vastly more appealing than the Patrick of legend. In his two surviving works, he includes details of his personal and spiritual life, his own statement of faith, his missionary call, and his theological understanding of and method for mission. The following account of Patrick's life and ministry is based largely on his *Confession*.

Patrick was a Briton born in the last decade of the fourth or early fifth century into a privileged and landowning aristocratic family. His name, Patrick, was "Patricius" in Latin, which means "noble" or "of the patrician class."

2. Thomas O'Loughlin, *Discovering Saint Patrick* (Mahwah, NJ: Paulist Press, 2005), 6, 123–26.
3. Richard Fletcher, *The Barbarian Conversion: From Paganism to Christianity* (Berkeley: University of California Press, 1997), 86.

His family's estate was in Bannaventa Berniae, a village in western Britain facing the Irish Sea. Patrick's family was Gallo-Roman, indicating that they had adopted aspects of Roman culture, including Latin, while retaining British elements, particularly the British (later Welsh) language. Patrick took pride in his Roman citizenship. In the *Confession*, he emphasizes that his father Calpurnius was a decurion, or city counselor—in other words, a local Roman official, possibly entrusted with the collection of taxes. This civil office (and his married status) did not hinder Calpurnius from holding the church office of deacon, as it had not hindered his father Potitus, Patrick's grandfather, from being a priest. Celibacy for church clergy was strongly encouraged but not insisted on at this time. Thus, Patrick grew up in a decidedly Christian family. Nevertheless, according to his own account, in his youth he was merely a nominal Christian. "I was then ignorant of the true God," he wrote. "I was like a stone lying in the deepest mire."[4] In this period, he committed an unspecified shocking sin that was brought up against him later in life.

Patrick's life changed dramatically when he was sixteen years old. Irish slave raiders attacked the family estate and took him captive to Ireland. Pirates and slave traders had been raiding the western seaboard of Britain since the third century. This trend only increased after the government of Emperor Honorius withdrew the Roman military and administration from the frontier of Britain in 410 in order to consolidate power at the core of the empire. Unlike Britain, Ireland had never belonged to the Roman Empire; nevertheless, a certain degree of cultural interaction existed between the two islands.[5] Archaeological evidence points to the extensive trade relationships that existed between this westernmost island and both Britain and the Continent. Not just goods but ideas were exchanged prior to the introduction of Christianity. The Irish Sea in this era was a "Celtic Mediterranean" that united more than it divided territories.[6]

Patrick was the victim of a common but illegitimate form of trade—the trade in human beings. "I was led as a slave to Ireland as were so many thousands of others." He was sold to a master, whom he served for the entire time of his captivity. For six years he herded sheep, the lowest form of servitude for a slave. Patrick's master probably lived close to the Wood of Foclut near the Western Sea (Atlantic Ocean) in what is today County Mayo in western Ireland. Close contact with the locals enabled the youth to learn Irish customs and to acquire the Irish language, which was similar to his native British. The

4. St. Patrick, *Confessio* 1, 12, in O'Loughlin, *Discovering Saint Patrick*, 142, 148; cf. 47–51.

5. Fletcher, *Barbarian Conversion*, 79–80.

6. Peter Brown, *The Rise of Western Christendom*, 2nd ed. (Malden, MA: Blackwell, 2003), 129–32.

SIDEBAR 2.1

Confession of Saint Patrick

I saw a vision of the night, a man named Victoricus, like one from Ireland, coming with innumerable letters. He gave me one of them and I began to read what was in it: "The Voice of the Irish." And at that very moment as I was reading out the letter's opening, I thought I heard the voice of those around the wood of Foclut which is close to the Western Sea. It was as if they were shouting out in one voice, "O Holy Boy, we beg you to come again to walk among us." And I was broken-hearted and could not read anything more. And at that moment I woke up. Thank God after many years the Lord granted them what they called out for.

Source: St. Patrick, *Confessio* 23, in Thomas O'Loughlin, *Discovering Saint Patrick* (Mahwah, NJ: Paulist Press, 2005), 153.

hours of solitude while tending sheep provided Patrick with an opportunity to reflect on his former life. The nominal Christian experienced a spiritual awakening. "God used the time to shape and mold me into something better. He made me into what I am now—someone very different from what I once was." There in Ireland, "the Lord opened my understanding to my unbelief . . . and had mercy on the ignorance of my youth." Patrick took to praying frequently. His fellows, perhaps mockingly, gave him the nickname "Holy Boy."[7] After six years of servitude, Patrick had a dream that instructed him to escape from his master. A ship was waiting for him two hundred Roman miles away on the southern or eastern coast of Ireland. He caught the ship and returned to his family, where the twenty-two-year-old was welcomed as a long-lost son.

After an undisclosed period of time, Patrick had another momentous dream (see sidebar 2.1). In the dream he saw a man named Victoricus from Ireland carrying a large bundle of letters. Victoricus, whom Patrick may have known in Ireland, handed to him one of the letters titled the "Voice of the Irish." As he read it, he heard the voices of those who lived in the forest of Foclut near the Western Sea pleading with him to return to them. This was Patrick's Macedonian call (Acts 16:9–10), his call to serve as a missionary among the Irish people. On two further occasions, God confirmed his call through spiritual experiences, so that he could confidently state, "It is not my grace, but God

7. St. Patrick, *Confessio* 1, 2, in O'Loughlin, *Discovering Saint Patrick*, 142–43; cf. 53–56.

who conquered in me . . . that I might come to the Irish nations to preach the gospel."[8] After his missionary call, Patrick began to study for the ministry. There were no theological seminaries in Britain at this time. A candidate for the ministry studied theology with a local bishop and learned from him the duties of a clergyman. Patrick would have progressed steadily through the ranks of clergy—from layman to deacon, from deacon to priest (with its minimum age of thirty), and finally from priest to bishop. After his theological training, the former slave voluntarily "return[ed] to the land of his captivity . . . to labor among the Irish for the rest of his life."[9]

Patrick's call to minister to barbarians (the Irish) outside the Roman Empire was without parallel. E. A. Thompson notes that "not one . . . earlier Western Catholic bishop . . . planned to go across the Imperial Roman frontier into the lands of the barbarians for the specific purpose of winning over the heathen who were living there. His [Patrick's] mission was something dramatically new."[10] It was a turning point in the expansion of Christianity. To appreciate the "newness" of Patrick's mission, we first need to examine two issues, which will be unpacked in the next section of this chapter: (1) the view that the Roman Empire and Christianity were coextensive, and (2) the Roman distaste for barbarians. I then discuss Patrick's motivations for his mission to Ireland and the mission methods he employed there. Although Patrick was not the first to evangelize among the Irish, his was the first intentional and sustained mission. The second half of this chapter is devoted to the mission that Pope Gregory the Great sent to the Anglo-Saxons of Britain in 596. This was also an intentional mission outside the boundaries of the Roman Empire and similar in several ways to Patrick's mission. It was also unique, as it was the first mission to a pagan population that was both sent and directed by the pope in Rome. Furthermore, Pope Gregory's missionary instructions sent to the mission team in 601 were an early and important example of accommodation to aspects of Anglo-Saxon religious culture. The chapter ends with the completion of the evangelization of Britain by none other than Irish missionaries.

Mission to Barbarians outside the Roman Empire

An evangelistic mission to barbarians outside the Roman Empire was virtually unheard of in late antiquity. Prior to Patrick, there was not one example during

---

8. St. Patrick, *Confessio* 37, in O'Loughlin, *Discovering Saint Patrick*, 158–59; cf. 57–59.

9. Jehu J. Hanciles, *Migration and the Making of Global Christianity* (Grand Rapids: Eerdmans, 2021), 194.

10. E. A. Thompson, *Who Was Saint Patrick?* (New York: St. Martin's Press, 1986), 82.

the Roman period of a bishop being assigned the specific task of evangelizing non-Christians outside the empire. That did not mean that no Christian communities came into existence beyond imperial frontiers. They did. Through the effort of Christian merchants, veterans, or even slaves, churches arose, which then were entitled to request a bishop to be sent to minister to their pastoral needs. Such requests occasionally occurred in the fourth and fifth centuries and were fulfilled. For example, a bishop was requested for the Christians at Axum in Ethiopia, and Athanasius of Alexandria consecrated Frumentius as bishop and sent him there.[11] However, it was entirely unique for an individual such as Patrick to conceive of a mission to the Irish without a prior invitation from Christians living there.

The first Christian emperor, Constantine, ended the brutal persecution of Christians in 313 when he published the Edict of Milan, granting freedom of religion to beleaguered believers. Later he directly supported the Christian religion. Thus began the period of Christendom in which, increasingly, the boundaries of Western Christianity were identical to those of the Roman Empire. The empire and the church became two aspects of the same united reality. Romanness and Christianity were viewed as intrinsically linked. This meant that Spanish historian Orosius in 417 could unite his identity "as a Christian and as a Roman." The link between empire and church was an idealized impression that never actually corresponded to the reality of ongoing, persistent paganism. Nevertheless, it was a widely believed impression that attained the status of established truth. The result of this for mission outside the Roman Empire was devastating. Very few Christians in the three centuries after Constantine viewed mission to non-Christians outside the borders of the empire as part of the church's responsibility or mandate.[12]

The Greek term "barbarian" was originally not entirely pejorative; it meant all that was not Greek but rather foreign or strange. The Romans, who were technically barbarians themselves, adopted the term and applied it to all peoples and nations lacking the accomplishments of the Greek or Roman civilizations.[13] By the fourth and fifth centuries, the term had decidedly negative connotations. In general, all barbarians were lesser creatures and barely human in Roman eyes. Spanish Christian poet Prudentius famously noted in 390, "Romans and barbarians are as distinct from the other as are four-footed beasts from humans."[14] Barbarians were portrayed as violent, nomadic groups

11. Fletcher, *Barbarian Conversion*, 25, 66.
12. Fletcher, *Barbarian Conversion*, 19, 24–25.
13. Online Etymology Dictionary, "Barbarian," accessed October 17, 2020, https://www.etymonline.com/word/barbarian.
14. Fletcher, *Barbarian Conversion*, 25.

who violated the boundaries of the empire. This portrayal was inaccurate for northwestern Europe. There the barbarian populations living outside the empire were not largely nomadic. They were farmers, not so very different from Roman Mediterranean pastoralists. Roman distaste for barbarians, however, was prevalent and deep-seated. In this climate of opinion, mission to barbarians was out of the question for most Christians.[15]

Two lonely voices in this period, Augustine of Hippo and Prosper of Aquitaine, spoke out for mission to barbarians outside the Roman Empire and thus provide the intellectual background to Patrick's mission to the Irish. A devastating earthquake on July 19, 418, prompted Bishop Hesychius of Salona, which is located on the Dalmatian coast of Croatia, to consult Augustine regarding Daniel's prophecies of the end time. Was the end time imminent, as many people believed? Augustine pointed out that Matthew 24:14 indicated that the conversion of the nations would precede the end time. In a second response to Hesychius, he expanded on his initial letter with a fifty-four-chapter pamphlet titled "On the End of the World." In it he argues that it was not the case that the original twelve apostles had completed the task of world evangelization, as most contemporaries believed. Augustine, the North African, reminded Hesychius that in Africa alone there were numerous ethnic groups among whom the gospel had not been preached. He clarified that "the Lord did not promise the Romans but all nations to the seed of Abraham." All nations were created by God and should call on his name and worship him. Although he quotes Romans 10:14–15, Augustine stops short of calling for missionaries to preach the good news to non-Christians outside the Roman Empire.[16]

Prosper of Aquitaine was a poet, a lay theologian, and a younger contemporary of Augustine of Hippo. In the 440s, and most likely in Rome, Prosper penned *The Call of All Nations* (see sidebar 2.2). This treatise has been named the first Christian book to make an appeal for the salvation of peoples and nations outside the empire.[17] Prosper's line of reasoning began with the Pentecost event. Not all of the people groups present at Pentecost lived within the boundaries of the empire. Yet the gospel was preached to them, and they carried the message back to their home countries. Although the Roman Empire, according to Prosper, was part of God's good providence, grace and salvation could not be limited to its boundaries. Nations still existed that had "not yet seen the light of the grace of the Savior."[18] But a time had

15. Brown, *Rise of Western Christendom*, 43–45.
16. Fletcher, *Barbarian Conversion*, 31–32.
17. Fletcher, *Barbarian Conversion*, 32–33.
18. St. Prosper of Aquitaine, *The Call of All Nations*, trans. P. De Letter (Mahwah, NJ: Paulist Press, 1978), 120–21.

SIDEBAR 2.2

Prosper of Aquitaine, *The Call of All Nations*

Their [Jews and proselytes on the day of Pentecost] testimony was to spread far and wide also to the more distant nations. We believe that God's Providence had willed the expansion of the Roman Empire as a preparation for His design over the nations, who had been called into the unity of the Body of Christ: He first gathered them under the authority of one empire. But the grace of Christianity is not content with the boundaries that are Rome's. Grace has now submitted to the scepter of the Cross of Christianity peoples whom Rome could not subject with her arms. . . . There are in the remotest parts of the world some nations who have not yet seen the light of the grace of the Saviour. But we have no doubt that in God's hidden judgment, for them also a time of calling has been appointed, when they will hear and accept the Gospel which now remains unknown to them.

Source: St. Prosper of Aquitaine, *The Call of All Nations*, trans. P. De Letter (Mahwah, NJ: Paulist Press, 1978), 120–21.

been appointed when those remote nations would hear and accept the gospel. Like Augustine, Prosper did not draw the logical conclusion that missionary activity must be embraced both outside and inside the empire. Perhaps the two men were too Roman, too much men of their time, to move from abstract theologizing to actual practice. That would require a Patrick.

Patrick's Mission to Ireland

Patrick was not the first bishop to the Irish. That honor belonged to Palladius, a deacon, possibly of the church in Auxerre in northern Gaul. In 429, Palladius became concerned with the spread of the Pelagian doctrine in Britain. He urged Pope Celestine to send a staunchly orthodox cleric to Britain to combat the heresy. Celestine acted on his advice and sent Germanus, bishop of Auxerre, and Lupus, bishop of Troyes, that same year. Two years later, when a group of Irish Christians signaled to Pope Celestine their desire for a bishop, he turned to Palladius. Celestine ordained and sent him "as their first bishop, to the Irish who believe in Christ." Pope Celestine did not envision Palladius's ministry to be evangelistic or missionary. He had been sent to those "who believe in Christ" to organize the small Irish church and serve as pastor of the flock. Nevertheless, Prosper of Aquitaine indicated in 434, three years after Palladius's sending, that Palladius had "also made the barbarian island [Ireland] Christian."[19] Prosper's account was contemporary to Palladius's ministry, and although exaggerated (the whole island was by no means made Christian), it is reliable in its statement that Palladius sought and achieved the conversion of some formerly pagan Irish. His ministry most likely lasted two decades and was centered on Leinster, the area around Dublin on the east coast of Ireland. In the early seventh century, Irish missionary Columbanus still remembered the ministry of Palladius. Shortly thereafter, however, his accomplishments were subsumed into the tradition surrounding Patrick. Details of Palladius's ministry became lost to history.[20]

Roughly twenty years after Palladius, in around 450, Patrick began his mission to Ireland. His name had been put forward for the office of bishop when he was absent from Britain, presumably in Gaul. Despite some concerns about his youthful sin and his interrupted education, Patrick was chosen, consecrated as bishop, and sent to Ireland. His ministry was supported by the British church. In some ways Patrick was a logical candidate. He knew the Irish language and culture. He was a devout priest, and although his Latin skills were relatively poor, he knew the Latin Bible inside and out. Patrick's writings abound with biblical references. Finally, his appointment as bishop to Ireland coincided with his own strong conviction of being called there. "It is not I but Christ the Lord who has ordered me to come and be with these [Irish] people for the rest of my life."[21]

Patrick had another powerful motive for missionary service in Ireland. He was convinced that he was living in the last days before Christ's imminent return. It is not surprising that Patrick believed the end was near. The thousand-year-old Roman Empire was crumbling. Barbarian raids wreaked havoc on the frontiers. The Roman government was incapable of retaining the allegiance of its armies. From the mid-third century on, military coup followed military coup as ruthless generals used their troops to seize the imperial throne. The vast majority of both legitimate emperors and usurpers in this period died violently; the average length of reign was less than two and a half years. The world as Patrick knew it was coming to an end. In his *Confession*, Patrick, like Augustine, quotes the prophecy of Matthew 24:14 that the gospel would be preached to all nations before the end would come. Like the apostle Paul before him, Patrick desired to preach the gospel

19. T. M. Charles-Edwards, *Early Christian Ireland* (Cambridge: Cambridge University Press, 2000), 182, 204–5.
20. Charles-Edwards, *Early Christian Ireland*, 182–83, 237–39.
21. St. Patrick, *Confessio* 43, in O'Loughlin, *Discovering Saint Patrick*, 163; cf. 57–59.

where no one had preached before—to be, as he put it, the "letter of Christ for salvation to the uttermost parts of the earth." Ireland was located at the uttermost western end of the known inhabited world at that time. It would be centuries before Europeans discovered the Americas. In his itinerant ministry in Ireland, Patrick intentionally evangelized the remotest corners of western Ireland on the Atlantic coast so that he could boast, "I have gone to places beyond where anyone lived . . . where no one else had ever travelled . . . to baptize . . . or bring the people to completion." Preaching was central to Patrick's ministry to people at the ends of the earth. Although Bishop Patrick preached and provided pastoral care for Christian believers, he understood his mandate to be for the unconverted masses. "I came to the heathen Irish to preach the Gospel," he wrote.[22]

Ireland in Patrick's day was not a single, unified state. It is estimated that roughly 150 clans existed in Ireland at this time, each under a king or, in the case of smaller groups, a sub-king. In his largely itinerant ministry, Patrick worked his way step by step through perhaps dozens of different people groups. He followed the appropriate cultural practice of seeking permission from the local king before entering his territory and evangelizing. Frequently he paid the kings the customary tribute or gave presents in order to gain favor and protection. He also recruited the younger sons of kings to accompany him on his travels. This afforded an extra measure of credibility and protection. Two later hagiographical accounts of Patrick's life, by Muirchú and Tírechán, contain legends in which Patrick antagonized the local kings and druids. Patrick's own writings give a different picture. No power encounters with druids, the religious specialists of the day, are found in them. We discover instead a missionary who paid careful attention to the practical politics of Irish society.[23] That does not mean that no conflict occurred with the traditional Irish religion. In Patrick's estimation, the polytheistic traditional religion was idolatrous; it had no redeeming qualities. Before his ministry, the Irish, as he put it, "had no knowledge of God and until now they celebrated only idols." Yet Patrick rejoiced when these former idol-worshipers converted and became "a prepared people of the Lord. . . . They are now called the sons of God."[24] His negative estimation of Irish traditional religion was driven by his theology that all non-Christian religion was essentially demonic. It does not necessarily indicate a lack of respect for other aspects of Irish culture.

22. St. Patrick, *Confessio* 11, 37, 51, in O'Loughlin, *Discovering Saint Patrick*, 146–47, 158–59, 166; cf. Charles-Edwards, *Early Christian Ireland*, 215–16.

23. Charles-Edwards, *Early Christian Ireland*, 195, 239–40. Cf. Philip Freeman, *St. Patrick of Ireland: A Biography* (New York: Simon & Schuster, 2004), 84–106.

24. St. Patrick, *Confessio* 41, in O'Loughlin, *Discovering Saint Patrick*, 161–62.

Patrick most likely had a small group of British clergy to help him in his ministry in Ireland, at least in the beginning. But one clear goal of his mission, mentioned several times in the *Confession*, was to ordain Irish clergy so that they could be the ones to baptize, exhort, and provide pastoral care for the new converts. Patrick also baptized. In fact, he claimed that he had baptized many thousands of people, who now had become his brothers and sisters in the faith. Unlike his father and grandfather, who were married clergymen, Patrick most likely was celibate; there is no mention of his marriage in the historical record. He also gave enthusiastic support to the ascetic lifestyle in Ireland. It is fair to say that the dedication of some of his converts to the ascetic life as "monks and virgins of Christ" was for him the culmination of his ministry. The vocation of a beautiful young Irish noblewoman shortly after her conversion and baptism is particularly highlighted in his *Confession*. Like Patrick, this woman received a vision of an angelic messenger calling her to be a virgin of Christ, despite the opposition of her family and any ensuing persecution. Patrick rejoiced not just that noble sons and daughters embraced a monastic life but that widows and slaves did as well. Most of these ascetics, the women particularly, would have continued to live on the family estate while pursuing a stringent, austere life. Fully organized monastic communities, for the most part, were the product of a later date.[25]

What is the significance of Patrick, missionary to the Irish? First, Patrick certainly contributed dramatically to the Christianization of Ireland and the numerical growth of the Irish church. Perhaps he did not baptize the many thousands mentioned in the *Confession*, but his mission was successful, and a solid beginning was made to the large-scale conversion of the island. When Patrick died in 493, the nobility had not yet been won to Christianity. Ireland was still ruled by non-Christian kings and under the influence of druids. But within a generation, the Irish church had adopted its essential structure. By 550, or after roughly two generations, the task of conversion had been accomplished.[26] Second, Patrick was the first person to cross the imperial frontier in order to *convert* a nation to the Christian faith. His ministry centered on evangelistic goals outside the empire among non-Christians. This was radically new and a turning point in the expansion of Christianity. Finally, Patrick imparted a missionary spirit to the Irish church. The Irish church looked to his example and set a high value on foreign missionary activity.

25. St. Patrick, *Confessio* 14, 42, 50, in O'Loughlin, *Discovering Saint Patrick*, 149, 162, 166. Cf. Freeman, *St. Patrick of Ireland*, 107–9, 113–19.
26. Charles-Edwards, *Early Christian Ireland*, 239–40.

Prelude to Gregory the Great's Mission to England

Patrick was a missionary bishop who evangelized the Irish outside the Roman Empire. When Pope Gregory the Great sent a group of forty Benedictine monks under Augustine of Canterbury to England in 596 to convert the Anglo-Saxons, he was likewise initiating mission beyond imperial boundaries. Britain south of Hadrian's Wall had been under Roman rule for four centuries. Then, beginning in 405–406, the Roman troops and government were withdrawn from Britain to reinforce the center of the empire. Without the support of imperial taxation, the infrastructure in Britain quickly collapsed. The power vacuum that ensued was exploited by bands of Germanic Angles, Saxons, and Jutes, who settled in what became known as England, the land of the "Angles." By the time of the arrival of Gregory's mission team in 597, Anglo-Saxons controlled the eastern and southern third of Britain. This was mission outside the boundaries of Roman hegemony.

There were other similarities between Patrick's mission to Ireland and Gregory's to England. Both missions occurred in chaotic times. The reconquest of parts of Italy and their subsequent reincorporation into the East Roman Empire by Justinian from 533 to 540 brought an end to the ordered rule of the senatorial aristocracy in Rome. Three decades later, in Gregory's lifetime, the Lombards ravaged the Italian countryside and cities, ultimately gaining control of central Italy along the Apennine range. Natural disasters—earthquakes, tornadoes, and floods—brought famine and disease in their wake.[27] In his writings, Gregory describes the chaos of his age: "Towns are depopulated, fortified places destroyed, churches burnt, monasteries and nunneries destroyed; fields are deserted by men, and the earth . . . is desolate. . . . The world no longer announces its coming end, but shows it forth."[28]

Like Patrick, Gregory interpreted the political and natural disasters of his time eschatologically. These events were signs of the imminent return of Christ. Gregory's conviction of the nearness of the end shaped every aspect of his thought and ministry, including the need for universal mission.[29] He understood Romans 11:25–26 to mean that the conversion of the Gentiles was the necessary prelude to the return of Christ and the subsequent mass conversion of the Jews. Only when the message of the gospel had spread to the ends of the earth would Christ return for his church. The majority of the

---

27. Brown, *Rise of Western Christendom*, 190–94, 213.
28. R. A. Markus, *Gregory the Great and His World* (Cambridge: Cambridge University Press, 1997), 52.
29. G. R. Evans, *The Thought of Gregory the Great* (Cambridge: Cambridge University Press, 1988), 43.

ethnic groups within the Roman Empire had been nominally Christianized by this time. But beyond the fringes of the empire, at the very "ends of the earth," lived the unconverted Anglo-Saxons. According to Gregory's eschatology, their conversion might hasten the end and therefore must be embraced. A third similarity between Patrick's mission to the Irish and Gregory's to the Anglo-Saxons is that both missions led to the successful establishment of a national church within two generations.

The man who became Pope Gregory the Great was born around 540 into an ancient and wealthy Roman senatorial family. Gregory's aristocratic background made his appointment as prefect of the city of Rome a logical choice. But his family had a long legacy of service to the church as well. Gregory's grandfather was Pope Felix III, who reigned from 483 to 492. After Gregory inherited the ancestral villa on the Caecilian hill opposite the Circus Maximus in Rome in 575, he transformed the property into a monastery dedicated to Saint Andrew. His tenure as a monk there lasted but four years. In 579 Gregory was ordained a deacon and thus reentered the public life of the church. The following year he was sent as a papal representative or legate to the court of Constantinople. In 590 he was elected pope and served in that role until his death in 604. His commentary on Job, the *Moralia*, his *Dialogues*, and his *Pastoral Rule* for bishops were highly influential in the Middle Ages. Gregory's crowning achievement, however, was his mission to the Anglo-Saxons.[30]

In 589, shortly after Gregory returned to Rome from Constantinople, a dramatic event occurred that might have prompted the soon-to-be pope toward mission. The Arian Visigothic king in Spain, Reccared, along with his nobles, rejected the Arian form of Christianity, with its unorthodox view of Christ's deity, for the Roman faith. An entire nation thus joined the Roman Church without papal intervention. Gregory admitted in his congratulatory letter to Reccared his own "sluggishness" with regard to mission:

> This is a change [the conversion of the Visigoths] which the right hand of the Most High hath wrought. It was a new miracle in our time. My feelings are aroused against myself, because I have been so sluggish . . . while, to gain the heavenly Fatherland, kings [Reccared] are working for the gathering-in of souls.[31]

It was not long before the pope replaced "sluggishness" with action directed toward the conversion of the Anglo-Saxons.

We are not sure when Gregory's attention was first drawn toward England. In 599, ten years after the Visigoths accepted Catholicism, the pope

30. Brown, *Rise of Western Christendom*, 199–211.
31. Brown, *Rise of Western Christendom*, 214.

acknowledged that he had "long had in mind" a mission to England. His interest certainly was aroused no later than September 595. At that time, Gregory instructed Candidus, his agent for the Roman Church's lands in Gaul (present-day France), to use some of the generated revenues to buy seventeen- or eighteen-year-old Anglo-Saxon slave boys. They should then be trained in monasteries, presumably to serve later as missionaries to their own people. Gregory had contacts in Gaul not just with his agent; he was likewise in communication with the Frankish court. He was aware, therefore, that by 596 the pagan Anglo-Saxon King Ethelbert of Kent had been married to the Catholic Merovingian princess Bertha for roughly fifteen years. Part of the couple's marriage agreement was that Bertha would be allowed to practice her Catholic faith freely. She had brought with her to Canterbury, the capital of Kent, the Frankish chaplain Bishop Liudhard.[32]

Liudhard was granted the use of an old Roman church in Canterbury, St. Martin's, which Bertha arranged to have restored for divine services. This church had been used by British Christians prior to the influx of Anglo-Saxons into Kent. British Christianity continued to thrive in western Britain, but in Kent in the southeast of England, the British church was in sharp decline when Augustine and his band of missionary monks arrived. An organized British clergy was lacking in these Saxon areas. A "folk" form of Christianity, however, survived to a degree among the peasant class, as evidenced by the ongoing cult to British martyr Saint Sixtus. Lacking clerical leadership and ecclesiastical structures, the remaining British Christians in Kent were unable and unwilling to evangelize their Saxon conquerors. The Northumbrian church historian, Venerable Bede, lamented that the Christian Britons "never preached the faith to the Saxons—or English—who dwelt among them."[33]

The Anglo-Saxons most likely would not have been open to a mission from the conquered British in any case. They were, however, by 596 open to a Frankish mission or to a mission sent from Rome. This fact is evident from a letter that Gregory the Great sent to the Frankish kings Theuderic II and Theudebert II in July 596. In the letter, Gregory notes:

> It has reached us that the English nation, by the compassion of God, eagerly
> desires to be converted to the Christian faith, but that the neighboring bishops
> neglect it and refrain from kindling by their exhortations the desires of the

32. Fletcher, *Barbarian Conversion*, 112–16.
33. Brown, *Rise of Western Christendom*, 129, 341–42; Venerable Bede, *Ecclesiastical History of the English Nation* 1.22, Internet History Sourcebooks Project, accessed April 21, 2021, https://sourcebooks.fordham.edu/basis/bede-book1.asp. Hereafter cited in the text as *EH*.

English. On this account, therefore, we have arranged to send thither Augustine, the servant of God [monk] . . . along with other servants of God.[34]

The larger context of this letter makes clear that "neighboring bishops" does not refer to British bishops but Frankish ones. Gregory received word that the English desired a mission. Since the Franks were unwilling to accommodate this desire, the pope sent a Roman contingent under Augustine to Kent.

Gregory the Great's Mission to England

The Venerable Bede was a great admirer of Pope Gregory the Great. In his *Ecclesiastical History*, he downplays the role of Augustine of Canterbury and stresses in its place the crucial contribution of the pope in the mission to England. "We can and should by rights call him [Gregory] our apostle," Bede claims, for "he made our nation until then enslaved to idols into a church of Christ" (*EH* 2.1). Pope Gregory certainly had the vision and determination for the mission, but it was Augustine who bore the day-to-day responsibility of transforming that vision into practical reality. Before being assigned head of the mission, Augustine (not to be confused with his earlier and more famous namesake Augustine of Hippo) had been prior at Gregory's family monastery of St. Andrew's in Rome. Augustine was accompanied in 596 by a very large contingent of missionaries—forty monks. Somewhere in Gaul, the missionary troop became frightened about "going to the barbarous, fierce and unbelieving nation whose language they did not even understand" (*EH* 1.23). They sent Augustine back to Rome to request an abandonment of the mission. Pope Gregory declined. He remedied the language problem, however, by requesting that the missionaries engage Frankish interpreters on their way through Gaul. In the spring of 597, they arrived at the island of Thanet, off the coast of Kent.

King Ethelbert of Kent had the mission party initially remain on Thanet while he decided what to do with them. A few days later, the king visited the island and allowed the missionaries to preach their message—in the open air, however, since he feared that magic might be worked on him if the meeting took place in a closed building. The message was sufficiently agreeable to the king that Ethelbert not only permitted the mission band to settle in Canterbury in a dwelling place made available for them but he provided their sustenance as well. The missionaries might preach and make as many converts

34. Robin Mackintosh, *Augustine of Canterbury: Leadership, Mission and Legacy* (Norwich: Canterbury, 2013), 26.

as possible as long as no coercion was exerted. The grateful missionary party processed into Canterbury behind a silver cross and an image of Christ painted on a wooden plaque, all the while singing a litany.[35]

The following July (598), Gregory was able to report to his colleague Eulogius, the patriarch of Alexandria, that the mission had made significant inroads in Kent. He wrote:

> [Augustine] with my permission . . . reached the [English] people *at the ends of the earth*, and now we have received reports of his well-being and his work. . . . At the festival of Christmas this last year, more than ten thousand are reported to have been baptized by our brother and fellow bishop.[36]

The number ten thousand is most likely an exaggeration; nevertheless, a very encouraging beginning had been made. Interestingly, there is no mention in this letter of the conversion of King Ethelbert. One would expect Gregory to include such an important detail. Therefore, perhaps the king had not yet accepted the faith of his Catholic wife.

Anglo-Saxon kings were not just political warlords of a warrior society, which ninth-century Welsh historian Nennius calls a "nation of thugs."[37] The kings also played a semireligious or sacral role in society, perhaps even leading pagan rituals. Anglo-Saxon kings traced their ancestry back to the Germanic god Woden; thus their very identity was linked to the traditional religion. Ethelbert was the overlord (*bretwalda*) of all the Anglo-Saxon kingdoms south of the Humber estuary. His overlordship gave him more freedom to change religions without reprisals from his subjects. Nevertheless, he needed to be careful not to alienate his nobles. Ethelbert admitted to Augustine his reluctance to turn his back on the old gods. "The words and promises you bring are fair enough, but because they are new to us and doubtful, I cannot consent to accept them and forsake those beliefs which I and the whole English race have held so long" (*EH* 1.25). Changing religion was a decision not to be made lightly or quickly, especially for a king.[38]

Bede does not reveal when Ethelbert converted and received baptism, although it was certainly before 601. In that year Gregory wrote a letter to Ethelbert in which he gives instructions to the already-Christian king. In the same packet of letters was one addressed by Gregory to Queen Bertha,

---

35. Brown, *Rise of Western Christendom*, 344–45; cf. Fletcher, *Barbarian Conversion*, 123–24; and Markus, *Gregory the Great*, 175–77.

36. Markus, *Gregory the Great*, 179.

37. Brown, *Rise of Western Christendom*, 341.

38. Barbara Yorke, "The Reception of Christianity at the Anglo-Saxon Royal Courts," in *St. Augustine and the Conversion of England*, ed. Richard Gameson (Stroud: Sutton, 2000), 152–73.

acknowledging her important role in the conversion of her husband. Bertha represents just one of a number of Christian "royal brides" in the early Middle Ages who helped convert their unbelieving husbands in a foreign land.[39] Ethelbert's conversion did help to further spread Christianity in Kent. The monks "obtained greater liberty to preach everywhere. . . . Greater numbers began daily to flock together to hear the Word, and forsaking their heathen rites" to accept the Christian faith (*EH* 1.26). Many noblemen, and presumably commoners, converted in Kent. Despite Ethelbert's initial reticence, his conversion was undoubtedly sincere. The king continued to supply significant material support for the church, including the restoration of a Roman church in Canterbury to serve as a cathedral, which was dedicated to the holy Savior. He also arranged that he would be buried in the Christian manner in the annex of a church. Finally, Ethelbert issued a law code in 602 or 603 that, among other laws, protected the "teaching he had welcomed," as well as church property.[40]

Gregory's Missionary Instructions

In 601 a group of Augustine's missionaries returned to Rome to report in person to the pope how the mission was progressing. At this time Gregory learned that paganism was more strongly entrenched among the Saxons than he had previously realized. Gregory used this opportunity to send to England not only ecclesiastical supplies and missionary reinforcements under Abbot Mellitus but also a cache of letters. One letter, dated June 22, 601, was addressed to King Ethelbert. After congratulating him on his conversion, Gregory encourages the king to follow the example of Constantine. Ethelbert

> should increase his righteous zeal for their [his subjects'] conversion; persecute the cult of idols; overthrow the shrines; strengthen the morals of his subjects by great purity of life, by exhorting, by terrifying, by enticing [and] by correcting them.[41]

He should spread the faith by his good example and exhortation among all subjects under his overlordship. The use of force and coercion to suppress the pagan cult, however, was acceptable if necessary. It is important to note that coerced conversion as well as the enforcement of orthodox forms

39. Hanciles, *Migration*, 273–74, 278–79.
40. Brown, *Rise of Western Christendom*, 346–47; cf. Fletcher, *Barbarian Conversion*, 116–18.
41. Markus, *Gregory the Great*, 181; cf. 174, 179–84.

of Christianity was common in the post-Constantinian world (see chap. 4). Gregory was recommending only standard procedures. The spread of the faith in Anglo-Saxon England was especially urgent since the "end of this present world . . . is at hand" (*EH* 2.32).

About four weeks later, on July 18, 601, Gregory wrote a second letter, this time to Abbot Mellitus with instructions for Augustine (see sidebar 2.3). The letter was important enough to be sent by special messenger to Mellitus, who by now was "somewhere in Francia" en route to England with the other monks. This letter revised the earlier instructions to King Ethelbert. After careful consideration, Gregory had changed his mind regarding the best approach to convert convinced pagans. He now recommended that well-built pagan shrines should not be destroyed. Rather, only the idols within the temples should be destroyed. Then the temple should be consecrated for Christian use and no longer be used for the "cult of demons" but rather for the "worship of the true God." Gregory had become convinced that pagans would be "more inclined to come to the places they were accustomed" for worship. This would ultimately result in their conversion. The Anglo-Saxons would "banish error from their hearts" and recognize and adore the Christian God. Furthermore, Gregory recommended that Christian festivals be substituted "in a changed form" for pagan feasts. No longer would the Saxons "sacrifice animals to the devil, but slay animals to the praise of God for their own eating." Gregory was convinced that eliminating all of their former "joys" would be detrimental to the spread of the gospel.[42]

This pronounced change of policy "is powerful testimony to Gregory's pastoral flexibility, and constitutes a dramatic change of direction in papal missionary strategy."[43] Gregory's mission approach recommended in the 601 letter to Mellitus is characterized by accommodation. After further consideration, Gregory came to the conclusion that *outward* adaptation to Anglo-Saxon religious culture was legitimate and conducive to conversion as long as the *inward* content was Christian. This contrasts considerably with the confrontational method found in his letter to Ethelbert. The reality is that both approaches were employed in the mission in England. Accommodation is reflected in the adoption of pagan Anglo-Saxon terms for the days of the week in English. For instance, Wednesday was Woden's day, and Thursday Thor's day. Even the name of the central Christian holiday Easter was derived from the pagan goddess Eostre. In response to Augustine's query, Gregory authorized an indigenous

---

42. Gregory the Great, Letter 76, in *A Select Library of Nicene and Post-Nicene Fathers of the Christian Church*, 2nd series, ed. Philip Schaff and Henry Wace (New York: Christian Literature, 1890–1900; repr., Peabody, MA: Hendrickson, 1994), 13:85.

43. Markus, *Gregory the Great*, 184.

SIDEBAR 2.3

Gregory the Great, Letter to Abbot Mellitus (July 18, 601)

But when Almighty God shall have brought you to our most reverend brother the bishop Augustine, tell him that I have long been considering with myself about the case of the Angli; to wit, that the temples of idols in that nation should not be destroyed, but that the idols themselves that are in them should be. Let blessed water be prepared, and sprinkled in these temples, and altars constructed, and relics deposited, since, if these same temples are well built, it is needful that they should be transferred from the worship of idols to the service of the true God; that, when the people themselves see that these temples are not destroyed, they may put away error from their heart, and, knowing and adoring the true God, may have recourse with the more familiarity to the places they have been accustomed to. . . . Nor let them any longer sacrifice animals to the devil, but slay animals to the praise of God for their own eating, and return thanks to the Giver of all for their fulness, so that, while some joys are reserved to them outwardly, they may be able the more easily to incline their minds to inward joys.

Source: Gregory the Great, Letter 76, in *A Select Library of Nicene and Post-Nicene Fathers of the Christian Church*, 2nd series, ed. Philip Schaff and Henry Wace (New York: Christian Literature, 1890–1900; repr., Peabody, MA: Hendrickson, 1994), 13:85.

liturgy suitable for the English church rather than merely appropriating the Roman liturgy. Confrontational approaches also abound in the historical record. King Eorcenbert of Kent (r. 640–664) ordered that all the idols in his kingdom be destroyed and abandoned by his subjects. A forty-day fast was called for his kingdom; those who failed to comply were punished. After his conversion, Coifi, formerly a pagan high priest in Northumbria, destroyed not just the idols in the temple at Goodmanham but the entire structure.[44]

Like Patrick, Pope Gregory the Great's motivation for mission was an outgrowth of his eschatological conviction that the conversion of pagan Gentiles was a prelude to the imminent return of Christ. Like the apostle to Ireland, he initiated mission among Anglo-Saxons outside the borders of the now-defunct Roman Empire. Gregory was unique in that he was the first pope to dispatch missionaries from Rome for the purpose of converting non-Christians. He not only dispatched a mission team; he also directed their mission endeavor through personal consultation (601) and letters in which he theorized over the

44. Brown, *Rise of Western Christendom*, 346–48; cf. Fletcher, *Barbarian Conversion*, 160.

most effective mission methods. His vision was broad. Unlike others before him, Gregory was able to conceive of converting the entire English nation to Christ. In an addendum to his *Moralia of Job*, Gregory rejoiced at the success of the English mission. "Britain's tongue, which had known nothing other than to rage with barbarian fury, now begins to echo the Hebrew Alleluia in the divine praises," he writes.[45]

Mission Threatened, Then Accomplished

Gregory's rejoicing in the *Moralia* was prudently tempered by the recognition that the English mission had only begun. After the deaths of Augustine of Canterbury in 604 and King Ethelbert in 616, the Roman mission to England not only ground to a halt; it suffered reversals. Most of the Anglo-Saxon royal families (East Anglia, Essex, Wessex, Northumbria, and Kent) reverted to paganism. Ethelbert's son and successor, Eanbald (r. 616–640), married his father's second wife in order to strengthen his claim to the Kentish throne. This action reaped the strong disapproval of local priests. Eanbald in return began to participate in pagan sacrifices for a time. Raedwald, the king of East Anglia (r. 599–624), assumed the overlordship of the kingdoms south of the Humber estuary after Ethelbert's death. He hedged his bets and promoted the worship of both Christ and pagan deities. Bede reports that "in the same temple he [Raedwald] had one altar for the Christian sacrifice and another small altar on which to offer victims to devils" (*EH* 2.15). Saberht of Essex (r. 604–616) was persuaded by Ethelbert in 604 to convert to Christianity. His three sons remained pagans. Ethelbert's daughter, Ethelburga, was given in marriage in 625 to Edwin, the powerful king of Northumbria and overlord of northern England. Paulinus, an Italian disciple of Augustine and part of the Roman missionary reinforcements sent with Mellitus in 601, accompanied the bride northward. Edwin converted in 628, but his death in battle in 633 led to a collapse of Christianity and a resurgence of paganism in his kingdom. Paulinus and Ethelburga were forced to flee back to the safety of Kent.[46]

Patrick, far more than his predecessors, furthered the conversion of Ireland and instilled a missionary spirit in the Irish church. His mission impulse came full circle when Irish missionary monks re-evangelized Britain, particularly Northumbria and much of southern England. It came about in this way. Oswald (r. 634–642), Edwin's successor to the Northumbrian throne, and his brother Oswy (r. 643–670) and their retainers, sought asylum in the

45. Markus, *Gregory the Great*, 186.
46. Brown, *Rise of Western Christendom*, 347–50.

Irish-Scottish kingdom of Dalriada on the west coast of Scotland during
Edwin's reign. During their exile, the entire retinue accepted the Christian
faith preached by the Irish monks from the island monastery of Iona. In 635,
the newly crowned King Oswald naturally turned to his spiritual roots, Iona,
to recruit Irish missionary monk Aidan and twelve companions to come to
Northumbria to reinitiate the Christianization process begun by Paulinus.
Aidan founded an Iona-styled Irish monastery on the island of Lindisfarne
off the coast of Northumbria near Oswald's royal fortress of Bamburgh.
From Lindisfarne, Bishop Aidan evangelized on foot throughout northern
England. Bede reports:

> He [Aidan] used to travel everywhere, in town and country . . . on foot . . . in
> order that, as he walked along, whenever he saw people whether rich or poor,
> he might at once approach them, and if they were unbelievers, invite them
> to accept the mystery of the faith; or, if they were believers, that he might
> strengthen them in the faith. (*EH* 3.5)

Aidan and his fellow Irish monks not only actively evangelized and planted
churches. They also established a school at Lindisfarne for Anglo-Saxon boys
to train them for the ministry. Some played pivotal roles in the evangelization of neighboring kingdoms (e.g., Cedd). The close proximity of royal
residence and monastery was no accident. The Northumbrian kings Oswald
and Oswy contributed to the mission activities emanating from Lindisfarne.
Oswald played a part in the conversion of the West Saxon king Cynegils. His
brother Oswy, during his reign, convinced the Mercian prince Peada to accept
the Christian faith. Oswy then arranged for four Lindisfarne monks (which
included the Anglo-Saxon Cedd) to complete the task of Christianization
in Peada's realm. Later Oswy sent Cedd to evangelize Essex, where he also
founded two monasteries. By the 680s, with the support of Anglo-Saxon kings,
Irish (and Anglo-Saxon) missionaries completed the task of evangelization
that Gregory's mission to England had inaugurated.[47]

In conclusion, Patrick's mission to Ireland was a pivotal event in the history of the expansion of Christianity. Like Augustine of Hippo and Prosper of
Aquitaine, Patrick recognized that the New Testament mission mandates had
not been fulfilled, since the pagan Irish living at the ends of the earth outside
the Roman Empire had not been converted. Like Augustine and Prosper, Patrick
was also convinced that he was living in the last days before the imminent return
of Christ. Unlike his predecessors, Patrick did not just theorize about mission

47. Fletcher, *Barbarian Conversion*, 163–70.

but launched a successful mission to Ireland. Although his role as bishop included some pastoral care for believers, Patrick's focus remained missional—leading unconverted Irish into the fold of the church. He accomplished this not through power encounters with druidic priests but through preaching, baptizing converts, ordaining Irish clergy, and encouraging the ascetic lifestyle. Like Patrick, Gregory the Great also inaugurated a mission among the polytheistic Anglo-Saxons beyond imperial boundaries. He was unique as the first pope to send and direct a Roman mission with the intention of winning an entire nation to Christ. Gregory also theorized on how best to evangelize. Patrick's impact on the Irish church came full circle when Irish missionaries completed the task of evangelizing Britain begun by Pope Gregory.

We end this chapter with an Old Irish prayer, traditionally attributed to St. Patrick. Although the prayer was probably written a century after the apostle's death, the sentiments included in it are archaic and reflect Patrick's missionary experience. Known as the Breastplate, the prayer calls for protection from the "whole armor of God" (Eph. 6:10–18) against the wiles of Satan in a pagan land.

> I arise today
> > through God's strength to pilot me:
> > God's might to uphold me,
> > God's wisdom to guide me,
> > God's eye to look before me,
> > God's ear to hear me,
> > God's word to speak for me,
> > God's hand to guard me,
> > God's way to lie before me,
> > God's shield to protect me. . . .
>
> I summon today all these powers between me (and these evils)—
> > . . . against incantations of false prophets,
> > against black laws of heathenry,
> > against craft of idolatry,
> > against spells of women and smiths and wizards,
> > against every knowledge [that endangers] man's body and soul. . . .
>
> Christ with me, Christ before me, Christ behind me,
> Christ in me, Christ beneath me, Christ above me,
> Christ on my right, Christ on my left,
> Christ where I lie, Christ where I sit, Christ where I arise.[48]

48. Bieler, *Works of St. Patrick*, 70–71.

Expanding Eastward

The East Syrian Mission to China (635)

(If) the highest heavens with deep reverence adore,
(If) the great earth earnestly ponders on general peace and
  harmony,
(If) man's first true nature receives confidence and rest,
(It is due to) Aluohe [Elohim], the merciful Father of the universe. . . .

We now all recite (your) mercy and kindness,
Sighing for your mysterious joy to enlighten our realm,
Honoured Mishihe [Messiah] most holy Son,
Widely delivering (from?) the region of bitterness, saving the helpless.

Merciful joyful Lamb of the everlasting King of life,
Generally and universally accepting pain, not refusing toil,
Be willing to put away the collected weight of sin of all living,
Mercifully save their souls that they may obtain rest.[1]

A remarkable religious and cultural encounter occurred in 635 in Xi'an, the capital of China during the Tang dynasty (618–907). The history

1. This hymn was originally written in Syriac around the year 800 by an anonymous Syrian monk and missionary in northwestern China. Translation from A. C. Moule, *Christians in China before the Year 1550* (London: SPCK, 1930), 53–54.

of this encounter and the subsequent spread of Christianity to China is most fully recorded on the famous Nestorian Stele, erected near Xi'an in 781. The stele describes the arrival of a group of East Syrian monks under the leadership of the "highly virtuous man . . . Alopen" (see sidebar 3.1). Bishop Alopen and his monks traveled roughly twenty-five hundred miles from eastern Persia along the Silk Road to Xi'an, located at its eastern terminus, most likely accompanied by Christian Persian merchants. The journey along the trade route had begun under auspicious signs in the heavens (a blue sky and favorable winds), but soon it exposed Alopen and his entourage to "difficulties and perils." Finally, they arrived at a western suburb of Xi'an. Emperor Taizong honored the visitors by dispatching not only his minister of state but also an imperial guard to escort the East Syrian delegation to the imperial palace. Alopen arrived bearing numerous Christian texts as well as religious images.

The bishop was then commissioned by the emperor to translate some of the texts into Chinese, which, with the help of Chinese Buddhists and Taoists, Alopen undertook in the imperial library. Emperor Taizong was persuaded by these translations that the Christian "Way" (or *Tao*) was morally sound and beneficial for the Chinese people. In fact, it exemplified "correctness and truth." Therefore, he issued an edict in 638 in which he granted the East Syrian monks freedom to preach the Christian message and to found a monastery in the imperial capital. A monastery in the I-ning quarter of Xi'an was established and soon occupied with twenty-one monks. That same year, the first Christian church in China was built in the capital city. Taizong himself gave the order for its construction and paid for it with funds from his own treasury. A portrait of the emperor was given to the missionaries and displayed prominently in the new church; it was a "sign of official recognition by the government."[2]

Taizong's successor, Gaozong (r. 656–684), honored Alopen by designating him as a great spiritual ruler and a guardian of the country (see sidebar 3.1). During his reign, Gaozong "caused monasteries of the Luminous Religion," as the East Syrian Christian religion was known in China, "to be founded in every prefecture"—in other words, in all ten provinces of China. This statement, found on the stele, is certainly an exaggeration. We only have firm evidence of eleven such monasteries or churches founded in this period. Nevertheless, it testifies to the spread of the Christian faith and the favor that

2. P. Y. Saeki, *The Nestorian Monument in China* (London: SPCK, 1928), 165–67; Wilhelm Baum and Dietmar W. Winkler, *The Church of the East: A Concise History* (New York: Routledge Curzon, 2003), 47; Li Tang, *A Study of the History of Nestorian Christianity in China and Its Literature in Chinese*, 2nd ed. (New York: Peter Lang, 2004), 92; Jehu J. Hanciles, *Migration and the Making of Global Christianity* (Grand Rapids: Eerdmans, 2021), 346.

SIDEBAR 3.1

Nestorian Stele (AD 781)

When the accomplished Emperor Taizong began his magnificent career in glory and splendor . . . behold there was a highly virtuous man named Alopen in the Kingdom of Da Qin [Syria]. Auguring from the azure sky he decided to carry the true Sutras with him, and observing the course of the winds, he made his way through difficulties and perils. Thus, in the ninth year of the period named Chen-Kuan [635] he arrived at Xian. The Emperor dispatched his Minister, Duke Fang Xuan-ling, with a guard of honor, to the western suburb to meet the visitor and conduct him to the Palace. The Sutras were translated in the Imperial Library. [His Majesty] investigated "the Way" in his own forbidden apartments, and being deeply convinced of its correctness and truth, he gave special orders for its propagation. . . . The following Imperial Rescript was is-sued: . . . "Having carefully examined the scope of his [Alopen's] teaching . . . we reached the conclusion that they cover all that is most important in life. . . . This teaching is helpful to all creatures and beneficial to all men. So let it have free course throughout the Empire." . . . [Gaozong] added new ornaments to the True Religion. He allowed for the establishment of the Luminous monastery in each prefecture. He added new favor to Alopen, conferring on him the title of *Great Lord of the Law, Guardian of the Realm*. The law spread through the ten provinces, and the empire enjoyed immense happiness. Monasteries were built in a hundred cities, and families prospered with great blessings.

Source: P. Y. Saeki, *The Nestorian Monument in China* (London: SPCK, 1928), 165–67 (spelling has been modernized).

the Church of the East enjoyed in China during the reign of Tang Emperors Taizong and Gaozong.[3]

What accounts for this early and extraordinary expansion of Christianity into China? Two key historical factors should be noted. First, both lay Christians and clerics (monks and priests) of the Church of the East exhibited strong missionary zeal. Both were a driving force behind the expansion of Christianity in Tang China.[4] The Church of the East refers to an ancient branch of Christianity that arose in the Eastern Aramaic, later Syriac-speaking, region of eastern Syria. Located outside the Roman Empire, it retained its Semitic character and did not adopt either the Latin or Greek language and culture. In

---

3. Samuel Moffett, *A History of Christianity in Asia* (San Francisco: Harper, 1992), 1:293.
4. Hanciles, *Migration*, 324–25, 328–29.

fact, even to this day, the Church of the East reflects an "East Syriac liturgical, linguistic, spiritual and theological heritage." Prior to a synod held in 424 at Markabta, when the church formally separated from the Byzantine church, it is more appropriate to use the geographical term "East Syrian," or the linguistic-cultural term "East Syriac," rather than "Church of the East." After that date, the terms are suitable synonyms of one another.[5] Although the church is commonly called the Nestorian Church in the West in both church-historical and theological literature, that term is avoided by its adherents. Some scholars have concluded that the christological position attributed to the erstwhile bishop of Constantinople Nestorius (ca. 386–451) was not "Nestorian" in the classic sense that it was (mis)understood, condemned, and anathematized at the Council of Ephesus in 431. Nestorius's adherence to the Antiochene theology of Diodore of Tarsus and Theodore of Mopsuestia meant that he stressed a literal-historical biblical exegesis and a precise differentiation of the divine and human natures of Jesus Christ, but perhaps not a division of Christ into two persons or two Sons, as classical Nestorianism claimed.[6]

It is likely that Alopen did *not* introduce Christianity into China as its first missionary, although he is frequently credited with doing so. It is more likely that "numerous Christians (and perhaps even some clergy) were already living in China when Alopen arrived" in 635. These lay Persian and Turkic Christians certainly gathered together for worship and probably shared their Christian faith with other immigrants and even the local Chinese. It would have been in keeping with common practice in the West and also within the Church of the East for these Christian immigrants to request that clergy be sent to Xi'an to administer the sacraments and shepherd the flock. Irish Christians in the West had done just that two centuries earlier; they requested that the pope send them a bishop to minister to their needs (see chap. 2). Similarly, in 549 Christian Hephthalites, a nomadic Hunnic people in central Asia, requested that the East Syrian patriarch appoint a bishop for them. Although no record of such a request exists from the Christian immigrants in Xi'an, we do know that Persian Patriarch Ishoyahb II (628–646) dispatched bishops to India, present-day Iran (Hulwan), Afghanistan (Herat), and Uzbekistan (Samarkand), where they pursued a ministry of outreach, as well as church organization and consolidation. Therefore, it is also likely that Ishoyahb II, in 635, responded to an appeal from Xi'an and sent missionary Bishop Alopen

5. Baum and Winkler, *Church of the East*, 1–5; cf. Hanciles, *Migration*, 327.

6. Baum and Winkler, *Church of the East*, 4, 19–25; Samuel N. C. Lieu and Ken Parry, "Deep into Asia," in *Early Christianity in Contexts: An Exploration across Cultures and Continents*, ed. William Tabbernee (Grand Rapids: Baker, 2014), 147–48; Moffett, *Christianity in Asia*, 1:507.

and his entourage to meet the pastoral needs there. Some scholars suggest that Alopen and his monks were the religious convoy associated with a larger, official state delegation sent by King Yazdegerd III of the Persian Sassanian dynasty. This interpretation is strengthened by the fact that Emperor Taizong sent a state minister and honor guard to greet and accompany Alopen and his companions to the imperial court.[7]

Missionary zeal burned within the bosoms of many lay Christians in Xi'an and was a driving force in the spread of Christianity. It was "the laity, and not the clergy, who first spread the faith from Persia to China [and] this is undoubtedly how Christianity continued to grow within China itself."[8] Unlike some immigrant groups, it appears that Christian Persians lived among the Chinese and not in segregated enclaves; this situation was conducive for evangelism among their neighbors. Emperor Gaozong asserted that at the time of his reign, the East Syrian religion had spread to "ten provinces" in China and that monasteries had been "built in a hundred cities" (see sidebar 3.1).[9] If his statement, although hyperbolic, is accurate in its broad strokes, this implies that the "Christian message had reached hundreds of families and had a grass-root level of believers."[10] This interpretation gains more credence if numerous Persian lay Christians had been evangelizing in China, presumably for decades. Furthermore, Alopen and his brother monks "probably did encourage (and perhaps even engage in) more basic evangelistic mission work," not just pastoral care of immigrants. That would be in keeping with the missionary zeal within the East Syrian Church and with Alopen's mandate.[11] That Alopen was praised by Gaozong as a great spiritual ruler means that he was still ministering in China when Gaozong's reign began, roughly twenty years after his arrival in 635. Thus, Alopen had a sustained ministry in China of evangelism, church planting, Bible translation, and the founding of monasteries. Lay Christians, monks, and clergy associated with the Church of the East all exhibited missionary zeal and contributed to the spread of the gospel in Tang China.

The second and perhaps more important factor in the widespread expansion of Christianity was that Alopen and his monks arrived in Xi'an at a providentially favorable time, during a new era of Tang dynasty cultural openness. The remarkably warm welcome by the emperor would not have occurred ten

7. Glen L. Thompson, "Was Alopen a 'Missionary'?," in *Hidden Treasures and Intercultural Encounters: Studies on East Syriac Christianity in China and Central Asia*, ed. Dietmar W. Winkler and Li Tang (Vienna: LIT Verlag, 2014), 272–76; cf. Hanciles, *Migration*, 337–40, 343–44.

8. Thompson, "Was Alopen a 'Missionary'?," 276.

9. Saeki, *Nestorian Monument in China*, 165–67.

10. Tang, *Nestorian Christianity in China*, 92.

11. Thompson, "Was Alopen a 'Missionary'?," 276.

years earlier during the reign of Taizong's father, Gaozu, the first Tang emperor. Despite the fact that Buddhists were prevalent in northern China, Gaozu issued an anti-Buddhist imperial edict in 626. He argued that Buddhist beliefs were foreign and alien to Chinese culture. Therefore, he secularized many Buddhist priests and drastically reduced the number of Buddhist temples. That same year, with the help of militant Buddhist priests, his son Taizong staged a coup and seized power. He reversed the anti-foreign, anti-Buddhist policies of his father and introduced a "golden age" of cosmopolitanism. During this early Tang period, China not only experienced a flowering of its own art and culture. It also benefited from close contact with foreign peoples and cultures radically different from its own. Tang China expanded the boundaries of its influence or control to include northern Vietnam, Korea, and vast tracts of central Asia, including Manchuria. It welcomed "large numbers of [foreign] merchants, students, and pilgrims," who made China their home due to "the growing importance of international trade and Buddhism." Concentrated primarily in large cities, these foreigners dominated both banking and trade. Rulers of the earlier Han dynasty had viewed the ethnic minorities on China's northern borders as distinctly inferior to their own population. In contrast, until at least the mid-ninth century, Tang emperors pursued a policy of cultural openness.[12]

The Tang dynasty was likewise a period of religious toleration in China. Emperor Taizong was very receptive to other religious traditions deemed worthy of propagation, whether Buddhist, Manichaean, Taoist, *or* East Syrian Christian. Though the first three religious traditions had been introduced earlier into China, they all gained traction during the first two centuries of Tang rule.[13] One additional reason for Taizong's tolerant attitude toward Alopen and his entourage of East Syrian monks was "the emperor's intense interest in a revival of learning." Taizong had a massive library built next to his palace, which reportedly housed two hundred thousand books. At the

12. Mark Edward Lewis and Timothy Brook, *China's Cosmopolitan Empire: The Tang Dynasty* (Cambridge, MA: Belknap, 2009), 145–47, 173–76; see Moffett, *Christianity in Asia*, 1:292–93.

13. Buddhism and Taoism were not labeled and constructed by Westerners or local observers as specific, distinct world religions with essentialized content until the late eighteenth and nineteenth centuries. Therefore, as these terms are anachronistic, they are generally avoided in this chapter. This does not imply, however, that Buddhist or Taoist practitioners in imperial China did not observe what we today understand by the concept of religion: "a belief in the supernatural; a set of beliefs regarding life and the world; a set of ritual practices manifesting the beliefs; and a distinct social organization or moral community of the believers and practitioners." Fengyang Yang, *Religion in China: Survival and Revival under Communist Rule* (New York: Oxford University Press, 2012), 36. Cf. Harold A. Netland, *Christianity and Religious Diversity* (Grand Rapids: Baker Academic, 2015), 10–30.

emperor's order, eighteen prominent scholars worked in the library to produce a standard edition of the Confucian classics. When Taizong "discovered that the new faith the Persian missionaries had brought was the religion of a book," his interest was immediately piqued. Alopen was escorted to the library to translate the Christian writings. "It was an auspicious beginning for the Christian mission to China."[14] The scholarship of the East Syrian missionaries and their successors continued to be appreciated by the Tang imperial court. Their political connections to the government, although a double-edged sword, benefited the mission at this point in its development.[15]

The East Syrian mission to China by Alopen and his successors was a turning point in the history of the expansion of Christianity for a number of reasons. First, it was the high point and culmination of a widespread mission eastward into East, Central, and South Asia by an Eastern, rather than the Western, branch of Christianity. Not only was it an early effort, but the mission enterprise of the Church of the East surpassed comparable efforts in the West. Due to its missionary zeal, the Church of the East "achieved the greatest geographical scope of any Christian church until the Middle Ages."[16] As early as the third century, East Syrian Christianity had reached Persia; by the fourth and fifth centuries, it had gained a foothold in India and parts of central Asia and the Arabian peninsula; and in the seventh century, during the Tang dynasty, it reached the imperial Chinese court at Xi'an. Second, the mission of the Church of the East demonstrates the important early roles of both laymen and clergy/monastics in the propagation of the Christian faith. This missional expansion of East Syrian Christianity was accomplished primarily by Christian laymen in the first three centuries. After the rise of the monastic movement in the fourth century, monks and clergy played an increasingly important role in the missionary outreach of the Church of the East. Third, the Church of the East's mission to China is an important early encounter of Christianity with a sophisticated and totally foreign religious context. The China mission of the East Syrian Church attempted to understand and to appropriately adapt the Christian message to the Chinese cultural context.

This chapter is roughly chronological but also thematic. I will focus first on the role of lay Christians in the expansion of Christianity in the first section, followed by a focus on the role of monastics in the second section, even though there is considerable chronological overlap between the two. The first section provides an overview of the early spread of the gospel eastward from western Syria to Persia, to central Asia, and finally to India. The chief agents of

14. Tang, *Nestorian Christianity in China*, 81–83; Moffett, *Christianity in Asia*, 1:293.
15. Hanciles, *Migration*, 321, 344–47.
16. Baum and Winkler, *Church of the East*, 1.

evangelization were lay Christians, immigrants, and refugees, who plied their occupations as merchants, physicians, and diplomats in new locations. The second section of this chapter will provide an overview of the distinctives of East Syrian monasticism, particularly how and why monastics of the Church of the East embraced mission. I highlight the mission theology of Narsai, as well as the eastward expansion of Christianity by monks and clerics. The final section of this chapter examines whether and to what degree the Church of the East compromised aspects of Christian doctrine in the process of transmitting the faith into the Chinese context. Furthermore, I will suggest factors for the decline of East Syrian Christianity in China by the end of the Tang dynasty.

Early Syrian Christianity Expands Eastward

Ancient Christianity was anything but a Western or European phenomenon. The Christian faith originated in West Asia among Jews speaking the Western Aramaic language, the vernacular of Jesus. As early as the day of Pentecost, East Syrian Jews heard the gospel preached to them in their own languages: Parthians from northeastern Iran, Medes from northwestern Iran, Elamites from the region north of the Persian Gulf, and residents from Mesopotamia all heard the apostles "declaring the wonders of God in [their] own tongues" (Acts 2:9–11). It is likely that some of these East Syrian Jewish pilgrims converted and brought the gospel back to their homelands.

The earliest firm evidence of Christianity in Asia outside the Roman Empire was found in Edessa (modern Urfa in eastern Turkey, just north of the Syrian border). Edessa was the capital of Osrhoene, a small buffer state between Rome and Persia. Despite intermittent periods of Roman rule, the culture of Edessa did not become Roman but remained Semitic (although later in the fourth century, Greek influence made inroads). Edessa was the cradle of the East Syrian Church and of Syriac, the East Syrian Aramaic language. Syriac became the lingua franca for diplomacy and commerce. It also became the biblical and liturgical language of this branch of the Christian church. Tradition has linked both the apostle Thomas and Thaddeus (Syriac *Addai*), one of the seventy (or seventy-two) disciples mentioned in Luke 10:1, with the conversion of Edessa. This tradition claims an apostolic foundation for the church in Edessa. Since it lacks historical confirmation, it must be viewed as questionable.[17]

Conclusive documentary evidence reveals that Christianity gained a foothold in Edessa during the second and not the first century. A later document, the *Doctrine of Addai* (dated ca. 390–430), contains the account of the found-

---

17. Moffett, *Christianity in Asia*, 1:46–50; Hanciles, *Migration*, 218–19, 227, 319.

ing of the church by a missionary named Addai. Since both Eastern and Western writers support the view that (an) Addai evangelized Edessa, it is not at all unlikely that this tradition is correct. However, the Addai in question was not one of the seventy of Luke 10:1 but a Palestinian Jew who preached the gospel in Edessa in the mid-second century. The *Doctrine of Addai* probably correctly records that the advance of Christianity in Edessa was not without setbacks. Initially, upon hearing the gospel, both Jews and Gentiles (including some nobles) believed in great numbers. Pagan priests converted and tore down the altars to the gods Bel and Nebo, although the "great altar" was spared. However, by the time of Addai's death, his charge to his similarly named successor, Aggai, reveals a less triumphal picture. Edessa was now a "difficult country" in which to minister. Aggai should take heed of the Jews, the "crucifiers" of Christ, and of the "heathen, who worship the sun and the moon, and Bel and Nebo." It is quite likely that Christianity initially made significant inroads in both the Jewish and Gentile communities, followed by setbacks, albeit in the second century rather than in the first. The *Doctrine of Addai* makes clear that not only two named missionaries, Addai and Aggai, but also a host of unnamed lay "Christians in Edessa were active in evangelization and . . . made a great contribution to the spreading of Christianity" in that city.[18] The same was true for the expansion of Christianity in the Western Roman Empire during the same time period, as noted in chapter 1.

Christianity was well established in Edessa by no later than the reign of King Abgar VIII (r. 177–212). Abgar most likely became a Christian, since a coin with his portrait was found with a cross on his headgear. The *Chronicle of Edessa* provides the first reliable chronological dating for the spread of Christianity. This source reports that the great flood that ravaged the city in 201 (a historically well-established date) destroyed the "temple of the church of the Christians," the "great and beautiful palace" of Abgar VIII, and the "desirable and beautiful edifices of the city." Interestingly, the Christian church is mentioned along with other beautiful buildings in Edessa destroyed by the flood. This implies that the church building was impressive—in other words, no small house church, but a cathedral-like structure. Christianity was thus already well established by at least the second half of the second century. That does not mean, however, that Abgar VIII adopted Christianity as the *state religion* of Edessa during his reign, as some scholars have argued. This theory, although appealing, cannot be substantiated one way or another.[19]

18. Moffett, *Christianity in Asia*, 1:50–52; Tang, *Nestorian Christianity in China*, 51–56, 62; George Phillips, ed. and trans., *The Doctrine of Addai the Apostle* (London: Trübner, 1876), 31–32, 41.
19. Moffett, *Christianity in Asia*, 1:56–59; Tang, *Nestorian Christianity in China*, 51–52, 55.

The church in Edessa was ruled by a bishop during this period. We know this since Bardaisan (154–222), a native of Edessa and a member of Abgar VIII's court, was converted in 179 through the preaching of Hystasp, the bishop of Edessa. After his baptism and training by the bishop, Bardaisan was made a deacon in the church. He went on to compose 150 hymns (in imitation of the Davidic Psalter) as well as dialogues against the Marcionite and Valentinian Gnostic heresies. Other noteworthy early Christians were associated with Edessa. Tatian (ca. 120–175) wrote his popular harmony of the gospels, the *Diatessaron*, at Edessa. Ephrem the Syrian (306–373) became one of the most celebrated fathers of the East Syrian Church. He wrote numerous biblical commentaries, dogmatic works against heresies, sermons, and countless hymns and poems. Ephrem founded the influential theological School of the Persians at Edessa, which provided the Syriac-speaking clergy with solid biblical and theological training in a semimonastic setting.[20]

Lay Christians played a crucial role in the evangelization of Edessa and also in the eastward advance of the gospel from Edessa to Persia. Christianity most likely spread from Edessa and Nisibis (today Nusaybin, in southeastern Turkey) into the Persian Parthian Empire (247 BC–AD 224) during the second century. The first Christians to bring the faith eastward from Edessa were lay merchants, who utilized one of the two important trade routes that intersected at Edessa— the one that ran southeastward to the Persian Gulf. The first Christian congregations in Persia emerged among the Aramaic-speaking Jewish population. Judaism had been present in Mesopotamia since the Babylonian exile. It was natural for Christians to spread the faith first among monotheistic Jews. Although there were some conversions among the Zoroastrian Persian population, the majority of Christians had an Aramaic Jewish background. Another group of lay Christians contributed to the expansion of Christianity in Persia—refugees. The second king of the Sassanian dynasty (224–651), Shapur I, during his war against Byzantium in 258–259, occupied Antioch and besieged Edessa. This resulted in a large number of Christians from Antioch, Cappadocia, Cilicia, and Syria being deported as prisoners of war into Persian territory. These lay Christians propagated the faith in their new environment. Among the refugees was Bishop Demetrius of Antioch, who subsequently served as the first bishop of Gundeshapur, Shapur's new capital north of the Persian Gulf.[21]

Due to intermittent persecution from the Zoroastrian majority within the Persian Empire during the Sassanian dynasty, Persian Christians, who had a

---

20. Tang, *Nestorian Christianity in China*, 56–60.
21. Tang, *Nestorian Christianity in China*, 65; Cornelia Horn, Samuel N. C. Lieu, and Robert R. Phenix Jr., "Beyond the Eastern Frontier," in Tabbernee, *Early Christianity in Contexts*, 96–98; Baum and Winkler, *Church of the East*, 8–12.

long-standing tradition of trading, often sought a more peaceful or prosperous life eastward in the oases along the Silk Road, which ran from Edessa through central Asia and all the way to Xi'an, China. Christian documents and archaeological evidence of churches and monasteries indicate that lay Christian merchants and their families were perhaps the largest group of Persian Christians who settled along the Silk Road. They not only settled in central Asia, but shared their faith and gathered for worship. In fact, "among Syrian Christians, the word 'merchant' become a metaphor for 'missionary.'" In a fourth-century poem, Syriac poet Cyrillona equates the two: "Travel well girt like merchants, That we may gain the world. Convert men to me [Jesus], Fill creation with teaching."[22]

It is also well documented that East Syrian Christian medical doctors held influential positions as court physicians to Muslim caliphs after the Arab conquest (630 on). It is likely that they also settled along the Silk Road, practiced their occupation, and shared their faith. Some lay Christians as well as members of the East Syrian Church hierarchy "played an essential role" on diplomatic missions from the Persian king to places such as Byzantium, Aleppo, and Xi'an. While doing so, many took the opportunity to evangelize.[23] The *Book of the Laws of Countries*, attributed to Bardaisan of Edessa but probably penned by his pupil Philip, documents the expansion of Christianity into central Asia. He notes that by the early third century, the "new race of ourselves who are Christians" were in "every country and in every region" that the "Messiah established at His coming." The writer then lists the countries: Persia, Media, Parthia, and as far east as Bactria in northern Afghanistan.[24] Lay Christian merchants, physicians, and diplomats were important agents of evangelization in central Asia.

That was also true for the early spread of the gospel into India. There are two main traditions for the establishment of Christianity in India, both of which have links to the East Syrian Church and a "Thomas." The first tradition is based on the apocryphal early-third-century *Acts of Thomas*, which originated in Edessa. According to this tradition, the apostle Thomas landed on the southwestern coast of India around AD 52. He evangelized and founded seven churches in the Kerala district and then moved to the eastern Coromandel coast, where he was martyred in AD 68. Several facts make the Thomas tradition plausible, though it has not been historically verified. It

22. Hanciles, *Migration*, 322–24.

23. Hanciles, *Migration*, 246, 259; Baum and Winkler, *Church of the East*, 14–17, 34–37, 40–41, 46, 60–69; Thompson, "Was Alopen a 'Missionary'?," 268–70, 273.

24. William Cureton, *Spicilegium Syriacum: Bardesan, Meliton, Ambrose, and Mara Bar Serapion* (London: Riverton, 1855), 32–33.

was indeed possible to travel to India—either overland or by sea—in the apostolic age. There is much evidence of trade with India from the West, from Egypt, and from Syria during the first century. Furthermore, at least one element of the legendary *Acts of Thomas* rests on solid historical data. The apostle is said to have visited the Indo-Parthian king Gundophares. His reign in the upper Indus valley in present-day Pakistan has been historically verified by coins.[25] Another prominent tradition claims that a merchant, Thomas of Cana, landed on the Kerala coast of India with seventy-two Christian families from Mesopotamia, as well as a bishop and four priests, either in the fourth or in the eighth century. This tradition is much more doubtful, since it was first reported in the sixteenth century during the Portuguese period. Today, two ethnically distinct communities of Saint Thomas Christians in Kerala are associated with the Thomas traditions. Both groups use Syriac as their liturgical language.[26]

The role of the Church of the East in the early evangelization of India is certain, although documentary evidence is scant. The medieval Arabic *Chronicle of Seert* reuses sources written several centuries before and therefore has historical value. It may be accurate in its account that Bishop David of Basra evangelized in India from around 295 to 300. The *Chronicle of Seert* likewise testifies to the interest of various patriarchs in the health of the Syriac church in India. Joseph of Edessa was appointed bishop of India by the East Syrian Church in 345. At different junctures during the fifth century, patriarchs sent to India Syriac translations of theological works—for example, by Diodore of Tarsus—as well as translations of Bible books in order to ensure that the Indian clergy was well-trained in correct theology. Patriarch Ishoyahb II, who most likely sent Alopen to China in 635, also sent additional bishops to India. His successor, Ishoyahb III (d. 658), established definitively the jurisdiction of the Church of the East over Indian Christians on the Malabar coast around 650. A series of copperplate inscriptions from the ninth century found in India provides hints to the character of the ancient Christian communities in the subcontinent. The Christians, for the most part, were aristocratic, belonging largely to the merchant-ruler class. The copperplates record privileges granted by local rulers to the Christians in Kerala—the right to sit on carpets and ride elephants, privileges normally reserved for high-caste individuals. They were also given a monopoly on public weights and measures. The Thomas

25. Lieu and Parry, "Deep into Asia," 171–73; Moffett, *Christianity in Asia*, 1:29–32; Robert Eric Frykenberg, "Christians in India: An Historical Overview of Their Complex Origins," in *Christians and Missionaries in India: Cross-Cultural Communication since 1500*, ed. Robert Eric Frykenberg (Grand Rapids: Eerdmans, 2003), 34–36.

26. Lieu and Parry, "Deep into Asia," 172–73, 177–80; Frykenberg, "Christians in India," 36.

Christians of India were "Hindu in culture, Christian in faith, and Syrian . . . in doctrine, liturgy and ecclesiology."[27]

This chapter section has outlined the eastward advance of the East Syrian Church from its early center in Edessa. The founding of the church in Edessa is associated with a missionary named Addai, a Palestinian Jew who evangelized in the mid-second century. Edessa was not only the location where the Syriac language arose. It was also home to the influential theological School of the Persians and several noteworthy Christians, and the launching pad from which primarily lay Christian merchants and refugees brought the gospel further eastward into Persia and central Asia. The church in India may have first-century roots if the apostle Thomas tradition is accepted. It is certain that the East Syrian Church played a key role in the evangelization of the subcontinent from the third century on. After the rise of monasticism in the early fourth century, monastics increasingly played a prominent role in the mission enterprise of the Church of the East, as the following section will demonstrate.

Monasticism and Mission in the Church of the East

Throughout its history, Christianity has spread to new peoples and lands at times through ordinary laypeople but often through smaller groups of highly committed Christians devoted to the spread of the faith. From the fourth century on, East Syrian monastics were one of those groups of radical Christians who zealously spread the gospel eastward across new frontiers. The roots of monasticism were located in the practice of asceticism, which both predated the monastic movement and was the cradle in which it was nurtured. A native tradition of asceticism flourished early in the Nile valley, but also in Syria and Persia. In fact, some scholars contend that the earliest forms of "ascetic monasticism . . . may actually have originated in Syria rather than in Egypt," although the reverse is often claimed.[28] Tatian (ca. 110–180) not only produced a gospel harmony at Edessa; he also promoted a form of rigorous asceticism that condemned marriage and procreation outright—a view associated with Encratism, which was rejected as heterodox by the Western church. Practicing a second premonastic form of Syrian asceticism were the Sons and Daughters of the Covenant, a largely informal group of

27. Moffett, *Christianity in Asia*, 1:100–101; Frykenberg, "Christians in India," 36–37; Lieu and Parry, "Deep into Asia," 175–76.

28. Malcolm Choat, Jitse Dijkstra, Christopher Haas, and William Tabbernee, "The World of the Nile," in Tabbernee, *Early Christianity in Contexts*, 201–3; Moffett, *Christianity in Asia*, 1:75–76.

male and female Christians who covenanted at the time of their baptism to live lives of celibacy and single-minded devotion to Christ. This form of asceticism fit within parameters acceptable to the Syrian church. The origins, not just of asceticism but also of monasticism in its various forms, are all traditionally ascribed to Egyptian ascetics: the hermit or anchoritic type, characterized by living alone in the wilderness, is typically associated with Anthony of Egypt (251–356); and communal monasticism, centered on the monastery, with Pachomius (ca. 292–348). Nevertheless, both Syria and Persia developed their own indigenous tendencies toward communal monasticism, for the most part independent of Egypt. Early Syrian developments can be traced to Syrian Antioch. In Persia the origins of communal monasticism have been attributed to Aphrahat, a Son of the Covenant and later bishop of Mar Mattai, a monastery formed north of Mosul in about 340.[29]

The Syrian ascetic and monastic movement contrasted with the Egyptian movement in one very important way: it was less concerned with separation and withdrawal from the world. Rather, "there was a missionary dynamic also in its faith that sent believers out into the pagan world to preach the gospel. . . . In the very earliest Christian documents of the East [Syrian Church], the call to ascetic self-denial is almost always associated with the call to go and preach and serve."[30] Many Syrian ascetics and monastics lived near villages, where they established regular pastoral and preaching ministries among the local population. This contrasted with the Egyptian practice, which stressed withdrawal from outside contacts. Furthermore, Syrian ascetics and monastics were influenced by the prominence of trading, travel, and itinerancy in their culture. Most early Syrian ascetics were not fixed to one locality. In contrast, Egyptian ascetics and monastics valued stability and agriculture, not itinerancy. This Syrian focus on mobility, when combined with the biblical example of the itinerant ministry of the seventy disciples in Luke 10, helped to make the Syrian monastic movement a powerful force for evangelism. The Syrian ascetic or monastic was under obligation "to traverse the cities and villages as traveling missionaries, expanding the gospel."[31] They accomplished this evangelistic mandate both far and wide.

Many of the wandering Syrian ascetics evangelized non-Christians not only with words but with symbol-laden actions. Most Christians in this age viewed paganism as a demonic force that must be resisted and perhaps even

29. Moffett, *Christianity in Asia*, 1:75–77, 97–100, 123–25; S. P. Brock, "Early Syrian Asceticism," *Numen* 20, no. 1 (April 1973): 3.

30. Moffett, *Christianity in Asia*, 1:77–78.

31. Arthur Vööbus, *History of Asceticism in the Syrian Orient* (Louvain: Secrétariat du CorpusSCO, 1958), 1:97.

attacked. The hostility between Christianity and paganism, which is well documented in early Syrian writers, almost exclusively took the form of destroying pagan sites. Such acts were intended to convincingly demonstrate to non-Christian observers that the Christian God was stronger than their own gods (see chap. 4). By the fourth century, this approach was well established. Late in his reign, the first Christian emperor, Constantine, ordered the pillaging and destruction of pagan temples. His son, Constantius II, enacted laws against pagans. It was during his reign that ordinary Christians began to vandalize pagan temples and shrines. Some Syrian monastics likewise participated in this destruction. Pagan Syrian philosopher Libanius complained about the illegal vandalism perpetrated by monks in a letter to Roman Emperor Theodosius in 386:

> This black-robed tribe [monks] . . . hasten to attack the temples with sticks and stones and bars of iron . . . in contravention of the law. . . . Utter destruction follows, with the stripping of roofs, demolition of walls, the tearing down of statues and the overthrow of altars, and [pagan] priests must either keep quiet or die.[32]

Rabbula, a Syrian hermit, and his friend Eusebius of Tella attacked a pagan temple at Baalbek in present-day Lebanon. Rabbula's attack did not achieve his wished-for martyrdom. He survived being thrown down the temple steps by the enraged crowd.[33] We do not know whether the common practice of destroying pagan sites convinced many onlookers of the superior power of the Christian God. We do know that it was a well-entrenched Christian practice in both the West and the East for the entirety of late antiquity and beyond.

The lives of Rabbula and others point to an interesting phenomenon in the East Syrian Church: the subordination of radical asceticism to the service of the church. Very shortly after Rabbula's attack on a pagan temple at Baalbek, he was appointed bishop of Edessa, a position he held from about 411 until his death in 435. During his tenure as bishop, Rabbula pursued mission; he evangelized and baptized thousands of Jews. Aphrahat left the solitary life of a Son of the Covenant to serve the church as a monk-bishop at Mar Mattai. Jacob of Nisibis devoted himself early to an ascetic life in the mountains and caves around Nisibis. Yet he left his solitude and answered the call to

32. Michael Maas, *Readings in Late Antiquity: A Sourcebook* (New York: Routledge, 2003), 187, 197.

33. "The Destruction of Pagan Temples," Encyclopaedia Romana, accessed August 20, 2020, https://penelope.uchicago.edu/~grout/encyclopaedia_romana/greece/paganism/temple.html; Francis C. Burkitt, *Early Eastern Christianity* (Eugene, OR: Wipf & Stock, 2005), 49–51.

become bishop of Nisibis. In 325 he signed the roster as a participant at the Council of Nicaea.

> Time and again, when the church needed them, the greatest of the ascetics put the call to service above the claims of separation. Purified by prayer and privation, they moved beyond the compulsions of self-discipline to the no less demanding task of reviving and leading the church.[34]

Monastics of the Church of the East served the church as bishops and missionaries.

The Church of the East had a strong tradition of theological education for both pastors *and* missionaries. Many East Syrian missionaries received their training at the theological school at Nisibis. This school was founded as a replacement for the theological school in Edessa (mentioned above), which had been closed by Byzantine Emperor Zeno in 489 as part of his campaign to suppress Nestorianism. The school moved 125 miles farther east to Nisibis in Sassanian Persia, where it became the Church of the East's premier theological institution. Narsai (d. ca. 503), a Persian poet, preacher, exegete, and theologian, either founded the theological school at Nisibis or assumed its leadership soon thereafter. During his tenure as head of the school, Narsai combined an emphasis on biblical exegesis and spiritual discipline with a focus on missionary outreach. The students studied the Antiochene theology of Theodore of Mopsuestia while living in a close-knit, semimonastic community. The twenty-two canons of the school adopted under Narsai in 496 required the students to remain celibate during their tenure at the school, relinquish half or all of their belongings to the common treasury, and participate in the daily antiphonal chanting. Later, under school director Henana (571–610), monastic garb and the tonsure were required.[35]

Narsai ensured that "the church's sense of mission" was "not . . . stifled." He articulated the motivation for mission and developed his mission theology in several of his extant sermons. Narsai's mission sermons are the oldest documents to encourage world evangelization within the Church of the East; they are also virtually unprecedented for all Christian groups in this era. Furthermore, his mission theology affected the practical mission outreach of the Church of the East. "No other explanation of the subsequent astonishing expansion of Nestorian missions is satisfactory" to account for this phenom-

34. Burkitt, *Early Eastern Christianity*, 49–51; Tang, *Nestorian Christianity in China*, 61; Moffett, *Christianity in Asia*, 1:123.
35. Lieu and Parry, "Deep into Asia," 147–48; Moffett, *Christianity in Asia*, 1:200–202; Arthur Vööbus, *The Statutes of the School of Nisibis* (Stockholm: Este, 1961), 75–77, 79, 99–100.

SIDEBAR 3.2

Narsai, Liturgical Sermon for Ascension Day

Your task is this: to complete the mystery of preaching! And you shall be witnesses of the new way I have opened up in my person. . . . You I send as messengers to the four quarters of the earth, to convert the Gentiles to kinship with the House of Abraham. You I have clad with the armor of the all-prevailing Spirit to engage in a contest with the strong one who has enslaved men. By you as the light I will banish the darkness of error, and by your flames I will enlighten the blind world. By you I will uncover the veil of iniquity which the evil one has spread and rip asunder the hateful garment which he wove in Eden. You I will set as a mirror before viewers, so that men might see their persons which iniquity has made hateful. By you I will open up the treasury of the all-enriching Spirit. Go forth! Give gratis the freedom of life to immortality! . . . Explain and make clear for the ears of everyone the intent of the parables! By you, I will open up the way to heaven for earthly ones. Show them the path to this incorruptible fashioning! By you, I will reveal God's stern judgment and abounding mercy. Correct and reprove men so that they will not be declared guilty by a sentence of condemnation!

Source: Frederick G. McLeod, trans., *Narsai's Metrical Homilies on the Nativity, Epiphany and Ascension: English Translation* (Turnhout, Belgium: Brepols, 1979), 165–66.

---

enon except Narsai alone.[36] In a sermon in commemoration of the apostles Peter and Paul, Narsai stresses that Jesus chose the twelve apostles as well as the seventy disciples (Luke 10) to carry the gospel two by two to all corners of the earth. The apostles and disciples obeyed this call, with the result that people of all ethnicities were brought to the eucharistic "banquet of Christ's love." Saul, the persecutor of the church, became Paul, the missionary par excellence to the Gentiles. According to Narsai's sermon, Paul—not Peter, who ironically is never mentioned—was also the primary apostle to the Jews. He successfully used Old Testament Scriptures to point the people of Israel to the Jewish Messiah. He tore down the walls that the Mosaic law had erected and led the Gentiles into fellowship with the house of Abraham. Paul warned sinners of the coming judgment and brought the world under the gentle yoke of the Savior's love. Narsai's application for his hearers is twofold. A harvest of souls was languishing in the fields for lack of workers. The hearers should pray that the Lord of the harvest would send out workers. They should also

36. Moffett, *Christianity in Asia*, 1:202.

pray that *they* might follow Paul's example, who preached the gospel to the "people" (Jews) and the "peoples" (Gentile nations). Narsai particularly has monastics in view. These "good ones" in their communities, like the apostles and disciples before them, had been chosen for a ministry of spreading the truth and "of bringing hope to those without hope."[37]

In a liturgical sermon for Ascension Day, Narsai challenges the theological students at Nisibis to evangelize using paraphrases of New Testament injunctions (see sidebar 3.2). In the sermon, Jesus himself calls his followers to be "messengers" and "witnesses" of the gospel throughout the four corners of the earth. Their mandate was to convert Gentiles and thereby bring them into the "House of Abraham," a theme that was likewise found in the prior sermon. This conversion would come about through preaching and by the convincing witness of a holy life. The missionary was to be a burning "light" that "enlightens the blind" and "banishes error" from his hearers. This was a noble task; the missionaries were offering "freedom" in this life and "immortality" in the next to those who accepted the Christian message.[38] Narsai's leadership at the school at Nisibis furthered the early mission zeal of the Church of the East; his mission sermons bore testimony to it.

In the previous section, we emphasized the undeniably significant role of lay Christians in the eastward expansion of Christianity. Nevertheless, in the period from Constantine until the decline of the Chinese Tang dynasty in 907, "Christian missions from Persia and Central Asia" were, for the most part, "monastic missions" and East Syrian monks the "primary agent[s] for mission." Monasteries of the Church of the East became centers of local "evangelization and the Christian life." They also became launching pads for missionary outreach farther afield. Patriarch Timothy I notes in a letter from the 790s that "many [East Syrian] monks cross the seas in the direction of India and China, bearing with them only a stick and saddle-bag." In this statement, Timothy stresses the extent of their mission (Central, South, and East Asia) and their motivation: the biblical example of Christ and his disciples (Luke 10).[39]

East Syrian monks and clerics were an active force in the evangelization of central Asia. The starting point for mission to central Asia and Chinese

---

37. Moffett, *Christianity in Asia*, 1:202; Paul Krüger, "Ein Missionsdokument aus Frühchristlicher Zeit: Deutung und Übersetzung des Sermo de memoria Petri et Pauli des Narsai," *Zeitschrift für Missionswissenschaft und Religionswissenschaft* 42, no. 4 (1958): 271–91.

38. Frederick G. McLeod, trans., *Narsai's Metrical Homilies on the Nativity, Epiphany and Ascension: English Translation* (Turnhout, Belgium: Brepols, 1979), 165–66.

39. Stephen B. Bevans and Roger P. Schroeder, *Constants in Context: A Theology of Mission for Today* (Maryknoll, NY: Orbis, 2004), 102; Matteo Nicolini-Zani, "Eastern Outreach: The Monastic Mission to China in the Seventh to the Ninth Centuries," in *Mission and Monasticism*, ed. Conrad Leyser and Hannah Williams (Rome: Pontificio Ateneo S. Anselmo, 2013), 64–65, 67.

Turkistan was probably from Merv, an oasis on the Silk Road in present-day Uzbekistan. The surviving legendary accounts of Bishop Bar Shaba (d. ca. 366) claim that he was the evangelizer and first bishop of Merv in the 360s. These accounts are of questionable historicity. Reliable synodical lists, however, indicate that the bishopric of Merv was established by 424 at the very latest.[40] From Merv, Christianity spread to central Asia to the Huns and Turkic peoples. In 403 Saint Jerome wrote from his monastery in Bethlehem that "the Huns learn the psalter, and the chilly Scythians are warmed with the glow of the faith." Early Christianity was further advanced among the Huns in 498, when the Persian king Kavad I temporarily sought refuge from political intrigue among the White Huns (Hephthalites) in Bactria. Two lay Christians formed part of this entourage. They were soon joined by Bishop Karadusat of Aran (west of the Caspian Sea) and four priests, who evangelized and baptized converts. In 549 the church among the Huns in Bactria was sufficiently developed that their request for a permanent bishop was fulfilled by Patriarch Aba I. A later metropolitan bishop of Merv named Elijah reportedly won a large number of Turks to the Christian faith in 644. One source recounts that Elijah, reminiscent of his biblical namesake, brought about the conversion of the khan of the ethnic group by miraculously dispelling a storm conjured up by the khan's magicians. Elijah then baptized the khan and his army in a nearby stream. A letter written by Patriarch Timothy in 781 affirms that another Turkic khan and his ethnic group had converted. The patriarch promptly complied with their request for a bishop.[41]

By the ninth century at the latest, archaeological and documentary evidence proves that Christianity had reached Chinese central Asia (Xinjiang). Two churches were excavated in Khotan on the southern Silk Road, as was a Syriac monastery in Bulayiq on the northern Silk Road. In Turfan, near Bulayiq, a large cache of "Nestorian" and other documents from the ninth and tenth centuries was found. This evidence confirms that the area was evangelized by missionary monks of the Church of the East from Merv or perhaps Samarkand, their major centers of missionary activity. The "dynamic missionary movement" of the Church of the East resulted in "tens, perhaps hundreds of thousands, of converts among the diverse peoples of central Asia."[42]

Early East Syrian monasticism differed from the Egyptian form. It was characterized by a focus on theological training and missionary engagement. Narsai, the head of the semimonastic theological school of Nisibis, articulated

---

40. Lieu and Parry, "Deep into Asia," 153.
41. Lieu and Parry, "Deep into Asia," 151–53; Tang, *Nestorian Christianity in China*, 75.
42. Daniel H. Bays, *A New History of Christianity in China* (Malden, MA: Wiley-Blackwell, 2012), 7; cf. Lieu and Parry, "Deep into Asia," 155–56, 164–70.

a biblical mission theology common within the Church of the East. It was based on the New Testament apostolic commissions and the ministries of the apostle Paul and the seventy disciples of Luke 10. East Syrian monastics and clerics were key agents of evangelization in central Asia and Chinese Turkestan among the Hunnic and Turkic populations. Alopen and his band of monks brought the gospel all the way to the Chinese imperial capital at Xi'an. The question of how successful that mission was in adapting the Christian message to the Chinese context is the focus of the remainder of this chapter.

East Syrian Christianity in the Chinese Context

Wherever the Christian faith has encountered new cultures and other faith traditions, missionaries have had to decide how to best communicate their message. How should the name of God be translated? How much of the local religious culture can be integrated into the beliefs, life, and liturgy of the church? To discover how the East Syrian missionaries during the Tang dynasty accommodated the gospel to the Chinese context, we turn to the extant Chinese documents and monuments (e.g., the Nestorian Stele) they produced. The extant documents fall into two distinct groups: a seventh-century group of texts and an eighth-century group. There are considerable differences between the two.

The seventh-century group consists of two texts, the *Jesus-Messiah Sutra* (*JM*) and the *Discourse on Monotheism* (*DM*). These two texts may have been written by Alopen or a member of his party; the *DM* is explicitly dated to 641, six years after Alopen's arrival in China.[43] These two texts are the most explicitly biblical of the Chinese "Nestorian" documents. The *JM* includes key elements of Christian dogma: monotheism, the evils of idolatry, and Christian ethical principles found in the Ten Commandments and the Sermon on the Mount. Both documents include the suffering and death of Jesus the Messiah and uphold substitutionary atonement. The *JM* affirms, "He gave up his life for the sake of all mankind, suffering death for them." The *DM* proclaims that "only . . . through the Messiah can all people be saved" (see sidebar 3.3). There is "no other way of salvation except this." Furthermore, salvation must be received, not through human effort (an "act requiring strength"), but through grace.[44] In these seventh-century documents,

---

43. Tang, *Nestorian Christianity in China*, 104–5, 108–9; Steve Eskildsen, "Christology and Soteriology in the Chinese Nestorian Texts," in *Chinese Face of Jesus Christ*, ed. Roman Malek (New York: Routledge, 2017), 1:181, 186–87.

44. P. Y. Saeki, *The Nestorian Documents and Relics in China*, 2nd ed. (Tokyo: Tokyo Institute, 1951), 145, 211–28.

SIDEBAR 3.3

Discourse on Monotheism (AD 641)

What the Messiah did was all in accordance with what had been foreordained. . . . In his own death He was hanged on high [crucified]. . . . Thereby all men without exception might be raised from the dead and ascend up to Heaven even as He [did]. . . . The Messiah Himself did the work of the Sanctifying Transformation in a limitless measure. What He did shows that He is not the seed of man. On the contrary, what he did shows that He is the seed of the Lord (of the Universe). . . . Only He was like a sheep that was led to the slaughter, and He opens not His mouth nor does He bleat and complain. So, He did not open His mouth but remained so silent when He was examined and He came to suffer the punishment on His body in accordance with the law. . . . Only by the succor of the Holy Mystery through the Messiah can all people be saved. Now, in such a convenient way, the Messiah is to be received (as the Savior) by all mankind through his sufferings. To receive Him, however, is not to remain without strength (i.e., effort). But to receive Him is not the act requiring strength (i.e., effort). . . . And because of the fact that the Messiah was hanged on high, He is acknowledged to be the true Lord of [the] Universe. For instance, everything (in His life) took place as it had been written [in the Scriptures].

Source: P. Y. Saeki, *The Nestorian Documents and Relics in China*, 2nd ed. (Tokyo: Tokyo Institute, 1951), 211–16.

we find orthodox Christian theology expressed in a way that would resonate with a Chinese audience. The *JM*, for example, in its ethical section, makes specific reference to the Confucian virtue of filial piety. Both texts made use of Taoist (*Tianzun*) and Buddhist (*fo*) terms for God. Other Syriac terms, however, such as Elohim (*Aluohe*), Jesus (*Yishu*), and Messiah (*Mishihe*), are not translated but merely transliterated into Chinese phonetics (see the hymn that opens this chapter). In these early texts, orthodox Christian content prevails, despite the use of Taoist and Buddhist terminology.[45]

In contrast, some scholars argue that Taoist and Buddhist beliefs have overshadowed or replaced Christian doctrines in eighth-century texts such as

45. Saeki, *Nestorian Documents and Relics in China*, 131–35; Lieu and Parry, "Deep into Asia," 167–70; Yves Raguin, "China's First Evangelization by the 7th and 8th Century Eastern Syrian Monks," in Malek, *Chinese Face of Jesus Christ*, 161; Tang, *Nestorian Christianity in China*, 129–30, 142.

the Nestorian Stele.[46] The author of the Nestorian Stele, the East Syrian monk Adam, utilized imagery found in Buddhist traditions and emphasized those aspects of Jesus's life that resembled the legendary Taoist teacher Laozi, in order to make the "Luminous Religion" less foreign to Chinese sensibilities. Furthermore, the stele lacks any mention of Christ's salvific death on the cross. Rather, the cross, when mentioned, "no longer symbolized the divine historical saving act, but had become an abstract symbol of the scheme of the universe and the transcendent principle or power that pervades it." In another eighth-century text, *The Scripture on the Relaxed Enjoyment of Aspiring towards Profundity*, salvation is attained by "relaxed enjoyment" through the "Method of the Ten Observations" and the "Four Superior Methods." This is essentially a Taoist or Buddhist form of salvation through meditation and self-effort, not an approach consistent with traditional orthodox Christianity.[47]

This does not necessarily mean that all adherents of Syriac Christianity in China in the eighth century had compromised orthodox Christian doctrines. It merely means that the admittedly meager number of late extant texts portray Christianity in a nontraditional or heterodox fashion. It is possible that the eighth-century texts downplayed the crucifixion in order to curry favor with the imperial court and to avoid persecution. The first round of persecution occurred during the reign of Empress Wu Hou. In 691, the staunchly pro-Buddhist empress declared Buddhist religious traditions the state religion. Seven years later, in 698, mobs sacked the church and monastery in the eastern capital of Luoyang. Then, in 845, Taoist Emperor Wuzong issued an edict against all foreign religious traditions, whether Buddhist, Manichean, or Christian. Buddhist and Christian monasteries were closed and the monks expelled during this "great persecution." All traces of the Church of the East in China disappeared until the Mongolian conquest in the thirteenth century brought a new influx of foreigners, including "Nestorians," into China. The meager historical record makes it extremely difficult to ascertain the reasons for the demise of Christianity in China. It is possible that the adherents of the Christian church were largely foreign merchants, diplomats, and monks, rather than indigenous Chinese. Almost all of the names listed on the Nestorian Stele are Syriac or the Chinese equivalents of Syriac names. This suggests that the church may have failed in its goal to form an indigenous church under indigenous leadership. The church was likewise dependent on the good will and patronage of the Tang emperors, which proved to be inconsistent. Finally,

---

46. Lieu and Parry, "Deep into Asia," 159–67; Tang, *Nestorian Christianity in China*, 111–14.

47. Eskildsen, "Chinese Nestorian Texts," 188, 194–201, 206–8; Raguin, "China's First Evangelization," 165–67, 176–79; Johan Ferreira, "Tang Christianity: Its Syriac Origins and Character," *Jian Dao* 21 (2004): 144–46, 150–54.

a further factor in the demise of the church may have been the theological compromise reflected in the eighth-century "Nestorian" texts.[48]

In conclusion, this chapter has demonstrated that ancient Christianity was anything but a Western or European phenomenon. Eastern Aramaic-speaking Syrian laymen (primarily merchants) and wandering ascetics spread the gospel eastward into the Persian Parthian Empire as early as the second century. An early native tradition of asceticism blossomed into a monastic movement in the fourth century. Monks of the Church of the East became an important force for evangelization in central Asia and China. The East Syrian advance into China was a turning point in the expansion of Christianity in this sense; it was the high point and culmination of the early and remarkable mission enterprise of the Church of the East. In China, East Syrian monks encountered a highly sophisticated culture and a totally foreign religious context, making it even more necessary to accommodate the gospel to the Chinese cultural environment. The extant "Nestorian" documents in China reveal that they did just that. East Syrian Christianity in China may have disappeared with the demise of the Tang dynasty in 907 due to persecution, the lack of a well-established indigenous church, and theological compromise.

We end this chapter with the "Anaphora of the Apostles Addai and Mari." This anaphora, or prayer of consecration for the eucharistic elements, is part of a very early East Syrian liturgy, possibly dating back to third-century Edessa. It is traditionally attributed to the apostles (missionaries) Addai and his successor, Mari.

> We give thanks to You, O my Lord, even we Your servants weak and frail and miserable, for that You have given us great grace past recompense in that You did put on our manhood that You might quicken it by Your Godhead.
>
> And have exalted our low estate and restored our fall and raised our mortality and forgiven our trespasses and justified our sinfulness and enlightened our knowledge, and, O our Lord and our God, have condemned our enemies and granted victory to the weakness of our frail nature in the overflowing mercies of Your grace. . . .
>
> And for all this great and marvelous dispensation towards us we will give You thanks and . . . with undisclosed mouths and open faces [lift] up praise and honour and confession and worship to Your living and life-giving Name now and ever and world without end. Amen.[49]

48. Lieu and Parry, "Deep into Asia," 170–71; Moffett, *Christianity in Asia*, 1:294–95, 302–5, 312–14; Hanciles, *Migration*, 351–55.
49. Gregory Dix, *The Shape of the Liturgy* (London: Dacre, 1945), 179–80 (modernized).

Confronting Pagan Gods

Boniface and the Oak of Thor (723)

Praise we the Lord
Of the heavenly kingdom,
God's power and wisdom,
The works of His hand;
As the Father of glory,
Eternal Lord,
Wrought the beginning
Of all His wonders!
Holy Creator!
Warden of men!
First, for a roof,
O'er the children of earth,
He established the heavens,
And founded the world,
And spread the dry land
For the living to dwell in.
Lord Everlasting!
Almighty God![1]

In 723 an Anglo-Saxon missionary bishop named Boniface rallied a large group of Hessian Christian converts and led them to a sacred grove dedicated

---

1. This poem was written in Anglo-Saxon in the late seventh century by Caedmon, a lay brother at the monastery of Whitby. Translation from Charles W. Kennedy, *The Caedmon Poems* (London: Routledge, 1916), 3.

to Thor. At the time Boniface was about fifty years old. Five years earlier, in 718, he had left his monastery in Wessex, England, to serve as a missionary and church reformer in Germany for the remainder of his long life. His first self-appointed task was to journey to Rome to win papal approval and authority for his mission. Pope Gregory II willingly gave his full support. Boniface then traveled to Germany, where he ministered briefly in Thuringia, followed by a three-year mentorship under Willibrord, a fellow Anglo-Saxon missionary, in Frisia (present-day Netherlands). Unlike in the former locations, Boniface's evangelistic efforts in Hesse in 721–722 met with considerable success. However, his second trip to Rome in the winter of 722 left his fledgling converts without pastoral care, and some returned to pagan practices. Paganism in this case refers to the "richly diverse" Germanic traditional pre-Christian religion. While it is virtually impossible to "(re)construct anything resembling a [coherent] pagan belief structure," evidence of ritual practices survives.[2] In the early Middle Ages, the "real battle with paganism in western Europe had only begun . . . a battle for the imaginative control of the *mundus* [world]." The pagan natural world needed to be "demystified" or purged of its nature deities and "filled up again . . . with Christian figures." Pagans were deeply religious and "alert entrepreneurs of the supernatural." Their "zest for new forms of access to the supernatural," particularly when tangible rewards in the present life were promised, made them frequently receptive to Christian rituals and sources of power.[3] When Boniface arrived back in Hesse in 723, he sought the "counsel and advice" of the local believers. It was decided that a dramatic confrontation with the pagan gods was needed to bolster the faith of vacillating converts and to convince the pagans that Christ was stronger than Woden or Thor.

The confrontation took place in a sacred grove near Geismar in Hesse. An enormous ancient oak tree there had received the nickname "Oak of Thor." Thor, the god of thunder, lightning, and rain, needed to be appeased with regular sacrifices to guarantee that adequate rain resulted in bountiful harvests and that epidemics were averted. At the site of the mighty oak, offerings of crops, livestock, or other valued objects (such as weapons or jewelry) were dedicated to the thunder god. Divination and magic were practiced under its branches. Boniface had probably announced to the local pagan population his intention to desecrate the sacred grove, since "a great crowd of pagans stood by watching and bitterly cursing in their hearts the enemy of the gods" (see

2. James Palmer, "Defining Paganism in the Carolingian World," *Early Medieval Europe* 15, no. 4 (November 2007): 407–8; cf. Richard Fletcher, *The Barbarian Conversion: From Paganism to Christianity* (Los Angeles: University of California Press, 1997), 4, 6.

3. Peter Brown, *The Rise of Western Christendom*, 2nd ed. (Malden, MA: Blackwell, 2003), 146, 340–41.

sidebar 4.1).[4] The confrontation was public and decisive; it was also some-what dangerous. Although Boniface was understandably nervous during this confrontation, he nevertheless "took his courage into his hands" and with an ax struck a blow to the giant oak. The *Life of Boniface*, written in 760 by Willibald, six years after his mentor's death, emphasizes that immediately the oak was "shaken by a mighty blast of wind from above." The tree crashed to the ground and burst asunder into four equal pieces. Once again, Boniface consulted with the "brethren" before using the wood from the desecrated tree to build a small oratory dedicated to Saint Peter in nearby Fritzlar. Reuse of the wood of the Oak of Thor for a Christian church symbolized the victory of Christ over pagan gods.[5]

The watching pagans were duly impressed by the dramatic power encounter. The visible demonstration of the powerlessness of Thor to strike down Boniface, the defiler of his shrine, with a bolt of lightning did more to convince them that the Christian God was superior than words could have ever done. Willibald reports that "at the sight of this extraordinary spectacle the heathens who had been cursing ceased to revile and began, on the contrary, to believe and bless the Lord."[6] Though aspects of Willibald's account might well be exaggerated, the response of the onlookers certainly was not. The felling of the Oak of Thor was a huge success. It resulted in the mass conversion of thousands. Conversion in this case signified a communal contractual agreement to change religion and to adopt Christianity rather than a true change of heart by all participants. That would require intensive follow-up instruction in the Christian faith. The astounding success of the event, however, is the reason it has been fondly remembered ever since the saint's martyrdom in 754—not because it was the only power encounter of its kind. "It symbolizes the achievement which posterity has granted Boniface in the label 'Apostle of Germany': namely the overthrow of the pre-Christian gods in what is now Germany, and their replacement by Christ."[7]

Several qualifications are necessary to nuance Willibald's recounting of Boniface felling the Oak of Thor. In the first place, the biographer in his account "downplayed any pre-Bonifatian missionary work and church building. . . . [His] narrative masks some of the groundwork laid for Boniface's

---

4. Thomas F. X. Noble and Thomas Head, eds., *Soldiers of Christ: Saints and Saints' Lives from Late Antiquity and the Early Middle Ages* (University Park: Pennsylvania State University Press, 1995), 126–27.

5. John-Henry Clay, *In the Shadow of Death: Saint Boniface and the Conversion of Hessia, 721–54* (Turnhout, Belgium: Brepols, 2010), 288; Lutz von Padberg, *Wynfreth-Bonifatius* (Wuppertal: Brockhaus, 1989), 72–74.

6. Noble and Head, *Soldiers of Christ*, 127.

7. Clay, *In the Shadow of Death*, 5.

SIDEBAR 4.1

Willibald, *Life of Boniface*, chap. 6 (760)

Now many of the Hessians who at that time had acknowledged the Catholic faith were confirmed by the grace of the Holy Spirit and received the laying-on of hands. But others, not yet strong in the spirit, refused to accept the pure teachings of the church in their entirety. Moreover, some continued secretly, others openly, to offer sacrifices to trees and springs, to inspect the entrails of victims; some practiced divination, legerdemain, and incantations; some turned their attention to auguries, auspices, and other sacrificial rites; while others, of a more reasonable character, forsook all the profane practices of the Gentiles [i.e., pagans] and committed none of these crimes. With the counsel and advice of the latter persons, Boniface in their presence attempted to cut down, at a place called Gaesmere, a certain oak of extraordinary size called in the old tongue of the pagans the Oak of Jupiter. Taking his courage in his hands (for a great crowd of pagans stood by watching and bitterly cursing in their hearts the enemy of the gods), he cut the first notch. But when he had made a superficial cut, suddenly the oak's vast bulk, shaken by a mighty blast of wind from above, crashed to the ground shivering its topmost branches into fragments in its fall. As if by the express will of God (for the brethren present had done nothing to cause it) the oak burst asunder into four parts, each part having a trunk of equal length. At the sight of this extraordinary spectacle the heathens who had been cursing ceased to revile and began, on the contrary, to believe and bless the Lord. Thereupon the holy bishop took counsel with the brethren, built an oratory from the timber of the oak and dedicated it to Saint Peter the Apostle.

Source: Thomas F. X. Noble and Thomas Head, eds., *Soldiers of Christ: Saints and Saints' Lives from Late Antiquity and the Early Middle Ages* (University Park: Pennsylvania State University Press, 1995), 126–27.

successes." Boniface was *not* the first missionary in the area. Two missionary bishops, Franconian Kunibert of Cologne and the Irishman Kilian of Würzburg, had evangelized and converted many communities between the Rhine and Thuringia already in the seventh century. Kilian or one of his disciples may have established the small church adjacent to the hilltop fortress of Büraburg, just a short distance from Geismar and Fritzlar, where the drama at the Oak of Thor took place.[8] Kilian serves as an example of the early Celtic missionaries who preceded and paved the way for the Anglo-Saxon mission to the Continent.

8. James T. Palmer, *Anglo-Saxons in a Frankish World, 690–900* (Turnhout, Belgium: Brepols, 2009), 154; cf. 128, 160; and Fletcher, *Barbarian Conversion*, 209.

Due to the prior Celtic mission, it is not surprising that some, perhaps many, Hessians were already to some degree Christianized when Boniface arrived in the region. The disarray of the church in Hesse, however, is apparent in Willibald's *Life*. Some of the locals had forsaken all pagan practices, but others, either secretly or openly, "continued . . . to offer sacrifices to trees and springs. . . . Some practiced divination, magic, and incantations; some turned their attention to auguries, auspices, and other sacrificial rites." Others "acknowledged the Catholic faith," but had only been baptized, presumably by earlier missionaries, and not confirmed—a task that Boniface completed (see sidebar 4.1).[9] In other words, when Boniface arrived on the scene, not all Hessians were adherents of the pre-Christian religion; many were either consistent *or* nominal *or* syncretistic Christians. It is possible that paganism in Hesse was in decline, as some scholars have argued. This would explain why the pagan onlookers at the felling of the giant oak only muttered curses under their breath and did not attack the defilers of their sacred grove.[10]

Boniface and his compatriots had reason to be nervous during the confrontation in the grove. None of the monks present at the event were armed. Boniface was well aware that fellow missionary Willibrord had been nearly murdered by irate pagans when he destroyed an idol in Frisia. Nevertheless, Boniface was never in grave danger. While in Rome the previous winter, the Anglo-Saxon had received from Pope Gregory II a letter of commendation to the Frankish ruler, Charles Martell. The pope's letter asked Charles "to help [Boniface] in all his needs and to grant him *your constant protection* against any who may stand in his way."[11] After returning from Rome, Boniface visited the Frankish ruler in the spring of 723 and received from Martell a letter of protection: "Be it known . . . that wheresoever he [Boniface] may choose to go, he is to be left in peace and protected as a man under our guardianship and protection."[12] The Franks had established direct control of Hesse in the period 690–720. Around 690 the fortress of Büraburg, which was only a little more than a mile from Geismar, was occupied by Franks. Therefore, the felling of the Oak of Thor took place but a stone's throw from a Frankish military installation. It was no wonder that the pagan onlookers muttered under their breath but did not attack Boniface's entourage.[13]

9. Noble and Head, *Soldiers of Christ*, 126.

10. Padberg, *Wynfreth-Bonifatius*, 73.

11. Pope Gregory II, Letter 20, in *The Letters of Saint Boniface*, trans. Ephraim Emerton (New York: Columbia University Press, 1940), 45.

12. Charles Martel, Letter 22, in *Letters of Saint Boniface*, 47.

13. Clay, *In the Shadow of Death*, 159, 168–76.

The mission of Boniface, exemplified by the felling of the Oak of Thor, was a turning point in the expansion of Christianity. This confrontation with pagan gods typified in dramatic fashion the struggle inherent in the conversion and Christianization of the primarily Germanic, Slavic, and Scandinavian peoples of western, northern, and central Europe from 400 to 1200. Boniface was not the first to confront pagan gods with power encounters. The "apostle to Germany," however, is an especially good representative of the conversion and Christianization of "barbarian" Europe for two reasons: In the first place, it is possible to know more about Boniface than almost any other missionary churchman in the early Middle Ages. Numerous historically reliable primary sources are available—particularly Willibald's *Life of Boniface*, written shortly after the saint's death and thus trustworthy, as well as 150 letters from, to, or concerning Boniface and his immediate disciples. Second, Boniface reflected deeply on the task of converting pagans. His correspondence with Bishop Daniel of Winchester, as well as other sources, reveals key aspects of his motivation for mission as well as the methods he employed in his mission. Once again, this was unique in the early Middle Ages.

In this chapter, we will first discuss the Celtic mission to the Continent, which predated the Anglo-Saxon mission by a hundred years. It is impossible to rightly understand the Anglo-Saxon mission of Boniface and his compatriots without a recognition of how that mission was an outgrowth of the prior Celtic endeavor. Both the Celtic and Anglo-Saxon missions to the Continent were motivated by the uniquely Irish penitential practice of *peregrinatio*, or pilgrimage for the sake of Christ. Both confronted the pagan gods in dramatic power encounters. Yet the Anglo-Saxon approach was more intentionally missional than the earlier Celtic movement. The discussion of the Celtic mission is followed by a brief survey of Boniface's Anglo-Saxon missionary predecessors, primarily his mentor, Willibrord. Then I examine Boniface's missionary career, which culminated in the martyrdom of the octogenarian missionary in 754 on his final evangelistic excursion to Frisia. The ministry of the apostle to Germany, like that of his missionary predecessors and successors, was most often characterized by patient itinerant evangelism and preaching, not confrontations with pagan gods. Therefore, the chapter ends with an analysis of Boniface's dual approaches to polytheistic paganism.

Celtic Mission to the Continent

In chapter 2 we noted the missionary zeal of Irish monks such as Aidan, who completed the work of evangelizing Britain begun by Pope Gregory the

Great. Aidan's mission, begun in 635, was not the first one undertaken by Irish monks. That honor falls to Columba (ca. 520–597), who, seventy years earlier in 563, left Ireland with twelve missionary companions to evangelize the Picts in Scotland. The traditional reason given in Irish sources for Columba's departure is both dramatic and not very flattering, though perhaps accurate in its broad strokes. The story goes that Columba, an Irish nobleman of the Neill clan, came into sharp conflict with Diarmait, the high king of Ireland, over several of the king's wrongdoings. Columba informed his clan of these offenses, and a battle ensued in 561 between the Neills and the high king at Cooladrummon, near Sligo. Three thousand warriors died. In a vision, the archangel Michael condemned Columba to lifelong exile for his role in the conflict. Then Columba's spiritual confessor, Molaise, ordered him, as an act of penance, to bring as many souls to Christ as had died in the battle.[14]

Columba's actual motivation and the circumstances surrounding his self-exile (or *peregrinatio*) from Ireland in 563 are ultimately unknown.[15] It was, however, most likely a penitential act first and foremost, which resulted secondarily in evangelistic activity. He first founded the monastery of Iona off the western coast of Scotland, which he used as a base for his periodic mission work. The conversion of the Picts was Columba's initial evangelistic goal. To that end, he visited the pagan Pictish king Brude at his royal residence near present-day Inverness, Scotland. There a mighty power encounter transpired between Columba on the one hand and the chief royal druid, Broichan, on the other. The Christian God prevailed, druidism was overthrown, and the way was opened for the spread of the Christian faith among the Picts. The death of King Brude in 584 brought about a union of the northern and southern Pictish kingdoms. The new king was a Christian and eager to cooperate with Columba in advancing the Christian faith. Though most of his remaining life was spent at his monastic retreat of Iona, Columba undertook periodic evangelistic voyages to the Hebrides. Columba died at Iona in June 597.[16]

Columba's self-exile from Ireland points to two characteristics of Celtic Christianity that were closely linked—penitential discipline and *peregrinatio*, which literally means "pilgrimage," though "exile for the sake of Christ" better captures its distinctive Irish connotation. The cornerstone of Celtic monastic spirituality in the early Middle Ages was penitential discipline, an

---

14. John Godfrey, *The Church in Anglo-Saxon England* (Cambridge: Cambridge University Press, 1962), 49–51.

15. Jehu J. Hanciles, *Migration and the Making of Global Christianity* (Grand Rapids: Eerdmans, 2021), 287.

16. Godfrey, *Church in Anglo-Saxon England*, 51–55; Fletcher, *Barbarian Conversion*, 92–93.

innovation of the Irish church. Prior to this time, the Roman Church had limited penance for the contrite sinner to a once-in-a-lifetime public ceremony administered by a bishop. This practice left a burden of guilt for subsequent sins and resulted in spiritual malaise for many Christians. The Irish solution was repeatable, private confessions made to any priest, who was sworn to secrecy. This form of confession was gradually spread to the Continent by Irish monks and was officially adopted by the Roman Church in 1215 at the Fourth Lateran Council.[17]

Confessors made use of "penitentials," small booklets written by revered spiritual guides, which correlated lists of sins with appropriate, recommended penances. Typical penances included the reciting of psalms, fasting, vigils, flagellation, monetary contributions, and pilgrimages. The strictest penance of all was *peregrinatio*, a penitential, ascetic form of voluntary banning from kin and country "in order to live a purer life, free of earthly connections and possessions."[18] For an Irishman, to leave one's beloved homeland and clan was a stiff penance indeed. The severity of this penitential act is reflected in ancient Irish law, according to which banishment from kinship groups, or in the worst cases from Ireland, was the most extreme punishment. Columba's alleged complicity in the slaughter of three thousand men was a grievous offense, which required the severest penance—*peregrinatio*—according to his spiritual counselor and the archangel Michael himself. Although *peregrinatio* was primarily a penitential deed, in practice it was frequently, though secondarily, linked with missionary outreach. *Peregrinatio* played an important role in the conversion of Europe. In fact, "the ideal of pilgrimage was absolutely central to the mission impulse of the early medieval period."[19]

The monastic founder and missionary Columbanus (ca. 543–615), not to be confused with his earlier contemporary Columba, was the author of an important penitential; he has also been referred to as the "father of *peregrinatio*." Born in Leinster in the mid-sixth century, he became a monk at Bangor in northern Ireland. There Abbot Comgall ruled the monastery with a firm hand, and the strictly enforced asceticism affected the young monk. In 590, when Columbanus was in his forties, he requested that Comgall release him from the monastery in order to live as a pilgrim in self-exile on the Continent. For Columbanus, the inspiration for this lifestyle was found in the life of Abraham. Jonas of Bobbio, his biographer, records, "He longed to go into strange lands, in obedience to the command which the Lord gave Abraham: 'Get thee out of thy country, and from thy kindred, and from thy

17. Godfrey, *Church in Anglo-Saxon England*, 55–56.
18. Palmer, *Anglo-Saxons in a Frankish World*, 61.
19. Fletcher, *Barbarian Conversion*, 138–40, 232.

father's house, into a land that I will show thee.'"[20] With a retinue of twelve companions, he set sail for Gaul.

Columbanus was primarily a monastic founder in the lands of his exile: first in eastern France and later in northern Italy. His most influential monastic foundation was at Luxeuil in Burgundy, which he founded around 590 in the ruins of a sturdy Gallo-Roman castle. Luxeuil was located on the margins of established Christendom, where many of the locals were Christians in name only. It served as Columbanus's base of operations for the first twenty years of his exile. There is no evidence that Columbanus or the monastery pursued active, intentional evangelization in the region. In fact, Columbanus's "missionary work, in the sense of converting pagans to the faith, was probably negligible at best."[21] Nevertheless, some pastoral care of local Christians is likely, which served to deepen their faith and ultimately further the Christianization of the area. The *Life of Columbanus* reports that after the founding of the monastery, "people streamed in from all directions in order to consecrate themselves to the practice of religion." The strict asceticism of Luxeuil was appealing especially to the Frankish nobility, who, according to the biography, "spurned trappings of the world and the pomp of present wealth . . . [and] sought . . . the remedy of penance."[22] Frankish nobles ruled over and were part of a brutal and violent warrior society. The private penitential discipline of this transplanted Irish-style monastery was balm for guilt-ridden Frankish souls. It was not long before a second monastery at Les Fontaines was founded to meet the demand of those pursuing the monastic life.[23]

In 610 Columbanus and his Irish monks were banished from France because he refused to bless the sons born to the concubines of Merovingian king Theuderic II. Columbanus used this banishment from France as an opportunity for direct evangelism, something he had not actively pursued previously. His (newfound?) desire to evangelize non-Christians was reflected in a letter he wrote to the monks at Luxeuil soon after his banishment.

> You know I love the salvation of many and seclusion for myself, the one for the progress of the Lord, that is, of His church, the other for my own desire. . . . It was in my wish to visit the heathen and have the gospel preached to them by us.[24]

20. Jonas of Bobbio, *Life of Saint Columban* 9, ed. Dana C. Monroe, https://sourcebooks.fordham.edu/basis/columban.asp; Godfrey, *Church in Anglo-Saxon England*, 45–46.

21. Hanciles, *Migration*, 290.

22. Jonas of Bobbio, *Life of Saint Columban* 17.

23. Fletcher, *Barbarian Conversion*, 136–39; Brown, *Rise of Western Christendom*, 248–54.

24. *Letters of Columbanus* 4.3–4, trans. G. S. M. Walker, https://celt.ucc.ie/published/T201054/index.html.

In this passage Columbanus admits that his own personal desire was life in a secluded monastery. Nevertheless, for the "progress" of the church, and because of his love for the "salvation of many," he desired to preach the gospel to the unconverted.

Columbanus used his southward wanderings to put his expressed intentions into practice. During a sojourn in Bregenz, in present-day Austria, in 611, the "man of God" sowed "the Christian faith in the heathens thereabout." One day Columbanus came upon the local Swabians as they were about to sacrifice a large cask of beer to the god Woden. He breathed on the cask, and immediately it burst asunder. Then "he rebuked them and preached the word of God to them and urged them to refrain from these sacrifices. Many of them were persuaded by his words and turned to the Christian faith and accepted baptism." Somewhat later Columbanus was gripped with a strong longing to go to the land of the Slavs "in order to illuminate their darkened minds with the light of the Gospel and to open the way of truth to those who had always wandered in error."[25] A vision revealed that this was not God's will for him. By 613 the three years of Columbanus's missionary travels had come to an end. At Bobbio in northern Italy he established his last monastery on a site given to him by Agilulf, king of the Lombards. He died at Bobbio in 615. The Irish monasteries of St. Gall (in Switzerland) and Luxeuil produced a new generation of disciples, some of whom spent part of their careers in missionary work.

Celtic monks on the Continent were motivated by the ascetic practice of *peregrinatio* (1) to found monasteries, (2) to further the Christianization of nominal Christians, and (3) to a lesser degree, to evangelize non-Christians. Their evangelistic ministry took place during itinerant wanderings. The monks seldom remained long in one place, frequently just long enough to baptize the converts before journeying on. This meant that their results were often not preserved, as Boniface discovered in Hesse and Thuringia. Like Boniface, Irish monks preached to the local population and, at times, destroyed their pagan temples and idols. They also sought and valued the protection of local rulers.

Anglo-Saxon Mission to the Continent before Boniface

One hundred years after Columbanus left for Gaul in 590, a new wave of missionaries, motivated in part by their Celtic predecessors, began to arrive on the European mainland. They were Anglo-Saxons from Britain, who between

25. Jonas of Bobbio, *Life of Saint Columban* 53, 56; Fletcher, *Barbarian Conversion*, 142; cf. Brown, *Rise of Western Christendom*, 248, 253–54.

690 and 770 migrated in large numbers to the Continent. Willibrord, Boniface's mission mentor in Frisia, was the most important of the pre-Bonifatian missionaries. These Anglo-Saxons did not come to eradicate the outposts of Celtic Christianity there but to evangelize those still bound by paganism and to organize the surviving Christian presence, particularly on the northern and eastern borders of the Frankish kingdom. Unlike the earlier Irish monks and missionaries, the Anglo-Saxons cooperated intentionally with the papacy in their mission work.

Anglo-Saxon missionaries to the Continent were driven by two strong motivations. The first was a fervent desire to convert pagan Germans, whom they believed to be their blood relatives. This presumed bond of ethnic brotherhood that Anglo-Saxons sensed with the "Old Saxons" on the mainland is reflected in a 738 letter from Boniface to his English mission supporters.

> We beg you to be instant in prayer that God and our Lord Jesus Christ . . . may convert the hearts of the pagan Saxons to the faith. . . . Remember them, because they themselves are accustomed to say: "we are of one blood and one bone."[26]

Boniface stresses blood kinship when he asks for prayer for the continental Saxons.

The ideals of *peregrinatio* were a second motivation for Anglo-Saxon missionaries. All of the earliest group of Anglo-Saxons connected with the mission to Frisia in present-day Netherlands (Wilfrid, Egbert, and Willibrord) had either studied in Ireland or were monks in an Irish monastery. Egbert's desire to be a missionary was related to his vow to live in permanent exile from his native England if he survived an outbreak of the plague. His self-exile was clearly motivated by Irish ideals of renunciation. Willibrord spent twelve years as a student at the monastery at Rath Melsigi in southern Ireland, where he adopted and became "a representative of the Irish ascetic practice of *peregrinatio*."[27] Later, Boniface, in a letter to an English abbess, combines both motivations (the desire to convert fellow Germans and *peregrinatio*) when he describes himself as "a *Germanic exile* who has [been sent] to enlighten the dark corners of the [Continental] *Germanic peoples*."[28] Irish *peregrinatio* had a great influence on Anglo-Saxon monks and missionaries. Nevertheless, *peregrinatio* as conceived and practiced by Anglo-Saxons

26. Boniface, Letter 46, in *Letters of Saint Boniface*, 74–75.
27. Michael Richter, "The Young Willibrord," in *Willibrord: Apostel der Niederlände*, ed. Georges Kiesel and Jean Schroeder (Luxembourg: Saint-Paul, 1989), 26.
28. Boniface, Letter 30, in *Letters of Saint Boniface*, 60–61.

differed fundamentally from those of their Irish predecessors, who were more concerned with personal penance and establishing monastic centres than with evangelization. Mission as *peregrinatio* . . . was a uniquely Anglo-Saxon concept. . . . For Boniface and his companions, *peregrinatio* was not merely about seeking a foreign wilderness and suffering the misery of exile according to the Irish model. . . . [It] also involved challenging and defeating paganism in accordance with the Great Commission.[29]

For Anglo-Saxon missionaries, mission was not an incidental or secondary aspect of their exile on the Continent; it was the reason they were there.

The beginnings of the Anglo-Saxon mission enterprise on the Continent were almost accidental. Wilfrid, a bishop from Northumbria, was on his way to Rome when he was forced by inclement weather to spend the winter of 678–679 in Frisia. He used his delay to preach to the local Frisians and to baptize a large number of converts. He observed that the Frisian king Aldgisl was open to receive missionaries in his kingdom. After his return to Northumbria, Wilfrid spread the news of an open door for mission in Frisia. Egbert was a Northumbrian studying in a monastery in Ireland when he developed a desire to be a "soldier of Christ"—that is, a missionary to the continental Saxons. Ultimately a vision convinced Egbert that his duty was to remain in Ireland. Although he did not serve as a missionary, Egbert could and did send others. He first sent Wigbert, who discovered that the political climate in Frisia had changed considerably since Wilfrid's visit. King Aldgisl, who had viewed a Christian mission favorably, had been succeeded by the adamantly pagan king Radbod. After two years of fruitless ministry, Wigbert returned to Ireland. In 690 Egbert sent a second mission consisting of twelve disciples, including the missionary priest Willibrord.[30]

By the time Willibrord (658–739) and the mission team arrived in Frisia, once again the political situation had changed—this time positively for Christian outreach. One year earlier the Frankish ruler, Pippin II, had conquered the southern portion of Radbod's Frisian kingdom. Pippin was well aware of the advantages of Christianizing the newly conquered territory; baptism was widely regarded in this era as a symbol of subjection to the Franks. Therefore, soon after his arrival in 690, Willibrord received from Pippin southern Frisia as his mission territory. Powerful secular support for the mission, something Wigbert had lacked, proved to be one key to its success. Pippin, and later Charles Martell, granted property to the mission. They used their armies to protect the missionaries and to expand mission territories through annexation

29. Clay, *In the Shadow of Death*, 247–48.
30. Godfrey, *Church in Anglo-Saxon England*, 135–37, 220–22.

of new lands. This was an early medieval example of mutual cooperation between mission and empire, church and state.

Support by Frankish rulers was not all that was needed for successful ministry. In 692, two years into the mission, Willibrord journeyed to Rome to seek the support and approval of Pope Sergius (r. 687–701) for his work in Frisia, which the pope readily granted. On his return from Rome, Willibrord began to systematically visit various locations within Frisia on evangelistic preaching tours. Then, in 695, Pippin sent Willibrord again to Rome, this time to be consecrated as archbishop. Pippin's role in Willibrord's consecration as archbishop was highly significant. "It is the earliest known case of cooperation between a Carolingian ruler . . . the pope . . . and the Anglo-Saxon missionary."[31] When Willibrord returned from this second trip to Rome, Pippin gave him the castle at Utrecht as his archepiscopal see.

Utrecht was at a strategic location within Frankish Frisia yet close to pagan territory under King Radbod. Willibrord first evangelized among the nominal Christians in Frankish-held territory. He vigorously "preached the Word of God" to them, and the people in the cities and villages, "through the help of divine grace . . . he brought to a knowledge of the truth and the worship of Almighty God."[32] Willibrord founded churches and monasteries to anchor the work. The archbishop then attempted to evangelize pagans outside the Frankish realm, first at Radbod's court, then at the court of the Danish ruler Ongendus. Both attempts were completely unsuccessful: the pagan rulers and their subjects showed no inclination to exchange their traditional religion for Christianity. In sharp contrast with Boniface's experience at the Oak of Thor, Willibrord's staged confrontations with pagan gods had little effect. Willibrord desecrated a pagan cultic site dedicated to a local god on the island of Heligoland off the western coast of Denmark. The defilers of the sacred spring (Willibrord and his entourage) did not "become mad or [get] struck with sudden death" as the pagans had expected; nevertheless the pagans did not convert. Instead, they reported to Radbod the sacrilege done to their sacred site. Radbod cast rune stones as lots to discover which of the missionaries would be executed for the desecration of the sacred spring. Providentially for Willibrord, the lot did not fall on him; another of his company won a martyr's crown. Willibrord's mission excursions outside Frankish territory met with little success.[33] The Frisians there remained stubbornly pagan until the time of Charlemagne, when they were converted only at the point of a

---

31. Godfrey, *Church in Anglo-Saxon England*, 225.

32. Noble and Head, *Soldiers of Christ*, 198.

33. Noble and Head, *Soldiers of Christ*, 198–99; Palmer, *Anglo-Saxons in a Frankish World*, 106–8, 133; Padberg, *Wynfreth-Bonifatius*, 32.

sword. Willibrord remained active in missionary work and episcopal duties until 728, when at the age of seventy he retired to his monastery at Echternach, where he died in November 739.

The Mission of Boniface to Germany

The man we know as Boniface was born in 672 into a landowning, prosperous family in Wessex, England. At his baptism he received the name Wynfrith. Wynfrith's father housed itinerant preachers on the family estate, and it was through these preachers that Wynfrith received his first spiritual impulses. When he was seven, his parents dedicated him to the monastic life as an oblate at the monastery in Exeter. Wynfrith was a clever and diligent student and by the age of twenty had outgrown the limited scholarly resources at Exeter. He moved to the larger monastery at Nursling to further his studies in sacred Scripture under Abbot Winbert. At the canonical age of thirty, Wynfrith was ordained a priest. In the following decade, he became a regular member at ecclesiastical synods, something that served him well later in life. The broad respect that he gained in this period meant that a public career in the English church was a viable option.[34]

Wynfrith's heart, however, was set on a missionary vocation. He shared his desire with Abbot Winbert, who initially refused to release him from the monastery. Finally, in 716 Winbert relented. Wynfrith, with several fellow monks, traveled to Frisia, intending to join Willibrord's mission. Circumstances prevented the accomplishment of their goal. Pippin had died in 714, and Radbod was launching a determined effort to regain the territory he had lost and destroy the Christian presence. By the time of Wynfrith's arrival, many Frisian churches had been destroyed and some pagan shrines restored. Wynfrith recognized that a mission to Frisia at this time was futile. He returned home to the monastery at Nursling, where he remained for another two years.[35]

In autumn 718, armed with letters of recommendation from his ecclesiastical superior, Bishop Daniel of Winchester, Wynfrith left England, never to return again. His first task was to present himself to Pope Gregory II in Rome to seek his approval and support for the mission. The pope took his time deciding whether and how best to utilize the talents of Wynfrith. Finally, on May 15, 719, the pope formally commissioned Wynfrith, who was given

34. Padberg, *Wynfreth-Bonifatius*, 46–58.
35. Padberg, *Wynfreth-Bonifatius*, 59–60.

SIDEBAR 4.2

Pope Gregory II Entrusts Boniface
with a Mission to the "Heathens" (719)

Gregory, the servant of the servants of God, to Boniface, a holy priest.

Your holy purpose, as it has been explained to us, and your well-tried faith lead us to make use of your services in spreading the Gospel, which by the grace of God has been committed to our care. Knowing that from your childhood you have been a student of Sacred Scripture and that you now wish to use the talent entrusted to you by God in dedicating yourself to missionary work, we rejoice in your faith and desire to have you as our colleague in this enterprise. . . .

Therefore, in the name of the indivisible Trinity and by the authority of Saint Peter . . . we now . . . decree that you go forth to preach the Word of God to those people who are still bound by the shackles of paganism. You are to teach them the service of the kingdom of God by persuading them to accept the truth in the name of Christ, the Lord our God. You will instill into their minds the teaching of the Old and New Testaments, doing this in a spirit of love and moderation, and with arguments suited to their understanding.

Source: Gregory II, Letter 12, in *The Anglo-Saxon Missionaries in Germany*, trans. and ed. C. H. Talbot (New York: Sheed and Ward, 1954), 68.

the new name Boniface. A written copy of Boniface's apostolic commission was preserved (see sidebar 4.2).

The apostle of Germany was commissioned to use the "talent entrusted to [him] by God" and his knowledge of Scripture to preach and teach the gospel to those "still bound by the shackles of paganism."[36] Boniface was not commissioned to force the Christian faith on the populace in Germany. Rather, he was called to *persuade* pagans to accept the gospel message through use of the biblical texts and appropriate arguments delivered in a spirit of love.[37] Boniface's papal mandate to use *persuasive* evangelistic methods is noteworthy, since in the post-Constantinian era, coercive methods were at times employed in the conversion of pagans and the Christianization of nominal Christians. This coercion was for the most part indirect and consisted of negative conse-

36. Gregory II, Letter 12, in *The Anglo-Saxon Missionaries in Germany*, trans. and ed. C. H. Talbot (New York: Sheed and Ward, 1954), 68.
37. Padberg, *Wynfreth-Bonifatius*, 62–63; Gregory II, Letter 12, in *Letters of Saint Boniface*, 32–33.

quences for nonconversion (increased taxation, shunning, or punishments).[38] Though milder than later forms, it was coercive nevertheless. Boniface took the pope's commission to heart and focused his ministry on persuading non-Christians through preaching and occasional power encounters.

The newly commissioned missionary had a short sojourn in Thuringia during the summer of 719. When he heard the news that the Frisian king Radbod had died, Boniface decided to join forces with Willibrord. Frisia, after all, had been the mission field that had first drawn him to the Continent. Boniface's three years (719–722) spent under the seasoned missionary Willibrord marked the completion of his practical training in mission methods. The two mission leaders took advantage of the new openness to the gospel in Frisia after Radbod's demise. They scattered "abroad the seed of Christian teaching to feed . . . those who had been famished with pagan superstitions." The influx of new converts into the church had one other result: "The authority of the glorious leader Charles [Martell] over the Frisians was strengthened."[39] Boniface's biographer candidly acknowledged the role of Christianization in subjugating a territory within the Frankish realm. Frankish rulers of the rising Carolingian dynasty were well aware that the Christianization of recently conquered areas effectively destroyed resistance to their rule. This was one key reason that they supported mission work, both during and after the conquest of new territories.

A half century later, however, during Charlemagne's conquest of Saxony (772–804), a fundamental shift occurred from the indirect pressure common in the post-Constantinian period to direct coercion to adopt the Christian faith. The conquered Saxons were forced to convert, often on pain of death. A ninth-century Saxon forthrightly reported that Charlemagne, their "apostle . . . preached with an iron tongue [the sword] in order to open up for us [Saxons] the gates of faith."[40] This degree of direct, as opposed to indirect, coercive Christianization was exceptional, though not unknown in the following centuries. There were two other key periods of Christian expansion where, like under Charlemagne, the "dominant face" of the church "justified the violence, oppression, and destruction" of non-Christians "in the name of evangelization." These two periods were the Crusades (1095–1291) and during the conquest and conversion of the New World (1492 to ca. 1550). During each of these periods there was a small minority of Christians who,

38. Ramsay MacMullen, "Christianity Shaped through Its Mission," in *The Origins of Christendom in the West*, ed. Alan Kreider (Edinburgh: T&T Clark, 2001), 102.

39. Noble and Head, *Soldiers of Christ*, 122.

40. H. Mayr-Harting, "Charlemagne, the Saxons, and the Imperial Coronation of 800," *English Historical Review* 111, no. 444 (November 1996): 1115, 1129.

through their example or writings, served as "voices of prophetic protest"[41] against coercive evangelism and for a persuasive approach: Alcuin during the reign of Charlemagne, Francis of Assisi during the Crusades, and Bartolomé de Las Casas and others during the conquest of the New World.

During Boniface's tenure on the Continent, Frankish rulers were actively involved in missionary and later church affairs, a trend that the papacy embraced. In a letter dated October 29, 739, Pope Gregory III rejoiced that one hundred thousand German souls had entered the church "through your [Boniface's] efforts *and those of Prince Charles* [Martell]," an acknowledgment that political patronage was just as crucial in missionary success as Boniface's preaching.[42]

Although Willibrord desired that Boniface remain in Frisia for the long term, Boniface's understanding of his apostolic commission did not allow him to be tied permanently to one locality. In 722, Boniface left for Hesse. He did not return to Frisia until after the death of Willibrord. Boniface's first station in Hesse was at Amöneburg, within (but on the edge of) Frankish-controlled territory. After Frisia, Hesse, particularly the borderlands to Saxony, was the most pagan portion of Germany. Most of the locals were still not Christians, since the Franks had made no attempt to convert them. It was therefore a logical location for Boniface to implement his apostolic commission to those still "bound by the shackles of paganism." The region had passed into Frankish control around 690–720 without rebellion on the part of the indigenous rulers, who continued to govern. When Boniface arrived, Amöneburg was ruled from a hilltop fortress by the twin brothers Dettic and Deorulf. It was common mission practice to first approach local leaders with the gospel. Dettic and Deorulf responded promptly to Boniface's preaching. The conversion of the two chiefs resulted in a mass conversion of many locals, though probably not the "many thousands" that Boniface's biographer reports. A church dedicated to Saint Michael was built at Amöneburg, as was a "little monastery" (*monasteriola*), to complement the church. Boniface went on to establish several "little monasteries," each positioned together with a church in the immediate area: first at Amöneburg, and, after the felling of the Oak of Thor, at Fritzlar and Büraburg. These small Hessian monasteries had both priests who provided pastoral care to the local population and a small contingent of monks. All three monasteries were used as centers for both

41. Justo González and Ondina González, *Christianity in Latin America: A History* (Cambridge: Cambridge University Press, 2008), 3–4. The Gonzálezes are referring specifically to the church in Latin America, but I would argue that the "two faces of the Church" are applicable for Charlemagne's Saxon wars and the Crusades as well.
42. Gregory III, Letter 45, in *Letters of Saint Boniface*, 72; see also Letters 20 (p. 45), 22 (p. 47).

the recruiting and training of indigenous and Anglo-Saxon missionaries and became bases for evangelizing the surrounding area. Institutions with mixed pastoral and monastic functions were common in eighth-century England, though not in the Frankish realm. They were used by Boniface as anchors for his missionary work.[43]

Boniface sent a messenger to Rome to report to Pope Gregory his successes in Hesse. The pope promptly summoned him to Rome. Boniface willingly complied, arriving in the eternal city in fall 722. While there, Boniface submitted a written copy of his theological beliefs to the pope for his perusal. Boniface passed the test for theological orthodoxy and on November 30, 722, was ordained bishop. At that time Boniface swore an oath of loyalty to the pope.

> I, Boniface, by the grace of God bishop, promise to you . . . the blessed pope Gregory . . . that I will uphold the faith and purity of holy Catholic teaching. . . . In all things I will show . . . complete loyalty to you and to the welfare of your Church on which . . . the power to bind and loose has been conferred.[44]

With this oath, Boniface placed himself firmly under the papacy as the pope's loyal servant. After this second trip to Rome, Boniface continued his mission work in Hesse. He challenged the pagan gods by felling the Oak of Thor. Until 732 Boniface evangelized and founded churches in Hesse and Thuringia. Boniface continued to nurture a close relationship with the papal successors of Gregory II; he ultimately served as a loyal servant under four popes.

In 732, Gregory III, Gregory II's successor, made Boniface archbishop. At this time (732–744) Boniface's ministry shifted from direct evangelism and church planting to the reform and organization of the church. In Bavaria, Hesse, and Thuringia, the apostle of Germany disciplined errant priests (of whom there were many), established and organized dioceses, consecrated bishops, and established monasteries. The task of evangelization was entrusted to new Anglo-Saxon missionary recruits, who, inspired by Boniface, flocked to the Continent to convert the Old Saxons. Monks such as Wigbert, Burchard, Denehard, and Lull, and nuns such as Leoba and Thecla, furthered the evangelization and Christianization of Germany.[45]

Boniface's heart's desire, however, lay in direct missionary work. In 737 Charles Martell planned a military campaign against the Saxons. Boniface recognized that the potential inclusion of Saxony into the Frankish kingdom

---

43. Palmer, *Anglo-Saxons in a Frankish World*, 147–53.
44. Boniface, Letter 16, in *Letters of Saint Boniface*, 41.
45. Padberg, *Wynfreth-Bonifatius*, 77–80; cf. Hanciles, *Migration*, 299–300.

provided a golden opportunity for mission among the kin of the Anglo-Saxons. So, in 738, Boniface wrote to England asking for prayer for the conversion of the Saxons, their blood brothers (quoted above). From 737 to 738, Boniface paid his third and last visit to Rome. This trip sprung from his aspiration to secure papal approval for a mission to the Saxons. Permission from Pope Gregory III for the Saxon mission, however, was not forthcoming. Instead, Boniface was instructed to return to southern Germany to organize the church on a diocesan basis. Boniface, ever the loyal papal servant, obeyed. Boniface never worked among the Saxons.[46]

Throughout his ministry on the Continent, Boniface confronted pagan beliefs: directly in his missionary endeavors and indirectly as a church reformer. In his organizational and reforming work in Thuringia and Bavaria, Boniface worked to eliminate the all-too-prevalent vestiges of pagan practices among church members and clergy alike. Then, at the very end of his life, the eighty-year-old Boniface returned once more to direct mission work among pagans. In early summer 753, the archbishop and his ministry companions returned to the place where the Anglo-Saxon mission had begun—Frisia. The mission among the Frisians prospered that first summer. Thousands were baptized, and sacred sites were destroyed and replaced with churches. The following summer, on the feast of Pentecost, a second large group of converts was baptized. Several days later, on June 5, 754, the mission entourage was attacked by a band of armed robbers. The robbers were infuriated when they discovered that the chests where they hoped to find gold and silver contained mainly books. Boniface's companions reached for arms, but the archbishop forbade resistance. Boniface attempted to shield his head from the sword blows of his attacker with a Gospel codex he was then reading. The octogenarian missionary and thirty of his companions were butchered by the robbers. Boniface's "murder on the mission field" was "one kind of martyr's death that continued throughout the Middle Ages . . . outside the old imperial boundaries," where "those preaching the word often encountered violent opposition from armed and hostile pagans."[47] The following day, Boniface's body and those of his companions were retrieved and brought to the monastery of Fulda. Also retrieved were several books, including the Ragyndrudis Codex. It had sword cuts on it and might very well be the book Boniface held up at the time of his death. Almost immediately after his death, Boniface was revered as a martyr, a saint, and the apostle to Germany.[48]

46. Padberg, *Wynfreth-Bonifatius*, 80–82.
47. Robert Bartlett, *Why Can the Dead Do Such Great Things? Saints and Worshippers from the Martyrs to the Reformation* (Princeton: Princeton University Press, 2013), 177.
48. Padberg, *Wynfreth-Bonifatius*, 99–103.

Confronting Pagan Gods

This chapter began with Boniface's dramatic felling of the Oak of Thor. For Germanic pagans, rituals performed in sacred spaces composed the core of their religiosity. They took place at sacred springs or groves, in temples or before idols. Therefore, the desecration or destruction of such sites struck at the very heart of their religion. It constituted a direct confrontation between two religious traditions (paganism and Christianity) in a battle waged for adherents. Local pagans usually became convinced of the frailty of their gods and the superiority of the Christian God when their gods failed to annihilate the defilers of their shrines. For this reason, both Celtic and Anglo-Saxon missionaries staged confrontations with pagan gods in their mission work.

Nevertheless, the desecration or destruction of pagan religious sites occurred much less frequently than might be assumed. Only about fifty instances of such confrontations are found in the primary sources for the 550 years between Gregory the Great's mission to England (597) and the completed conversion of the Slavs and Scandinavians (ca. 1150). These instances are minimal in comparison to the number of accounts of missionary preaching activity in the sources for the same time range. Furthermore, preaching was almost always part and parcel of a staged confrontation with the gods.[49] Therefore, while confrontations were dramatic, convincing, and had their place within the missionary's arsenal of tactics, the majority of Boniface's mission work consisted of patient, itinerant preaching. Interestingly, a letter from Pope Gregory II to Boniface shortly after the felling of the Oak of Thor emphasizes that "by your *preaching* great numbers have been converted to the faith."[50] No mention is made of the dramatic power encounter as the cause of conversion; the focus is on preaching.

Missionary preaching was the premier method of confronting pagan gods. Unfortunately, no missionary sermons from Boniface are extant. Nevertheless, some hints are found in the primary sources that cast light on the subject. In the first place, Boniface had mastered the Frankish language and preached to non-Christians in the vernacular. Boniface was also a student of the Bible. He was "inflamed with a love of the Scriptures" and daily committed "to memory the writings of the prophets and apostles . . . and the Gospel teaching of Our Lord." Boniface's sermons were based on the Scriptures and adapted to his hearers. "Those matters that were written for the instruction of the peoples [Gentiles or pagans] he paraphrased and explained to them with striking

49. Lutz von Padberg, *Die Inszenierung religiöser Konfrontationen: Theorie und Praxis der Missionspredigt im frühen Mittelalter* (Stuttgart: Anton Hiersemann, 2003), 246–50.
50. Gregory II, Letter 24, in *Letters of Saint Boniface*, 51.

Bishop Daniel of Winchester, *The Method of Converting the Heathen* (723–724)

Do not begin by arguing with them about the genealogies of their false gods. Accept their statement that they were begotten by other gods through the intercourse of male and female and then you will be able to prove that, as these gods and goddesses did not exist before, and were born like men, they must be men and not gods. When they have been forced to admit that their gods had a beginning, since they were begotten by others, they should be asked whether the world had a beginning or was always in existence. . . . If they maintain that the universe had no beginning, try to refute their arguments and bring forward convincing proofs. . . . Do they think the gods should be worshipped for the sake of temporal and transitory benefits or for eternal and future reward? If for temporal benefit let them say in what respect the heathens are better off than the Christians. . . . These and similar questions, and many others that it would be tedious to mention, should be put to them, not in an offensive and irritating way but calmly and with great moderation. From time to time their superstitions should be compared with our Christian dogmas and touched upon indirectly. . . . This conclusion also must be drawn: If the gods are omnipotent, beneficent and just, they must reward their devotees and punish those who despise them. Why then, if they act thus in temporal affairs, do they spare the Christians who cast down their idols and turn away from their worship the inhabitants of practically the entire globe? And whilst the Christians are allowed to possess the countries that are rich in oil and wine and other commodities, why have they left to the heathens the frozen lands of the north, where the gods, banished from the rest of the world, are falsely supposed to dwell? The heathens are frequently to be reminded of the supremacy of the Christian world and of the fact that they who still cling to outworn beliefs are in a very small minority.

Source: Daniel of Winchester, Letter 23, in *Christianity and Paganism, 350–750: The Conversion of Western Europe*, rev. ed., ed. J. N. Hillgarth (Philadelphia: University of Pennsylvania Press, 1986), 172–73.

eloquence, shrewdly spicing it with parables," or illustrations from the lives of martyrs.[51]

The content of Boniface's missionary preaching was very likely similar to that found in a letter to the Old Saxons written in 738–39 by Pope Gregory III.

---

51. Noble and Head, *Soldiers of Christ*, 115; Padberg, *Wynfreth-Bonifatius*, 66, 124.

Gregory starts by reminding the Saxons that the end of the world, and hence judgment, is at hand. The Saxons should no longer worship idols, which are demons, but believe in the monotheistic Creator God. They must renounce the many gods of their ancestors, embrace the Christian faith and its moral standards, and be baptized in the name of Jesus Christ. Then they will be set free from eternal damnation and enter eternal life. Boniface's missionary preaching was first and foremost a call to repentance. It included a critique of polytheism and an apologetic for Christian monotheism.[52]

Bishop Daniel of Winchester was Boniface's spiritual superior, his colleague, and his spiritual friend. The bishop followed with interest Boniface's missionary career in Germany. In a letter written in 723–724, most likely after the felling of the Oak of Thor, Daniel takes "the liberty of making a few suggestions, in order to show you how, in my opinion, you may overcome . . . the resistance of this barbarous people." This letter is highly significant since it is one of very few reflections from the early medieval period on how best to convince pagans of the errors of their religious beliefs (see sidebar 4.3). Daniel proposes two main arguments: First, Boniface should avoid confrontation with his audience over the origins and "genealogies of their false gods." He should allow them to continue in their belief that their gods were engendered by human propagation but show them the logical consequence of this belief—their gods had a definite beginning; they were not eternal; and therefore they were human and not divine. Bishop Daniel suggests that Boniface use a series of questions to engage his listeners and to demonstrate the logical inconsistencies of their beliefs. This should be done "not in an offensive and irritating way but calmly and with great moderation." Daniel's second argument is to demonstrate the relative weakness of paganism as compared to the power and cultural superiority of Christendom. Boniface should point out that "Christians are allowed to possess the [southern] countries that are rich in wine and other commodities" whereas the countries that are "left to the heathens [are] the frozen lands of the north." The apostle to Germany should point to the "supremacy of the Christian world," which contrasts sharply with the "worn-out beliefs" of the "very small minority" of pagans.[53]

Bishop Daniel's (and Pope Gregory III's) suggested approach for evangelizing pagans was based on the presupposition that conversion occurred through

---

52. Pope Gregory III, Letter 21, in *Letters of Saint Boniface*, 45–47; cf. Lutz von Padberg, "Die Missionarische Arbeit des Bonifatius," *Zeitschrift für Missionswissenschaft und Religionswissenschaft* 88, no. 2 (2004): 129.

53. Daniel of Winchester, Letter 23, in *Christianity and Paganism, 350–750: The Conversion of Western Europe*, rev. ed., ed. J. N. Hillgarth (Philadelphia: University of Pennsylvania Press, 1986), 172–73.

persuasion and intellectual assent. Pagans were not deficient intellectually. They had the cognitive ability to understand and respond to logical arguments. Therefore, they should be persuaded by reason to adopt the Christian faith. Furthermore, pagans deserved respect and must not be mocked for what the missionaries viewed as their inadequate beliefs. Boniface's response to the bishop's letter unfortunately no longer exists. It would have been fascinating to know what the Anglo-Saxon missionary with a half dozen years of practical ministry among pagans thought of Daniel's admittedly theoretical reflections.

In conclusion, the mission of Boniface on the Continent was a turning point in the expansion of Christianity in this sense. Boniface's felling of the Oak of Thor was a well-documented and representative example of the mission approach used during the conversion and Christianization of the pagan peoples of western, northern, and eastern Europe between 400 and 1200. Yet Boniface's mission was not without precedence. One hundred years prior, the first Irish monks, motivated by the penitential practice of *peregrinatio*, had arrived on the European mainland, where they founded monasteries and furthered the Christianization of western and central Europe. Like Boniface, the Celtic missionaries staged confrontations with pagan gods when appropriate. Nevertheless, for Boniface and his compatriots, the main means of confronting paganism was through patient, ongoing itinerant preaching. The content of his missionary preaching included a call to renounce paganism, to repent of one's sins, and to accept salvation in Jesus Christ with its attendant ethical standards.

We end this chapter with an Advent prayer, written in Anglo-Saxon around 800 by an anonymous poet:

> As You, begotten God of God, Son of the True Father, without beginning abode ever in the splendour of heaven, so now for need Your handiwork beseeches boldly that You send the bright sun unto us; that You come and shed Your light on those who long ere this, compassed about with mist and in the darkness, clothed in sin, sit here in the long night, and must needs endure the dark shadow of Death. Now are we full of hope and put our trust in Your salvation, heralded to the hosts of men by the word of God, which in the beginning was with God, with the Almighty Father coeternal, and afterward was made flesh unstained of sin, which the Virgin bare, a solace unto wretched men.[54]

---

54. Charles W. Kennedy, trans., *The Poems of Cynewulf* (London: Routledge, 1910), 156.

Accommodating Culture

Jesuits and the Chinese Rites Controversy (1707)

Before more than a thousand five hundred and ten years ago,
The invisible God resides in heaven,
But now he appears as a child to whom we should pay our respect.
Why is it that the Chinese people show no devotion? . . .
He who serves God will possess eternal happiness. . . .
Believe and adore the Supreme God. . . .
If the people of China understand the meaning of the profession of
    the faith,
It would be good to prepare themselves to embrace the [Catholic]
    religion.
The evildoers will meet their fate in the place of [eternal] torment,
While the good will merit eternal happiness in heaven.[1]

In December 1705, the Kangxi emperor of China (1654–1722) held the first of two audiences with the papal legate and cardinal Charles-Thomas Maillard de Tournon. Tournon, an official representative of Pope Clement XI,

---

1. The text above includes excerpts from two poems by Michele Ruggieri, a sixteenth-century Jesuit missionary to China. Albert Chan, "Michele Ruggieri, S.J. (1543–1607) and His Chinese Poems," *Monumenta Serica* 41 (1993): 163, 166 (poems 16.1–2; 18.2–3).

had been sent to China to communicate to the Roman Catholic missionaries Clement's 1704 decree (*Cum Deus optimus*) concerning the Chinese rites. Tournon was well aware that Kangxi, the "final arbiter in ethical matters" in China, had made his position regarding the rites abundantly clear in his own imperial decree in 1700. Ritual ceremonies in honor of Confucius or one's ancestors were not superstitious or even religious in nature, the emperor asserted, since they did not seek benefits or blessings. Rather, such acts of veneration merely expressed in Confucian fashion filial piety, gratitude, and devotion.[2] Kangxi's stance on the rites was diametrically opposed to the official position stipulated in Pope Clement's 1704 decree, which Tournon had been sent to promulgate and uphold. Clement categorically mandated that it was "not permissible on any ground for [Chinese] Christians to be present at or take part in the solemn rites in honor of Confucius or the ancestors."[3] Due to their different stances on the issue, it is not surprising that Tournon's audiences with the Chinese emperor went poorly. His papal legation from 1705 to 1707 once again brought tensions over the Chinese rites, which had been simmering for nearly a century, to a boil. There were disastrous results, both immediate and long-term, for the Roman Catholic China mission.

I will discuss the long-term impact of the Chinese Rites controversy on the China mission later in this chapter. Three immediate results are relevant here. First, the Kangxi emperor expressed his displeasure with Tournon by banishing him to Portuguese-held Macau on the Chinese coast. There he remained under house arrest until his untimely death in 1710. Second, in December 1706 the emperor mandated that all European missionaries must receive an imperial certificate of residence in order to remain in China. Such certificates would only be issued to those who upheld Confucian and ancestor-veneration rites. Last, Kangxi's edict of April 19, 1707, identified his own understanding of the rites with the approach followed by pioneer Jesuit missionary to China Matteo Ricci (d. 1610) a century before. Kangxi required that "henceforth those who do not follow the rules of Ricci [on the Chinese rites] are not permitted to stay in China."[4] The Kangxi emperor claimed that Ricci had correctly understood the rites, whereas Pope Clement XI and the papal legate Tournon had not. He also affirmed Ricci's cultural accommodation approach.

2. Liam Matthew Brockey, *Journey to the East: The Jesuit Mission to China, 1579–1724* (Cambridge, MA: Harvard University Press, 2007), 187, 190–92.
3. George Minamiki, *Chinese Rites Controversy: From Its Beginning to Modern Times* (Chicago: Loyola University Press, 1985), 47.
4. Quoted in John Dragon Young, "Chinese Views of Rites and the Rites Controversy, 18th–20th Centuries," in *The Chinese Rites Controversy: Its History and Meaning*, ed. D. E. Mungello (Nettetal: Steyler Verlag, 1994), 94.

This raises the questions: What was it about Ricci's approach to the Chinese rites and culture that so impressed Kangxi? Why would the Chinese emperor only allow pro-Riccian missionaries to remain in the country? This chapter seeks to answer these questions.

The Chinese Rites controversy raised crucial questions not only about ancestor veneration but also about the relationship between Christianity and non-Western cultures. Were the Chinese rites inherently superstitious or idolatrous and therefore inappropriate for Chinese Christians? More broadly, was it necessary for converts to reject much of their own culture and to adopt Western customs in order to embrace the Christian faith? Many Jesuit missionaries in the sixteenth to eighteenth centuries would answer both questions with a resounding no! They would develop "methods of the apostolate [mission] which demonstrated a sharp break with the dominant spirit of the age." In doing so, they "restored the concept of cultural adaptation to a central position in the world mission of Christianity."[5] The approach to other cultures developed by Ignatius Loyola, the founder of the Jesuits, and his later missionary compatriots—Alessandro Valignano, who was the visitor (or head) of the Asian mission, and Matteo Ricci in China—was unique, innovative, and groundbreaking. With but a few exceptions, nothing similar to the radical Jesuit approach to culture was implemented by missionaries of the contemporary Roman Catholic mendicant orders (Dominicans and Franciscans) or even by Protestant missionaries until the eighteenth or nineteenth centuries. Jesuit cultural accommodation, though controversial, was truly a turning point in the expansion of Christianity. Not only did it challenge the dominant and prevailing mission mindset, but during the ensuing Rites controversy, it forced both adherents to the Riccian approach and their opponents to take a stand on the issues of cultural adaptation it raised.

In order to understand the uniqueness of the Jesuit approach to culture that so impressed the Chinese emperor, we must first unpack what early Jesuits understood by the concept of cultural accommodation. Then I will summarize the development of Ricci's innovative missionary strategy in China, including both its strengths and weaknesses, in order to better understand why his accommodational approach garnered both exuberant praise and fierce condemnation. Furthermore, I will note areas where Ricci's method succeeded and where it failed to produce his desired outcomes. Finally, the chapter ends with an overview of the Chinese Rites controversy and a brief discussion of its broader, long-term impact.

5. George H. Dunne, *Generation of Giants: The Story of the Jesuits in China in the Last Decades of the Ming Dynasty* (Notre Dame, IN: University of Notre Dame Press, 1962), 12–14.

Jesuit Cultural Accommodation

In 1540 a minor Spanish noble and erstwhile soldier named Ignatius Loyola (1491–1556) founded a new religious order, the Society of Jesus, or the Jesuits. The founding document of the order stressed that individual members were obliged to take a special oath of obedience to the pope and to be ready to be sent instantly to any country where the pontiff might command them. The Jesuits were "engaged in a conflict for God" for souls "among the Turks or other heathen . . . or among whatsoever heretics and schismatics, or among any believers whatsoever."[6] This document makes explicit that the Society of Jesus was committed to missionary outreach among all peoples, whether non-Christians overseas ("Turks or other heathen") or Protestant heretics and schismatics in Europe. They experienced considerable success in both ventures. In the sixteenth century, the Jesuit order was still in its youth and full of energy, idealism, and missionary zeal. It played a significant role in revitalizing the spirituality of the Roman Catholic Church and in relaunching its missionary endeavor. Unlike the mendicant orders, which were established three centuries earlier, Ignatius Loyola founded the Society of Jesus in the era of Renaissance humanism, when openness and respect for indigenous cultures was on the rise. Loyola capitalized on this new modern spirit. He insisted that Jesuit missionaries learn not only the language of the country in which they served but also the customs and patterns of thought—an approach that was not universally practiced at this time. In doing so, he laid the theoretical groundwork for Jesuit cultural accommodation.

The term "accommodation" was frequently used by sixteenth- and seventeenth-century Jesuits (e.g., Ignatius Loyola, Matteo Ricci, and Roberto de Nobili), although the term is not common in mission circles today. Instead, "inculturation" (among Roman Catholics) or "contextualization" (among Protestants) have replaced this more archaic term. "Accommodation" as a technical historical term referred to a "typically Jesuit or, more specifically, Ignatian spirit that subsumed the means of sparking conversions . . . to the ends" in order to achieve the "ultimate goal of their mission: the conversion of the Chinese to Christianity."[7] In other words, on one level, accommodation was essentially a practical, goal-oriented mission strategy to clear away unnecessary cultural hindrances to conversion for the target population. Ignatius Loyola claimed in a September 1541 letter that accommodation was necessary in order to "meet with better [evangelistic] success." "Whenever

---

6. Quoted in John C. Olin, ed., *The Catholic Reformation: Savonarola to Ignatius Loyola, Reform in the Church, 1495–1540* (New York: Harper & Row, 1969), 204–5.

7. Brockey, *Journey to the East*, 44.

SIDEBAR 5.1

Definitions of Cultural Accommodation

Ignatius Loyola, Letter to Fathers Broët and Salmerón (1541)

In dealing with men of position or influence—if you hope to win their affection for the greater glory of God our Lord—first consider their temperaments and adapt yourselves to them. . . . Whenever we wish to win someone over and engage him in the greater service of God our Lord, we should use the same strategy for good that the enemy employs to draw a good soul to evil. The enemy enters through the other's door and comes out his own. He enters with the other, not by opposing his ways but by praising them. He acts familiarly with the soul, suggesting good and holy thoughts that bring peace to the good soul. Then, little by little, he tries to come out his own door, always portraying some error or illusion under the appearance of something good, but which will always be evil. So, we may lead others to good by praying or agreeing with them on a certain good point, leaving aside whatever else may be wrong. Thus after gaining his confidence, we shall meet with better success. In this sense we enter his door with him, but we come out our own.

Duarte de Sande

In truth, among these nations that are so different from ours, and have laws and customs so different, it is necessary to enter with theirs to come out with ours, *accommodating ourselves* to them in what our Holy Faith permits, in this way to divulge and teach our holy doctrine, which they would receive in no other way.

Source: Ignatius Loyola, Letter to Fathers Broët and Salmerón, September 1541, available at http://www.library.georgetown.edu/woodstock/ignatius-letters/letter1; Duarte de Sande, quoted in Liam Matthew Brockey, *Journey to the East: The Jesuit Mission to China, 1579–1724* (Cambridge, MA: Harvard University Press, 2007), 44.

we wish to win someone over [i.e., convert them] . . . we enter his door with him, but we come out our own" (see sidebar 5.1).[8]

Duarte de Sande (1547–99), Jesuit missionary and mission superior of China, defended and elaborated on Loyola's concept of accommodation in 1595, using Loyola's terminology (see sidebar 5.1). Both Jesuits held that the "laws and customs" of other nations were radically "different from ours."

8. Ignatius Loyola, Letter to Fathers Broët and Salmerón, September 1541, available at http://www.library.georgetown.edu/woodstock/ignatius-letters/letter1.

This cultural distance made it imperative for missionaries to adapt as much as possible to the foreign culture in order to successfully evangelize the locals. Only when the missionaries entered fully through the door of the receiving culture by adapting themselves to their customs would they be able to entice members of the target population to follow them into the Christian faith. It is important to note that Loyola and de Sande were not stating that Christian converts would retain all aspects of their culture or that their Christian faith would be wholly dissimilar to that of the missionaries. After all, the converts "come out our own" (European) Christian door. In practice, accommodation meant that missionaries demonstrated a willingness to adopt all local customs "unless they are clearly against divine law." "When preaching the Gospel, we should avoid mixing in European customs not needed for the salvation of souls," advised Valignano, visitor of the Jesuit Asian missions.[9] Furthermore, the similarities (and not the differences) between the Christian faith and the cultural/religious traditions in China (Confucianist, Taoist, and Buddhist) or South Asia (Hindu) were stressed.[10]

Valignano's admonition above brings us to a second aspect of accommodation. It was an intentional "style of mission that attempted to break free from both European political imperialism and, what was even more powerful and longer lived, Europeanism—the belief that the European experience is the Christian experience and is definitive for all humanity."[11] This approach to the missionary task diverged radically from standard contemporary procedures. Many mendicant missionaries, and even some Jesuits, upheld the tabula rasa or "blank slate" approach to culture. Missionary adherents to this viewpoint were convinced that potential converts must adopt European ways in order to become Christians. Indigenous culture, it was believed, had little to recommend itself and had to be virtually eliminated, erased clean like a blank slate prior to conversion. This approach was common in the sixteenth and seventeenth centuries in the overseas possessions of Portugal and Spain in both the Americas and Asia. In a series of papal bulls (from 1455 on), the Iberian monarchs were granted the "right of dominion" over their territories abroad "in exchange for the responsibility . . . to Christianize" the indigenous population. This system was referred to as royal patronage (*padroado real* in

---

9. R. Po-chia Hsia, *Matteo Ricci and the Catholic Mission to China: A Short History with Documents* (Indianapolis: Hackett, 2016), 66.

10. For Confucianism, Taoism, and Buddhism as modern constructs, see Tomoko Masuzawa, *The Invention of World Religions* (Chicago: University of Chicago Press, 2005), 1–33, 121–46; Anna Sun, *Confucianism as a World Religion: Contested Histories and Contemporary Realities* (Princeton: Princeton University Press, 2013).

11. Andrew Ross, *A Vision Betrayed: The Jesuits in Japan and China, 1542–1742* (Maryknoll, NY: Orbis, 1994), xv.

Portuguese; *patronato real* in Spanish). Not only were the Iberian monarchs entitled to levy tithes to fund their missionary activities, but they also could appoint clerics to all ecclesiastical posts. This meant that "there was virtually complete royal control of the ecclesiastical structure" of the church and "an unparalleled union between crown and cross."[12] One attendant result of this system was that Iberian political control and culture were conflated with the Christian faith. In contrast, accommodation proclaimed that a non-European could be authentically Christian while retaining elements of his or her indigenous culture that were not idolatrous.

It is important to note that accommodation was not consistently practiced by all Jesuits. It was most common among Italian Jesuits, since many of them had been educated in institutions influenced by Renaissance humanism. Hence they were more likely to adopt a tolerant attitude toward cultural differences. This open-minded approach to other cultures was found not only in the Jesuit China mission. Italian Jesuit Roberto de Nobili, in his ministry among high-caste Tamil Hindus in South India, embraced key aspects of Brahmin culture (the ocher dress of a guru, vegetarianism, and caste separation). He wrote a lengthy defense of his accommodational approach titled *Adaptation* (1619). In this work he argues that a missionary must emulate the apostle Paul and "adopt the social customs of the people he has come to evangelize." All customs that were not contrary to the Catholic faith were legitimate; in fact, even those customs that were "mixed with various superstitious elements" had in the past been adopted by Christianity and "made . . . honorable by simply changing their purpose."[13] In contrast, many Spanish and Portuguese Jesuits accepted the basic premises of the *patronato real* approach discussed above. One glaring example is the Spanish Jesuit Alonso Sanchez, who wrote a memorandum to King Philip II of Spain recommending that an armada be sent from Spain to conquer China. The advantage of the conquest, he wrote, was that "innumerable souls will come to know and adore their creator, who are now in a state of blindness, ignorance and servitude to the devil."[14] This suggestion sounds remarkably similar to the coercive approaches to evangelism practiced during the Crusades and in the conquest of the New World (see chap. 4). Fortunately for the China mission, no such conquest took place. Under the leadership of Valignano and Ricci, the China mission pursued persuasive evangelism and a policy of cultural accommodation.

12. Justo González and Ondina González, *Christianity in Latin America: A History* (Cambridge: Cambridge University Press, 2008), 28.
13. Roberto de Nobili, *Adaptation*, ed. S. Rajamanickam, SJ (Palayamkottai: De Nobili Research Institute, 1971), 11, 37, 43.
14. Hsia, *Ricci and the Catholic Mission to China*, 68.

Matteo Ricci and the Jesuit Mission to China

Matteo Ricci was born in 1552 to a prosperous family in Macerata, Italy. At age nine he began seven years of classical preparatory education at a Jesuit school in his hometown. This early association with the order provided an excellent education; it also bore spiritual fruit in the young pupil. In August 1571, shortly before his nineteenth birthday, Matteo Ricci joined the Jesuit order. The six years Ricci then spent as a Jesuit novice in Rome (1571–77) were foundational for his future life. He completed his formal studies in liberal arts and philosophy at the Jesuit Roman College (*Collegio Romano*). He developed important and influential friendships with, among others, Alessandro Valignano, who supervised first his novitiate and later his mission work. Then, in 1576, Ricci responded to the call for missionary candidates for the order's Asian fields.

After a brief stint in Portugal, Ricci and the other missionary recruits set sail for the Portuguese colony of Goa on the west coast of India, where they arrived in September 1578. Ricci spent four years in Portuguese India (1578–82). Then, in 1582, Valignano—now the visitor of the Jesuit missions to India, Japan, and China—assigned the young missionary to a new post. Ricci was to join his older colleague Michele Ruggieri (who wrote the Chinese poems that opened this chapter) in a lifelong mission to mainland China. On Valignano's orders, this mission, as well as that to Japan, was to differ significantly from the mission efforts common in the Portuguese settlements under the patronage system. Valignano insisted that the China missionaries take the time to learn the Chinese language well. Without a high level of proficiency in Mandarin, he argued, evangelistic effectiveness would be thwarted, and true accommodation of the Christian message to Chinese culture could not be achieved. Ricci embraced Valignano's vision of cultural accommodation. Later, as head of the Jesuit China mission, Ricci expanded that vision even further.

Ricci's compatriot, Michele Ruggieri, had launched the mission on the Chinese mainland and secured permission for himself and a companion to reside in Zhaoqing, the capital of Guangdong province. This was an accomplishment in and of itself, since the residence of foreigners within the Ming Empire was seldom allowed. After a short period of expulsion from the city, Ruggieri was allowed to return to Zhaoqing in September 1583, this time with Ricci in tow. There the two Jesuit missionaries enjoyed the patronage of Wang Pan, a local magistrate. Wang encouraged them to adopt the dress of Chinese Buddhist monks, something Ruggieri readily agreed to, since he had already for some time identified himself as a monk from India. A plaque was placed at the entrance to the Jesuit residence with the words "temple of the Flower of the Saints" in Chinese, thus confirming their identification with Buddhist traditions.

This identification with Buddhist traditions proved to be both a benefit and a liability. One positive result was that it provided protection for the Christian mission in these early years. Association with Buddhism, a very popular and accepted religious tradition in China, meant that Christianity avoided "outright confrontation" in the religious sphere. Furthermore, Roman Catholicism paralleled some Buddhist practices and doctrines (monasticism, fasting, rosary beads, images of saints, heaven and hell). Therefore, it was not surprising that the vast majority of the eighty Christian converts in Zhaoqing were former Buddhists. Identification with Buddhist traditions also proved to be a liability. It is questionable whether the Buddhist-background converts in Zhaoqing clearly differentiated Christianity from their former religious beliefs, in part because Buddhist terminology abounded in the first Christian catechism in the Chinese language, prepared by Ruggieri.[15]

During his years in Zhaoqing (1583–89), Ricci acquired an astonishing level of competency in the written and spoken Chinese language, soon surpassing the ability of Ruggieri (see sidebar 5.2 for Li Zhi's impression of Ricci). Valignano had commissioned Ricci to translate the *Four Books* (Confucian Classics) into Latin both to improve his language skills and to deepen his understanding of Chinese Confucian thought. This exercise contributed to Ricci's growing conviction that the Jesuit association with Buddhist traditions was a serious mistake and a hindrance to conversion. In 1589, Ricci and fellow Jesuit António de Almeida were forced to relocate to a provincial town in northern Guangdong, Shaozhou, where Ricci remained until 1595. There he became the lifelong friend of scholar Qu Rukei. Qu advised him to abandon his association with Buddhism, arguing that Buddhist clergy, in contrast to Ricci himself, had low social status and intellectual ability. He would be better served by associating with and dressing like the Confucian literati. "Literati" in this context refers to a large elite group of Chinese scholars who took at least one of the triennial examinations on the Confucian classics, which were a prerequisite for holding an official office in the local, provincial, or imperial government.[16] Ricci's identification with the literati coincided with a growing aversion to Buddhist religious traditions. In time, this aversion increased to outright hostility, which Ricci expressed in his apologetic as well

15. Ross, *Vision Betrayed*, 118, 123, 126. Cf. Hsia, *Ricci and the Catholic Mission to China*, 22–24.

16. Nicolas Standaert, ed., *Handbook of Christianity in China*, vol. 1, *635–1800* (Leiden: Brill, 2001), 474.

Letter of Chinese Scholar Li Zhi
with His Impressions of Ricci (ca. 1599)

You asked about Ricci: he is a Westerner from the Extreme West, and traveled for over one hundred thousand *li* to reach China, sailing first to south India, where he learned of Buddha. . . .

When he reached Guangzhou and South Sea, he found out that our Great Ming realm has had the virtuous kings Yao and Shun, and the sages Zhou and Confucius. He lived in the south and in Zhaoqing nearly two decades, reading every book of our nation, asking teachers to help him note the pronunciations and meanings of the words . . . so that now he is fluent in speaking and writing our language, and following our rituals. . . . I have never seen anyone more impressive. . . . But I have no idea why he is here. I have met him three times already and still do not know his intention in coming here. Perhaps he wants to use his teachings to change our Confucian learning, but that would be silly, and must not be the case.

Source: Po-chia R. Hsia, *Matteo Ricci and the Catholic Mission to China: A Short History with Documents* (Indianapolis: Hackett, 2016), 89.

as in specifically anti-Buddhist writings. Thus, Ricci's advocacy of religious accommodation was selective; he accommodated Confucian beliefs, but not Buddhist.

Ricci's years in Guangdong province convinced him that the future of the Jesuit mission lay elsewhere. Anti-European feeling was rife in Guangdong due to the ongoing presence of foreigners at the Guangzhou (Canton) trading fairs as well as its proximity to Portuguese Macau. On several occasions, the Jesuit residence in Zhaoqing was barraged with stones. In Shaozhou the missionaries were the victims of sporadic acts of violence and vandalism. The need for protection for the mission was a key reason for a radical change of mission strategy from an identification with Buddhist traditions to an identification with the Confucian literati. This change could only be achieved by promoting good relationships with local literati magistrates, and later with the Chinese imperial court in Beijing.[17]

The year 1595 was a pivotal one in the development of the Jesuit China mission. In that year Ricci was asked to accompany a high-ranking Confucian

17. Dunne, *Generation of Giants*, 226.

magistrate to Beijing. Though he left the magistrate before reaching Beijing, he settled in the important second capital city of Nanjing. This northward movement from Guangdong was viewed as a godsend. Already in late 1592, Ricci had met personally with Valignano in order to discuss the next stages of the China mission. The two men agreed that it was imperative for the success of the mission to move away from Guangdong and closer to the centers of political power. Ricci explained to Duarte de Sande in a letter: "Until we have a foothold in one of these two royal cities [Beijing or Nanjing] we will always live in fear of losing this mission to China."[18] At this meeting Ricci also raised the issue of changing his dress from that of a Buddhist monk to that of the Confucian educated elite. Valignano gave Ricci the green light to identify himself with the literati.[19] So, on his way north in 1595, Ricci donned the robes of the mandarins and grew his hair and beard to emulate the Chinese elite (see the 1610 portrait of Ricci on this book's cover). This change of dress and move to an imperial capital, Nanjing, was the first step in his "ascent to Beijing," as it is often called, where Ricci arrived in January 1601. It was also the culmination of his developing missionary strategy.

A year before his death, on February 15, 1609, Ricci wrote a letter to his colleague Francesco Pasio, then the vice principal of the Jesuit Japan mission. In the letter Ricci outlines in eight points the key elements of his mature mission method. These eight points reveal his conclusions on the best way to evangelize the Chinese, drawn from his nearly thirty years of experience. The points overlap one another considerably and, therefore, like some other scholars, I will combine them into four elements.[20] The first key element of Ricci's mature mission method is his identification with the Confucian literati. After 1595, when Ricci distanced himself and the Jesuit mission from Buddhist religious traditions, these elite scholars and magistrates became the mission's principal evangelistic target group. In his letter to Pasio, Ricci rejoices that some Jesuit missionaries are viewed as "learned and virtuous men"—in other words, as literati.[21] This focus on the literati had monumental consequences for the day-to-day activities of the missionaries. Much of the missionaries' time was occupied with nurturing social relationships with the literati through the obligatory rounds of hospitality. During these visits, the literati desired

18. Brockey, *Journey to the East*, 35, 43.

19. Standaert, *Handbook of Christianity in China*, 1:474; Liam Brockey, *The Visitor: Andre Palmeiro and the Jesuits in Asia* (Cambridge, MA: Harvard University Press, 2014), 215–17.

20. Ross, *Vision Betrayed*, 143–45; Standaert, *Handbook of Christianity in China*, 1:310–11; Nicolas Standaert, "Jesuits in China," in *The Cambridge Companion to the Jesuits*, ed. Thomas Worcester (Cambridge: Cambridge University Press, 2008), 172–73.

21. Hsia, *Ricci and the Catholic Mission to China*, 121.

primarily to discuss philosophical and scientific topics. Thus, focus on the scholarly class frequently served to distract from the task of preaching, and "the work of conversion that was the goal and primary fruit for which we had come," as Jesuit missionary Feliciano da Silva (1579–1614) frankly admitted.[22] Both Valignano and Ricci were taking a long view of the China mission. Ricci's task was not "to build up worshipping communities" or "initiate . . . [a] mass conversion movement." Rather, the goal was to carefully "lay the foundation" for a "truly Chinese and Christian Church" in the future.[23]

The reality was that only a very small number of literati converted. "It was not that the Jesuits were failing to make converts; rather they were making the wrong sort of converts." There was a "profound mismatch between the Jesuits' stated aims" and the actual results.[24] During the seventeenth century, the number of literati converts (including their family members) was roughly 1 percent of the Chinese Catholic population.[25] The key reason for so few literati conversions was the negative impact that Christian faith could have on the lives *and careers* of the educated elite. The actual social background of Chinese converts was quite different from the intended target group. Ninety percent of the newly baptized were illiterate. The vast majority were not only uneducated but were common people with an "idolatrous" Buddhist background. They adopted the Christian faith, not because it convinced them rationally, but because it met their emotional and spiritual needs. Healing from illness, freedom from evil spirits, and miraculous events involving images of Christ, the Virgin Mary, or a crucifix were common reasons for conversion. While the handful of literati converts were widely and publicly celebrated by the Jesuits, "it is clear from their writings that the Jesuits sought to make new Christians from all ranks of Chinese society and that they proselytized the lower orders whenever it was possible for them to do so."[26]

The second element of Ricci's mature mission method, and a clear corollary of the first element, was a top-down evangelistic approach. By 1609, when the Pasio letter was written, Jesuit missionaries had regular contact at the imperial courts in Beijing and Nanjing. Since scholarship was "highly esteemed" in China, Ricci was convinced that "it will thus be easy to persuade the leaders of the realm that the things of our holy faith are confirmed with rational evidence. With the most important of the leaders agreeing with us, it

22. Quoted in Brockey, *Journey to the East*, 60.

23. Ross, *Vision Betrayed*, 135.

24. Mary Laven, *Mission to China: Matteo Ricci and the Jesuit Encounter with the East* (London: Faber and Faber, 2011), 52, 196.

25. Standaert, *Handbook of Christianity in China*, 1:387; cf. 1:474–87.

26. Brockey, *Journey to the East*, 48; cf. Standaert, *Handbook of Christianity in China*, 1:390–91; Standaert, "Jesuits in China," 175–77; and Laven, *Mission to China*, 48, 55, 227–33.

will be easy to convert the rest of the people."[27] This method held that if the "leaders of the realm," ideally the Chinese emperor and his court, converted, then the entire country would ultimately be won for the Christian faith. As noted above, it was considerably more difficult to win Chinese elites to the gospel than anticipated, and a mass conversion of the Chinese never occurred. Nevertheless, a focus on the "leaders of the realm" was not ill-conceived. Ricci's "ascent to Beijing," and his growing network of relationships with members of the Chinese governmental bureaucracy, provided credibility and protection for Catholicism in China. His residence at the capital also furthered the geographic expansion of the Jesuit mission. This occurred naturally when members of the Confucian bureaucracy, who had befriended the Jesuits, were transferred to a new government post—something that transpired with regularity. Magistrates who were Jesuit allies, even if they were not baptized Christians, often aided conversion efforts in the provinces.[28]

The third key element of Ricci's mature mission method was the so-called scientific apostolate. This refers to the use of Western knowledge, and particularly mathematics, astronomy, and cosmography, to interest Chinese intellectuals in a relationship with the Jesuits and ultimately in conversion to Christianity. This method can be viewed as an indirect approach to the propagation of the faith. Chinese intellectuals were first drawn to the Jesuits as purveyors of exotic Western knowledge, which they desired to acquire. Then, ideally, once an ongoing relationship of dialogue and discussion of more secular topics had been established, an interest in the Christian message would develop. Ricci was convinced of the efficacy of the scientific apostolate. He wrote Pasio: "We have opened the blind eyes of the Chinese" through "teaching on the natural science of mathematics. What would they say if they knew about the more abstract subjects such as physics, metaphysics, theology, and the supernatural?" "If we can teach them our science, they would not only succeed in being eminent men, but we could also easily induce them to embrace our holy law."[29] The Jesuit mission was committed to the scientific apostolate as a valid and effective means of evangelizing Confucian intellectuals. Throughout the seventeenth century, they recruited well-trained Jesuit mathematicians, astronomers, and scientists to serve at the imperial court in Beijing.

The writing and translating of books on both scientific and apologetic/religious topics was an important aspect of the indirect method of evangelization the Jesuits pursued among the literati. During the seventeenth century, roughly 120 texts on science and the West were published in Chinese

27. Hsia, *Ricci and the Catholic Mission to China*, 120.
28. Brockey, *Journey to the East*, 50.
29. Hsia, *Ricci and the Catholic Mission to China*, 120.

by missionaries and Chinese Christians. During the same century, 470 texts on apologetics and religious or moral topics were printed.[30] In the letter to Pasio, Ricci lists some of the advantages of the print medium. "Books . . . can travel everywhere without hindrance . . . reach more people, more often, than we can, and can provide greater detail and precision than we can orally."[31] The written word could also be read by speakers of various Chinese dialects.

The fourth key element of Ricci's mature mission method was accommodation to Chinese Confucian cultural customs and religious beliefs. True accommodation, according to Ricci, required an in-depth knowledge of the Chinese language. Early along, a strategic decision was made to learn Mandarin, the language of the literati, rather than Cantonese or another Chinese dialect. During Ricci's tenure as head of the China mission, new Jesuit recruits for the mission underwent a two-phased program of study: the first phase focused on spoken Mandarin; the second was dedicated to a serious study of the *Four Books* of Confucianism. Ricci was convinced that the Confucian beliefs found in "the most ancient and most authoritative . . . books of the literati," the *Four Books*, were not idolatrous. This contrasts sharply from his evaluation of both Taoist and Buddhist beliefs, which, in Ricci's estimation, were clearly "idolatrous." Ricci distinguished between a pristine ancient or *original* Confucianism (as he called it) and later neo-Confucian beliefs. In the Pasio letter and in his book of Christian apologetics titled *The True Meaning of the Lord of Heaven*, Ricci argues that original Confucianism was essentially monotheistic and not polytheistic, since it was free of the idolatrous, Buddhist accretions prevalent in neo-Confucian thought. "No worship" of polytheistic gods was found in the ancient Confucian canon. Instead, "they venerate only Heaven, Earth and the Lord of both."[32]

Ricci believed that the transcendent Lord of Heaven in the ancient Confucian canon could be identified with the Christian God of the Bible. The Jesuits admitted that the divine truth found in the earliest Confucian writings was incomplete and only a prelude to the fuller revelation found in Christianity. Nevertheless, Ricci and his compatriots gave high value to the Truth content (with a capital *T*) about God and morality in original Confucianism, making a synthesis of this ancient system with Christianity possible. Ricci boldly claims in the Pasio letter that, by God's "divine mercy and grace" many of the ancient Confucian "natural philosophers . . . who observed natural law were saved."[33] Furthermore, Ricci believed that ancestor veneration was a

30. Standaert, *Handbook of Christianity in China*, 1:600.
31. Hsia, *Ricci and the Catholic Mission to China*, 120.
32. Hsia, *Ricci and the Catholic Mission to China*, 121.
33. Hsia, *Ricci and the Catholic Mission to China*, 121.

legitimate expression of filial piety for Chinese Christians, since such rites were neither idolatrous nor superstitious. Filial piety was the foundation of all Confucian morality, was consistent with Christian ethics, and therefore should be allowed. Ricci's positive assessment of original Confucianism as essentially monotheistic, and of the veneration rites in honor of Confucius and the ancestors as not idolatrous, aligned with the Kangxi emperor's own stance on these issues. The Kangxi emperor was rightly impressed by Ricci's command of the Chinese language and his understanding of the Confucian classics. As a result, only those missionaries who adopted Ricci's views on the rites were welcome in his kingdom.

The Chinese Rites Controversy

Ricci's mature cultural accommodation policy prompted praise from the Kangxi emperor. It also inadvertently triggered the Chinese Rites controversy, which culminated in the papacy's condemnation of those rites—first in 1704, then in 1715 and 1742. The Chinese Rites controversy refers to a century (1630s to 1742) of animosity and debate between Jesuits and the mendicant orders concerning whether the veneration of Confucius and the ancestors was idolatrous. A succession of popes and papal legates as well as Chinese intellectuals and the emperor contributed their voices to the controversy.

After the death of Ricci in 1610, some cracks developed in the unity among Jesuits over Ricci's accommodational approach. Nicolo Longobardi (1559–1654) had been handpicked by Ricci to be his successor as head of the China mission. Between 1611 and 1613, Longobardi was ordered by two successive visitors of Japan and China to reexamine the so-called term question: Were the terms *Shangdi* (High Lord) and *Tian* (Heaven) found in the Confucian classics legitimate translations for the Christian God, as Ricci claimed? Longobardi launched a full investigation but ultimately came to an anti-Riccian position. In his *Response* published in 1623, he notes that there is wide discrepancy within the Confucian classics and between the classics and neo-Confucian commentaries on the meaning of *Shangdi*. He argues that most contemporary Confucian literati follow the neo-Confucian interpretation of the divine name, which, in his opinion, was antithetical to a Christian understanding of God. Longobardi condemns not just the use of *Shangdi* but also the notion that original Confucianism is far more compatible with Christianity than later neo-Confucianism, which was also a Riccian conviction. The majority of the Jesuit China missionaries rejected Longobardi's stance, and he was ordered to destroy all of his anti-Riccian writings. However, a copy of the *Response* survived. It made its way into the hands of Dominican missionary Domingo Navarette, who used it as a powerful weapon against the Jesuits during the Rites controversy.[34]

During this same period, a number of Chinese intellectuals, independently of one another, rejected either Ricci's presentation of Christianity or his understanding of Chinese religious traditions. The Jesuits had learned early on that certain key Christian doctrines, particularly Christ's salvific death on the cross, were offensive to the Chinese. For this reason, Ricci is silent on the cross in apologetic writings (e.g., his key apologetic work, *The True Meaning of the Lord of Heaven*) and in evangelistic contexts. Only when a prospective convert had become a baptismal candidate (catechumen) was the full range of Christian doctrines revealed. This procedure came back to haunt Ricci's successors after his death in 1610. Shen Que petitioned the emperor in 1616 against the Jesuit missionaries for encouraging the people to worship an executed criminal. Yang Guangxian stated it more pointedly in 1664: "In his books, Ricci took very good care not to speak of the lawful execution of Yesu [Jesus]. Thus, all the literate elite have been duped and deceived." Zhang Chao, who had been a friend and collaborator of some prominent Jesuits, called into question Ricci's understanding of Confucian beliefs. Zhang rejected the conflation of the personal Christian God, the Lord of Heaven (*Tianzhu*), with the impersonal Confucian Heaven (*Tian*).[35] Finally, there was also pushback regarding Ricci's understanding of Buddhist thought. In *The True Meaning of the Lord of Heaven*, Ricci launches a direct attack on traditional Buddhist beliefs. In response, Yu Chunxi, a Mandarin and devout Buddhist, wrote an open letter in which he faulted Ricci for his obvious lack of familiarity with the Buddhist sutras and his prejudicial attitude toward Buddhist religious beliefs.[36]

Pope Gregory XII in 1585 had granted to the Jesuits the exclusive right to send missionaries to China. This gave them the opportunity to develop their accommodation strategy free of interference from other religious orders. This Jesuit missionary monopoly was gradually rescinded by a series of papal decrees between 1600 and 1633. The Rites controversy broke out in the mid-1630s, when Dominican and Franciscan missionary friars began arriving in larger numbers to the Chinese mainland. It was not long before

34. Sangkeun Kim, *Strange Names of God: The Missionary Translation of the Divine Name and the Chinese Responses to Matteo Ricci's "Shangti" in Late Ming China, 1583–1644* (New York: Peter Lang, 2005), 167–68, 178, 222; J. S. Cummins, *A Question of Rites: Friar Domingo Navarette and the Jesuits in China* (Brookfield, VT: Ashgate, 1993), 61, 96.

35. Laven, *Mission to China*, 223–24.

36. Hsia, *Ricci and the Catholic Mission to China*, 32, 115–17.

disagreements between the mendicants and the Jesuits arose over accommodation. The mendicant friars were strongly influenced by their collective mission experience in the Americas and the Philippines. All too often they had needed to root out syncretistic aspects of indigenous religious customs that converts had retained alongside the Christian faith. This made them cautious and leery of Jesuit accommodation. They were convinced that the Chinese rites must be forbidden for Christian converts. It is important to note that the mendicant friars had a different evangelistic target group than the Jesuits had. They aimed to reach the poor and not the educated elite—although, as noted above, the Jesuits themselves reached vastly more commoners than elites. Interestingly, even the Jesuits admitted that the common people's view of ancestor veneration was usually superstitious and perhaps idolatrous. Most mendicant missionaries believed that the "Jesuits had expanded the limits of acceptable Catholic practice so far as to be abetting paganism among their flocks."[37] The Dominicans and Franciscans "were prepared to be unpopular rigorists" and to err on the side of caution. Domingo Navarette observed: "We say that the gate is strait [narrow], but then so did Christ."[38]

The first salvo of the Rites controversy was fired by the Dominican Juan Bautista de Morales. Morales (1597–1664) had served first as a missionary in the Philippines; in 1633 he arrived in China as one of the first Dominicans to enter the country. In 1643 his superior sent him to Rome to present to the pope "Seventeen Questions" regarding the Jesuit approach to the Chinese rites. Morales's choice of Latin terms in his memorandum to describe ancestor veneration (sacrifice, priest, altar, temple) underscored its religious nature and ultimately biased Rome's view. Therefore, Pope Innocent X in 1645 condemned the rites for Chinese Christians. In 1651, the Jesuits dispatched their own representative, Martino Martini, to Rome to present counterarguments against Morales's depiction of Jesuit mission practice. Martini successfully defended the Jesuit position and received approval from Pope Alexander VII in 1656 for their understanding of the rites. To complicate the matter further, Pope Clement IX in 1669 declared that both earlier (and diametrically opposed) rulings were still in effect and that final judgment belonged to the missionaries on the ground in China. Both mendicants and Jesuits rightly viewed this proclamation as a mandate to understand the rites as they saw fit.

Dominican Domingo Navarette initiated the next round of controversy. In late 1672, he arrived in Rome, intent on having the Martini decree overturned. While in Rome he translated key Chinese texts into Latin, including Chinese

---

37. Brockey, *Journey to the East*, 11.
38. Cummins, *Question of Rites*, 59.

rituals in honor of the ancestors, which he supplemented with illustrations. In 1676 he published his *Treatise* (*Tratados*), which included an engaging description of his missionary journeys as well as criticisms of Jesuit accommodation, bolstered by the inclusion of Longobardi's suppressed *Response*. Navarette's second unpublished volume, *Controversies*, dealt exclusively and in strongly polemical terms with the Chinese Rites controversy and Jesuit errors. Navarette did not succeed in his goal to have the Martini decree annulled. That honor fell to Charles Maigrot.

Maigrot was a Paris Foreign Mission Society missionary and vicar apostolic of Fujian. On March 26, 1693, he issued a mandate consisting of seven articles to which the China missionaries under his jurisdiction had to adhere. Articles 3–6 condemned the Martini decree and forbade Christians to attend or perform veneration rituals in honor of Confucius or their ancestors, or to have ancestor tablets in their homes. Maigrot's mandate was then submitted to Rome for evaluation. A commission of cardinals studied the mandate and the supporting documents. Their conclusions were expressed in the decree *Cum Deus optima*, approved by Pope Clement XI on November 20, 1704. This was the decree that papal legate Cardinal Tournon brought to China in 1705 and that provoked such a negative response from the Chinese emperor, Kangxi. The 1704 papal decree, which officially condemned the Chinese rites,

---

SIDEBAR 5.3

Decree of Pope Clement XI, *Ex illa die* (1715)

1. Since the word *Deus* does not sound right in the Chinese language, the Westerners in China and Chinese converts to Catholicism have used the term "Heavenly Lord" for many years. From now on such terms as "Heaven" and "Shangti" should not be used.
2. The spring and autumn worship of Confucius, together with the worship of ancestors, is not allowed among Catholic converts.
3. Chinese officials . . . if they have been converted to Roman Catholicism, are not allowed to worship in Confucian temples.
4. No Chinese Catholics are allowed to worship ancestors in their familial temples.
5. Whether at home, in the cemetery, or during the time of a funeral, a Chinese Catholic is not allowed to perform the ritual of ancestor worship.

Source: "Modern History Sourcebook: The Chinese Rites Controversy, 1715," Fordham University, https://sourcebooks.fordham.edu/mod/1715chineserites.asp.

was reiterated in 1715 and 1742. The papacy mandated that only the term "Heavenly Lord" (*Tianzhu*) might be used for the Christian God; *Shangdi* and *Tian* were rejected. All expressions of Confucian or ancestor veneration were categorically forbidden (see sidebar 5.3).

Kangxi responded vigorously to the papal decrees. As noted above, in 1707 the emperor allowed only those missionaries to receive the required residence permits and to remain in China who "followed the rules of Ricci" with regard to the Chinese rites. The imposition of this requirement decimated the ranks of China missionaries. The majority (over thirty missionaries) were banned from China by the end of 1708; only a small number of Jesuits remained. After Kangxi died in 1723, his son and successor, Yongzheng, took his religious policies one step further. In 1724 he issued an edict that ordered all missionaries, except those who served in the Bureau of Astronomy in Beijing, to be banished to Portuguese-held Macau. Catholicism was forbidden, churches were confiscated and transformed into government offices, and Chinese Christians were persecuted. In 1742, after the final papal decree was issued against the rites, Emperor Qianlong repeated and strengthened the imperial Chinese proscription of Catholicism and missionary presence.

There is no doubt that Roman Catholicism suffered gravely in China as a result of the Chinese imperial prohibitions. The Chinese Rites controversy proved to be "the most damaging controversy to shake the Catholic world in modern times, for it scandalized both China and Europe."[39] The infighting between European missionaries became manifestly evident to the Chinese elite and dealt a serious blow to the reputation and progress of the Christian faith in China. Furthermore, it blackened the reputation of the Jesuits among many members of the European Catholic hierarchy and was one factor in the (temporary) suppression of the mission-oriented Jesuit order in 1773.

In light of these setbacks due to the Rites controversy, is it still legitimate to view Jesuit cultural accommodation as groundbreaking, innovative, and a turning point in the expansion of Christianity? I would argue that it is, although with some reservations. First, the reservations: The seventeenth-century Chinese critiques of Ricci's presentation of Christianity and his understanding of Chinese religious traditions outlined above are valid. Ricci was silent on the cross in apologetic writings and in evangelistic contexts. Furthermore, Ricci's construct of "original Confucianism" was quite arbitrary. All religion is fluid and changing, and it is highly questionable whether the Chinese separated "original Confucianism" from its later neo-Confucian accretions (Longobardi's argument). Finally, given the large number of

39. Cummins, *Question of Rites*, 70.

Buddhist-background converts in China, hindsight suggests that Ricci's aversion to Buddhist religious traditions and lack of accommodation to them were regrettable.

On the positive side, the Jesuits

> by their readiness to put aside European prejudices, by their adaptability . . . their alertness to discover the good and reluctance to note the bad, by the sympathy and understanding they brought to their contact with China . . . pointed the way, and their example still points the way, to cultural rapprochement between the peoples of the world.[40]

Ricci and his compatriots did serve as powerful examples of successful enculturation for generations of Roman Catholic and Protestant missionaries. Ricci's mature mission method and the accommodation it promoted demonstrated a high level of interaction with and appreciation for Chinese Confucian culture. In order to win the right to share the Christian faith, Ricci and his followers adapted themselves to the Chinese people, rather than expecting the Chinese to conform to them. They immersed themselves in the Confucian canon and were willing to affirm truth content in original Confucianism, albeit to a degree that made many mendicant and some Jesuit missionaries uncomfortable. This approach was revolutionary in the era of the Portuguese *padroado real*, when a tabula rasa mindset toward indigenous cultures and a disdain for non-Christian religions was the norm. Jesuit cultural accommodation proclaimed that it was possible to be authentically Chinese and truly Christian. Such an approach was ahead of its time and innovative. It was also a turning point in the expansion of Christianity, not because it convinced all missionaries to adopt their (admittedly) controversial understanding of cultural accommodation. Rather, it was an important turning point in this sense: the issue of cultural adaptation was once again front and center in most discussions over mission methods going forward, even among those missionaries who rejected the Jesuit approach as too radical.

In 1939 the Roman Catholic Church reversed its policy on the Chinese rites. The papal edict (*Plane compertum est*) promulgated by Pope Pius XII recognized that the significance of the rites in honor of Confucius and ancestors had changed over time. They were now deemed as civil and social in function (and not religious or superstitious) and therefore allowable for Chinese Christians. It is thus appropriate that we close this chapter with a prayer from the Chinese Catholic ancestral liturgy, which has been used in Taiwan since 1974:

40. Dunne, *Generation of Giants*, 370.

Celebrant: My dear people, God's command is that we honor our parents and revere our ancestors. Today we recall our forebearers with grateful hearts, [and] specially pray for them before our Heavenly Father.

Let us pray for our ancestors and all our deceased relatives, beseeching the Lord to unite them together in heaven to enjoy eternal happiness.

Response: Lord, hear our prayer. . . .

Celebrant: Most merciful Heavenly Father, You are the God of Abraham and Jacob, and the God of our ancestors. We beseech you to hear the prayers of us your family and grant to our ancestors eternal rest in Your bosom, forever sharing in your love. Through Christ our Lord.[41]

41. Beverly Joan Butcher, "Remembrance, Emulation, Imagination: The Chinese and Chinese American Catholic Ancestor Memorial Service" (PhD diss., University of Pennsylvania, 1994), 475.

6

Pioneering a Global Outreach
Zinzendorf and Moravian Missions (1732)

There's but a small beginning made,
The earth is still o'ercast with shade:
Break forth, You Sun of Righteousness,
With healing beams the nations bless.

Lord of the harvest, laborers send,
Who willing are their lives to spend
In scorching heat and chilling cold,
To bring the heathen to your fold.[1]

Count Nikolaus Ludwig von Zinzendorf (1700–1760) seemed predestined for Christian mission from his earliest years. Born into the German aristocracy, he was raised by his maternal grandmother, Henriette Katharina von Gersdorf (1648–1726), on her estate in southeastern Saxony. Zinzendorf, looking back on his life, credited his grandmother with planting in him the desire

---

1. This hymn was written by Matthäus Stach (1711–1787), the first Moravian missionary to Greenland. *Hymnal and Liturgies of the Moravian Church* (Bethlehem, PA: Provincial Synod, 1920), 245 (#358) (modernized).

"to witness to Christ in the world."[2] Baroness von Gersdorf was a vigorous supporter of the new German Pietist movement and its leaders, Philip Jakob Spener and August Hermann Francke. Pietism represented a "new paradigm" within German Protestantism that "encouraged personal renewal and new birth," small group Bible studies, "social activism," "ecumenical cooperation," and, most importantly for this chapter, "worldwide mission."[3] Zinzendorf's mission interest may have been ignited by his grandmother, but the influence of both Spener and Francke kept the fires burning. Spener was not only the godfather of the young count but also a frequent visitor to his grandmother's estate. The young Zinzendorf was impressed by Spener's spirituality.

Likewise, Count Zinzendorf's early missionary zeal owed much to the influence of his schoolteacher, Francke, and the brand of Pietism associated with the eastern German city of Halle. Even as a young lad, the count had heard reports of the first Pietist missionaries, Bartholomäus Ziegenbalg and Heinrich Plütschau, who served in India with the Danish-Halle mission after graduating from the University of Halle. Then, from age ten to sixteen, Zinzendorf attended Francke's recently founded school for aristocrats in Halle. During his school years at Halle, the count's interaction with Francke's sermons and other Pietist instructors furthered his religious and missionary zeal. There, over the period of nearly a year, he interacted personally with the missionaries Ziegenbalg and Plütschau, who were home from India and who brought vividly to life for the young count the need for world mission. Also while at Halle, Zinzendorf covenanted with one of his school friends, Friedrich von Watteville, to work for the conversion of non-Christians. He reasoned that "the heathen would certainly not all be converted by the time we were grown. Those who remained, *we* wanted to bring to the Savior."[4] While studying at Wittenberg University, the bastion of German Lutheranism, Zinzendorf formed a mission-oriented voluntary society, the Society of the Confessors of Christ.

Two key events were necessary, however, to enable Zinzendorf's vision for mission to gradually take on concrete form. The first occurred in 1722, when a group of Bohemian refugees from Moravia settled on Zinzendorf's estate in Saxony and with the count's assistance founded the community of Herrnhut (meaning the "Lord's watch"). A second event was necessary to

2. Dietrich Meyer, "Zinzendorf und Herrnhut," in *Geschichte des Pietismus*, vol. 2, *Der Pietismus im achtzehnten Jahrhundert*, ed. Martin Brecht and Klaus Deppermann (Göttingen: Vandenhoeck & Ruprecht, 1995), 9.

3. Douglas H. Shantz, *An Introduction to German Pietism: Protestant Renewal at the Dawn of Modern Europe* (Baltimore: Johns Hopkins University Press, 2013), 7.

4. Peter Zimmerling, *Gott in Gemeinschaft. Zinzendorfs Trinitätslehre* (Giessen: Brunnen Verlag, 1991), 68–69; cf. Ron Davies, *A Heart for Mission: Five Pioneer Thinkers* (Fearn, UK: Christian Focus, 2001), 100–102; and Meyer, "Zinzendorf und Herrnhut," 11.

turn the bickering Herrnhuters into a mission dynamo. That occurred five years later, in August 1727, when a spiritual revival rocked the community. The transformed congregation reinstituted the ancient Moravian Brethren Church (*Unitas Fratrum*) and embraced Zinzendorf's missionary vision. It was natural for Zinzendorf to look toward Lutheran Denmark for help in turning his mission goal into a reality. The count was related to the pietistically inclined crown prince of Denmark and throughout the 1720s had corresponded frequently with the Danish court. Denmark had colonial territories with non-Christian inhabitants, and it had cooperated with Halle in launching the Danish-Halle mission to Tranquebar, India, with Ziegenbalg and Plütschau as its first missionaries. Just one month after the "Moravian Pentecost," in September 1727, Zinzendorf took advantage of his strong links to Denmark and sent two Moravians to Copenhagen to inquire about possible missionary work in Danish-held territories. Then, on February 28, 1728, at the monthly church meeting, the Moravian Brethren discussed how they might "risk something significant for God" for the conversion of non-Christians, whether among Muslims in Turkey or the Inuit in the frozen wastes of Greenland and Lapland. The following day, twenty-six of the single Moravian men under the leadership of Leonhard Dober covenanted to pray regularly for world mission and to serve as missionaries if called.[5]

A concrete mission opportunity presented itself several years later, when Zinzendorf and several Moravians attended the coronation of the Danish king Christian VI in Copenhagen in June 1731. There the count met two Greenlanders and learned that the Greenland mission of Dano-Norwegian Hans Egede required immediate reinforcements to survive. Even more influential was Zinzendorf's encounter with a black slave, Anton Ulrich, from the Caribbean island of St. Thomas in the Danish West Indies. Anton had recently converted to Christianity and been baptized. He reported to the count the dire circumstances under which plantation slaves lived and worked in the West Indies. Besides physical slavery, the slaves were also kept in spiritual bondage. They were forbidden to learn to read or write or to attend Christian preaching. Anton pled with Zinzendorf to send missionaries to preach to his brother Abraham and his sister Anna, as well as to other slaves in St. Thomas who longed to hear the Christian message. Back in Herrnhut, on July 23, Zinzendorf recounted Anton's story to the assembled community. That night, both Leonhard Dober and Tobias Leupold felt called to be missionaries to St. Thomas. On July 25, in a letter to the count, they offered themselves for

5. Hartmut Beck, *Brüder in vielen Völkern: 250 Jahre Mission der Brüdergemeine* (Erlangen: Verlag der Ev.-Luth. Mission, 1981), 23–24; Davies, *Heart for Mission*, 118–19.

missionary service, the first recorded instance in Moravian history. Then, on July 29, Anton arrived in Herrnhut and shared his own story. He made clear that no one could evangelize slaves without becoming a slave himself.[6]

Nearly a year went by and no decision had been made by the Herrnhut community regarding a mission to the West Indies. On June 16, 1732, Leonhard Dober wrote the count again: "If another brother will go with me, I am ready to become a slave myself." That same day it was decided to send Dober and David Nitschmann to St. Thomas. The community had cast lots, and the lot decided that Tobias Leupold would not be sent at that time, although he was one of the reinforcements dispatched the following year. On August 21, 1732, after a rousing send-off by the Herrnhut congregation, the two men, with thirty shillings in their pockets, were driven the first fifteen miles in the count's carriage. Then they set out on foot to walk the remaining 425 miles to Copenhagen, where they caught a ship to St. Thomas. In January 1733, less than a year later, Matthäus Stach (who wrote the hymn that opens this chapter), Christian Stach, and Christian David departed Herrnhut for a ministry among the Inuit in Danish-held Greenland. Within a decade, Moravian missionaries were serving on five continents: Europe (Greenland and Lapland), North America (the West Indies, among Native Americans), South America (Surinam), Asia (Ceylon), and in South Africa. By the time of Zinzendorf's death in 1760, 226 missionaries had been sent to twenty-eight different mission fields.[7]

Zinzendorf's encounter with Anton Ulrich and the black slave's subsequent visit to Herrnhut effectively launched the Moravian Church's mission enterprise. This mission endeavor was unique and a turning point in the development of Protestant mission for several key reasons. First, unlike the tepid response to cross-cultural evangelism within Protestantism at this time, foreign mission was a key priority for the Moravian Church and central to its self-understanding. A Moravian synod in the mid-1760s expressed it thus: "Our missions are the most important work of God, entrusted unto the [Moravian] Brethren by our Lord himself." "To be a Moravian and to further foreign missions are identical," affirmed Moravian Bishop E. R. Hassé.[8] Mission strongly influenced all aspects of Moravian life—how they spent their finances, the founding of communities, and even the decision of some individuals to remain single in order to serve as missionaries.

6. A. J. Lewis, *Zinzendorf, the Ecumenical Pioneer: A Study in the Moravian Contribution to Christian Mission and Unity* (Philadelphia: Westminster, 1962), 78–80.
    7. Lewis, *Zinzendorf, the Ecumenical Pioneer*, 78–80; Davies, *Heart for Mission*, 122.
    8. J. C. S. Mason, *The Moravian Church and the Missionary Awakening in England, 1760–1800* (Rochester, NY: Boydell, 2001), 16, 24.

Second, the Moravian Church had a strong, visionary advocate for mission in the person of Zinzendorf. Without his influence, it is unlikely that the Moravian Church would have developed into the eighteenth-century mission dynamo it became. The count reflected biblically and theologically on the task of mission. He was intimately involved in the financing and planning of new missions and in the development and implementation of new methods. Zinzendorf is rightly credited with having "made the [Moravian] community a missionary movement. He had a global vision that was ahead of its time and is rightly described as 'a pioneer of world mission.'"[9] Finally, the Moravians did more than any previous Protestant group to make mission an evangelical concern. Certainly, it is impossible to envision the development of the Moravian missions apart from the theology of the Reformers or from the prior Danish-Halle mission, which significantly affected the count. Nevertheless, the Moravians *put into practice* the Reformers' teaching on mission. They soon far outstripped their Pietist predecessor, the Danish-Halle mission, in international influence, in the number of missionaries, and in the geographic breadth of their mission outreach.

In order to rightly assess the significance of the eighteenth-century Moravian mission enterprise, it is imperative to contrast it with the relative lack of concrete foreign mission engagement by the magisterial Reformers and their immediate successors. That topic will be discussed first in this chapter. It will be followed by a survey of both early Lutheran and Reformed mission activities, with special focus on the most significant early mission: John Eliot's mission to Native Americans. Next, the focus will shift to the Danish-Halle mission, which, in contrast to Eliot's mission, was a sustained Protestant mission with dozens of missionaries over decades and resulted in the still-existent Tamil Lutheran Church. Finally, our attention will turn to the unique mission of Zinzendorf and the Moravian Church, truly a turning point in the worldwide expansion of Christianity. I will note differences between the Danish-Halle mission and Moravian mission practices. I give special attention to Zinzendorf's developing mission theology and how that theology influenced Moravian mission methods.

The Magisterial Reformers and Mission

Sixteenth-century magisterial Reformers Martin Luther and John Calvin were just that: reformers. Both key leaders of the Protestant movement pursued an

9. Shantz, *German Pietism*, 258.

agenda to "Christianize Christendom." In other words, their primary aim was not to convert non-Christians, such as Jews or Muslims, to the Christian faith but to "convince people who had already been baptized to believe and practice the faith in a way judged by Protestants to be more valid."[10] For the Reformers, a more valid faith included correct biblical doctrine and holy living. Luther was convinced of the necessity of the task of "re-Christianizing" Europe. In his estimation, the German churches were filled with "many who have not yet believed or become Christians. . . . [It is] just as if we were holding divine services among the Turks or heathen."[11] Nominal European Christians were just as much in need of regeneration and in danger of eternal punishment as any Muslim, Jew, or Hindu.

Luther viewed his mandate of reform and re-Christianization as applying primarily to the German territories, and he and his colleagues were preeminently successful in spreading Lutheranism in central and northern Europe. Similarly, while Calvin worked to establish "true Christianity" throughout Europe, he was particularly concerned with his home country of France. Calvin played a key role in the rapid development of French Calvinism by sending pastors trained at his academy in Geneva to evangelize and plant churches in France. The success of this venture is manifest. In 1555 there was only one fully organized Reformed church in France; in 1562 there were two thousand, with roughly 10 percent of the French population being members of those churches.[12]

Certainly Europe at the time of the Reformation was desperately in need of widespread evangelization and was, in that sense, a legitimate mission field. Furthermore, one should not maintain too sharp a division between home and foreign mission, or between mission among nominal Christians and mission among non-Christians. Nevertheless, the task of the expansion of Christianity, which is the topic of this book, concerns the advance of the Christian faith across cultural, linguistic, ethnic, and religious frontiers into territories where there was little or no Christian presence. That was not the case in Reformation-era Europe, where there was a significant Christian presence. Furthermore, evangelistic outreach by first- and second-generation Lutheran and Reformed Christians remained primarily within their own cultural and linguistic groups, and almost exclusively among nominal Christians, meaning

10. Scott H. Hendrix, *Recultivating the Vineyard: The Reformation Agendas of Christianization* (Louisville: Westminster John Knox, 2004), xvii, 18.

11. Gordon D. Laman, "The Origin of Protestant Missions," *Reformed Review* 43, no. 1 (1989): 56.

12. Ingemar Öberg, *Luther and World Mission: A Historical and Systematic Study*, trans. Dean Apel (St. Louis: Concordia, 2007), 6, 325; Hendrix, *Recultivating the Vineyard*, 39.

that a religious boundary was not crossed. There is, therefore, considerable legitimacy to the claim by Glenn Sunshine and others that "foreign missions were thus a weakness for the sixteenth-century Protestants" and that the magisterial Reformers "displayed neither missionary vision nor missionary spirit."[13]

It is certainly true that foreign missions were not actively pursued by Protestants in the sixteenth century. There were some valid reasons for this lack of mission activity outside of Christian Europe; other reasons are less convincing. First, the earliest generations of Protestants had their hands full with the task of reform, the re-Christianization of unregenerate churchgoers in Europe, and the organization and establishment of Reformation churches—and therefore can be excused for not immediately pursuing foreign mission. Second, in contrast to Spain, Portugal, and the Italian city-states, in the sixteenth century, Protestant countries were not maritime powers with trading relationships or colonies in the New World, Asia, or Africa; in other words, they had little natural access to foreign mission fields. Even if they had so desired, Protestants were prohibited by the pope, the Holy Roman Emperor, and the Iberian monarchs from missionizing in Roman Catholic overseas possessions regulated by patronage agreements. It was not until the early seventeenth century that Protestant countries such as Britain, Denmark, and the Netherlands formed East India trading companies.[14] Nevertheless, even when they had access to foreign mission fields, these countries began only very slowly to missionize. For example, the Danish East India Company received the right to trade in Tranquebar on the east coast of India in 1621. It was not until almost a century later, in 1706, however, that the first missionaries of the Danish-Halle mission were sent there.

Third, both Luther and Calvin believed that kings and princes bore a key responsibility in their territories to support gospel ministers financially, to safeguard correct doctrine, and to ensure the spread of the gospel. In the sixteenth-century Holy Roman Empire, in order to prevent ongoing wars of the religion between Catholics and Protestants, the political leaders of the German territories were granted the privilege to determine whether the Roman Catholic or Lutheran faith would be practiced in their realm, a privilege known by the Latin phrase *cuius regio, eius religio*, which translates as "whose region, his religion." This relationship between church and state had

13. Glenn S. Sunshine, "Protestant Missions in the Sixteenth Century," in *The Great Commission: Evangelicals and the History of World Missions*, ed. Martin I. Klauber and Scott M. Manetsch (Nashville: B&H, 2008), 12, 15.

14. Sunshine, "Protestant Missions in the Sixteenth Century," 14; Öberg, *Luther and World Mission*, 6.

a detrimental impact on foreign mission, since German princes were understandably only concerned with the faith in their own, often small, territories. "A church with such geographical/psychological limitations was unlikely to develop a dynamic missionary motivation."[15] Finally, Protestants lacked a ready-made workforce for mission. Roman Catholicism in the same era had a huge cadre of monastics (Jesuits, Franciscans, and Dominicans), whom they could *and did* send as missionaries to the ends of the earth. It was not until the eighteenth century, when Protestants developed the voluntary missionary society, that they had a comparable workforce at their disposal.

Did Luther and Calvin lack "missionary vision and missionary spirit," as some scholars suggest? That claim is somewhat misleading without qualification. Both magisterial Reformers did theorize about mission—not in a systematic manner, but scattered throughout their commentaries, sermons, and letters. The apostolic commission of Matthew 28:16–20 was not an important element of Luther's mission theory. However, other commissions in the New Testament—particularly John 14–16, but also Mark 16:15–16 and Matthew 22:9—were significant for the Wittenberg Reformer. In commenting on these passages, Luther emphasizes that

> preaching the Word was begun by the apostles, and it constantly goes forward, and is pushed on farther and farther by the preachers, driven hither and thither into the world, yet always being made known to those who have never heard it before.[16]

For Luther, the Word of God was unstoppable. Like a stone that had been tossed into a lake, the message of the gospel would continue to spread out its influence into all the world until the end of the age. For Calvin, the office of an apostle was a temporary one, found only in the primitive church. Through the preaching of the early apostles, all the nations of the earth had already been offered the gospel. Yet, like Luther, Calvin also claimed that the apostles began but did not complete the missionary task. "The kingdom of Christ was only begun in the world, when God commanded the gospel to be everywhere proclaimed, and . . . at this day its course is not as yet completed."[17] Both Luther and Calvin theorized about the need for mission to the ends of the earth. They laid the theoretical and doctrinal foundation on which later generations built. In that sense, they did exhibit a level of missionary vision

15. Laman, "Origin of Protestant Missions," 53–54.
16. Öberg, *Luther and World Mission*, 146.
17. John Calvin, *Commentaries on the Twelve Minor Prophets*, trans. John Owen, vol. 3 (Grand Rapids: Christian Classics Ethereal Library), https://ccel.org/ccel/calvin/calcom28/calcom 28.iv.4.iv.html. Cf. Calvin, *Institutes of the Christian Religion* 4.3.4.

and spirit. However, neither Luther nor Calvin translated mission theory into concrete foreign mission practice. That would be the task of later generations.

Early Lutheran Mission

The first concrete foreign mission efforts by Lutherans took place after Luther's death in 1546. In the following decades, there were several small conversionary efforts across cultural and linguistic boundaries. Primus Truber and Baron Hans Ungnad von Sonegg from Württemberg, Germany, formed the Uracher movement in the 1560s to translate and then distribute Bibles and evangelical literature among the southern Slavs and Turks. Unfortunately, the twenty-five thousand volumes printed for this purpose were confiscated by Roman Catholic authorities, thus bringing the Uracher movement to an abrupt and unsuccessful end. Lutherans in this era considered mission to be the responsibility of kings and princes. Two such Lutheran political leaders did demonstrate a heart for cross-cultural mission. King Gustaf I of Sweden (1496–1560) in 1559 ordered a mission among the Lapps/Sami within his territory in northern Sweden. Despite his order, mission work was only half-heartedly pursued. Duke Ludwig of Württemberg sent Valentin Cless to Morocco in 1583 to learn Arabic in order to evangelize Muslims. This is noteworthy, since Ludwig showed concern for the eternal fate of non-Christians *outside* his dukedom of Württemberg. Nevertheless, little came of the mission.[18]

These early foreign mission attempts within Lutheranism were dealt a death blow by Lutheran Orthodoxy in the seventeenth century. Lutheran Orthodoxy refers to an era (ca. 1580–1730) within Lutheranism when theologians stressed the formulation of precise doctrinal statements based on scholastic, Aristotelian methodology. Theologian Johann Gerhard (1582–1637) and the faculty at Wittenberg University believed that, since all people had been Christianized by the apostles, it was no longer compulsory for Christians of their day to spread the gospel globally. The New Testament apostolic commissions had been intended for the apostles alone and were no longer mandated for Christians in the postapostolic period.[19] Pastors were to remain in their pulpit and not concern themselves with foreign mission outreach. In 1722, Lutheran Orthodox hymn writer Erdmann Neumeister expressed it thus: "'Go out into

18. Öberg, *Luther and World Mission*, 498–500.
19. Calvin's successor and interpreter, Theodore Beza, strengthened Calvin's more ambiguous view. Like Gerhard, Beza argued that the missionary mandate in Matt. 28 applied only to the original apostles.

the world,' the Lord of old did say; But now: 'Where God has placed thee, *There* he would have thee stay!'"[20] Pastors were to remain in their parishes, but princes who ruled over non-Christian peoples, such as King Gustaf I of Sweden, had a duty to missionize. Lutheran "Orthodoxy soon squelched mission involvement," and in doing so, it distanced itself from Luther's own mission theory.[21] Orthodoxy discouraged mission through its theology and denigrated early mission efforts. For example, the Jesus-Loving Society, founded by Justinian E. von Welz in 1663 to promote mission among both Christians and non-Christians, was officially rejected by Lutheran Orthodoxy. Johann Georg Neumann, in his work *Dissertation against False-Apostles* (1708), branded the Danish-Halle missionaries as false apostles who had gone to the mission field merely for the sake of monetary gain.[22]

Early Reformed Mission

Foreign mission efforts by Reformed Christians in the sixteenth century were also infrequent. However, when an opportunity for mission presented itself to Calvin in 1556, he and the Genevan church responded. In that year, French naval officer Nicolas Durand de Villegaignon requested that Calvin provide ministers and laymen to accompany his colonial expedition to Brazil. Persecuted French Huguenots were also recruited. One of the Genevan laymen, Jean de Léry, recorded the response of his church.

> Upon receiving these letters and hearing this news, the church of Geneva at once gave thanks to God for the extension of the reign of Jesus Christ in a country so distant and likewise so foreign and among a nation entirely without knowledge of the true God.[23]

The two ministers and eleven laymen sent from Geneva faced numerous difficulties from the outset of their mission among the Tupinamba people. They found the Tupinamba to be barbaric and their language impossible to learn; furthermore, the mission work was hindered by pro-Catholic colonists. The mission was short-lived, lasting not much more than a year (1557–58), and it

---

20. Quoted in A. J. Lewis, *Zinzendorf, The Ecumenical Pioneer: A Study in the Moravian Contribution to Christian Mission and Unity* (Philadelphia: Westminster, 1962), 78n1.

21. Öberg, *Luther and World Mission*, 501.

22. Andreas Gross, Y. Vincent Kumaradoss, and Heike Leibau, eds., *Halle and the Beginning of Protestant Christianity in India*, vol. 1, *The Danish-Halle and the English-Halle Mission* (Halle: Franckeschen Stiftungen, 2006), 14.

23. R. Pierce Beaver, "The Genevan Mission to Brazil," *Reformed Journal* 17, no. 6 (July–August 1967): 16.

did not result in any converts. Villegaignon soon became disenchanted with the Reformed colonists. Three were murdered in February 1558, and soon thereafter, the Portuguese attacked and destroyed the remainder of the settlement near Rio de Janeiro. "This first Protestant attempt at mission overseas ended with three martyrs, a journey home, and a powerful backlash in the Reformed Church against similar undertakings."[24] Nevertheless, several notable individuals kept the cause of world mission alive.

In 1602, the Dutch East India Company (DEIC) was founded. This sparked a desire among a small group of Dutch Reformed Christians to pursue mission among non-Christians in the overseas possessions of the DEIC, particularly in Ceylon and Indonesia. In 1618, Dutch medical doctor and pastor Justus Heurnius (1587–1651) wrote "An Exhortation to Embark upon an Evangelical Mission among the Indians," in which he argued that the missionary mandate was still valid in that day. He urged the DEIC to support mission in those areas under their colonial control. In 1624 he was sent by the presbytery of Amsterdam to serve as a missionary, primarily in Batavia (Jakarta) in Indonesia, where he established the Dutch East Indies Church, but also briefly in India and on other islands of the East Indian archipelago. After serving fourteen years in the East Indies, conflict with the DEIC forced him to return to the Netherlands. Gisbert Voetius (1589–1676), a Dutch Reformed professor at the University of Utrecht, elaborated a theology of mission. It included the conversion of the non-Christian Gentiles (*conversio gentilium*) and the establishment of a mission church for the glory of God and his divine grace. Johannes Hoornbeek (1617–66), a pupil of Voetius at Utrecht, authored four books on missiology. He even suggested that a Protestant organization be founded to promote foreign missions in the same manner as the Roman Catholic Congregation for the Propagation of the Faith.[25]

The most significant early Reformed mission by far was that of Puritan John Eliot in colonial New England. The charter of the Massachusetts Bay Colony claimed that the conversion of the Natives was the "principal end of this plantation." According to John Winthrop, the first governor of the Bay Colony, mission to Native Americans would not only lead to the conversion of some, but it would also remove the "scandal to our religion that we show not as much zeal in seeking the conversion of the heathen as the papists do"—a frequent rebuke of Protestants by Roman Catholics in this era. There proved to be a wide gap between their statements of intention to engage in mission and what was actually accomplished. The majority of the first generation

24. Öberg, *Luther and World Mission*, 500.
25. Laman, "Origin of Protestant Missions," 63–64.

of Puritan immigrants were focused on the construction of towns and the establishment of economic, political, and ecclesiastical institutions—not on the evangelization of Native Americans.[26]

Other factors also contributed to the lack of mission among Native Americans in the first fifteen to twenty years of the Massachusetts Bay Colony. First, the Algonquin language was much more difficult to learn than anticipated. Second, the congregational church polity adopted in the Bay Colony did not allow ordination to full-time missionary service. Ministers such as John Eliot were required to serve a local English congregation full time and pursue mission work on the side. This church policy was not conducive to a robust mission effort. Third, the eschatology of Puritan John Cotton, the leading theologian of the Massachusetts Bay Colony, had clear "anti-missionary implications" and was "one of the factors that postponed the mission." Cotton held to a Jews-then-Gentiles eschatological scheme. In the end times, first Roman Catholicism, which Protestants identified as the antichrist, must be destroyed at the battle of Armageddon. Then the Jews would convert en masse. Only then would the non-Christian Gentile nations, which included Native Americans, respond to the gospel. This meant that prior to the end of the age, only isolated Native Americans could experience salvation. Clearly, this theology was demotivating for mission.[27] Interestingly, John Eliot adopted a different, mission-friendlier eschatology in 1649. He came to believe that the indigenous population were Jews descended from the ten lost tribes of Israel, not Gentiles. A larger harvest of Native souls could be expected, since contemporary events in England (the execution of King Charles I that year) had convinced Eliot that Christ would return imminently. Finally, New England Puritans, including Eliot, believed that the Native Americans had to adopt English civilization before conversion was even possible. Civilization included the renunciation of most Native customs in exchange for English ones. For example, they believed that English grooming habits must be adopted and a nomadic lifestyle exchanged for a settled and industrious life of agricultural pursuits. This approach was ethnocentric, since it assumed that English culture was inherently superior. It was also "the major reason for the postponement of the mission" to Native Americans since relatively few of them desired to adopt English ways.[28]

Eliot, the "apostle to the Indians," immigrated in 1631 to Roxbury, Massachusetts, where he served as pastor. He soon developed an interest in the local Native American population. In 1646, fifteen years after his arrival in

26. Richard Cogley, *John Eliot's Mission to the Indians before King Philip's War* (Cambridge, MA: Harvard University Press, 1999), 3; cf. 1–4.

27. Cogley, *John Eliot's Mission to the Indians*, 18; cf. 9–18, 21–22, 76–77.

28. Cogley, *John Eliot's Mission to the Indians*, 22; cf. 6–9, 18–22.

New England, he began preaching to the Algonquin, first in English, but within a year in their own language. His sermons were long (an hour and a half on average), doctrinal, and evangelistic—they aimed to convince his hearers to repent. Eliot often employed contextual illustrations in his sermons. For example, he compared eternal punishment in hell to the Native American practice of torturing enemy captives, the sacraments to a place of refuge, and the new birth to the cleaning of dirty ceremonial pipes. However, in the Eliot tracts, a series of ten published progress reports on the mission, he interacts very little with the indigenous culture. Eliot was "not a perceptive student of traditional native culture," and he often "misconstrued culture." Nevertheless, he "had a greater respect for the Indians' intelligence and character than did his contemporaries."[29] One outstanding achievement of John Eliot was his translation of the Bible into the Algonquin language, which he completed in 1663, and the production of an Algonquin grammar.

"Praying towns" were a chief characteristic of the Puritan mission. The term refers to a group of fourteen Christian Native American communities in the Bay Colony between 1650 and 1675, where roughly 3,500 "praying Indians" lived segregated from the broader Algonquin society. The goal was to enable the inhabitants to more easily adopt Christianity, as well as the requisite aspects of English culture (work habits, gender roles, sexual norms, and grooming). Eliot gradually came to appreciate aspects of traditional Native customs that he had earlier repudiated in the name of "civilization." In the praying towns, the indigenous language, traditional ornaments, Native medicine, forms of indigenous leadership, residence in wigwams, and hunting and fishing (rather than just agriculture) came to be allowed. The Algonquin had their own legitimate reasons for residing in praying towns: a desire for literacy, English goods and skills, and protection from their enemies were key motivations. Ultimately the "praying Indians" stressed those aspects of Christian belief that correlated with Algonquin traditional religion: for example, Jesus's healing ministry, which correlated with that of a traditional shaman, and souls being transported to heaven, which correlated with the Algonquin belief in dream souls. Most of the praying towns were destroyed and their residents scattered during a military conflict in 1675 between the settlers and Native Americans called King Philip's War.[30]

In conclusion, John Eliot's mission to the Algonquin was a notable effort among an indigenous population. However, it was largely an individual endeavor. Eliot had very few compatriots; the most notable were the father-and-

29. Cogley, *John Eliot's Mission to the Indians*, 243–44; cf. 61, 124.
30. Cogley, *John Eliot's Mission to the Indians*, 56–59, 108, 140, 243, 248.

son team of Thomas Mayhew Sr. and Jr. on Martha's Vineyard. Eliot's tracts put the cause of world mission before an Anglo-American Christian populace. This proved more influential on later generations than the actual mission itself, which was largely destroyed by King Philip's War. It was German Pietists, however, who launched a more sustained mission involving numerous missionaries in many lands among indigenous populations as yet untouched by the Christian gospel.

The Danish-Halle Mission

Pietism was a distinctly German renewal movement that arose in the 1670s in reaction to the perceived deadness of Lutheran Orthodoxy. German Pietists rejected the overintellectualizing of faith and the polemical, doctrinal sermons common in Lutheran churches in favor of warm heart-religion. Philip Jakob Spener, the founder of German Pietism, refuted the Orthodox claims that the apostolic commissions were no longer valid and that Jesus's command in Matthew 10:5–6 to concentrate on the "lost sheep of Israel" meant that mission outside Germany was not mandated. Now was the time, Spener argued, to embrace worldwide mission and to bring the gospel to non-Christian Gentiles of all nations.[31]

Denmark was the only Lutheran land that possessed overseas territory with non-Christian inhabitants: 25,000 local Tamils along with 250 Europeans resided in the small trading colony of Tranquebar on the east coast of India. The Danish king Friedrich IV (the father of Christian VI, mentioned above) concluded that it was his obligation as sovereign to promote the evangelization of the Tamil population there. He asked his German Pietist court preacher, F. J. Lütkens, to recruit missionary candidates from Germany. The two missionaries chosen, Heinrich Plütschau (1677–1746) and Bartholomäus Ziegenbalg (1683–1719), had both studied under A. H. Francke at the University of Halle, the key center of pietistic Lutheranism at that time. After ordination in Copenhagen in November 1705, the two missionaries sailed to Tranquebar, where they arrived in July 1706.[32]

Although the initiative for the mission came from the Danish king, the wide-ranging institutions founded by Francke at Halle ensured the success and longevity of the Danish-Halle mission, as it came to be called. The Theological College of Oriental Studies at Halle taught key languages necessary for mission work in Asia. The pharmacy produced a variety of medicines that

31. Gross, *Danish-Halle and English-Halle Mission*, 15–17.
32. Shantz, *German Pietism*, 237–38, 241–42.

were sent to the mission field and also sold for profit to support the mission and other diaconal efforts. The publishing house edited and published news from Tranquebar: letters from Ziegenbalg and the first Protestant missionary magazine, titled *Remarkable Reports from East India*. Francke raised money and acted as publicist for the mission. He arranged for a printing press with Tamil script to be sent to India and gave regular advice and encouragement to the missionaries. Without his global vision and efforts, the mission may not have succeeded. This support from Halle, as well as from the English Society for Promoting Christian Knowledge (SPCK), was even more crucial due to the ongoing conflict between the Danish East India Company and the Tranquebar mission in its first decade. The business objectives of the trading company were sharply at odds with the mission's goals. In November 1708, the Danish governor of Tranquebar arrested and imprisoned Ziegenbalg for four months—clear evidence that the Danish-Halle mission was not merely an extension of colonial power, at least at this early date. This "persecution" of the missionaries had an unexpected result: the local Tamil population differentiated them from other Europeans and viewed the missionaries more sympathetically.[33]

Bartholomäus Ziegenbalg was the younger of the two missionaries, but he, being more gifted linguistically, soon outshone his older colleague Plütschau. Within about six months, Ziegenbalg was able to read, write, speak, and preach in the difficult Tamil language. In January 1707, he began to translate Martin Luther's *Smaller Catechism*. With the assistance of Tamil language helpers, Ziegenbalg and Plütschau produced Christian prayers and wrote or translated one hundred hymns that were set to either European or Tamil melodies. Then, in 1708, Ziegenbalg began translating the New Testament into Tamil. Two and a half years later, the first draft was finished.

Parallel to his linguistic and translation work, Ziegenbalg sought to understand the Tamil Hindu culture through sensitive conversations with Tamil language helpers, converts, and other partners. He collected and studied Tamil classics, which, prior to his own introduction of paper, were written on palm leaves. On the basis of this research, Ziegenbalg wrote two lengthy ethnological works: *Malabarian Heathendom* (1711) and *Genealogy of the Malabarian Gods* (1713).[34]

33. Martin Brecht, "August Hermann Francke und der Hallische Pietismus," in *Geschichte des Pietismus*, vol. 1, *Der Pietismus vom siebzehnten bis zum frühen achtzehnten Jahrhundert*, ed. Martin Brecht (Göttingen: Vandenhoeck & Ruprecht, 1993), 527–29; Shantz, *German Pietism*, 245.

34. Daniel Jeyaraj, *Bartholomäus Ziegenbalg: The Father of Modern Protestant Mission* (New Delhi: Indian SPCK, 2006), 66, 72, 78, 198–200, 216–17, 252.

SIDEBAR 6.1

Bartholomäus Ziegenbalg,
A Translation of Two Speeches (1716)

If we consider the success of this Mission from its first beginning; it hath not yet indeed been answerable to our desires. . . . The seed of the Word sown here and there would have seemed as dead to us, unless we had *believed in hope even against hope*, that after so many tempests and commotions, it would in time spring up, and bring forth fruit abundantly. Almighty God, who is the waterer, can give that increase to us, or to those who may come after us in this arduous affair. In this sure hope of the conversion of the Gentiles, I leave *Europe*, to return to the *Indies* again, imploring the Divine Majesty, that He would be graciously pleased to conduct me safe thither, through all the perils of the deep, and to direct and prosper my endeavors of guiding many souls to salvation.

Source: Daniel Jeyaraj, *Bartholomäus Ziegenbalg: The Father of Modern Protestant Mission* (New Delhi: Indian SPCK, 2006), 104.

Ziegenbalg's main goal in leaving Europe was evangelistic: with God's help to bring about "the conversion of the Gentiles . . . and to . . . [guide] many souls to salvation" (see sidebar 6.1).[35] Nine months after his arrival in Tranquebar (May 1707), the first five Indian converts were baptized. By October of the same year, the newly formed New Jerusalem Church had forty Indian members; five years later, it boasted 202 members. Within a decade, the church building needed to be enlarged. This modest success was more remarkable since Ziegenbalg and the Danish-Halle mission—unlike Jesuits since Roberto de Nobili—"deplor[ed] caste observances." Ziegenbalg's ethnological research had convinced him that the caste system was rooted in Hindu religious doctrines and therefore was not merely a set of social divisions based on class and occupation. Nevertheless, Ziegenbalg pursued a "mild policy with regard to caste," which allowed "concessions to the prejudices of the weaker brethren." Some caste distinctions were allowed in worship services.[36] These minor concessions were not enough for many higher-caste

35. Jeyaraj, *Bartholomäus Ziegenbalg*, 104.
36. Duncan B. Forrester, *Caste and Christianity: Attitudes and Policies on Caste of Anglo-Saxon Protestant Missions in India* (New York: Routledge, 2017), 120–21; D. Dennis Hudson, *Protestant Origins in India: Tamil Evangelical Christians, 1706–1835* (Grand Rapids: Eerdmans, 2000), 50, 90–91, 108.

Tamils, who were unwilling to accept baptism and church membership in the Tamil Lutheran Church if any renunciation of caste was required. Ziegenbalg became convinced that conversion efforts would bear more fruit among those less indoctrinated into Hindu religious traditions. He argued, therefore, that "we must inculcate Christian principles into the hearts of children and youth."[37] To achieve this end, he replicated closely the educational system established by Francke in Halle. Schools were formed for boys as well as for girls—something that was unheard of at that time in Hindu culture. Both boys and girls were taught in cross-caste classes. In order to allay the fears of Hindu parents, Ziegenbalg advertised that children would not be overly influenced to convert to Christianity. Pupils would be taught not only the Bible and Lutheran doctrine but also the Tamil Hindu classics.

The Tranquebar missionaries soon realized that they needed Indian co-workers and catechists in order to accomplish the evangelistic goals of the mission. In May 1708, they appointed the first Indian catechist. The job description of a catechist, according to a 1712 mission report, included instructing catechumens (baptismal candidates), providing pastoral care for church members and the sick, and evangelizing non-Christians. Male and female prayer leaders led worship and Bible study and provided pastoral care in rural and unevangelized areas. In 1716, Ziegenbalg founded a theological seminary to train Tamil pastors and catechists. Eight graduates of the Tamil boys' school formed the first class. In time, there were four or five Tamil mission associates for every European missionary. Ziegenbalg died in 1719 at the young age of thirty-six, but the mission he had valiantly served did not. He was succeeded by a series of remarkable German missionaries and linguists (e.g., Benjamin Schulze, Johann Phillip Fabricius, and Christian Friedrich Schwartz), who trained several generations of Tamil mission associates to evangelize their own people. By 1845, when the Danish colony of Tranquebar was absorbed into British India, more than fifty European missionaries and over two hundred Tamils had served the local population.[38]

The Danish-Halle mission was "disproportionally influential in the history of Protestant missions because of its methods, connections and timing." Its groundbreaking mission methods included the use of vernacular language, Bible translation, cultural sensitivity, and the establishment of an indigenous church. The mission forged international connections between Halle, Copenhagen, and London, which became a "source of inspiration for [later] Danish, German and English missionary societies." Its opportune timing as the first

37. Jeyaraj, *Bartholomäus Ziegenbalg*, 63–69, 168.
38. Jeyaraj, *Bartholomäus Ziegenbalg*, 68; Shantz, *German Pietism*, 249–52.

sustained Protestant mission allowed it to shape broader "public opinion" and put "foreign missions on the mental map of European Protestants."[39] Nevertheless, the Danish-Halle mission soon paled in comparison to the foreign mission endeavor of Zinzendorf and the Moravian Church.

Early Missions of the Moravian Church

Zinzendorf's developing mission interest owed much to the influence of August Hermann Francke, to missionary reports about the Danish-Halle mission, and to personal contact with the Tranquebar missionaries Ziegenbalg and Plütschau. Thus, in one sense, the Moravian mission was both inspired by and an outgrowth of the earlier Danish-Halle mission. There were some significant similarities between the Danish-Halle mission approach and that of the Moravian mission during the three decades of Zinzendorf's leadership (1732–60): the use of the vernacular, cultural sensitivity, and indigenous leadership. Despite these similarities, the early Moravian mission approach differed in several important ways from the Danish-Halle mission.

Leonhard Dober and David Nitschmann, the first missionaries to St. Thomas, were deeply religious Christians who felt a strong call to mission work. They volunteered to serve overseas, and their appointment was confirmed by the casting of lots, an early Moravian practice. Unlike the Danish-Halle missionaries, they were neither theologically trained nor ordained. The majority of Moravian missionaries during Zinzendorf's lifetime were members of the artisan class, who worked a trade for their living. While Zinzendorf provided the necessary funds for travel to St. Thomas, once there, Dober and Nitschmann were required to earn their own economic support. In some mission locations, agriculture or plantation work was common (North America, West Indies, Surinam). Alongside other occupations, crafts and small industry were plied in Surinam, trade and commerce in Greenland and Labrador. A 1756 letter from Solomon Schumann in Surinam describes the variety of occupations the Moravian missionaries pursued there. "Brother Kamm is picking coffee; Brother Wenzel is mending shoes; Brother Schmidt is making a dress for a customer; Brother Dörfer is digging a garden; Brother Brambly is working on the canal."[40] One key advantage of missionary self-support was that the Moravians lived in close contact with the people they hoped to convert. Working alongside the locals enabled the missionaries to

39. David Hempton, *The Church in the Long Eighteenth Century* (London: I. B. Tauris, 2011), 80–81.
40. Lewis, *Zinzendorf*, 92.

acquire the language naturally and to demonstrate that they were useful and productive members of society. It also meant that the Moravians, as political and ecclesiastical "outsiders," were "low-impact missionaries," who operated for the most part independent of colonial structures. They "were not concerned with furthering imperial projects, although their work often did in fact facilitate the spread of European settlement."[41] In contrast, Halle only sent well-educated, ordained missionary theologians to serve in the Tranquebar mission. Contact with locals was less frequent and normally limited to religious functions. Indian catechists, and not the Danish-Halle missionaries, were the ones who rubbed shoulders regularly with the Tamil population as they ministered in rural settings. Halle's later cooperation with the English SPCK had positive benefits, but also the negative side effect of creating a closer affiliation of the mission with the political goals of the East India Company.[42]

The early Moravian mission enterprise also reflected key aspects of Zinzendorf's developing mission method and theology. The first Moravian mission to St. Thomas prompted the count to reflect biblically and theologically on the task of mission and to develop new mission theories and methods. During his lifetime, he published at least fourteen pamphlets containing instructions for Moravian missionaries. Like Puritan theologian John Cotton before him (discussed above), Zinzendorf held to a Jews-then-Gentiles eschatological scheme, which expected few Gentile converts in the present era. The count expressed the Moravian position thus: "We believe in general that the Time of the Heathen is not yet come. For it is believed in our Church that the Conversion of the Jews, and of all Israel must needs go before, ere the proper Conversion of the Heathen can go forward."[43] Zinzendorf believed that prior to the end times, only individual converts or "first fruits" among the Jews and Gentiles could be expected. Therefore, in his 1738 *Instructions to All Missionaries*, he writes, "We gave this instruction to our first missionaries to St. Thomas: to bring here and there a soul to the Savior, and how many more the Savior might give." After all, "it is not our commission, it is not part of our instruction, that we should convert nations, lands and islands. Rather just as we are a chosen people, so we also only hope here and there

41. Rachel Wheeler, *To Live upon Hope: Mohicans and Missionaries in the Eighteenth-Century Northeast* (Ithaca, NY: Cornell University Press, 2008), 84–87.

42. Hermann Wellenreuther, "Pietismus und Mission," in *Geschichte des Pietismus*, vol. 4, *Glaubenswelt und Lebenswelten*, ed. Hartmut Lehmann (Göttingen: Vandenhoeck & Ruprecht, 2004), 168–72; Penelope Carson, *The East India Company and Religion, 1698–1858* (Woodbridge, UK: Boydell, 2012), 10–14.

43. William C. Reichel, ed., *Memorials of the Moravian Church* (Philadelphia: Lippincott, 1870), 1:116; cf. Wheeler, *To Live upon Hope*, 88–91.

for a first fruit from the heathen."[44] This theology was potentially, and often actually, demotivating for the cause of mission, as was seen in the relative lack of mission in Puritan New England. In contrast, despite a demotivating mission theology, the Moravians' passionate love for the "crucified Savior" resulted in active mission work. The Savior had a deep desire for converted souls, and they felt obligated out of love for the "Lamb" to be his messengers and witnesses to a needy world that needed redemption (see the prayer at the end of the chapter).

Zinzendorf's "first fruits" theology had in some cases a negative effect on Moravian mission efforts. After six years (1732–38) of ministry on St. Thomas, there were seven hundred converts—a number far too high in the count's estimation. August Gottlieb Spangenberg, Zinzendorf's successor, reported the latter's reaction.

> And hearing that so many were baptized at once in St. Thomas . . . Count Zinzendorf, was apprehensive lest the labour of the Brethren on the souls of the heathen should not have a sufficient foundation. He therefore did everything that lay in his power to bring it to pass that only few might be gathered, but that those few might be well-attended to.[45]

As a result, Moravian missionaries on St. Thomas after 1740 were instructed to concentrate their efforts on those perceived to be "first fruits" rather than on all baptized converts, to the detriment of the mission's work. With time, however, the number of converts won by the Moravian missions forced a theological reevaluation. Zinzendorf's last words (1760), recorded in Spangenberg's *Life of Zinzendorf*, state this poignantly: "I only asked for first fruits among the heathen, and thousands were granted me. What a great caravan there must be now before the throne of the Lamb."[46] In 1764, four years after the count's death, a synod of the Moravian Church officially abandoned the "first fruits" theology.

The second Moravian mission was to Greenland, where the early years proved extremely difficult for the missionaries. The Inuit were hostile, the language near impossible to learn, and much time was needed to procure

44. Werner Raupp, *Mission in Quellentexten* (Erlangen: Verlag der Evang.-Luth. Mission, 1990), 166, 170.

45. August Gottlieb Spangenberg, *An Account of the Manner in Which the Protestant Church of the Unitas Fratrum, or United Brethren, Preach the Gospel, and Carry Out Their Missions among the Heathen* (London: H. Trapp, 1788), 52, available at https://www.wmcarey.edu/carey /spangenberg/ags.htm.

46. Quoted in Jon Hinkson, "Mission among Puritans and Pietists," in Klauber and Manetsch, *Great Commission*, 43.

food. Not one convert was won to Christ in the first five years. A break-through came on June 2, 1738, when missionary Johannes Beck resisted his natural inclination to use dogmatic theological argumentation to present the gospel to a group of Inuit. Instead, he felt inspired to slowly read and explain St. Matthew's account of Christ's agony in Gethsemane. The Inuit listened to the story of the Savior's suffering for hours, and the first convert was won. On Easter Sunday the following year, Kayarnak and his family were baptized. "Where argument had failed, the story of the Suffering Savior prevailed—a lesson the Moravian missionaries never forgot."[47] A strongly Christocentric approach with a focus on Christ's passion was adopted as part of official Moravian mission method after Zinzendorf's rousing *Statement at the Synod of Marienborn* in December 1740 (see sidebar 6.2). This approach was reflected in the *Plan of a Catechism for the Heathen*, published that same year. Zinzendorf maintained that it was wrong to begin the task of evangelization with the doctrine of God's existence, the Trinity, and creation, as was common in mission efforts among indigenous populations at that time. Instead, one should begin with Jesus's suffering and death and "when they believe in his death and wounds, one tells them that this God [Jesus] has a father."[48]

Another aspect of Moravian Christocentrism in mission was their conviction that Jesus was the actual missionary, who prepared and called individuals prior to the arrival of Jesus's human helpers. The job of the human witness was merely to identify those souls that, like Cornelius in Acts 10, had been prepared in advance. This meant that Moravians could approach their mission activity with confidence and composure. They did not expect large numbers to convert. Furthermore, if Moravian missionaries failed to discover souls prepared by the Holy Spirit, they were encouraged to move on to a new field of mission activity. An official decision to discontinue work among the Copts in Egypt was made in 1782, when it became clear that the unfruitful ministry was a misuse of scarce human and monetary resources.[49]

In his 1738 *Instructions to All Missionaries*, Zinzendorf specifies that Moravian missionaries were expected to practice a communal lifestyle on the mission field, just as they did in Saxony. A number of early Moravian missions imported the fellowship structures developed at Herrnhut to their overseas locations. In 1741, a Moravian Christian community of four hundred Inuit was established in Nuuk, which ultimately became the capital of Greenland. Named New-Herrnhut, the Greenland community adopted the so-called choir

47. Lewis, *Zinzendorf*, 84.
48. Raupp, *Mission in Quellentexten*, 167.
49. Mason, *Moravian Church*, 15.

SIDEBAR 6.2

Nicholas von Zinzendorf, *Statement at the Synod at Marienborn* (1740)

There are two false methods to preach the Gospel to the heathen: 1) That one speaks too much about God and not from the Lamb and his propitiation . . . 2) That in the preaching of the gospel one speaks first of the Father and then of the Son. In this case they must first believe the Trinity before one declares the word concerning the wounds of the Lamb. Therefore, we want to preach first to the heathen, that the creator of all things, God, whom they from nature believe in, became man and his blood was poured out for us. Then when they believe in his death and wounds, one tells them that this God [Jesus] has a father, and so forth. . . . It's best in the beginning not to preach the deity of the Savior to them. . . . One merely tells them about his merits and death, and calls the Savior by his name Jesus. When one tells them, that he created the world, then it becomes clear that he is God. One leaves it to the Holy Spirit to preach the deity of the Son in their hearts. When one has truly spoken to their hearts about Jesus, his cross and death, then one asks them: Did you know that Jesus has a Father? And then you tell them something of the deity of the Father and the Holy Spirit. . . . The Savior has kept closed to us the doors to other heathens, since we did not have the right method. When we no longer convert . . . the heathen wrongly, then soon the door and gate will be opened to us.

Source: N. L. von Zinzendorf, *Texte zur Mission*, ed. Helmut Bintz (Hamburg: Wittig, 1979), 63–64.

system of its German model, in which residents were divided by gender, age, and marital status into fellowship groups that both lived and worked together. Fifty-five single men and boys, and over seventy single women, lived in separate residences or "choir" houses, thereby giving up their formerly nomadic lifestyle. Intense fellowship was furthered in all the Moravian missions through the introduction of extended periods of hymn singing (*Singstunden*), likewise mirroring rituals at Herrnhut.[50]

In other locations, mission stations became Christian villages, where converts lived and worked alongside Moravian missionaries. Mission work in the Dutch colony of Surinam on the northern coast of South America first began in 1735 among black plantation slaves in Paramaribo. Hostility

50. Mason, *Moravian Church*, 20–21.

from local slave owners and clergy forced the early German missionaries to relocate further south, where the native Arawak became the focus of their preaching. In 1740 the mission station Pilgerhut ("pilgrim's watch") was formed. There, missionary linguist Solomon Schumann baptized four hundred Arawaks in twelve years, the majority of whom took up residence at Pilgerhut. In 1753, a "new direction in the work of the Moravians" was initiated there. The missionaries recognized that the Arawak understood their own language and culture considerably better than the missionaries did. Therefore, they encouraged the locals to not only lead worship but also to undertake evangelistic mission trips into surrounding territories.[51] The empowerment and training of indigenous workers was replicated on the other mission fields. This was also the case in the Danish-Halle mission to Tranquebar.

This overview of the early Moravian mission enterprise during Zinzen-dorf's lifetime has demonstrated that these missions differed in important ways from the Danish-Halle mission. The Moravians primarily employed artisan missionaries, who were neither theologically trained nor ordained. The missionaries practiced self-support; they lived and worked alongside the local population. This approach meant that they were not linked with colonial agendas. Zinzendorf was the chief theologian and mission strategizer for the Moravian mission in the first decades. His eschatology prompted him to expect only few conversions of Gentiles during the current church age. The count developed this conviction in his "first fruits" theology. Zinzendorf promoted a Christocentric evangelistic approach; missionaries should first preach the passion of the Savior before tackling the doctrine of the Trinity and of creation. Finally, the early Moravian missions imported elements of Herrnhut practice into their mission contexts: communal living; fellowship groups based on age, gender, and marital status; and Christian villages.

In conclusion, the Moravian mission endeavor proved to be a giant leap forward for the global witness of Protestants. Previously, Luther and Calvin had theorized about the need for worldwide mission. However, the focus of both Reformers remained on converting nominal Christians within Europe, for the most part within their own ethnic and linguistic territories. They thus failed to put their mission theory into concrete foreign mission praxis. In the generations after Luther, there were several unsuccessful cross-cultural at-tempts, until Lutheran Orthodoxy rejected out of hand the mission mandate and squelched mission motivation. On the Reformed side, the cause of world

---

51. Franklin Steven Jabini, *Christianity in Suriname: An Overview of Its History, Theologians, and Sources* (Carlisle, UK: Langham, 2012), 67.

evangelization was kept alive by several Dutch Reformed mission theologians and one missionary (Justus Heurnius) to the Dutch East Indies. The mission of John Eliot to the Algonquin in Puritan New England was by far the most significant Protestant mission effort to date. However, it too was short-lived and the effort of only a few select individuals. In contrast, German Pietists in the early eighteenth century launched more sustained missions involving numerous missionaries. The Danish-Halle mission to India, with its later English partner, the SPCK, lasted roughly 140 years (1706–1843) and employed over fifty missionaries. Arno Lehmann claims that prior to the Danish-Halle mission, "nothing was done which could even be charitably called the beginning of [Protestant] mission work."[52]

Yet the Moravian mission effort soon eclipsed all predecessors and caused them to pale in comparison. Within one decade, Moravian missionaries were serving on five continents in twenty-eight countries, a geographic extension unparalleled by any previous and many later Protestant groups. Moreover, "no Protestant Church had ever directed her efforts to so many different races" and ethnicities as the Moravians.[53] During Zinzendorf's lifetime, 226 Moravian missionaries were sent out, equaling roughly one missionary for every sixty church members. In contrast, other Protestant churches in the same time frame averaged one missionary for every five thousand members.[54] Moravian missions also won a considerable number of converts. Despite the early Moravian "first fruits" theology, over six thousand souls were won for the crucified Savior on the various mission fields in Zinzendorf's lifetime; by 1822 they had thirty-three thousand non-Western converts and catechumens.[55] Finally, the Moravian mission enterprise influenced the rise of the missionary movement in England and in Germany in the 1790s. Key individuals, including William Carey, were inspired by the Moravian example to embrace world mission. The founding of the most important British and German missionary societies (the Baptist Missionary Society, London Missionary Society, Church Missionary Society, Basel Mission, and Leipzig Mission) were all directly influenced by the Moravian mission. To a greater or lesser degree, these missions adopted elements of the Moravian mission model (their approach to preaching, communalism, and nonordained artisan missionaries). For these reasons, the Moravian mission enterprise was indeed a turning point in the history of the expansion of Christianity.[56]

52. Jeyaraj, *Bartholomäus Ziegenbalg*, xiii.
53. Lewis, *Zinzendorf*, 91.
54. Shantz, *German Pietism*, 449n93.
55. Mason, *Moravian Church*, 199.
56. Mason, *Moravian Church*, 1–4.

We end this chapter with a prayer from Zinzendorf that reflects his strong Christocentric focus and his commitment to Moravian missionary outreach:

> My dearest Savior! We beg of you this same blessed look, this same irresistible look, which you always fix upon the souls who like to look upon you, who like to receive you. . . . And to this look help, according to your wisdom, all souls, high and low, rich and poor . . . at the moment of their willingness. In the meantime, let us witness so long and, as far as possible, propagate our testimony among mankind so long, until you have gradually accomplished the number of those [souls] who want to and will see your saving Cross's image here in time . . . so that your witnesses, before they rest, may be able to bring you the answer: Lord, what you have commanded is done.[57]

---

57. Peter C. Erb, *Pietists: Selected Writings* (New York: Paulist Press, 1983), 323–24.

Launching a Mission Movement

William Carey and the
Baptist Missionary Society (1792)

> Go bear the Saviour's name to lands unknown,
> Tell to the Southern world His wondrous grace;
> An energy Divine your words shall own
> And draw their untaught hearts to seek His face.
>
> Many in quest of gold and empty fame
> Would compass earth, or venture near the poles;
> But how much nobler your reward and aim
> To spread His praise, and win immortal souls.[1]

In many respects, William Carey (1761–1834) seemed an unlikely candidate to launch a mission movement. Unlike Count Zinzendorf, who was born to wealth and privilege, Carey's family was not socially prominent. He was born the eldest son to impoverished parents in the small Northamptonshire village of Paulerspury in 1761. The Careys' situation improved somewhat

---

1. This hymn was penned in 1788 by John Newton (1725–1807), the former slave trader turned evangelical advocate for world missions, on the occasion of Richard Johnson's commissioning as chaplain to Botany Bay, Australia. Michael Hennell, *John Venn and the Clapham Sect* (London: Lutterworth, 1958), 222–23 (modernized).

in 1767, when his father Edmund was appointed Anglican parish clerk and schoolmaster. Nevertheless, as William later acknowledged in a letter to his friend and colleague Andrew Fuller, "My parents were poor and unable to do much for me."[2] With a schoolmaster father, William Carey most likely received a better-than-average elementary education. But he lacked the higher learning necessary to become, among other things, an Anglican clergyman. Carey's formal schooling was over when, in his mid-teens, he was apprenticed to a shoemaker in the nearby village of Hackleton.

This brings us to a second reason—this time a religious one—why Carey seemed an unlikely candidate to launch a mission movement: he was affiliated with a dissenting denomination that was inhospitable to mission. Carey was still a staunchly committed Anglican when he moved to Hackleton for his apprenticeship. That would soon change. John Warr, a fellow apprentice, was a devout Christian who persistently shared the gospel and invited Carey to midweek meetings at the Congregationalist church he attended. The Congregationalists, Presbyterians, and Baptists were "dissenters"—that is, not in communion with the established Church of England. Although they had been granted the freedom to worship by the Toleration Act of 1689, dissenters continued to face prejudice and limitations to their civil liberties. In 1779 Carey became convinced that he must be willing to "bear the reproach of Christ among the dissenters."[3] Gradually, over the next four years, Carey came to reject his formerly held views on infant baptism. In October 1783, William Carey was baptized by John Ryland Jr. in Northampton. Carey and his wife Dorothy moved to Moulton in March 1785 to begin his first residential pastorate with the Particular Baptist Association of Northamptonshire. One notable advantage of Carey's association with the Baptists was that this denomination accepted pastors who, in some cases, were self-taught as Carey was and were not trained at the Bristol Baptist Academy. Many Particular Baptists in the eighteenth century reacted sharply to the liberalizing and rationalistic theological tendencies gaining currency at the time, especially the rise of Unitarianism. They responded with a form of hyper-Calvinism, which rejected evangelism and mission out of hand as "an attempt to usurp God's prerogative of salvation."[4] Only a small group of Particular Baptist pastors,

2. Mary Drewery, *William Carey: A Biography* (Grand Rapids: Zondervan, 1979), 9; cf. Brian Stanley, *The History of the Baptist Missionary Society, 1792–1992* (Edinburgh: T&T Clark, 1992), 6–7.
3. Stanley, *History of the Baptist Missionary Society*, 2–3, 6–7; Michael Haykin, "Just before Judson: The Significance of William Carey's Life, Thought and Ministry," in *Adoniram Judson: A Bicentennial Appreciation of the Pioneer American Missionary*, ed. Jason G. Duesing (Nashville: B&H Academic, 2012), 12–14.
4. Stanley, *History of the Baptist Missionary Society*, 2–3.

which included William Carey and his friends and colleagues John Ryland Jr., John Sutcliffe, and Andrew Fuller, rejected the anti-missionary tenets of hyper-Calvinism and espoused a moderate, mission-friendly form of Calvinism.

If Carey's social, educational, and religious background made him an unlikely candidate to launch a mission movement, his character qualities more than outweighed such factors. In the first place, from a young age, Carey was a self-learner and a voracious reader. As a boy, he devoured books on science, navigation, history, and voyages of exploration. Later, he studied Latin, Hebrew, and Greek under the tutelage of John Sutcliffe. His self-education paid off. In 1808, Carey was awarded an honorary doctorate of divinity from Brown University in Providence, Rhode Island. Second, Carey exhibited an unusual degree of persistence when he put his mind to something. He told his nephew, Eustace Carey, that a person would judge him correctly "if he gives me credit for being a plodder. . . . Anything beyond this is too much. I can plod. I can persevere in any definite pursuit. To this I owe everything."[5] Carey's accomplishments were certainly due to more than mere plodding; he was a gifted linguist and missionary. But there is much truth in his statement that it was his persistent and tireless pursuit of goals, particularly for the advance of world mission, that was the key to his success.

Carey has frequently been hailed as the "father of the modern Protestant missionary movement." Carey was certainly not the first Protestant missionary to minister to indigenous peoples, as we saw in chapter 6. In section two of his important volume, *An Enquiry into the Obligations of Christians to Use Means for the Conversion of the Heathens* (1792), he clearly acknowledged that he and others of his generation stood on the shoulders of numerous missionary predecessors: John Eliot, Ziegenbalg and the Danish-Halle mission, the Moravians, and the Wesleyans in the West Indies. Nevertheless, it is accurate to say that Carey did more than any other single individual to turn the previously sporadic Protestant mission efforts into a growing and thriving movement. Carey's launching of the modern mission movement was a turning point in the expansion of Christianity. He launched the movement through several key endeavors.

In the first place, Carey's *Enquiry*, with its clarion call for global evangelism, played a pivotal role. In sections 1 and 4, Carey persuasively rebuts theological and practical objections to mission and thereby clears the way for a robust growth in worldwide evangelization. The fifth and final section of the *Enquiry* challenges Christians not only to pray for foreign mission but also to put their prayers into action. "We must not be contented however with

5. Eustace Carey, *Memoir of William Carey* (London: Jackson and Walford, 1836), 623; cf. Stanley, *History of the Baptist Missionary Society*, 7–9.

praying, *without exerting ourselves in the use of means* for the obtaining of those things we pray for," he writes.[6] The *Enquiry* played a significant role in the rise of the mission movement in both Great Britain and the United States by increasing both prayer for mission *and* missionary recruits.

Second, Carey gave the mission movement its organizational structure—the missionary society (discussed more fully below)—by adapting the previously existing voluntary society for the specific needs and cause of mission. In 1792, Carey and his pastoral colleagues founded the Baptist Missionary Society (BMS). Brian Stanley correctly notes that the formation of the BMS "marks a turning-point in the history of the Christian missionary endeavor. . . . Its foundation was one of the first indications in Britain of the self-confidence and breadth of vision" that had been nurtured on both sides of the Atlantic for world mission.[7] Within the next two decades, a whole crop of important new missionary societies were founded, among them the London Missionary Society (1795), the Church Missionary Society (1799), and the American Board of Commissioners for Foreign Missions (ABCFM, 1810)—a clear sign that Carey's founding of the BMS had launched a movement.

Third, Carey's missionary service became an inspiration and his mission methods a model for the current and next generation of Protestant missions. Among other things, Carey laid the foundation for the translation of the Bible into vernacular languages worldwide, which became a hallmark of evangelical missions. He continued and furthered the training and empowerment of indigenous church leaders begun by the Danish-Halle and Moravian missions. He tackled social injustices head-on. During his missionary career, Carey waged a successful protest against some of the human injustices he encountered in India—caste discrimination, the forcible burning of widows (*sati*), and female infanticide. To sum it up, the modern missionary movement launched by William Carey

> made of Christianity a truly global faith and must be regarded as the most salient event in the history of Western churches since the Reformation. . . . The energy with which and scale upon which Western Christian missionaries set out to evangelize the world was a tremendously important turning point in the history of Western Christianity.

Indeed, "Carey played a major role in the genesis of the modern missionary movement" through his promotion of world mission in his *Enquiry*, through the establishment of the missionary society, and as a model for later missionaries.[8]

6. Stanley, *History of the Baptist Missionary Society*, 13.
7. Stanley, *History of the Baptist Missionary Society*, 2.
8. Haykin, "Just before Judson," 9–10.

In this chapter, we will examine several of the key moments in the early Protestant mission movement. First, I will survey significant factors leading to the rise of the mission movement. Then I will discuss the founding of the BMS and the missionary career of William Carey. I will give special attention to the Serampore Covenant for several reasons: it was the clearest and the most concise statement of Carey's mission method; it was remarkably advanced for its time; and it had considerable impact on the nascent mission movement. This is followed by an overview of two other early mission efforts—that of Adoniram Judson and his colleagues in Burma and that of the American Board of Commissioners for Foreign Missions (ABCFM) to the Sandwich Islands (today Hawaii). These last two examples provide a fuller picture of the range of mission methods and outcomes within the newly launched mission movement. Judson observed firsthand the ministry of Carey and the Serampore Baptists and successfully applied many of those methods in Burma. The mission of the ABCFM to Hawaii likewise drew inspiration from Carey. However, a unique set of circumstances there resulted in a remarkably different outcome.

Factors for the Rise of the Mission Movement

"The modern missionary movement" was, according to Andrew Walls, "an autumnal child of the Evangelical Revival." This transatlantic revival, which swept Great Britain and the American colonies from the 1720s to the 1760s, created the conditions necessary for the rise of the mission movement. The revival generated religious excitement and energy as well as a renewed concern for the eternal destiny of the unconverted. This concern for the salvation of the neighbor one could see soon expanded to include the far-off stranger in distant lands. As a result, the revival supplied missionaries willing to evangelize overseas. It also forged logistical and communication networks between evangelicals on both sides of the Atlantic. Advice and information were shared internationally through letters as well as in missionary magazines that collected and disseminated news from a wide variety of denominations and countries. Such sharing of information fanned mission interest in Great Britain and North America. Similarly, missionary biographies, beginning with Jonathan Edwards's influential *Life and Diary of David Brainerd* (1749), created evangelical missionary heroes and stimulated enthusiasm and involvement in the mission enterprise.[9]

9. Andrew F. Walls, *The Missionary Movement in Christian History* (Maryknoll, NY: Orbis, 1996), 79–80.

Finally, the transatlantic revival spawned a mission prayer movement. In 1741, Philip Doddridge, a dissenting pastor at an independent church in Northampton, called on Christians to gather four times a year to pray for missions. Scottish evangelicals issued a similar appeal in 1744, which encouraged churchgoers to assemble locally at regular intervals to pray for the outpouring of the Holy Spirit on all nations of the world. In New England, Jonathan Edwards, in his pamphlet *A Humble Attempt* (1747), proposed a continuance of the Scottish concerts of prayer. He reminded Christians that it was only through "extraordinary and united prayer" that the "promised glorious and universal outpouring of the Spirit of God" throughout the world would come about.[10] Edwards's pamphlet had a deep impression on the circle around Carey—John Ryland Jr., John Sutcliffe, and Andrew Fuller—both for its call for united prayer and for its carefully balanced tension between God's sovereignty and human responsibility in mission. The prayer movement, and Edwards's pamphlet in particular, shaped the rise of the Protestant mission movement by stimulating a "world-wide vision," by "linking . . . mission with the *eschaton*," and by "giving the Christian disciple a share in God's own mission."[11]

A second factor needed for the rise of the mission movement has been alluded to several times in this chapter: the resolution of theological objections to foreign missions. The primary theological issue that needed to be resolved was the hyper-Calvinism prominent among the Particular Baptists and other dissenters. Joseph Hussey, an English Congregationalist minister, published a book in 1707 titled *God's Operations of Grace but Not Offers of His Grace*. In it he claims that it is inconsistent to uphold God's election to salvation and at the same time to call the lost to accept Christ. Such "promiscuous" offers of salvation are to be rejected, since they are nothing more than "rank Arminianism."[12] Other ministers claimed that it was *not* "the duty of poor unconverted sinners, who hear the gospel preached and published, to believe in Jesus Christ"—an assertion that independent pastor Matthias Maurice challenged in his 1737 pamphlet "A Modern Question Modestly Answered."[13]

This form of hyper-Calvinism had clear anti-missionary implications and needed to be resolved in order to allow the Protestant mission movement to ad-

10. *The Works of Jonathan Edwards*, ed. Anthony Uyl, vol. II-I (Woodstock, Ontario: Devoted Publishing, 2017), 455; Stanley, *History of the Baptist Missionary Society*, 4–5.

11. R. Pierce Beaver, *Pioneers in Mission* (Grand Rapids: Eerdmans, 1966), 24; cf. Walls, *Missionary Movement*, 244–45.

12. Joseph Hussey, *God's Operations of Grace but Not Offers of His Grace* (Scotts Valley, CA: CreateSpace, 2017), 96, 101.

13. Matthias Maurice, *A Modern Question Modestly Answered* (London: James Buckland, 1737), 3, 28.

vance and flourish. Andrew Fuller had grown up in a Particular Baptist church where the pastor did not call people to conversion. Three major influences led Fuller to adopt a more evangelical form of Calvinism: (1) admonitions in the Bible calling sinners to repent; (2) the example of John Eliot and David Brainerd, who did just that; and (3) Jonathan Edwards's *Inquiry into the Freedom of the Will* (1754), which reconciled divine sovereignty and human free will. Fuller's volume *The Gospel Worthy of All Acceptation* (1785) rejected the central tenets of hyper-Calvinism. "Unconverted sinners are commanded, exhorted, and invited to believe in Christ for salvation," he proclaims. Furthermore, "the Gospel, though a message of pure grace, requires the obedient response of faith."[14]

In September 1785, William Carey was a young and not-yet-ordained pastor within the Northamptonshire Baptist Association. At their regular pastors' meeting, Carey suggested as a topic for discussion a second theological issue that needed to be resolved for the mission movement to take flight: whether the "command given to the apostles to 'teach all nations'" found in Matthew 28 and elsewhere was still binding on Christians in the postapostolic era. John Ryland Sr. dismissed this question out of hand, with a stern rebuke that may well be apocryphal: "Young man, sit down. When God pleases to convert the heathen, he will do it without your aid or mine!"[15] Even if the rebuke is not authentic, it does reflect the predominant hyper-Calvinist theology within the Particular Baptist denomination. In the title and in the text of his *Enquiry*, Carey counters Ryland Sr.'s assertion that God works without human aid. He stresses that it is the "obligation of Christians to *use means* for the conversion of the heathen." It is not adequate to just pray. Means such as the formation of a missionary society, the recruitment and sending of missionaries, and the provision of financial support must be implemented to advance the gospel around the world. Likewise, in section 1 of the *Enquiry*, Carey gives convincing biblical arguments why the "commission given by the Lord to his disciples" is still binding. Since baptism, the instruction of nonbelievers, and the divine presence mentioned in Matthew 28 are still applicable in the present era, so is the apostolic commission to "go and make disciples of all nations" (v. 20).[16]

14. Timothy George, *Faithful Witness: The Life and Mission of William Carey* (Worcester, PA: Christian History Institute, 1998), 55–56.

15. Stanley, *History of the Baptist Missionary Society*, 6–7.

16. William Carey, *An Enquiry into the Obligations of Christians to Use Means for the Conversion of the Heathens* (London: Hodder and Stoughton, 1891), 7–12, 81. Cf. David F. Wright, "The Great Commission and the Ministry of the Word: Reflections Historical and Contemporary on Relations and Priorities," *Scottish Bulletin of Evangelical Theology* 25, no. 2 (Fall 2007): 154, who notes that Carey did not use the term "Great Commission," which did not gain widespread use until the late nineteenth century.

A third key factor in the rise of the mission movement was the so-called second age of discovery and the electrifying new information about foreign lands and peoples that it brought. Captain James Cook's three voyages (1768–71, 1772–75, 1776–79) captured the evangelical imagination and were a contributing factor in the formation of a number of missionary societies.[17] George Burder, an independent minister and cofounder of the London Missionary Society (LMS), credited the "modern discoveries in geography" with increased interest in missions among Christians.

> Captain Cook and others have transversed the globe . . . and as it were presented to us a new world, a world of islands in the vast Pacific Ocean. . . . May we not reasonably hope that a well-planned and well-conducted mission to one or more of these . . . will be attended with the blessing of God and issue in the conversion of many souls?

He challenged his readers: if "Cook and other navigators have voluntarily exposed their lives" to perilous danger in their voyages, should not "ministers and pious youth" gladly bear the tidings of salvation to the "heathen" in "Africa, Indostan, China," and the "astonishing clusters of South Sea islands"?[18] Like many other evangelicals of his day, William Carey reported that "the first thing that engaged my heart to think of missions" was when, in 1784–85, he read the journals of Captain Cook.[19] Not surprisingly, his choice for the first mission field of the BMS was Tahiti, until Dr. John Thomas convinced the new society that Bengal in India was the better choice. Tahiti, however, was the first mission field of the LMS. In 1796 thirty men and six women were sent as missionaries to that island on the mission ship *Duff*.

William Carey and the Baptist Mission to India

Carey's growth of interest in mission was not only influenced by his reading of Cook's journals. He was also significantly influenced by Moravian missions. Carey and his colleagues were acquainted with Moravian mission literature, particularly David Crantz's *History of Greenland* (1765) and A. G. Spangen-

---

17. Kathleen Wilson, "The Island Race: Captain Cook, Protestant Evangelicalism and the Construction of the English National Identity, 1760–1800," in *Protestantism and National Identity*, ed. Tony Clayton and Ian McBride (Cambridge: Cambridge University Press, 1998), 270–71, 284–85.

18. "Religious Intelligence," *Evangelical Magazine* (1795): 161, 163, available at http://www .sierra-leone.org/Books/The_Evangelical_Magazine-1795.pdf.

19. Stanley, *History of the Baptist Missionary Society*, 8.

berg's *Instructions* to missionaries (1785) and *Account of the . . . [Moravian] Missions* (1788). Such writings were considered required reading for Christians interested in foreign mission, and they were eagerly consumed by early BMS and LMS missionaries and supporters. In fact, the BMS and LMS "were formed . . . due in part to the example of the Moravian Church and its missions." Their example "provided the founders of the BMS and LMS with the very necessary evidence with which to convince their followers that they too could maintain foreign missions, and be successful overseas."[20] The Moravians proved that mission to non-Christians throughout the world was possible and achievable. They also had significant impact on the early mission theory and practice adopted by the BMS, as I will demonstrate below.

Armed with the Moravian example, William Carey transformed his burgeoning interest in foreign mission into concrete practice. His compelling burden that "something should be done for the heathen" to bring them the message of salvation convinced him by 1787–88 "to do all in his power to set on foot [establish] a Baptist mission." At the 1791 Easter meeting of the Northamptonshire Baptist Association, Carey proposed the formation of a "society for propagating the gospel among the heathen." Carey was well aware that he must develop "the appropriate means to accomplish the task" of world mission. "The simple fact was that the Church as then organized . . . could not effectively operate mission overseas. Christians had accordingly to 'use [other] means' to do so."[21] The appropriate means embraced by Carey to provide the organizational structure for the missionary movement was the voluntary society. Voluntary religious societies were a distinctly Anglo-American Protestant form of organization dating back to the early eighteenth century. They consisted of a group of individuals or congregations who would enter into an agreement as volunteers to form an organization around a common interest, be it moral (temperance, abolition of slavery) or religious (Bibles, tracts, or Sunday schools). In his *Enquiry*, Carey suggests that a group of "serious Christians, ministers and private persons . . . form themselves into a society." Their task would be to develop regulations regarding "the persons who are to be employed as missionaries [and] the means of defraying the expense."[22] Thus was born the voluntary missionary society, and the organizational structure of the missionary movement.

On May 31, 1792, Carey preached a stirring sermon to the Baptist Association of ministers at Nottingham. His Bible text was Isaiah 54:2–3: "Enlarge

20. J. C. S. Mason, *The Moravian Church and the Missionary Awakening in England, 1760–1800* (Rochester, NY: Boydell, 2001), 144–47, 168–69.
21. Stanley, *History of the Baptist Missionary Society*, 9–10; Walls, *Missionary Movement*, 246.
22. Walls, *Missionary Movement*, 241–47; William Carey, *Enquiry*, 82–83.

the place of your tent." Although a copy of the sermon does not exist, its main points were well-remembered. God was about to enlarge his church by the conversion of Gentiles. Christians were called not to sit by passively but to "expect great things" from God and to "attempt great things" for God to advance his kingdom. The following day, the Baptist Association resolved to prepare a plan to form a "Baptist society for the propagation of the Gospel among the Heathen." At the next association meeting, on October 2, 1792, in Kettering, the BMS came into existence. The first order of business for the new society was to establish an adequate base of financial support and to choose and send out the first missionaries. John Thomas, a medical doctor who had served on an East India Company ship since the 1780s and who knew Bengal well, was appointed in January 1793 to be the BMS's first missionary. Carey volunteered to accompany Dr. Thomas to India. Andrew Fuller, the newly appointed secretary of the BMS, and the other members of the leadership committee were delighted, since they had "long considered him [Carey] as a person peculiarly formed and fitted for so arduous an undertaking."[23]

John Thomas and William Carey and family arrived in Bengal in November 1793. Carey's wife Dorothy had initially refused to accompany her husband to India—not surprisingly, since Carey had made the decision to go to India without consulting her. Furthermore, the Careys had four children at the time, including a newborn. She ultimately agreed to embark on the journey after insistent pleading on the part of her husband and Dr. Thomas and after her sister consented to accompany her. Unfortunately, Dorothy never adjusted to life in India. She lost her grip on reality after the death of the Careys' third son Peter in 1794 and never really recovered. She died of fever on December 8, 1807. William Carey's second and third marriages, in 1808 to Charlotte Emilia Rumohr (1761–1821) and in 1823 to Grace Hughes (1777–1835), were happier.

The early years in India were difficult ones not only personally for the Careys but also for the BMS mission work. The problem was not the Bengali language, which Carey quickly mastered. Soon thereafter, he began to trans-late the New Testament into Bengali, a task he completed in 1797. Rather, the difficulty lay with the unexpected resistance of the Hindu population to Christianity. Both Carey and, later, William Ward found that the caste system, which permeated Hindu society and religion, had such a tenacious hold on the local population that conversions to Christ were rare. It was not until 1800, seven years after Carey's arrival in the country, that the first two Hindus converted and were baptized, Krishna Pal and his friend Gokul.[24]

23. Stanley, *History of the Baptist Missionary Society*, 14–17.
24. Stanley, *History of the Baptist Missionary Society*, 36–37.

SIDEBAR 7.1

Krishna Pal, "O Thou, My Soul"

O thou, my soul, forget no more
The friend who all thy misery bore;
Let every idol be forgot,
But, O my soul, forget Him not.

Jesus for thou a body takes,
Thy guilt assumes, thy fetters breaks,
Discharging all thy dreadful debt;
And canst thou e'er such love forget?
Renounce thy works and ways, with grief,
And fly to this most sure relief;
Nor Him forget, who left His throne,
And for thy life gave up His own.

Source: *Grace Hymns* (London: Grace
Publications Trust, 1975), #145.

Krishna Pal (1764–1822) had been a "seeker after truth" for some time; he had first heard the gospel from Moravian missionaries at Serampore before they quit the field in 1792 due to the unresponsiveness of the people. In November 1800, Pal required medical assistance and contacted Dr. John Thomas. Thomas, along with Carey and his colleague Joshua Marshman, used this opportunity to explain the gospel to Pal. They left him with a pithy rhyme to ponder: "Sin confessing, sin forsaking, Christ's righteousness embracing, the soul is free."[25] Such a rhyme was culturally appropriate, since mantras (a syllable, word, or verse) were commonly employed in Hindu religious traditions to impart deeper spiritual understanding.[26] A month after his first contact with the BMS missionaries, Pal converted, and on December 28, 1800, he was baptized by Carey in the Hooghly River. Pal went on to become a very effective and eloquent preacher, who regularly preached a dozen times a week in Calcutta and its environs. He also wrote hymns in Bengali for use by local

25. Haykin, "Just before Judson," 26–27.
26. Hinduism is a modern construct developed by Westerners and Indian intellectuals in the nineteenth century to designate India's native religion. Geoffrey A. Oddie, "Constructing 'Hinduism': The Impact of the Protestant Missionary Movement on Hindu Self-Understanding," in *Christians and Missionaries in India: Cross-Cultural Communication since 1500*, ed. Robert E. Frykenberg (Grand Rapids: Eerdmans, 2003), 156–57; cf. Brian K. Pennington, *Was Hinduism Invented? Britons, Indians and the Colonial Construction of Religion* (Oxford: Oxford University Press, 2005), 167–89.

Christians. One hymn, "O Thou, My Soul, Forget No More" was translated into English by Joshua Marshman (see sidebar 7.1). The conversion of Krishna Pal set in motion modest growth in the number of baptized believers. Between 1800 and 1821, roughly fourteen hundred persons were baptized. Somewhat surprisingly, the majority of converts were not low caste or outcaste; in fact, a disproportionate number of Brahmins were found among the congregants.[27]

The conversion of Krishna Pal occurred at Serampore, a small Danish colony on the Hooghly River near Calcutta. In late 1799 Carey had moved there with his family, in part due to the already strained relationship of the BMS and other mission societies with the British East India Company (BEIC). In 1806 the BEIC unsuccessfully sought to have *all* missionaries expelled from BEIC territory, though only two new missionaries were forced to leave Bengal. Tacit toleration for missionary activity in India was not achieved until 1813, when parliamentary lobbying in Britain by William Wilberforce led to the inclusion of the "pious clause" in the charter of the BEIC. This ambiguously worded clause allowed missionaries and others interested in the "religious and moral improvement" of the local Indian population to apply for a permit to reside on BEIC territory in pursuance of missionary work.[28] Carey was joined in Serampore soon thereafter by two newly arrived missionaries, printer and preacher William Ward and educator and apologist Joshua Marshman and their families. The three men became the famed "Serampore Trio," a missionary "partnership that has few parallels in Christian history" for its remarkable unity of spirit and endeavor.[29]

Within weeks of the founding of the BMS mission station at Serampore, the mission family there adopted a set of rules for their community. The rules outlined what was to be one of their key guiding principles—a form of communalism strongly influenced by Moravian mission practice. Even before Carey had departed for India, he had proposed in his *Enquiry* that the best way to ensure the economic support of the mission community was to have a common purse. He suggested that two or more missionaries concentrate on preaching and evangelism while roughly an equal number of assistant missionaries "would be wholly employed in providing for them."[30] This was remarkably similar to the Moravian approach to missionary self-support, as Carey freely admitted in a letter to Andrew Fuller on November 16, 1796: "I will now propose to you what I would recommend to the Society [self-support]—you

27. Stanley, *History of the Baptist Missionary Society*, 56–57.
28. Penelope Carson, *The East India Company and Religion, 1698–1858* (Woodbridge, UK: Boydell, 2012), 3, 145–48, 250.
29. Haykin, "Just before Judson," 24.
30. William Carey, *Enquiry*, 72–73. Cf. Mason, *Moravian Church*, 150, 172–73.

will find it similar to what the Moravians do."[31] One modification from the Moravian model was that the Serampore Baptists brought their dissenting traditions of liberty and equality (rejection of ecclesiastical hierarchy, more stress on racial and gender equality), resulting in a more democratic scheme.

The set of rules adopted at Serampore in January 1800 was further modified by William Ward, one of the trio, in October 1805. The 1805 Form of Agreement, often referred to as the Serampore Covenant (SC), differs significantly from its earlier predecessor. The emphasis on communal self-support is retained, though it is made less stringent. In the 1805 document, "the emphasis shifted from *how* the missionaries lived to *what* they lived to accomplish."[32] It thus includes a succinct program in ten points of "the great principles upon which the brethren of the Mission at Serampore think it their duty to act in the work of instructing the heathen."[33] The Form of Agreement will be the main text for the following discussion of the early BMS mission goals and methods in India (see sidebar 7.2).

The 1805 Form of Agreement opens with a rousing reminder of the theological necessity of this "great and solemn work": the reality of eternal punishment for the unsaved. The Serampore Baptists are called to fix their minds on the "dreadful loss sustained by [each] unconverted soul launched into eternity" and on "the inconceivably awful condition of this vast country, lying in the arms of the wicked one" (SC, I). This opening reminder is followed by several points that address the appropriate missionary attitudes toward the local Hindu population, their religion, and their culture. Point II stresses the importance of the missionaries' informing themselves about the locals' "modes of thinking" (or worldview); their habits, likes, and dislikes (culture); the "nature of their idolatrous worship, feasts, songs" (religious practices); and the "way in which they reason about God, sin, holiness, the way of salvation, and a future state" (religious beliefs). They needed to understand these customs for pragmatic reasons, in order to "gain their attention to our discourse" about Christ and to "avoid being barbarians to them." Such information could be gained through conversations with Hindus, through reading their literature, and through carefully "observing their manners and customs" (SC, II). Furthermore, the missionaries should follow the example of the apostle Paul and abstain from those aspects of English culture that

31. Terry G. Carter, ed., *The Journal and Selected Letters of William Carey* (Macon, GA: Smyth & Helwys, 2000), 136–37.

32. Samuel Moffett, *A History of Christianity in Asia* (Maryknoll, NY: Orbis, 2005), 2:257.

33. William Carey, Joshua Marshman, William Ward, John Chamberlain, Richard Mardon, John Biss, William Moore, Joshua Rowe, and Felix Carey, "The Serampore Form of Agreement," *Baptist Quarterly* 12, no. 5 (1947): 129.

are offensive to Hindus and that would thereby "increase their prejudices against the gospel" (SC, III). After all, "it is absolutely necessary that the natives should have an entire confidence in us, and feel quite at home in our company." Therefore, "on all occasions [the missionaries ought] to treat them as our equals" (SC, VI).

These prescribed missionary attitudes and the resultant practices were quite advanced and enlightened in the early nineteenth century. The Serampore Baptists recognized that English culture was not inherently superior to Hindu culture; after all, the English could be viewed as "barbarians" by Hindus. Likewise, their desire to treat the local population as equals was quite revolutionary. Nevertheless, the BMS missionaries, like other evangelical missionaries in that era, viewed the Hindu religion, largely for theological

---

SIDEBAR 7.2

Serampore Covenant (1805)

In order to be prepared for our great and solemn work, it is absolutely necessary that we set an infinite value upon immortal souls; that we often endeavor to affect our minds with the dreadful loss sustained by an unconverted soul launched into eternity. . . .

It is necessary, in our intercourse with the Hindus, that as far as we are able to abstain from those things which would increase their prejudices against the gospel. Those parts of English manners which are most offensive to them should be kept out of sight as much, as possible. . . . Paul's readiness to become all things to all men, that he might by any means save some . . . are circumstances worthy our particular notice. . . .

Another important part of our work is to build up, and to watch over, the souls that may be gathered. . . . To bear the faults of our native brethren, so as to reprove them with tenderness, and set them right in the necessity of a holy conversation, is a very necessary duty. . . .

Another part of our work is the forming our native brethren to usefulness, fostering every kind of genius, and cherishing every gift and grace in them. In this respect we can scarcely be too lavish of our attention to their improvement. It is only by means of native preachers that we can hope for the universal spread of the gospel throughout this immense continent.

Source: William Carey, Joshua Marshman, William Ward, John Chamberlain, Richard Mardon, John Biss, William Moore, Joshua Rowe, and Felix Carey, "The Serampore Form of Agreement," *Baptist Quarterly* 12, no. 5 (1947): 125–38.

reasons, as idolatrous and satanic. They were convinced that "Hinduism was not merely devoid of salvific value but an idolatrous system that was an affront to God's sovereign rule of his world."[34] The negative view of Hinduism was exacerbated by Hindu religious practices that the missionaries viewed as both cruel and inhumane: *sati* (the forcible burning of widows, which Carey crusaded against for thirty years, until it was forbidden by the British government in 1829), female infanticide, the exposure of the sick and elderly, and the practice of hook-swinging at festivals. With time and increased knowledge of Hindu beliefs, some of the missionaries moderated their approach to Hindus. Attacks on Hindu religion and culture were replaced at times with "a more positive evangelistic approach which concentrated on preaching the distinctive Christian message of redemption."[35] This, however, was a change of strategy and not of theology.

Other points in the Form of Agreement described various aspects of missionary work. Point IV stressed the importance of taking advantage of every available opportunity to spread the gospel among the local population. The missionaries covenanted to "carry on conversations with the natives almost every hour in the day" in the villages and marketplaces. "This is the life to which we are called in this country . . . and we incur a dreadful woe if we proclaim not the glad tidings of salvation" (SC, IV). Furthermore, "the great subject of our preaching" is "Christ the crucified." Not only was "Christ's expiatory death . . . the grand means of conversion," but the "most successful missionaries in the world at the present day make the atonement of Christ their continued theme. *We mean the Moravians*" (SC, V). Evangelism and preaching the cross of Christ remained the central focus of the Serampore Baptists. The "European sisters" (female missionaries) were expected to acquire linguistic proficiency and "become instrumental in promoting the salvation of the millions of native women, who [for cultural reasons] are in a great measure excluded, from all opportunities of hearing the word from the mouths of [male] European missionaries" (SC, VII).

Translation of the Scriptures into all "the languages of Hindustan" was another key priority for the BMS in India. "We consider the publication of the divine Word throughout India as an object we ought never give up till accomplished" (SC, IX). William Carey was gifted in languages and, alongside his leadership and supervisory function within the BMS, his primary task was to put a translated Bible into the hands of as many Indians as possible. Carey (and Joshua Marshman) supervised teams of native-speaking

34. Stanley, *History of the Baptist Missionary Society*, 43.
35. Stanley, *History of the Baptist Missionary Society*, 46.

Indian assistants, who did the lion's share of the translations, which were then checked and edited by the missionaries. By the time of Carey's death in 1834, the complete Bible had been translated into five of the great languages of India (Bengali, Sanskrit, Marathi, Hindi, and Oriya) and partially translated into twenty-nine others. Despite being hasty, wooden, and "unidiomatic to the point of incomprehensibility, . . . Carey's . . . translations of the Bible remain perhaps the most remarkable individual achievement in the history of Bible translation."[36] The Serampore Baptists were aware that Bible translations alone were not adequate. Portions of the Bible and religious tracts needed to be distributed as widely as possible and then explained to the people. Furthermore, literacy was necessary so that the local population could read the Bible for themselves. To accomplish this goal, missionaries were encouraged to establish and promote "native free schools" (SC, IX). By 1818 ninety-two schools had been established with ten thousand pupils. These schools were "one of the most effectual means of spreading the light of the gospel."[37]

The two points (VII and VIII) that discuss the formation and mentoring of indigenous Christian leaders are the longest and most detailed points of the covenant, comprising four out of the document's nine pages. Early along Carey and his colleagues had become convinced that "it is only by means of native preachers that we can hope for the universal spread of the gospel throughout this immense continent" (SC, VIII). The vast population of the subcontinent, and the linguistic and cultural barriers that confronted the European missionaries, meant that the primary role of the BMS would be "forming our native brethren to usefulness, fostering every kind of genius, and cherishing every gift and grace in them" in order "to send forth as many native preachers as possible" (SC, VIII). The missionaries' role was not to pastor local churches but to "advise the native brethren" to form "separate churches, to choose their pastors and deacons from amongst their own countrymen." The word would be preached and the ordinances administered "by the native minister . . . without the interference of the missionary of the district," whose role was merely to supervise, advise, and correct any errors of the indigenous preachers. Furthermore, the European missionary ought "to direct his efforts continually to the planting of new churches *in other places*, and to the spread of the gospel in his district" (SC, VIII). The missionary goal of training and mentoring local preachers was put into practice. Serampore College was founded in 1818 in order to better train native clergy and thus further the establishment of an indigenous church. It was first and foremost

36. Stanley, *History of the Baptist Missionary Society*, 49.
37. Stanley, *History of the Baptist Missionary Society*, 51.

a missionary training institution, whose primary task was training Hindu converts to evangelize their own people. At the time of William Carey's death in 1834, forty-four out of the fifty workers serving nineteen mission stations connected with Serampore were Indians.[38]

William Carey became increasingly enfeebled during the last few years of his life (1831–34). Nevertheless, Carey the "plodder" continued to work as he was able. He finished his eighth revision of the Bengali New Testament in 1832 and continued to write and preach until shortly before his death on June 9, 1834. He instructed his sons to erect a simple tombstone with only his name and dates, and this verse from an Isaac Watts hymn: "A wretched, poor, and helpless worm, On Thy kind arms I fall."[39] More than that of any other individual, Carey's contribution launched the modern Protestant mission movement and shaped its early course. His contribution was pivotal and a turning point in the expansion of Christianity. We now briefly turn to two other early missions, the American Baptist Missionary Union (ABMU) mission to Burma and the American Board of Commissioners for Foreign Missions (ABCFM) mission to the Sandwich Islands, to examine their similarities and differences from the methods and vision cast by William Carey and the Serampore Baptists.

The ABMU Mission to Burma

Adoniram Judson (1788–1850) was born the son of a strict, devout Congregationalist minister in Malden, Massachusetts, in 1788. Adoniram was unusually gifted intellectually and excelled in school, particularly in literature and languages. Despite his Christian upbringing, he struggled spiritually and became an agnostic while a student at Providence College (later Brown University). Two professors at Andover Theological Seminary recognized his potential and encouraged Judson to enroll there, which he did in October 1808. Shortly thereafter he had a decisive conversion and in May 1809 was accepted as a member of the Third Congregationalist Church of Plymouth.

William Carey's direct and indirect influence on Adoniram Judson's missionary career is evident, starting with his call to mission. Carey's *Enquiry*, as well as his mission work in India, was known in evangelical circles in New England, as periodic references to him in the Boston-published evangelical publication *The Panoplist* indicate. Judson was almost certainly aware of Carey's ministry prior to reading in September 1809 an influential sermon

38. Stanley, *History of the Baptist Missionary Society*, 53.
39. Eustace Carey, *Memoir of William Carey*, 572–73.

by Claudius Buchanan titled "The Star in the East." Buchanan, an Anglican
BEIC chaplain in India, had become convinced of the centrality of Bible
translations for the conversion of Asians after personal conversations with
William Carey. Buchanan arranged for Carey to be appointed professor of
Bengali and Sanskrit at the newly formed College of Fort William in Calcutta,
a position Carey held from 1801 to 1807. Judson claimed that Buchanan's
sermon convinced him to pursue mission work in Asia. Buchanan's emphasis
on the important role of Bible translation in his sermon especially resonated
with Judson due to his own interests and giftedness.[40]

In 1811 Judson was appointed a missionary with the ABCFM, a Congregationalist mission society, for which he and other seminary students
at Andover had successfully advocated. In early 1812, Judson and his new
bride Ann embarked for Calcutta. The Judsons knew that they would be
in contact with Carey and the Serampore Baptists shortly after their arrival
in India. Therefore, while aboard ship, they studied the issue of believers'
baptism, and first Adoniram and then Ann came to the conviction that this
was the prescribed New Testament practice. On September 6, 1812, the
couple was baptized by immersion by William Ward at Serampore. Feeling
that he could no longer serve in a mission that supported infant baptism,
Judson resigned from the ABCFM. Shortly thereafter, Judson and fellow
missionary Luther Rice persuaded the Baptists of North America to form
their own missionary society, the American Baptist Missionary Union. Thus,
Judson had a significant role in the founding of the first two American missionary societies.[41]

The Judsons remained in India for just over a year (June 1812 to July
1813)—long enough to gain in-depth knowledge of the BMS mission approach. The BEIC at this time still determined which foreigners would be
licensed to reside in India.[42] Since the Judsons did not procure a license, they
chose to relocate to Burma, where William Carey's son Felix served as a government official. There the Judsons and their ABMU mission colleagues put
into practice a number of the mission methods outlined in the Serampore
Covenant. According to a mission strategy statement penned by Judson and
George Hough, the chief "means by which we hope . . . to introduce the
Religion of Jesus Christ into the empire of Burma . . . are translating, printing and distributing the Holy Scriptures, preaching the Gospel, circulating

40. Jason G. Duesing, "Ambition Overthrown: The Conversion, Consecration, and Commission of Adoniram Judson, 1788–1812," in Duesing, Adoniram Judson, 55–76.
    41. Nathan A. Finn, "'Until All Burma Worships the Eternal God': Adoniram Judson, the
Missionary, 1812–50," in Duesing, Adoniram Judson, 77–100.
    42. Carson, East India Company and Religion, 23.

religious tracts, and promoting the instruction of native children."[43] Like Carey, Adoniram and Ann Judson were gifted in languages and convinced of the importance of Bible translation in the task of mission. Judson made use of indigenous language helpers, as Carey did, to double-check his Bible translation, which was completed in 1834. Unlike Carey's translations, Judson's Burmese Bible survived the test of time and is still used in this century. Missionary printer George Hough arrived in Burma in 1816. Shortly after his arrival, he produced the first printed texts in Burmese: eight hundred copies of the Gospel of Matthew. By 1850, when Judson died, five million pages of Christian literature in the Burmese language had been printed and distributed.

Despite his commitment to Bible translation, Judson gave high priority to evangelism and preaching, since "the press can never supplant the pulpit."[44] Like Carey and the Serampore Baptists, Judson soon learned that Burmese Buddhists were more responsive to a positive explanation of the gospel than to anti-Buddhist polemics. Therefore, he attempted to make the gospel relevant to the Burmese mentality without compromising Christian doctrine. In an effort to adapt to the local context, Judson erected a Burmese-style bamboo-and-thatch reception shelter, called a *zayat*, to hold conversations with seekers and public worship meetings.

"Promoting the instruction of native children" was a commitment of the BMS mission to India and the ABMU in Burma. By 1852 there were twelve schools in three centrally located urban centers in Burma, and fifteen self-supporting village schools.[45] Establishing schools and teaching in them was one very common and important ministry of missionary wives and single missionary women in Burma. One further similarity in mission method between the BMS and ABMU was the strong emphasis on establishing an indigenous clergy. By the time of Judson's death, there were eleven Burmese pastors and more than 120 lay preachers. These numbers, while encouraging, were viewed by the mission as inadequate. At the first Baptist Missionary Convention in 1853, the ABMU adopted the goal to place an ordained Burmese pastor in every church in the near future.

The Judsons discovered what the Serampore Baptists had already learned—that mission work among Hindus and Buddhists was difficult and slow. It was four years after arrival in Burma (April 1817) that Judson first dared to hold semipublic meetings in his *zayat*, and two more years before the first Burmese convert (Moung Nau) was won to Christ. The evangelizing efforts of the

43. Keith E. Keital, "The Enduring Legacy of Adoniram Judson's Missiological Precepts and Practices," in Duesing, *Adoniram Judson*, 139.

44. Keital, "Enduring Legacy," 139.

45. Moffett, *Christianity in Asia*, 2:329.

ABMU team unfortunately resulted in a backlash from local Buddhist priests, who convinced the viceroy to prohibit proselytization in Rangoon, where Judson had been based. While conversions and church growth remained slow among the Burmese, another avenue of much more fruitful ministry opened up for the ABMU mission among the Karen people, a non-Buddhist ethnic minority group in Burma. The Karen had had prior contact with Anglicans and requested that missionaries be sent to work among them. In response, George and Sarah Boardman were sent as the first missionaries to the Karen in 1828. They were accompanied by Ko Tha Byu, an illiterate thief and murderer who, after a resounding conversion, became the "apostle to the Karen." His evangelistic success among his fellow clansmen had been prepared by ancient oral traditions among the Karen that bore remarkable similarity to the Old Testament. A largely indigenous-led Christian mass movement was launched. Today, less than 2 percent of Burmese are Christian, whereas 40 percent of the Karen claim faith in Christ. Adoniram's ministry focus continued to be on the Burmese population, although he contributed to the Karen work by developing an alphabet for their language and by training Karen leaders.[46]

Judson's enduring legacy is that he laid the foundation for the church in Burma. He accomplished this by adopting and adapting key principles pioneered by William Carey (preaching, Bible translation, schools). One chief difference between the two missionaries was that Judson, and particularly the ABMU in the years after his death, promoted ministry not just among the majority Burmese Buddhist population but increasingly among the more-responsive ethnic minorities. Unlike the Serampore Baptists, the ABMU did not pursue secular work to support mission activity.

The ABCFM Mission to the Sandwich Islands

The ABCFM mission to the Sandwich Islands (today Hawaii) displayed some of the characteristic elements of the early Protestant mission movement (Bible translation, schools, and native clergy). Like Carey and the founders of the LMS, American evangelicals also devoured Captain Cook's *Journals*. They were intrigued by Polynesian culture and desirous of mission work among Pacific Islanders. The serendipitous landing in 1809 of a young Hawaiian, Henry Opukahaia, in New Haven, Connecticut, set off a chain of events that led to the launching of the ABCFM's mission to the Sandwich Islands. After his arrival, Opukahaia was taken in by Timothy Dwight, the president of Yale University. He soon converted to Christianity and became the top

46. Finn, "Judson, the Missionary," 82, 93–94.

pupil and poster child at the ABCFM's Foreign Mission School in Cornwall, Connecticut. The school was founded in 1816 to train assistant missionaries to serve in their countries of origin. Opukahaia's early death in 1818, and particularly his inspiring and bestselling *Memoirs*, was the reason that at least four of the first company of ABCFM missionaries volunteered for the Hawaii mission.[47] This was just the first unique circumstance that attended the mission to the Sandwich Islands and that resulted in mission methods and outcomes not found in the missions of William Carey and Adoniram Judson.

A second remarkable circumstance transpired just four months before the arrival on March 30, 1820, of the first missionaries to the Sandwich Islands— the Hawaiian traditional religion, known as the *kapu* system (Hawaiian for "taboo"), was completely overthrown. The Prudential Committee of the ABCFM described the Hawaiian Cultural Revolution thus: "One of the strangest of revolutions . . . occurred just before their [the missionaries'] arrival. The national idols had been destroyed, the temples burned, the priesthood, tabus, and human sacrifices abolished" (see sidebar 7.3).[48] There had been a gradual weakening of the *kapu* system ever since Captain James Cook first made landfall in Hawaii in 1778 and thus introduced ongoing Western contact. This weakening came to a dramatic conclusion in October 1819, when King Kamehameha II (also known as Liholiho), his female coruler Ka'ahumanu, and the queen mother Keōpūolani publicly ate sacred foods forbidden by the *kapus*. The overthrow of the *kapu* system created a religious vacuum that was disorienting for Hawaiians and made them more receptive to Christianity. Reformed Protestantism not only reanchored them in a religious universe; it also provided new *kapus* for ethical behavior to replace the old ones.[49]

A third unique aspect of the ABCFM Hawaii mission was the extraordinary responsiveness of political elites to the Christian message in the first decades. An attempt to reach the elite classes was a common early modern mission strategy. However, this strategy was seldom very effective, as the example of the sixteenth-century Jesuit missions to Japan, China, and India demonstrate. The reality is that throughout the history of Christian expansion, the common people and *not the elites* have tended to be more responsive to the gospel.

47. Paul William Harris, *Nothing but Christ: Rufus Anderson and the Ideology of Protestant Foreign Missions* (Oxford: Oxford University Press, 1999), 40–41; cf. Mary Zwiep, *Pilgrim Path: The First Company of Women Missionaries to Hawaii* (Madison: University of Wisconsin Press, 1991), 14–15.

48. Rufus Anderson, *Memorial Volume of the First Fifty Years of the American Board of Commissioners for Foreign Missions*, 5th ed. (Boston: ABCFM, 1862), 253–55.

49. Jennifer Fish Kashay, "From Kapus to Christianity: The Disestablishment of the Hawaiian Religion and Chiefly Appropriation of Calvinist Christianity," *Western Historical Quarterly* 39 (Spring 2008): 18–25, 31–32.

Not so in the Hawaiian mission and in other Pacific contexts (e.g., Tahiti) in the early nineteenth century. Within roughly a decade, the majority of the Sandwich Islands' kings and queens, high chiefs and chiefesses had not only accepted Christianity but actively supported its propagation. This responsiveness to Christianity was not only due to the demise of the *kapu* system but also because the American missionaries were viewed as more benevolent Westerners than the merchants and sailors who visited their islands. They offered not only a soul-satisfying solution to the religious vacuum but also access to vernacular education for commoner and chief alike, something that

---

SIDEBAR 7.3

Statement of the Prudential Committee of the ABCFM (1853)

The SANDWICH ISLANDS have been thus Christianized. . . . God prepared their [the missionaries] way; one of the strangest of revolutions having occurred just before their arrival. The national idols had been destroyed, the temples burned, the priesthood, tabus, and human sacrifices abolished. . . . The horrid rites of idolatry had ceased; but the moral, intellectual, social desolation was none the less profound and universal. Society was in ruins. . . .

[But now] the Hawaiian nation is a Christian nation. . . . All the religion they now have claims the Christian name. A fourth part of the inhabitants are members in regular standing of Protestant Christian churches. The nation recognizes the obligations of the Sabbath. Houses for Christian worship are built by the people. . . . Christian marriage is enjoined and regulated by the laws. . . . The language is reduced to writing, and is read by nearly a third part of the people. . . . The Bible . . . was in the hands of the people before the year 1840. . . . Through the blessing of God . . . a beneficent change has occurred in all the departments of the government. . . . The very first article in the Constitution [1840], declares "that no law shall be enacted which is at variance with the word of the Lord Jehovah" . . . and that "all the laws of the Islands shall be in consistency with God's law." . . .

Here, then, let us, as a Board of Foreign Missions . . . proclaim with shoutings of grace, grace! that the people of the Sandwich Islands are a Christian nation, and may rightfully claim a place among the Protestant Christian nations of the world!

Source: Rufus Anderson, *Memorial Volume of the First Fifty Years of the American Board of Commissioners for Foreign Missions*, 5th ed. (Boston: ABCFM, 1862), 253–55.

was highly desired but denied to them by traders and merchants. Interest in literacy was a key factor in responsiveness to Christianity and instrumental in gaining the chiefs' support.[50]

After their conversion, the Hawaiian elites frequently directed the religious change. Beginning in 1822, Ka'ahumanu (d. 1832) made several tours of the islands on which she suppressed the traditional religion by destroying hundreds of wooden idols and exhorted the local population to worship the Christian God. She was one of several Hawaiian rulers who instituted Christian laws (called *kapus*) against theft, murder, infanticide, the drinking or distilling of alcohol, prostitution, and the profaning of the Sabbath. These laws culminated in the Hawaiian Constitution of 1840, which was drafted by a group of mission-educated Hawaiians. Article I of this document declares that "no law shall be enacted which is at variance with the word of the Lord Jehovah, or at variance with the general spirit of His word. All laws of the Islands shall be in consistency with the general spirit of God's law."[51] Although the explicit Christian elements were much reduced in the 1852 Constitution, it is nevertheless significant that a Christian constitution was promulgated in Hawaii just twenty years after the first missionary contact.

It was not just the elites who responded to the gospel; the commoners did likewise. Between 1831 and 1837, five new companies of ABCFM missionaries arrived in the Sandwich Islands, swelling the number of mission personnel to about ninety. These newcomers had been influenced by the Second Great Awakening in New England and Charles Finney's New [evangelistic] Measures. From 1837 to 1838, "one of the most remarkable conversion movements in the history of foreign missions" broke out.[52] Five to seven thousand Hawaiians were accepted as new church members in that period, which swelled church membership fivefold to sevenfold. Though some missionaries, particularly Titus Coan and Lorenzo Lyons, played an important role in the Hawaiian Great Awakening, as the revival was called, it was largely an indigenous grassroots movement led by Hawaiian commoners and not the ruling elite, as had previously been the case. Puaaiki, better known as Blind Bartimaeus, was an active indigenous leader of the revival on Maui.

A fourth unique element of the ABCFM Hawaii mission is that, after just thirty-five years of mission work, the ABCFM board publicly declared in 1853 that the task of mission on Hawaii was completed, since the "Sandwich Islands were Christianized." "Here then, let us, as a Board of Foreign Missions

50. Kashay, "From Kapus to Christianity," 33–39.
51. Kingdom of Hawai'i Constitution of 1840, available at http://www.hawaii-nation.org /constitution-1840.html; cf. Zweip, *Pilgrim Path*, 182–83, 203, 214–16.
52. Harris, *Nothing but Christ*, 67–68.

. . . proclaim with shoutings of grace, grace! that the people of the Sandwich Islands are a Christian nation, and may rightfully claim a place among the Protestant Christian nations of the world!" (see sidebar 7.3).[53] As justification for this bold statement, the document cited that Christianity was the only religion in Hawaii, one-quarter of the population were church members in good standing, the Bible had been translated, and society had been shaped by Christian values. Nevertheless, it is important to note that the Christianization was "extremely superficial" in places.[54]

Even prior to the 1853 declaration, the ABCFM had been working to dismantle the Hawaiian mission. One key issue to be resolved was the financial policy for missionaries. When the first missionaries arrived in 1820, a common-purse approach to missionary support was followed, modeled on that of the early Serampore Baptist mission. In 1842 a salary system was introduced. Then, in 1848, a new financial arrangement was promulgated. Missionaries were encouraged to remain in Hawaii for the purpose of Christian ministry but to become self-supporting, usually by persuading larger Hawaiian churches to furnish part or all of their support. Mission stations were dismantled, and former ABCFM personnel who continued in ministry were entitled to purchase the houses they lived in and to receive a portion of the station land. Many missionaries took advantage of these offers, remained in the islands, and became Hawaiian citizens. Their children and grandchildren became prominent citizens and wealthy landowners, proving true the common adage: "The missionaries came to do good, and they did very well!" The ABCFM Sandwich Islands Mission no longer existed in Hawaii after 1853. Its successor institution, the Hawaiian Evangelical Association, was viewed as a home mission consisting of former ABCFM missionaries and Hawaiian pastors.[55]

In conclusion, William Carey, more than any other individual, launched the modern Protestant mission movement and set its course. His pamphlet, the *Enquiry*, persuasively addressed theological and practical objections to global mission and challenged Christians to not only pray for the worldwide expansion of the gospel but to put feet to those prayers. He developed the organizational structure for effective mission, the voluntary missionary society. Carey's missionary service in India and his mission principles outlined in the Serampore Covenant motivated and inspired a generation of missionaries. Adoniram Judson's missionary career bore the fingerprints of William Carey. He observed firsthand the application of Carey's mission principles in

53. Anderson, *Memorial Volume*, 255.
54. Harris, *Nothing but Christ*, 47–50.
55. Harris, *Nothing but Christ*, 62–65, 117–22.

Serampore and applied them faithfully in Burma. The key difference between the two was Judson's and the ABMU's turn from the majority population (Burmese Buddhists) to the more responsive ethnic minorities. Finally, the ABCFM mission to Hawaii reflected common elements found in the early Protestant mission movement, including communal missionary support, vernacular education, Bible translation, and an interest in evangelizing the Pacific islands. Yet this mission was unique in many ways. The traditional religion was overthrown just months before the first missionaries arrived, creating a religious vacuum at just the right moment. Political elites converted en masse and frequently directed the religious change. A spiritual revival swept the islands in 1837–38 and resulted in a massive influx of new church members. Finally, the ABCFM was able to declare in 1853 that its job of evangelizing the Sandwich Islands was completed, thereby permitting it to dismantle the mission. Despite these unique elements, the shadow of William Carey looms large over the ABCFM as well as over the ABMU, LMS, and the other voluntary missionary societies of the first generation.

We end with a prayer from William Carey concerning the Hindu practice of widow burning and the conversion of many in India:

> I thank You, Father, for this surpassingly sweet promise which You did vouchsafe to me long ago, with its assurance of the ultimate banishment of all heathen devices and abominations, and of the ultimate winning of all hearts to Your allegiance. Use even Your unworthy servant to speed the day of fulfillment, the day when all the sons of men shall become Your people and all the kingdoms of this world shall become the kingdoms of Your dear Son.[56]

---

56. Eugene M. Harrison, *Giants of the Missionary Trail* (Chicago: Scripture Press, 1954), 18–19 (modernized).

Breaking the Chains of Sin and Slavery

British Abolitionism and Mission to Africa (1807)

Forced from home and all its pleasures
    Afric's coast I left forlorn,
To increase a stranger's treasures
    O'er the raging billows borne.
Men from England bought and sold me,
    Paid my price in paltry gold;
But, though slave they have enrolled me,
    Minds are never to be sold.
Still in thought as free as ever,
    What are England's rights, I ask,
Me from my delights to sever,
    Me to torture, me to task?
Fleecy locks and black complexion
    Cannot forfeit nature's claim;
Skins may differ, but affection
    Dwells in white and black the same. . . .
Deem our nation brutes no longer,
    Till some reason you shall find
Worthier of regard and stronger
    Than the colour of our kind.

Slaves of gold, whose sordid dealings
Tarnish all your boasted powers,
Prove that you have human feelings,
Ere you proudly question ours![1]

On May 12, 1789, the then twenty-nine-year-old member of Parliament William Wilberforce rose to address the House of Commons on the issue of the abolition of the slave trade. He spoke extemporaneously and eloquently for three and a half hours in what was hailed as one of his greatest speeches. Wilberforce was a slender, diminutive man, but according to his contemporary James Boswell, when he spoke this "mere shrimp . . . grew and grew until the shrimp became a whale."[2] His eloquence was legendary. Wilberforce had been elected to Parliament in 1780 at the age of twenty-one. After his conversion to evangelical Christianity in 1785, he considered resigning from political life but was encouraged by his friend, Prime Minister William Pitt the Younger, to remain in Parliament and devote himself to the cause of the abolition of slavery. Wilberforce agreed and soon became the undisputed leader of the campaign to abolish the slave trade. That goal was not achieved until 1807, nearly twenty years after his influential 1789 speech to the House of Commons.

In that speech, Wilberforce described with painstaking factual details the horrors endured by slaves during the "Middle Passage," as their transport from Africa to the Americas was called (see sidebar 8.1). He refuted the objections raised by British planters who utilized slave labor on their plantations in the West Indies. Yet Wilberforce did not point the finger at others or exonerate himself from culpability with regard to the slave trade. "I mean not to accuse any one, . . . for having suffered this horrid trade to be carried on under their authority," he proclaimed. "We are all guilty, we ought all to plead guilty, and not to exculpate ourselves by throwing the blame on others." Wilberforce announced in the speech that a Society for the Abolition of the Slave Trade had been founded that very month by the "most conscientious [Christians] of all persuasions"—dissenters, Quakers, and Anglicans. "Let not Parliament be the only body that is insensible to the principles of national justice." His call

1. John Newton, the author of "Amazing Grace," persuaded his friend William Cowper (1731–1800) to write a poem to encourage popular support of the antislavery movement in Britain. The result was "A Negro's Complaint," penned in 1788 and set to music, available at https://www.geneseo.edu/~easton/engl313/CowperNC.html.
2. Eric Metaxas, *Amazing Grace: William Wilberforce and the Heroic Campaign to End Slavery* (New York: HarperCollins, 2007), 37.

to Parliament: "Let us make a reparation to Africa. . . . Let us then make such amends as we can for the mischiefs we have done to that unhappy continent."[3]

Britain had indeed done "mischief" to Africa. In the mid-seventeenth century, Britain acquired colonies in the West Indies, most notably Barbados and Jamaica. This resulted in a sharp expansion of the British slave trade in the eighteenth century, since slave labor was viewed as essential for the cultivation of sugar cane, the chief cash crop on plantations in the West Indies. Mark Shaw reminds us: "For Europeans living between 1600 and 1800, sugar was king and slavery was its handmaid. Attempts to sever the link between sugar and slavery seemed doomed to failure."[4] By the end of the eighteenth century, over five thousand Englishmen were slave traders, one-half of all European slave ships were British, and 2.1 million slaves had been brought to English colonies. Profits from the lucrative slave trade furnished between 20.9 and 55 percent of Britain's gross fixed financial capital in 1770.[5] Due to these economic realities, the abolitionist movement faced a daunting task. The bill for the abolition of the slave trade was introduced into Parliament and then defeated eleven times before it ultimately passed in 1807. In 1833, Parliament passed the Abolition of Slavery Act, which emancipated all slaves in British dominions. The bill included compensation to slaveholders equaling twenty million pounds.

"The abolition of slavery must count as one of the greatest moral achievements in history."[6] It was accomplished by a coalition of reformers associated with William Pitt, deeply religious dissenting Christians (Quakers and Methodists), and evangelical Anglicans. Some of the latter were members of Parliament known as the "Saints." These were "political players" with deep roots in finance and business who generally voted in alignment with Wilberforce. Others were part of what came to be called in 1844 the Clapham Sect, a loose and amorphous group of roughly a dozen wealthy and politically influential evangelical activists in the 1790s to the early nineteenth century.[7] Many of them lived in Clapham, a village south of London (hence the name), and at-

---

3. William Wilberforce, "Speech and Resolutions on Abolition of the Slave Trade," May 12, 1789, http://www.emersonkent.com/speeches/abolition.htm.

4. Mark Shaw, *The Kingdom of God in Africa: A Short History of African Christianity* (Grand Rapids: Baker Books, 1996), 127.

5. Stiv Jakobsson, *Am I Not a Man and a Brother? British Missions and the Abolition of the Slave Trade and Slavery in West Africa and the West Indies, 1786–1838* (Uppsala: Almquist & Wiksells, 1972), 39; James Heartfield, *The British and Foreign Anti-slavery Society, 1838–1956: A History* (Oxford: Oxford University Press, 2016), 10.

6. Heartfield, *British Anti-slavery Society*, 13.

7. Gareth Atkins, *Converting Britannia: Evangelicals and British Public Life, 1770–1840* (Woodbridge, UK: Boydell, 2019), 1, 10–12, 78–79, 253.

William Wilberforce, Speech on the Abolition of the Slave Trade (1789)

I mean not to accuse any one, but to take the shame upon myself, in common, indeed, with the whole Parliament of Great Britain, for having suffered this horrid trade to be carried on under their authority. We are all guilty, we ought all to plead guilty, and not to exculpate ourselves by throwing the blame on others. . . . For my own part, so clearly am I convinced of the mischiefs inseparable from it, that I should hardly want any further evidence than my own mind would furnish, by the most simple deductions. . . . I must speak of the transit of the slaves in the West Indies. This . . . is the most wretched part of the whole subject. So much misery condensed in so little room is more than the human imagination had ever before conceived. . . . How then can the House refuse its belief to the multiplied testimonies . . . of the savage treatment of the negroes in the middle passage? Nay, indeed, what need is there of any evidence? The number of deaths speaks for itself, and makes all such inquiry superfluous. . . . It is now to be remarked that all these causes of mortality among the slaves do undoubtedly admit of a remedy, and it is the *abolition of the slave trade* that will serve as this remedy. . . . Let us make a reparation to Africa, so far as we can, by establishing a trade upon true commercial principles.

Source: William Wilberforce, "Speech and Resolutions on Abolition of the Slave Trade," May 12, 1789, http://www.emersonkent.com/speeches/abolition.htm.

tended the local Anglican church, where John Venn was pastor. Wilberforce was the central figure in the group. The group held meetings to discuss how they might implement practical solutions for a variety of social problems, including education of the poor, conditions in factories, care of the sick and handicapped, and prison reform. While their premier cause was the elimination of the "odious trade in human flesh," home and foreign missions formed a close second. In 1799 members of the Clapham Sect and their allies founded the Church Missionary Society (CMS) and in 1804 the British and Foreign Bible Society (BFBS).[8]

There was a clear link between the British abolition crusade and early Protestant missions to Africa. Many British Anglicans who supported abolition

8. Kenneth Hylson-Smith, *Evangelicals in the Church of England, 1734–1984* (Edinburgh: T&T Clark, 1988), 80, 85–93. Cf. Atkins, *Converting Britannia*, 50–51, 110–20.

had experienced conversion and adopted evangelical convictions during the revival that swept their land in the mid-eighteenth century. As we saw in the previous chapter, British evangelicals focused their first mission efforts in either Asia or the Pacific region. It was only as British evangelicals became involved in the abolitionist movement that their concern for the eternal fate of Africans deepened and that Africa came on their radar screen as a potential venue for missionary activity. While there were some notable exceptions prior to the antislavery campaign (such as the eighteenth-century Moravian mission to South Africa), abolitionist concerns in some cases generated and often accompanied most nineteenth-century Protestant missions in Africa. Evidence of this clear link between the abolition of slavery and mission to Africa was that the same activist British evangelicals were concerned about both issues. Andrew Walls notes, "The missionary movement and the movement for the abolition of slavery had grown up together, with constituencies that considerably overlapped."[9] This is nowhere more apparent than "in the Clapham Sect [where] interest in the abolition of the slave trade was combined with interest in missions." For example, William Wilberforce was not only the most important Claphamite and campaigner for the abolition cause in Parliament. He was also involved in early discussions that led to the founding of the CMS and was one of the CMS's first vice presidents. Granville Sharp was the first chairman of the Society of the Abolition of the Slave Trade (1787) *and* the BFBS (1804). In 1787 he also founded the Sierra Leone colony as a "'Province of Freedom' . . . and a bridgehead for the propagation of the Gospel in Africa."[10]

Members of the Clapham Sect felt called to support missions to all areas of the non-Christian world, yet "a feeling of compassion with the Africans who had suffered on account of the slave trade and slavery, [and] a wish to make restitution" made mission to Africa a central focus.[11] The need to make restitution for British complicity in the slave trade was a theme found in Wilberforce's 1789 speech but also in the founding documents of the CMS and the Society for the Extinction of the Slave Trade (1839). The CMS document (penned by John Venn, the rector at Clapham) noted that the "whole continent of Africa" was "still open to the missionary labors of the Church of England." The founders of the new missionary society hoped "that the wrongs which Africa has so long sustained will at length be repaired by the

---

9. Andrew Walls, "An Anthropology of Hope: Africa, Slavery, and Civilization in Nineteenth-Century Mission Thinking," *International Bulletin of Missionary Research* 39, no. 4 (October 2015): 225.

10. Jakobsson, *British Missions and Abolition*, 37, 579–80.

11. Jakobsson, *British Missions and Abolition*, 580.

offerings of spiritual peace and Christian freedom."[12] The abolition of the slave trade and the emancipation of slaves were essential first steps for many British evangelicals. But their ongoing responsibility required active support and involvement in missions to Africa.

Beginning with the founding of Sierra Leone in 1787, this pivotal new direction in mission, directed toward Africa, gradually took concrete form. However, this was more than just a geographical turning point in the global expansion of Christianity, though it was that as well. This new focus on mission in Africa was unique in two other ways. First, in the two representative mission societies that are the focus of this chapter, the CMS and the Universities Mission to Central Africa (UMCA), the focus on Africa was intimately linked with a desire to make national reparation for the collective sin of complicity with slavery; and second, it was joined with a clear humanitarian agenda to root out all remaining vestiges of slavery in Africa. In these ways, British abolitionism and the resultant mission to Africa was a turning point in the expansion of Christianity.

Each section of this chapter demonstrates the intersection between evangelical mission to Africa and the antislavery agenda, broadly understood. We will begin with a discussion of the early mission efforts in the Sierra Leone settlement prior to the founding of the CMS and the inauguration of its ministry there. After its first failed outreach among the Susu people in the Rio Pongas, the CMS achieved success when it shifted its ministry focus to the education and evangelization of freed slaves. In a second section, we will unpack a comprehensive mission goal frequently espoused by mid-nineteenth-century British evangelicals (including David Livingstone): Christianity, commerce, and civilization. As applied in nineteenth-century Africa, this mission approach included a distinct abolitionist goal: to not only evangelize (Christianity) and introduce education and literacy (civilization), but also to promote legitimate commerce to replace and eliminate all remnants of the slave trade in Africa. We will end the chapter with a discussion of the ministry of the UMCA, particularly their adaptation of the "three Cs" (Christianity, commerce, and civilization), the formation of freed-slave colonies, and the utilization of freed slaves as missionaries to their own and other African ethnic groups.

The Early CMS Mission to Sierra Leone

Sierra Leone was founded in 1787 as a British haven for freed slaves. Located on the coast of West Africa, the initial settlement was a small patch of land

12. Michael Hennell, *John Venn and the Clapham Sect* (London: Lutterworth, 1958), 282, 284.

consisting of but twenty square miles. In May 1787, the first contingent of settlers arrived, a group of about four hundred impoverished blacks from London. From the beginning, Granville Sharp's "province of freedom" was plagued with difficulties, largely due to inadequate preparations and insufficient resources. A trading company known as the Sierra Leone Company was formed in 1790 to address these issues and to help ensure the settlement's financial viability. Abolitionist members of the Clapham Sect, including Granville Sharp, Henry Thornton, and William Wilberforce, were closely involved in the Sierra Leone Company until it was disbanded when the enlarged settlement became a crown colony in 1808. According to its first report, "The leading object of the Company was to substitute, for that disgraceful traffic [in slaves] which has so long subsisted, a fair commerce with Africa, and all the blessings that might be expected to attend it." This commitment to legitimate commerce to replace the slave trade was an early precursor to the mid-century Christianity, commerce, and civilization scheme, which I will discuss more fully below. One other key goal for the settlement was missional. The company report for 1794 specified that it was "the duty of the directors" of the company "to embrace the opportunities that will arise of . . . promoting Christianity, as far as the Company's influence reaches."[13] In other words, the goal and hope was that the settlement would be a springboard for missionary activity in the surrounding region. Thus, "in the creation of the Sierra Leone colony the humanitarian [antislavery agenda] and missionary concerns of Clapham Evangelicalism . . . met together."[14]

By 1791, only forty-eight of the original settlers from London still lived in the settlement. The remainder had either died or moved elsewhere. The settlement was effectively reestablished as Freetown in 1792 when a group of nearly twelve hundred Nova Scotian immigrants of African descent arrived. Many of the immigrants were ex-slaves who had supported the British during the American Revolution. All of them were baptized Christians of either the Baptist or Methodist persuasion. They arrived as "a ready-made African Church" in Sierra Leone with a half dozen preachers and largely intact church organizational structures and congregations. Visitors to Freetown were uniformly impressed at the religious vitality of the Nova Scotians, who initially viewed mission outreach as part of their mandate. Nevertheless, only sporadic and rather feeble attempts were made by the Nova Scotians and the company governors in Freetown to evangelize the local populations. This was due in part to the pressing demands of life in the settlement, but also to the evangelistic

13. Jakobsson, *British Missions and Abolition*, 52–53.
14. Andrew Walls, "A Christian Experiment: The Early Sierra Leone Colony," in *Studies in Church History* 6 (1970): 108.

task being more daunting than anticipated. The nearest neighbors to Freetown were partly Islamicized. Some were middlemen in the slave factories on the Sierra Leone river. The black Nova Scotians also ran the additional risk of being taken prisoner and sold into slavery when outside the settlement. Other early mission efforts in the Sierra Leone settlement were likewise largely unsuccessful. The presence of Baptists and Methodists in Freetown encouraged both the Baptist Missionary Society (BMS) and British Methodists to send missionaries there. Two BMS missionaries were sent in 1795, and a group of six (unfortunately ill-prepared) Methodist laymen arrived the following year. Neither of these mission efforts proved successful; nor did the efforts of four other early missions to Sierra Leone, of the London, Glasgow, Edinburgh, and Church Missionary Societies.[15]

Although the initial focus of the CMS ministry in Sierra Leone proved ineffective and was abandoned, ultimately "no agency played a more crucial role" in the formation of Sierra Leone Christianity "than the Church Missionary Society."[16] The formation of a missionary society had been actively discussed for at least a decade before its actual founding in 1799 by Anglican clergymen in metropolitan London and throughout England, as well as by members of the Clapham Sect, including William Wilberforce.[17] Clapham member Charles Grant (1746–1823) was an influential figure in the establishment of the CMS. Grant had gone to India as a young man and served in the British East India Company (BEIC). After a dramatic conversion to evangelical faith, Grant became concerned that so little was being done for the evangelization of South Asians by chaplains of the BEIC or missionaries of the Anglican Society for Promoting Christian Knowledge (SPCK). Along with two friends (David Brown and George Udny), Grant proposed establishing a Protestant Mission to Bengal and Behar. In 1790 he returned to England, where he took up residence in Clapham and was elected to Parliament. Grant's ongoing promotion of missionary activity in India was one key factor in the later founding of the CMS. Nevertheless, by 1793 it became apparent that a mission work in India was impossible at that time, since the BEIC officially rejected the proselytization of Hindus.[18] Furthermore, by the late 1790s, Claphamites became increasingly convinced that a specifically evangelical Anglican missionary society was

15. Walls, "Christian Experiment," 108–13; Jakobsson, *British Missions and Abolition*, 81.
16. Jehu Hanciles, *Euthanasia of a Mission: African Church Autonomy in a Colonial Context* (Westport, CT: Praeger, 2002), 12; Walls, "Early Sierra Leone Colony," 112–13.
17. Atkins, *Converting Britannia*, 50–51.
18. Hylson-Smith, *Evangelicals*, 82–83, 87–88; Penelope Carson, *The East India Company and Religion, 1698–1858* (Woodbridge, UK: Boydell, 2012), 39–41.

needed alongside the dissenting BMS and LMS and the Anglican SPCK and the Society for the Propagation of the Gospel, particularly since the latter two missions concentrated their ministry on English settlers in colonies and not on indigenous peoples. On April 12, 1799, sixteen evangelical Anglican ministers and nine laymen met at an inn on Aldersgate Street, where the LMS had been founded four years earlier. The group resolved that since it was "a duty highly incumbent upon every Christian to endeavor to propagate the knowledge of the Gospel among the Heathen," a Church Missionary Society would be established employing episcopal-ordained missionaries who adhered to the "church principle, though not the high church principle." Since India was not a viable option, it was decided that Sierra Leone would be the new society's first mission field.[19]

The early enterprise of the CMS in Sierra Leone was inauspicious for a number of reasons. First, there was a dearth of British candidates willing to serve as missionaries with the CMS in Africa. The society was forced to fill its ranks with pietistic German Lutherans. Sixteen missionaries were sent to Sierra Leone by 1815; thirteen of them were Germans who had trained at missionary training schools such as those in Basel or Berlin.[20] The high mortality rate of CMS missionaries in Africa was a second factor contributing to its slow beginning. In its first twenty years, fifty CMS men and women died, most of them as a result of tropical diseases. Third, not all of the early missionaries were stellar. Peter Hartwig and Melchior Renner, both Germans, arrived in April 1804 as the first missionaries for the Sierra Leone field. Reports of Hartwig's idleness and public quarreling soon surfaced. After he was dismissed from the society in 1807, he took up slave trading.[21] Furthermore, the evolving relationship of the CMS to the Sierra Leone Company affected its mission policy, which changed "from one that was designed initially and solely to spread the Christian message in the interior of West Africa to one that included service to the colony of Sierra Leone." This service initially included providing a missionary to act as company chaplain for its English personnel. Soon after his arrival in Freetown, Melchior Renner accepted this position, albeit temporarily (1804–8). He did this in part because he had become convinced (as had company leadership) that it was "not yet the time of converting the Susoos [sic]," the first ethnic group targeted for CMS ministry,

19. Kevin Ward, introduction to *The Church Mission Society and World Christianity, 1799–1999*, ed. Kevin Ward and Brian Stanley (Grand Rapids: Eerdmans, 2000), 1; Hennell, *John Venn*, 216–19, 233, 241, 284; Atkins, *Converting Britannia*, 47–54.

20. Bruce L. Mouser, "Origins of CMS Accommodation to Imperial Policy: The Sierra Leone Quagmire and the Closing of the Susu Mission, 1804–17," *Journal of Religion in Africa* 39 (2009): 387.

21. Hanciles, *Euthanasia of a Mission*, 13.

because local slave trading had not been effectively outlawed.[22] This concern proved to be prescient.

The Rio Pongas Mission among the Susu people was launched by the CMS in 1808 in an area still rife with the slave trade. The Rio Pongas district was located 120 miles northeast of Freetown. Mission work there was in part an attempt by the CMS to operate far away from and independently of colonial interference. The choice of the Susu people as the mission's first evangelistic target was a logical one. The CMS had received an invitation from Susu chief Fantimani to commence a mission in his town on the Pongo River. Fantimani's son William was one of several Susu boys among the twenty Africans who attended the African Institute, a school located on Clapham Common near London. Since the Susu language was widely spoken in West Africa, the CMS's mission goal was to utilize Susu converts as a vanguard of African missionaries who would spread the gospel in West Africa. In 1808 Renner and fellow Germans Leopold Butscher and Johann Prasse inaugurated the mission in the Rio Pongas district. There, at five mission stations, the original missionaries and subsequent reinforcements established churches and schools. In order to accommodate the desires of local chiefs, education was given priority. Instruction for the children of headmen, local traders, and freed slaves was in English, not Susu.[23]

The mission among the Susu faced ongoing opposition throughout its short existence from both local Muslims and slave traders who operated on the Pongo River. The end of the Rio Pongas Mission was precipitated by a sequence of events that occurred in 1816–17. In late 1816, Renner reported to the governor of Sierra Leone, Charles MacCarthy, that a slave ship was collecting human cargo on the Pongo River. A skirmish ensued after British forces attempted to confiscate the slave ship, resulting in several deaths among the Fula people (overlords of the slave trade on the river). All missionaries, but especially Renner, were blamed by the locals for the crisis, and mission presence in the region became progressively more untenable. Then, in August 1817, the mission buildings were mysteriously burned to the ground. It was decided that it was not worthwhile to replace them. The CMS ended the Susu mission and moved its base of operations to the safer location of Freetown. In effect, "the British struggle against the slave trade in West Africa led to the end of the CMS mission in the Rio Pongas area."[24]

This retreat from upcountry ministry occurred at the time when a new, fruitful avenue of ministry was opening up in Freetown. In 1807 the British

22. Mouser, "Origins of CMS Accommodation," 375, 383.
23. Mouser, "Origins of CMS Accommodation," 378–87, 390.
24. Mouser, "Origins of CMS Accommodation," 388–93; and Jakobsson, *British Missions and Abolition*, 167.

Parliament abolished the slave trade. By 1808 British men-of-war ships were patrolling the coast of West Africa and seizing both British and foreign slave ships. The captured slave traders, their human cargo, and their ships were brought to Sierra Leone. There the slave traders were tried by an admiralty court, their confiscated ships sold, and the slaves freed. In 1808 alone, two thousand slaves were freed in Sierra Leone. By the 1840s, sixty-seven thousand freed slaves were settled in the colony. They are known in the historical literature either as "Liberated Africans" or, more often, as "recaptives" (even though they were *freed* in Sierra Leone after their recapture by the British). They were the fortunate ones who, with the help of the British Navy, escaped slavery. Unfortunately, the Liberated Africans represent only a small proportion of the slaves transported to the Americas (mainly Brazil and Cuba) in this time frame. The recaptives originated from a broad geographic swath of West Africa—from Senegal to the Congo. They represented over 120 languages and a diversity of ethnic groups, the most prominent being the Yoruba, Igbo, Hausa, Wolof, and Congo peoples. The "parish scheme" was inaugurated by the colonial government, whereby recaptives were settled in newly created villages on the Freetown peninsula. Some ethnic groups had their own separate villages: there was a Congo Town, a Kosso Town, and a Fula Town. Other villages were a conglomerate of ethnic groups. This broad diversity in such a small colony resulted over time in a partial breakdown of ethnic ties. A new common identity grew up around the shared experience of enslavement, recapture, and liberation in a new location. A distinctive *Krio* (or Creole) culture and language arose, formed of both indigenous and Western elements.[25]

The termination of the Susu mission and the massive influx of Liberated Africans into the colony led the CMS to revise its mission focus. Until at least the 1840s, first priority was given to the education of the recaptives rather than direct evangelism—to civilization before Christianization. This led to closer ties between the CMS and the colonial government of Sierra Leone. Governor Charles Maxwell in 1814, for example, assigned all Liberated Africans to the care of the CMS. In accordance with an 1824 agreement with the mission, the colonial government established and financed most chapels and schools in the villages. CMS missionaries, however, educated the Liberated Africans and provided pastoral care, first in conjunction with the Nova Scotians and later with the recaptives themselves.[26] The CMS educational plan called not only for day and grammar schools in the villages but for the best students

25. Lamin Sanneh, *Abolitionists Abroad: American Blacks and the Making of Modern West Africa* (Cambridge, MA: Harvard University Press, 1999), 110–12, 122–25.
26. Sanneh, *Abolitionists Abroad*, 124; Hanciles, *Euthanasia of a Mission*, 15.

among the Liberated Africans to be trained at the CMS Fourah Bay College (founded in 1827) to be teachers, catechists, pastors, and missionaries. The most influential of these recaptive pastors and missionaries was Samuel Ajayi Crowther (pictured on this book's cover); his ministry is discussed in chapter 9.

Not only were many recaptives educated; the majority of them also converted to Christianity. According to Jehu Hanciles, this "transformation of . . . pagan ex-slaves into assemblies of earnest converts is one of the most spectacular achievements in modern mission history, and 'the first mass movement to Christianity in modern Africa.'" By the 1850s, over two-thirds of the population were professed Christians, and the country was viewed by CMS leadership as Christianized. This is not to imply that Sierra Leone Christianity lacked weaknesses. Christianity in the colony was cast distinctly in an English mold, at least on the surface. Under the surface, troubling remnants of traditional religious practices, such as divination, witchcraft, healing rituals, burial customs, and idol worship, coexisted alongside outward forms of Christian piety and doctrine.[27] Despite these weaknesses, Sierra Leone Christians accomplished the mission goal that the CMS had set for Susu converts. The recaptives, unlike the Susu, did become a vanguard in the conversion of West Africa beginning in the 1840s (see chap. 9).

Antislavery ideology was a powerful motivation in the formation of the Sierra Leone settlement, the Sierra Leone Company, and the CMS. Each of these institutions was driven by a need to make "repayment for wrongs brought on Africa as a consequence of slave trading."[28] Abolitionist ideals brought the CMS to Sierra Leone and influenced its mission work. It was a local conflict over the ongoing slave trade that brought the Rio Pongas Mission to an abrupt end. The CMS's new and fruitful focus of ministry was educating and evangelizing survivors of the slave trade in Freetown, the Liberated Africans. In this case, the CMS prioritized education or civilization before Christianization, although both were simultaneously accomplished in a remarkable way, in large part due to the contribution of persons of African descent (black Nova Scotians and recaptives).

Christianity, Commerce, and Civilization

The relationship between Christianity and civilization had long been debated by Protestant mission practitioners and theorists. The prevailing viewpoint among New England Puritans from the 1640s until the 1760s was that

27. Hanciles, *Euthanasia of a Mission*, 7–11.
28. Mouser, "Origins of CMS Accommodation," 393.

civilization must precede Christianization. John Eliot (1604–90), like his contemporaries, believed that the first stage in the missionary process was to train Native Americans in "civility" (see chap. 6). Only when the Natives had adopted aspects of civilization could they be taught the gospel and convert to Christianity. By the late eighteenth century, this viewpoint had been rejected by the majority of evangelicals on both sides of the Atlantic, in part due to reports in Moravian mission publications. Their mission success demonstrated convincingly to the new societies of the burgeoning Protestant missionary movement that "no preparatory process of civilization was necessary before 'savages' could respond to the gospel." Although evangelicals upheld the value of civilizing indigenous people, the priority, at least in theory, remained the task of evangelization. By the 1830s, however, "experience suggested the wisdom of a practical partnership between the two."[29] Christianity and civilization, along with the third element of the "three Cs," commerce, reflected the Enlightenment conviction that there was "no essential contradiction between spheres of economics, politics and theology." Anglican clergyman Joseph Tucker affirmed in 1774 that they were "so many parts of one general Plan," due to "the unity of God's providential rule."[30] The three elements supported each other, since they had overlapping interests. Commerce became especially important in mid-nineteenth-century Africa as a potent antidote to the slave trade.

The abolition of the slave trade in 1807 was a momentous example of humanitarian reform in Great Britain and its colonies. The 1807 parliamentary decision only addressed the British slave trade. Not only did the transatlantic trade by other European powers (France, Netherlands, and Portugal) continue unabated, but the 1807 decision also failed to eliminate the British slave trade itself, much less the institution of slavery in British dominions of the West Indies. The trade in African slaves actually increased in the 1830s and continued throughout the nineteenth century. This trade was primarily centered in East Africa. Slaves from the interior were brought by Muslim and Swahili merchants to the East African coast and from there shipped to plantations in Zanzibar, Brazil, Cuba, and the Indian Ocean islands of Mauritius and Reunion.

In 1821 Thomas Fowell Buxton (1786–1845) assumed the mantle of William Wilberforce and became the champion in British Parliament for the eradica-

29. Brian Stanley, "Christianity and Civilization in English Evangelical Mission Thought, 1792–1857," in *Christian Missions and the Enlightenment*, ed. Brian Stanley (Grand Rapids: Eerdmans, 2001), 179, 192.

30. Brian Stanley, *The Bible and the Flag: Protestant Mission and British Imperialism in the Nineteenth and Twentieth Centuries* (Leicester: Apollos, 1990), 71.

SIDEBAR 8.2

Joachim Nettelbeck (1738–1824)
on the African Slave Trade (1821)

*Joachim Nettelbeck was a former slave trader on both Dutch and English slave ships. He documented the interdependence of trade that resulted from the traffic in slaves.

Here at one time human beings were seen as goods to be exchanged for the products of the European skilled industry, and so such articles would be chosen depending mainly on which need or luxury had become indispensable for the black Africans. Guns of all kinds and gunpowder in small barrels . . . were of prime importance. Almost as desirable was tobacco . . . and liquor. . . . Once accustomed to having these different articles from Europe, the Africans on the coast as well as those farther inland could not and would not do without them and thought incessantly about how to obtain the things which could be exchanged for the desired goods. Therefore, the entire land was from then on divided into small regions which were hostile to one another and all prisoners which they took were sold either to the black slave traders or were immediately taken away to the European slave ships. Sometimes, if spoils of war were lacking, and they needed new supplies of goods, their chiefs . . . would seize which of them was the most dispensable. . . . One can easily understand that all these lands found themselves in the most miserable state; but just as little could it also be denied that *the original reason for all this misery stemmed from the Europeans,* who up until then through their eager insistence had encouraged and undertaken kidnapping.

Source: Klaus Koschorke, Frieder Ludwig, and Mariano Delgado, eds., *A History of Christianity in Asia, Africa, and Latin America, 1450–1990: A Documentary Sourcebook* (Grand Rapids: Eerdmans, 2007), 161–62.

tion of slavery and the emancipation of slaves. Buxton's first resolution in the House of Commons in 1823 declared that slavery should be gradually abolished since it was "repugnant to the British constitution and Christian religion."[31] Not surprisingly, this resolution was unacceptable to West Indian planters and many members of Parliament. This initial salvo was followed by a decade of vigorous lobbying in lectures and public meetings, as well as pamphlets. In 1833 the Abolition of Slavery Act was passed, which declared all slaves in British colonies free on August 1, 1834. While this bill was an important milestone, the battle against slavery and the slave trade was not

31. Hylson-Smith, *Evangelicals*, 86.

yet won. As long as "there was still a transatlantic demand for slaves and a demand in Africa for manufactured goods that was supplied primarily by the slave trade," the trade would and did continue (see sidebar 8.2).[32]

In 1839 Buxton published the results of his extensive research into the current state of the African slave trade and his solution for it. In *The African Slave Trade and Its Remedy*, Buxton argued that the most effective way to eradicate the still-pervasive slave trade was to replace it with legitimate forms of commerce (see sidebar 8.3). This viewpoint was not original to Buxton. It had first been suggested in the writings of two African ex-slaves, Ottobah Cuguano and Olandah Equiano, in 1787 and 1789 respectively and was soon thereafter embraced by British abolitionists. Buxton, like his predecessors, envisioned that the rich bounty of Africa's agricultural products could be traded with Western partners for the desired manufactured goods, thus liberating Africans from dependence on the slave trade. In Buxton's view, commerce should never be separated from Christianity or from civilizing influences. Pursued together, the three Cs would not only introduce the gospel but help to end the slave trade and to improve the economic and social life of Africans. Buxton explained that while commerce might open the way for the gospel, ultimately only Christianity could heal the damage caused by the slave trade. Christianity remained the "proximate cause" of the "happy change" brought about by "missionaries and schoolmasters, the plow and the spade," since it alone unleashed a transformative power that could renew slave-ridden societies. Like previous abolitionists, Buxton was motivated by the need for reparation for the ills wrought by the slave trade. Buxton acknowledged that "one part of our national debt to Africa" had been discharged when all slaves in British territories had recently been emancipated. "There remains yet, however, a larger debt uncancelled—that of restitution to Africa itself," he wrote.[33] In his view, Christianity, commerce, and civilization were the very best way to make such reparation.

Buxton not only theorized about a solution to the African slave trade; he actively sought to turn his goals of Christianity, commerce, and civilization into reality in West Africa. At his urging, the British government authorized an expedition up the Niger River in 1841. Its explicit goal was to "establish new commercial relations with those African chiefs and powers within whose dominions" both the internal and external slave trade was still carried on. The goal was to replace the slave trade with legitimate commerce. The

32. Andrew Walls, "The Legacy of Thomas Fowell Buxton," *International Bulletin of Missionary Research* 15, no. 2 (April 1991): 75.
33. Thomas Fowell Buxton, *The African Slave Trade and Its Remedy* (London: John Murray, 1840), 511–12.

SIDEBAR 8.3

Thomas Fowell Buxton, *The African Slave Trade and Its Remedy* (1840)

The hope, therefore, of effecting Africa's civilization, and of inducing her tribes to relinquish the trade in man, is, without this assistance [Christianity], utterly vain. This mighty lever, when properly applied, can alone overturn the iniquitous systems which prevail throughout the continent. Let missionaries and schoolmasters, the plow and the spade, go together and agriculture will flourish; the avenues to legitimate commerce will be opened, confidence between man and man will be inspired, whilst civilization will advance as the natural effect, and Christianity operate as the proximate cause of this happy change. If, indeed, it is true that such effects will follow in the train of religion, and that Christianity alone can effect such changes, then we must pause before we take a single step without it. . . . One part of our national debt to Africa has already been acknowledged by the emancipation of our colonial slaves. There remains yet, however, a larger debt uncancelled—that of restitution to Africa itself. . . . I can form no conception of a stronger argument in favor of carrying thither civilization and Christianity, than the existence of the Slave Trade itself. . . . It is the duty of the people of this empire to take up the cause upon Christian grounds, as a measure of atonement for the injuries we have done to her, as the only means now of making restitution to her.

Source: Thomas Fowell Buxton, *The African Slave Trade and Its Remedy* (London: John Murray, 1840), 511–12.

expedition consisted of 145 Europeans, some of whom were scientists, commercial agents, government officials authorized to make treaties, members of the Agricultural Society commissioned to establish model farms, and two CMS missionaries: German linguist J. F. Schön and African recaptive Samuel Ajayi Crowther. Unfortunately, the expedition achieved but few of its objectives. The farms failed, no mission stations were established, and 130 of the Europeans contracted malaria, 42 of whom died. The chief lesson learned from the expedition was that the evangelization of Africa must be accomplished by her native sons and daughters and not Europeans. The disastrous outcome of the 1841 Niger Expedition "produced dramatic shifts in CMS policy," specifically "a new focus on African agency."[34]

34. Hanciles, *Euthanasia of a Mission*, 19, 21; Sanneh, *Abolitionists Abroad*, 150–51.

The failure of the Niger Expedition soured the British government on Buxton's Africa policy. That was not the case for most mid-nineteenth-century missions to Africa, which continued to espouse the principles of Christianity, commerce, and civilization. Renowned Scottish missionary David Livingstone (1813–73) embodied Buxton's principles for a new generation. Livingstone was born in the mill town of Blantyre, Scotland, to a devout but impoverished family. After an evangelical experience of conversion, twenty-one-year-old Livingstone read an appeal by China missionary Karl Gützlaff for medical missionaries for China. In response to that appeal, Livingstone entered medical school in 1836 in Glasgow, where he also studied Greek at the University of Glasgow and theology at the congregational church. Since China was closed to missionaries due to the Opium Wars, he applied and was accepted for missionary service with the LMS in southern Africa, where he arrived in 1841. Livingstone established a mission station in Mobatsa in 1843. Later, he pursued ministry among the Bakuena, where in 1848 he made his only known convert, the Bakuena king, Sechele. Livingstone was anything but a "traditional" missionary. He chafed under the restraints of a settled missionary existence.

Livingstone's entire missionary career is best defined by antislavery ideology and adherence to Buxton's principles of Christianity, commerce, and civilization. The Scottish missionary was convinced that the evangelization of Africa could only succeed with the destruction of the slave trade, and the key to its destruction was commerce. On December 4, 1857, Livingstone gave a famous clarion call for Christianity and commerce at the University of Cambridge. "I go back to Africa to try to make an open path for commerce and Christianity. Do you carry out the work which I have begun?" he challenged his contemporaries.[35] An open path for commerce, in Livingstone's view, necessarily required geographic exploration of the interior of Africa. Therefore, in 1857 he resigned from the LMS to pursue with less restraint his explorations of southern and central Africa, which he had already begun in 1852. Like Buxton, Livingstone believed that rivers were the ideal commercial highways from the interior of the continent to its coasts. Many of his explorations, including his ill-conceived, poorly executed, and unsuccessful Zambezi Expedition (1858–64), were vain searches for navigable waterways that could support viable trade with Western countries. Livingstone logged more than thirty thousand miles in his explorations, all the while documenting for his Western partners the extent of the slave trade. Most modern assessments of Livingstone note his many failures as a missionary and an explorer. His great

35. Andrew Walls, "The Legacy of David Livingstone," *International Bulletin of Missionary Research* 11, no. 3 (July 1987): 126.

"legacy," however, was "'to revive the commitment both to anti-slavery and to commerce' in late nineteenth century missionary work."[36]

Christianity and civilization, when combined with the essential element of commerce, was a mid-nineteenth-century attempt to eliminate the systemic social injustice of slavery and the slave trade in Africa. It was thus an early attempt at "holistic mission," although that was a term that neither Buxton nor Livingstone would know or use. The three Cs, as conceived by their mid-century advocates, were clearly linked to humanitarian (antislavery) and evangelical ideals. That would change in the last quarter of the century, "when the abolition of slavery was no longer a political concern." Then, "the entire argument [of Christianity and commerce] would be turned on its head and used to underpin European empire-building."[37] This was not Buxton's intention in the mid-nineteenth century. He made clear in *The African Slave Trade* that Western commercial countries were called to "raise up Africa—not to divide her broad territory amongst them, nor to enslave her people, but to elevate her [Africa] into something like an equality with themselves for their reciprocal benefit."[38]

The Early Ministry of the Universities Mission to Central Africa

The Universities Mission to Central Africa (UMCA) was founded in 1859 in response to lectures given by David Livingstone at Cambridge University two years prior. On that occasion, Livingstone challenged the Church of England to send missionaries to Africa who had been educated at Oxford or Cambridge (hence the name Universities Mission). UMCA mission personnel belonged to the high church, Anglo-Catholic wing of the Anglican Church and served under the leadership of a missionary bishop, who had considerable authority to develop his own distinctive strategies. The initial goal of the mission reflected Livingstone's emphases: to "establish . . . centers of Christianity and civilization, for the promotion of true religion, the encouragement of lawful commerce, and the ultimate extinction of the slave trade."[39]

The original goals of civilization and commerce, however, were soon given considerably less prominence by the UMCA, although the focus on antislavery remained strong. The first UMCA missionary bishop, Charles Mackenzie, and

---

36. Shaw, *Kingdom of God in Africa*, 170.
37. Hanciles, *Euthanasia of a Mission*, 17.
38. Buxton, *African Slave Trade*, 525.
39. Henry Rowley, *The Story of Universities' Mission to Central Africa from Its Commencement under Bishop Mackenzie, to Its Withdrawal from the Zambesi* (London: Saunders, Otley, 1866), 1.

three other mission colleagues succumbed to tropical diseases in the Zambezi region of East Africa in 1862–63. William G. Tozer was soon appointed as Mackenzie's episcopal successor (bishop, 1863–73). Tozer had already begun to entertain doubts about a "civilizing mission," even before he and fellow missionary Dr. Edward Steere moved the mission's base of operations in 1864 to a healthier location—the island of Zanzibar, off the coast of present-day Tanzania. By 1873, Tozer was convinced that the "aim" of Christian missionaries was "to Christianize the people—in other words, to save their souls."[40] Civilizing goals were subsidiary and must serve the greater purpose of evangelization.

Tozer also questioned whether English missionaries could evangelize Africa without serious risk to their lives. The recent deaths and ongoing health risks had convinced Tozer to adopt a revised mission strategy. The central tenet of the revised strategy prescribed that the "chief work of evangelization" would not be accomplished by Westerners but "must . . . be entrusted to a native ministry." "We must regard the training of native teachers . . . as a duty of primary importance," he concluded.[41] Serendipitously, a few weeks after the arrival of Tozer and Steere in Zanzibar, the sultan of Zanzibar-Oman, Majid bin Said, presented to the bishop five slave boys (aged eight to twelve) who had been recently confiscated from an Arab slave boat. Tozer was delighted to receive the freed-slave boys for two reasons: First, "as a mission dedicated to antislavery efforts, the UMCA considered it part of their calling to work among captives freed by the British."[42] Second, the ethnic backgrounds of four of the five freed slaves were from the UMCA's original target area near Lake Nyasa (today Malawi). "I look upon this acquisition as almost a providential one, giving us work just when we wanted it," Tozer enthused.[43] The five ex-slaves (along with three converts through the CMS) formed the core of the new school established by Tozer in September 1864 in Zanzibar to train African teachers. All of the freed slaves had converted and been baptized. In addition, four of the five "declared themselves desirous of becoming missionaries" on the African mainland and were "chosen as capable" by the mission for the further educational and ministry training it required.[44] Thus Tozer's aim to

---

40. *Report of the Universities' Mission to Central Africa* (London: The Mission, 1873), 11.

41. William G. Tozer, *Letters of Bishop Tozer*, ed. Gertrude Ward and Helen Tozer (London: UMCA, 1902), 86, 98.

42. Anne Marie Stoner-Eby, "African Leaders Engage Mission Christianity: Anglicans in Tanzania, 1876–1926" (PhD diss., University of Pennsylvania, 2003), 35.

43. Tozer, *Letters of Bishop Tozer*, 81.

44. Edward Steere, *Central African Mission: Its Present State and Prospects* (London: Rivington, 1873), 17. See also Alice T. Ott, "The 'Faithful Deacon' and the 'Good Layman': The First Converts of the UMCA and Their Responses to Mission Christianity," *Studies in World Christianity* 24, no. 2 (2018): 135–56.

utilize native-born teachers to evangelize East Africa and central Africa found a ready-made group of potential missionaries in the freed-slave population.

In the first two decades of the UMCA ministry, the majority of African teachers, missionaries, and clergy (reader, deacon, or priest) were freed slaves educated at the Kiungani boys' school in Zanzibar. Their role as teachers and missionaries in the Ruvuma region of present-day southeastern Tanzania remained crucial until at least 1897. Starting in the 1880s, however, there was a notable shift in the student population at Kiungani. Rather than freed slaves, many students who later became teachers and clergy were freeborn African converts from the Ruvuma district, a considerable number of whom were the progeny of chiefs.[45] This change reflected the laudable growth of local converts within the UMCA, as well as the growing conviction that freeborn Africans were better suited than freed slaves to serve as missionaries on the African mainland.

Tozer, as well as Steere, who succeeded the former as bishop in 1874, had long regarded Africans as the best qualified to reach their own people for the following reasons: they had "no new language to acquire"; they did not need to be acclimated to the climate; and they were familiar with the "modes of life" and the "habits and customs" they would encounter.[46] Experience proved that the freed slaves did not have the qualifications the bishops assumed and were therefore less effective evangelists than anticipated. Most of them had been enslaved as children, had lost their mother tongue, and were dependent on communication in Swahili. African missionaries also experienced significant bouts of illness on the mainland, although less frequently than their English colleagues. Finally, the bishops were naive to discount the considerable cultural differences between the various ethnic groups on the mainland. The relative lack of cultural competency of the freed-slave missionaries was exacerbated by the fact that a number of them had studied for a time in England and developed a taste for "all things English."[47] In contrast, local freeborn converts were, for the most part, intimately acquainted with the language and culture. They were embedded in kinship groups, which proved very significant in the spread of the gospel. And finally, some ethnic groups among whom the UMCA ministered, such as the Bondei people in the Usambara region of northeastern Tanzania, generally viewed freed slaves negatively. They preferred higher-status English missionaries, or at least freeborn Africans, rather than freed-slave workers. Beginning in the 1880s, ex-slave workers were increasingly

45. Stoner-Eby, "African Leaders," 120, 132–34, 140, 243.
46. Tozer, *Letters of Bishop Tozer*, 188–89; and R. M. Heanley, *A Memoir of Edward Steere* (London: George Bell, 1888), 245.
47. Tozer, *Letters of Bishop Tozer*, 137.

marginalized by UMCA leadership in favor of freeborn African missionaries, who were often better received and more effective.

One other UMCA mission policy influenced by its antislavery ideology was the formation of freed-slave colonies as a safe haven for slaves rescued from Arab slave boats by the East Africa Squadron of the British Navy. The slave market on Zanzibar was the center of the East African slave trade. Yearly, thousands of captives from the interior of Africa were sold into slavery there. In 1873 the British pressured Sultan Barghash to sign a treaty that forbade the transport of slaves by sea from mainland coastal towns to Zanzibar. Nevertheless, the illegal transport of captives and the slave trade continued unabated. That same year, Bishop Steere reiterated that it was "the duty of this Mission to be ready to give all such help as the men and money at its command may allow to any and every scheme for the benefit of the slave, and released slaves."[48] This duty stemmed from their concern to make reparation for the slave trade.

To this end, Steere established the Mbweni freed-slave colony in early 1874 on land purchased by the UMCA a few miles outside Zanzibar Town. The "Christian village" at Mbweni was created on the model of a similar colony founded six years prior by the Roman Catholic Holy Ghost Fathers in Baga-moyo on the east coast of Tanzania. The Mbweni colony grew rapidly from twenty inhabitants in 1874 to over 140 by 1876 and was soon at capacity. Therefore, Steere decided in 1875 to establish a similar settlement on the mainland near Lake Nyasa, David Livingstone's preferred location for UMCA ministry. This new settlement would achieve two goals: it would return some freed slaves to their former homeland, and it would allow Mbweni to accept more freed slaves. Steere, in line with the UMCA's antislavery concerns, viewed the repatriation of ex-slaves as a "great and glorious work."[49]

Fifty-five Nyasa freed slaves from Mbweni were chosen to spearhead this repatriation effort at the freed-slave colony at Masasi. All of them were up-right of character and desired to relocate, although very few of them were Christian converts when they left Zanzibar. At Masasi the UMCA revived Livingstone's goal to establish centers of Christianity, lawful commerce, and civilization, despite the disastrous results of a previous similar attempt in the Zambezi region. The UMCA's hope that the colonists, numbering 157 in 1881, would evangelize the largely traditional religionists of the area did not come to fruition. Rather, during the first six years of the settlement, evange-listic work focused on converting the freed slaves themselves, about half of

48. Stoner-Eby, "African Leaders," 36.
49. Stoner-Eby, "African Leaders," 71.

whom remained resistant to the gospel. The English missionaries expended much time and energy at Masasi developing the trappings of civilization—stone buildings, agriculture, husbandry, industrial arts, and a functioning government—to the detriment of the evangelization of Masasi's neighboring Yao-speaking villages. In September 1882, a large contingent of Magwang wara warriors attacked the village of Masasi, killed seven settlers, held others for ransom, burned several houses, and seized the village livestock and other goods. This attack dealt a death blow to the Masasi freed-slave colony. In 1884 the UMCA Synod passed a resolution that the UMCA would no longer receive adult freed slaves, nor again establish any freed-slave colonies on the mainland.[50] The mission got out of the business of creating freed-slave colonies, in large part because they entangled them in "civilizing" structures and the governance of villagers. Henceforth, at the Mbweni settlement and elsewhere, their role would be merely pastoral and evangelistic.

The mission policy of the UMCA evolved over time. Tozer early distanced himself from Livingstone's Christianity, commerce, and civilization approach, only to have the civilization aspect temporarily revived at Masasi during the tenure of Bishop Steere. The Magwangwara attack at Masasi served to refocus attention back on Tozer's primary goal of evangelization. Despite its ongoing commitment to antislavery, experience led the UMCA to disassociate itself from freed-slave colonies and even freed-slave missionaries. In the mid-1890s, roughly at the same time as the effective imposition of colonialism in East Africa, two missionary bishops of the UMCA, Dr. John Hine and Frank Weston, began to advocate slowing the process of ordaining African clergy until more European missionaries could be recruited to supervise them.[51] This was a partial reversal of Tozer's earlier policy that indigenous teachers should evangelize Africa. It was also evidence of reduced trust in African Christian workers.

In conclusion, many British evangelicals of the abolitionist movement were concerned not only with the elimination of the slave trade and the emancipation of slaves but also with mission. Not only did missions to the African continent become a new geographical focus for British evangelicals as a result of their abolitionist convictions, but these missions were motivated by a humanitarian desire to eliminate all vestiges of slavery as well as a compulsion to make restitution for British complicity in the slave trade. Antislavery ideology permeated the ministry focus of two of the major British missions to Africa during the nineteenth century, the CMS and the UMCA. Both of these missions intentionally pursued mission among freed slaves rescued by the British Navy

---

50. Stoner-Eby, "African Leaders," 104.
51. Andrew Porter, *Religion versus Empire? British Protestant Missionaries and Overseas Expansion, 1700–1914* (Manchester: Manchester University Press, 2004), 289.

patrolling the coasts of West and East Africa. For the CMS, ministry focus on Liberated Africans occurred after the slave trade interrupted its earlier mission among the Susu people. While the CMS gave higher priority to education in its ministry to the freed slaves, a civilizing goal, in reality its evangelistic goal was also achieved to a remarkable degree. The UMCA under bishops Tozer and Steere also focused its ministry on freed slaves rescued by the British Navy. The freed slaves were educated, and those who desired and were capable were trained to serve as missionaries on the African mainland. Unlike the CMS, the UMCA got into the business of forming freed-slave colonies for a time. The UMCA had been founded on Livingstone's conception of the triad of Christianity, commerce, and civilization. Nevertheless, the civilizing goal was for the most part subordinated to the evangelizing goal. Commerce, the third element of the triad, was not promoted consistently by either the CMS or the UMCA.

We end this chapter with a thanksgiving prayer on the occasion of the abolition of the slave trade in 1807. It was written by Absalom Jones (1746–1818), an ex-slave and ordained pastor of the African Episcopal Church of St. Thomas in Philadelphia.

> Oh, God of all nations upon the earth! We thank you, that you are no respecter of persons, and that you have made of one blood all nations of men. We thank you, that you have appeared, in the fullness of time, on behalf of the nation from which most of the worshiping people now before you [members of the African Episcopal Church], are descended. We thank you, that the sun of righteousness has at last shed morning beams upon them.
>
> Rend your heavens, O Lord, and come down upon the earth. . . . Send your gospel, we beseech you, among them. May the [African] nations, which now sit in darkness, behold and rejoice in its light.
>
> May Ethiopia soon stretch out her hands unto you, and lay hold of the gracious promise of your everlasting covenant. Destroy, we beseech you, all the false religions which now prevail among them; and grant, that they may soon cast their idols, to the moles and the bats of the wilderness.
>
> O, hasten that glorious time, when the knowledge of the gospel of Jesus Christ, shall cover the earth, as the waters cover the sea. . . .
>
> We pray, O God, for all our friends and benefactors in Great Britain, as well as in the United States: reward them, we beseech you, with blessings upon earth, and prepare them to enjoy the fruits of their kindness to us, in your everlasting kingdom in heaven; and dispose us, who are assembled in your presence, to be always thankful for your mercies, and to act as becomes a people who owe so much to your goodness.[52]

52. Christopher L. Webber, ed., *Give Us Grace: An Anthology of Anglican Prayers* (Harrisburg, PA: Morehouse, 2004), 198 (modernized).

Empowering Indigenous Churches

Henry Venn and Three-Self Theory (1841)

> Let me now urge on you a claim,
> The claim of Christ whom you should know,
> And though you do not know Him yet,
> His instant, urgent claim I press.
> His very name you do not know, so let me tell you who He is:
> No foreigner's ancestor He, nor Westerner's exalted saint,
> But God's own Son come down from heaven
> To bear man's guilt and pay its price.
> O ye who should revere His name, come trust Him now
>   to bear your sins;
> For they who put their trust in Him, have endless life and joy
>   in heaven.[1]

In 1841, Henry Venn was appointed the honorary secretary of the Church Missionary Society (CMS), a position he held until his retirement in 1872. The term "secretary" should not deceive us. Henry Venn was the virtual

---

1. This hymn, "A Song of Christ's Claims," was written by Xi Shengmo (1835–96), a former opium addict who became a Chinese evangelist, pastor, hymn composer, and founder of opium refuges. He collaborated with the ministry of Hudson Taylor's China Inland Mission. See *The Songs of Pastor Hsi*, trans. Francesca French (London: CIM, 1920), 17.

director of the CMS, although his secretaryship was "honorary" or unsalaried. He was the oldest surviving son of the Reverend John Venn, the Anglican rector at Clapham and early member of the Clapham Sect and the CMS, whom we met in chapter 8. Henry had not only impeccable evangelical credentials but also intimate knowledge of the CMS from his earliest days. Venn's tenure as head of the CMS distinguished him "as the most influential mission administrator and strategic thinker of his age."[2] The "chief work of his official life" was "his careful and prolonged labors for the organization of Native Churches" until they gradually became "in his own phraseology, self-supporting, self-governing, and self-extending."[3] Henry Venn crafted mission theory that aimed to develop independent and indigenous native churches by means of the "three selfs," as his approach came to be known. Venn's mission theorizing was groundbreaking, since prior to the 1840s, there was little strategic, missiological reflection on how to achieve the ultimate goal of missionary work—a culturally appropriate and independent national church. This is not to imply that all such reflection was entirely absent from deliberations by early Protestant mission leaders. Already at the very beginning of the modern missionary movement, William Carey and his colleagues Joshua Marshman and William Ward expressed three-self theory in incipient form in points VII and VIII of the 1805 Serampore Covenant (see chap. 7). Later, in 1817, Josiah Pratt, the second secretary of the CMS (1802–24), published an article in the CMS journal *Missionary Register* in which he advocates that native churches should assume the lion's share of financial responsibility (self-support) and utilize primarily native teachers and evangelists (self-governance and self-extension).[4] Furthermore, despite the lack of a fully developed mission theory, the Karen church in Burma put into practice three-self principles largely of its own volition beginning in the 1830s. Such early theorizing, however, did not reach its "mature form and become a dominant mission strategy" until the middle decades of the nineteenth century, simultaneous with the beginning of Venn's tenure as CMS secretary.[5]

There were reasons for the lack of early mission strategizing. During the first two generations of the Protestant mission movement, early missionaries in pioneering situations were occupied with more rudimentary matters. Mission

2. Andrew Porter, *Religion versus Empire? British Protestant Missionaries and Overseas Expansion, 1700–1914* (Manchester: Manchester University Press, 2004), 167; cf. Eugene Stock, *The History of the Church Missionary Society* (London: CMS, 1899), 67.

3. William Knight, *Memoir of the Rev. H. Venn* (London: Longmans, Green, 1880), 276.

4. Josiah Pratt, "Introductory Remarks," *Missionary Register* (January 1817): 5–6, available at https://archive.org/stream/1817CMSMissionaryRegister/1817_CMS_Missionary_Register.

5. Jehu Hanciles, *Euthanasia of a Mission: African Church Autonomy in a Colonial Context* (Westport, CT: Praeger, 2002), 25.

societies were focused on developing their own organizational structures and networks of support. Training schools for mission personnel stressed practical preparation rather than theoretical strategies. It was only after 1840 that the Protestant mission movement had developed and matured enough to enable certain mission leaders to reflect on their past field experience and to formulate strategic and systematic goals. Henry Venn of the CMS in Great Britain and Rufus Anderson of the American Board of Commissioners for Foreign Missions (ABCFM) in the United States became the key theorists of three-self principles in the mid-nineteenth century. These two men articulated remarkably similar three-self theories virtually simultaneously, although independently of each other, in response to similar experiences on their respective mission fields.[6]

There were reasons why mission theory not only failed to develop extensively before the 1840s; there were also two key reasons why it progressed rapidly after that date. The CMS and the ABCFM faced comparable pressures around 1840 for which the three selves were an attractive solution. First, both mission societies faced a shortage of funds. The CMS had developed more programs on its various fields than could be covered by its monetary resources. The Panic of 1837 plunged the United States into a financial depression that resulted in fundraising shortfalls for the ABCFM. An obvious solution to the inadequate finances of the two missionary societies was for native churches to bear a larger proportion of incurred expenses. Self-support "was essentially a product of exigency and self-preservation" designed to solve "the [Church Missionary] Society's financial predicament." It became the "centerpiece of Venn's new [three-self] scheme."[7] Second, both societies faced a dearth of missionary candidates. The CMS had difficulty from the outset recruiting ordained English missionaries and was forced in the first decades to rely on German Lutherans. The high mortality rate of CMS missionaries in West Africa exacerbated the problem. Furthermore, "popular enthusiasm for missions" and for a missionary career waned in the 1830s on both sides of the Atlantic. The difficulty of recruiting missionaries "accounts for much of the zeal to raise up a native agency through schools."[8] Not only were native teachers and catechists cheaper than Western missionaries, but they were also inured to the climate and considerably more effective.

Both Henry Venn and Rufus Anderson deserve credit as the primary theorists of three-self principles in the mid-nineteenth century. This chapter,

6. Hanciles, *Euthanasia of a Mission*; 25; Porter, *Religion versus Empire?*, 164–66.
7. Hanciles, *Euthanasia of a Mission*, 16, 26.
8. Paul William Harris, *Nothing but Christ: Rufus Anderson and the Ideology of Protestant Foreign Missions* (Oxford: Oxford University Press, 1999), 60–62.

however, will focus on the legacy of Henry Venn for several reasons. First, Venn was "the most articulate and systematic exponent of [three-self] ideas." He wrote a series of three highly influential policy papers (1851, 1861, 1866) on the development of an independent indigenous church that advanced "the accepted wisdom of the day to a more developed and worked out stage than anyone else had achieved hitherto."[9] Second, Venn's views influenced not only the CMS but other British mission societies, such as the China Inland Mission, as well. Venn's influence likewise spread beyond missionary circles and into the British public sphere. In conjunction with the humanitarian evangelical lobby in England, Venn "exercised great influence in [the] British colonial" arena and exerted a "powerful impact on African affairs," as well as on India.[10] This influence far outstripped that of Rufus Anderson and the ABCFM in the United States. Finally, Venn implemented his three-self theories in the Sierra Leone Native Pastorate of 1861. Although this effort was ultimately unsuccessful, it was the earliest and most radical attempt to invest a native church with "a substantial degree of independence."[11] The development of three-self principles for the advance of an independent and indigenous native church was a turning point in the history of the expansion of Christianity, and Henry Venn was its most important advocate. Never before had a mission leader reflected on indigenizing principles so deeply, articulated them so clearly, and put them into practice so resolutely as did the CMS leader. Venn began a development that over time enabled and empowered mission-founded national churches to become independent and equal partners in the Christian global community of faith.

In this chapter, I will first unpack the development of Venn's three-self principles as outlined in his three policy papers and briefly discuss their implementation in West Africa in the Yoruba and Niger Missions and the Sierra Leone Native Pastorate. I will address the issue of why the Native Pastorate was unsuccessful at some length. In a second section, I will describe the formation of the China Inland Mission (CIM) by Hudson Taylor and discuss the extent to which this highly influential faith mission employed three-self principles. Despite its early adoption of some indigenous principles, the CIM, like many other Protestant missions, failed to fully promote the three selfs during the nineteenth century. Finally, we end with John Nevius's adaptation

9. Peter Williams, "'Not Transplanting': Henry Venn's Strategic Vision," in *The Church Missionary Society and World Christianity 1799–1999*, ed. Kevin Ward and Brian Stanley (Grand Rapids: Eerdmans, 2000), 148, 157.

10. Wilbert R. Shenk, *Henry Venn: Missionary Statesman* (Eugene, OR: Wipf & Stock, 2006), xi–xii.

11. Williams, "Venn's Strategic Vision," 157.

of three-self theory to the Chinese context and its successful transplantation to the Korean peninsula. The Nevius Plan in Korea was the most effective implementation of three-self principles in the nineteenth century and a key factor in the rapid growth of Christianity there.

The Three-Self Theory of Henry Venn and Its Implementation

Henry Venn was well aware when he assumed the role of CMS honorary secretary that the beginnings of the mission movement were over and that a new era tasked with the identification and implementation of fundamental mission strategies had begun. In 1852 he freely admitted this to CMS Nigeria missionary Henry Townsend: "The fact is we are only beginning . . . to understand the true principles of Mission work," he wrote. Venn reiterated the sentiment to Rufus Anderson in 1854: "The present era is one for the development of Missionary principles in action," and would continue to be so for some time. In his October 1859 "Instructions to Missionaries," Venn notes that

> Missionary Societies were still in the era of the investigation of first principles; [and] that it would be some time yet before the great societies would have ascertained the most effective modes of missionary operations, the right organization of the native churches, and various other fundamental missionary principles.[12]

Venn was cognizant that the era in which he served was one of groundbreaking mission theorizing.

The CMS honorary secretary brought a broad range of resources to bear on the distillation and formation of mission policy. He carefully studied not only the mission approaches of eighteenth-century Moravian missionaries but also that of Jesuit missionary Francis Xavier, about whom he wrote an expansive three-hundred-page book. Venn acquainted himself thoroughly with the former policies of the CMS by scouring early documents. He devoured contemporary publications of other mission societies and corresponded with mission leaders such as Rufus Anderson of the ABCFM and Wilhelm Hoffmann of the Basel Mission. Finally, he required CMS missionaries to regularly submit honest and detailed written reports, which he read and utilized in the formation of policy.[13] One thing that Venn did not do was visit any CMS mission field personally during his tenure as honorary secretary. He relied instead

12. Wilbert R. Shenk, "The Contribution of Henry Venn to Mission Thought," *Anvil* 2, no. 1 (1985): 29.
13. Shenk, "Contribution of Henry Venn," 32–33.

SIDEBAR 9.1

Henry Venn, "The Employment and Ordination of Native Teachers," 1851

Regarding the ultimate object of a mission, viewed under its ecclesiastical result, to be the settlement of a native Church under native pastors upon a self-supporting system, it should be borne in mind that the progress of a mission depends upon the training up and location of native pastors; and that, as it has been happily expressed, the "euthanasia of a mission" takes place when a missionary, surrounded by well-trained native congregations under native pastors, is able to resign all pastoral work into their hands, and gradually relax his superintendence over the pastors themselves, till it insensibly ceases; and so the mission passes into a settled Christian community.

Source: Wilbert R. Shenk, *Henry Venn: Missionary Statesman*
(Eugene, OR: Wipf & Stock, 2006), 119–20.

on written reports and personal conversations with national Christians and missionaries on furlough.

Venn's three-self theory developed gradually and incrementally. In 1841 the newly appointed honorary secretary faced his first crisis: the CMS was strapped financially. In his first major policy decision (December 1841), he informed the field missionaries that they needed to encourage and develop local sources of revenue rather than rely on CMS funds. "Native Converts should be habituated to the idea, that the support of a Native Ministry must eventually fall upon themselves," he wrote.[14] Self-support by native churches was thus the first aspect to be addressed of the three-self triad, which also included self-governance and self-extension (or self-propagation). Venn was realistic enough to recognize that self-support by native churches was a goal that would require time to achieve. He also realized, as the quote above indicates, that self-support could not be separated from the formation of a native, indigenous ministry. Venn reported in 1846 to a meeting of clergy in the London suburb of Islington: "The Church Missionary Society has long given its most earnest attention and most strenuous support to plans for preparing and educating a Native Ministry, and for introducing a self-supporting principle into the Native Churches."[15]

14. Shenk, "Contribution of Henry Venn," 35; see also C. Peter Williams, *The Ideal of the Self-Governing Church: A Study in Victorian Missionary Strategy* (Leiden: Brill, 1990), 3–4.
15. Shenk, "Contribution of Venn," 36.

Venn's first official policy paper, penned in 1851, was titled "The Employment and Ordination of Native Teachers" (see sidebar 9.1). In it Venn draws a clear distinction between the role of Western missionaries and that of native teachers. The former were tasked with pioneer missionary work—evangelistic preaching to the unconverted, and the instruction of "inquirers" and "recent converts." In contrast, "as soon as settled congregations [were] formed, such pastoral care should be devolved upon native teachers." Native teachers were chosen from the ranks of the converts and "trained up" for the ministry. Those who had proven their ability to teach were first appointed to the office of catechist. Catechists evangelized the local population and ministered to congregations until they were provided with an ordained native pastor. The "ultimate object of a mission" was "the settlement of a native Church under native pastors upon a self-supporting system." Venn refers to this goal as the "euthanasia" (or happy death) of a mission. It occurred when the missionary was able to "resign all pastoral work" to native pastors and "gradually relax his superintendence over the pastors" until it completely ceased and the mission became an independent native church.[16]

In the first decade and a half of his administration, Venn was convinced that native pastors must be under European superintendence "for both financial and moral reasons."[17] Since the CMS was still providing some salaries and subsidies, it insisted on control of its investment. It was also concerned that educational and moral standards for native clergy be preserved. This approach of native ministry under European superintendence was evident in the CMS Yoruba Mission. The Yoruba Mission was inaugurated at the request of Sierra Leone recaptives of Yoruba ethnicity (see chap. 8), hundreds of whom had already resettled in their former homeland in western Nigeria between 1839 and 1842. They urgently pleaded that missionaries "come and provide Christian ministrations for them and teaching for the Heathen population."[18] In response, the CMS sent a large missionary party to Abeokuta, Nigeria, in 1845. Two European missionaries (British Henry Townsend and German C. A. Gollmer) supervised the large mission group of Christian Sierra Leoneans, who formed part of the contingent. The Yoruba Mission was distinctive in that Christian recaptives of Yoruba descent not only formed the nucleus of the church in Abeokuta; they also contributed significantly to local and regional missionary efforts. Mark Shaw notes:

Christianity was brought to the Yoruba by other Yoruba, returning exiles who had suffered much but who had found the Christian God an unequaled help

16. Shenk, *Henry Venn*, 118–20; see also Williams, *Ideal of the Self-Governing Church*, 5–9.
17. Shenk, *Henry Venn*, 43.
18. Hanciles, *Euthanasia of a Mission*, 28–29.

through their hardships. The foreignness of the Gospel was thus minimal, and its incarnation in a Christian community composed of their own kin proved too powerful a witness for the Yoruba to resist long.[19]

The spread of the gospel in Yorubaland was accomplished primarily through the ministry of native clergy and laymen, not European missionaries.

Samuel Ajayi Crowther (ca. 1807–91) was the most prominent African member of the Yoruba Mission. Crowther was born in Osogun to the Egba branch of the Yoruba people. At age thirteen, he was taken captive by Fulani and Yoruba Muslim traders. After serving as a domestic slave for several years in Abeokuta, in 1822 he was sold to Portuguese slave traders and was on his way to the Americas when the slave ship was intercepted by the West Africa Squadron of the British Royal Navy. He was freed in Sierra Leone and educated by the CMS. His participation in the 1841 Niger expedition convinced Venn of his abilities. In 1843 he was ordained an Anglican priest in England, prior to partnering with Townsend and Gollmer in the leadership of the Yoruba Mission.

In 1857 Venn launched a second mission in West Africa along the Niger River at Onitsha and its environs. The Niger Mission was decidedly different from the Yoruba Mission. By the mid-1850s, Venn had observed the ugly face of missionary paternalism frequently enough to convince himself that European superintendence of native clergy should be replaced with a "mutuality in relationship and equality in status. Experience had changed Venn's mind substantially" from the stance he espoused in the 1851 policy paper.[20] The Niger Mission embodied Venn's vision for a self-supporting, self-governing, and self-propagating native ministry. From the outset, Samuel Crowther had complete oversight of the Niger Mission—the ministry was self-governing. It was also a compelling example of self-propagation. The mission was staffed entirely by first- and second-generation Sierra Leonean Christians. Unlike the Yoruba Mission, the African missionaries of the Niger Mission served in a genuinely cross-cultural capacity in predominately Muslim territory. This required the African staff to learn previously unknown languages and customs. Their "record of translation and publication is remarkable." By 1888 Crowther and other African missionaries had translated portions of Scripture, the catechism, and hymns into the main dialects of the Niger (including Igbo and Idzo). Furthermore, the Niger Mission under Crowther's leadership represented the "first sustained missionary engagement with Afri-

19. Mark Shaw, *The Kingdom of God in Africa: A Short History of African Christianity* (Grand Rapids: Baker, 1996), 145.
20. Shenk, *Henry Venn*, 43.

SIDEBAR 9.2

Henry Venn, "The Organization of Native Churches" (1861)

The missionary, whose labours are blest to the ingathering of converts, naturally desires to keep his converts under his own charge, to minister to them as pastor, and to rule them as a native congregation. . . .

The evil incident to this system is threefold:

(1) In respect to the missionary: his hands soon become so full that his time and energy are wholly occupied by converts, and he extends his personal labours to the heathen in a continually decreasing ratio. . . . The character of the simple Missionary is complicated with that of the director and paymaster of the Mission.

(2) In respect to the converts: they naturally imbibe the notion that all is to be done for them—they are dependents upon a foreign Mission, rather than members of a native Church. . . . The principles of self-support, self-government and self-extension are wanting; on which depend the breath of life in a native church.

(3) In respect of the Missionary Society: the system entails a vast and increasing expense in its oldest Missions; so that instead of advancing to "the regions beyond," it is detained upon old ground.

Source: Wilbert R. Shenk, *Henry Venn: Missionary Statesman*
(Eugene, OR: Wipf & Stock, 2006), 120–21.

can Islam in modern times" and "one of the most notable periods of Christian expansion on the African continent."[21] The Niger Mission, however, was only partially self-supporting. Crowther himself was supported by the CMS throughout his life, even after he was consecrated as the first African Anglican bishop in 1864.

Venn's second policy paper, "The Organization of Native Churches" (1861), reiterates and extends his vision from ten years earlier with concrete, practical suggestions for its implementation. In this paper, Venn restricts European superintendence over native converts and pastors to the early stages of the development of a native church (see sidebar 9.2). Otherwise, if the missionary, "instead of advancing to 'the regions beyond,' . . . is detained [too long] upon old ground," the native church will fail to develop along three-self principles. An unhealthy dependence by native converts on the missionary and

---

21. Hanciles, *Euthanasia of a Mission*, 30, 33; Shenk, *Henry Venn*, 76.

mission society will develop, whereby they rely wholly on mission finances and passively "imbibe the notion that all is to be done for them."[22]

The second half of Venn's policy paper explains how these unhealthy outcomes are to be avoided. First and foremost, it was "expedient that native converts should be trained, at as early a stage as possible, upon a system of self-government, and of contributing to the support of their own native Teachers." Only when principles of independence were initiated at the very first stages of development, only when they were built into the DNA of the emerging native church, could they successfully take root. The native church should develop in this fashion. First, a small group of converts were formed into "Christian Companies" for the purpose of "mutual support and encouragement." These weekly meetings for Scripture reading and prayer would be led by one of the small group members, who was selected to serve as "elder" or "headman." Thus, from the beginning, self-government was instituted. Similarly, giving to the Native Church Fund was built into the weekly meetings of companies, "be it only a handful of rice, or more as God should prosper them." The headmen of Christian Companies would meet monthly with the local CMS missionary for "spiritual counsel and encouragement." A local congregation would be formed by uniting several neighboring companies into one body. A native teacher paid from the Native Church Fund would serve the newly formed congregation as pastor. Several congregations would be formed into a Native Pastorate under an ordained native pastor, also paid by the Native Church Fund. When a sufficient number of Native Pastorates had been formed, "foreign agency will have no further place in the work, and that district will have been fully prepared for a native episcopate."[23] For this Anglican mission, the ultimate sign of a mature, independent, and indigenous church was a Native Pastorate under an African bishop.

In 1861, Henry Venn placed nine churches in Sierra Leone under national pastors, withdrew financial support from them, and thereby established the Sierra Leone Native Pastorate. Venn viewed this occasion as a significant moment. It was, in his words, "the great experiment of modern missions, and if successful will be hailed as a triumph throughout the whole mission field."[24] Unfortunately, the first decade of the "experiment" was inauspicious. The Native Pastorate was placed under an English bishop, Edward Beckles (1860–70), not an African one. Despite Beckles's valiant efforts, he was frequently absent from the colony and often hindered by obstructionist CMS

22. Shenk, *Henry Venn*, 121.
23. Shenk, *Henry Venn*, 122–24; Williams, *Ideal of the Self-Governing Church*, 26–27.
24. Jehu J. Hanciles, "The Anatomy of an Experiment: The Sierra Leone Native Pastorate," *Missiology* 29, no. 1 (January 2001): 63.

missionaries, persistent racialism, and financial difficulties. The second European bishop in charge, Henry Cheetman (1871–81), brought energy and resourcefulness to the experiment and thus ensured the survival of the Native Pastorate. Under his watch, the remaining four Sierra Leonean churches were placed under African curates and added to the pastorate. At that time, the Sierra Leone church "became an all-African affair, with the exception of a European bishop."[25] Unfortunately, Cheetham's successor, Bishop Ernest Ingham (1883–96), disapproved of the objectives of the experiment, and during his tenure, the Native Pastorate began its slow demise. By the 1890s, Venn's ambitious scheme for an independent, indigenous African church had been all but abandoned by CMS leadership and missionaries alike.

What caused the slow demise of the Sierra Leone Native Pastorate? Why did this noble experiment, begun with such high hopes, lose its way? The death of Henry Venn in January 1873 was certainly a key factor in the waning of enthusiasm for an independent national church. The CMS honorary secretary had been the stalwart visionary and defender of three-self principles and their implementation. He was the one who countered the paternalistic and racist tendencies found all too often within the ranks of the CMS as well as in many Western missions in this era. As a child, Venn had played with Africans attending the African Institute in his home village of Clapham, England. Through that experience, he had developed a "lifelong affinity with Africa and Africans. . . . He saw Africans as equals, treated them with dignity and respect, and sought their advancement with unfailing zeal."[26] In his policy paper "On Nationality" (1868), he encouraged CMS missionaries to adopt a similar stance. They should "study the national character of the people" among whom they worked and show "utmost respect for national peculiarities." The missionaries should not transplant an English church on foreign soil but adapt church structures to the local environment and culture.[27]

Venn's cultural sensitivity was rare during his lifetime, and even more so in the decades after his death. The earlier mid-century era of humanitarianism was replaced with the high imperialist age (see chap. 10). This changed historical and intellectual context had great impact on Western Christian missions. There was a new breed of missionaries, who too often were influenced by social Darwinism and so-called scientific racism.[28] Native pastors

25. Hanciles, "Anatomy of an Experiment," 67.

26. Hanciles, *Euthanasia of a Mission*, 23, 34.

27. Williams, "Venn's Strategic Vision," 165–67; Williams, *Ideal of the Self-Governing Church*, 38–41.

28. Andrew C. Ross, "Christian Missions and Attitudes to Race," in *The Imperial Horizons of British Protestant Missions, 1880–1914*, ed. Andrew Porter (Grand Rapids: Eerdmans, 2003), 88–92.

were more frequently distrusted and their morality and work ethic called into question. In the 1880s–1890s, CMS mission leaders sought to wrest control of the West African church from the nationals by dismissing, suspending, and transferring local leaders and replacing them with European missionaries. Piece by piece, Venn's vision and legacy were dismantled in Sierra Leone. This trend was clearly seen in the persistently elusive goal of placing the Native Pastorate under an African bishop. Venn had viewed the 1864 consecration of Samuel Crowther as the first African Anglican bishop as the cornerstone of his implementation of three-self principles. However, several white CMS missionaries refused to serve under an African bishop. As a result, a compromise was struck whereby Crowther was granted authority over territory where no white missionaries served. Crowther's episcopal jurisdiction was thus not within Sierra Leone but in the undefined "countries of Western Africa beyond the Queen's dominions." Furthermore, Crowther was the first *and only* African Anglican bishop affiliated with the CMS in the nineteenth century.[29] It was not until 1937 that T. S. Johnson was appointed as the first Sierra Leonean *assistant* bishop to the Sierra Leone church.[30]

CMS historian Eugene Stock acknowledges in his massive four-volume *History of the CMS* that the "Sierra Leone Pastorate was not a fully organized Native Church; but its formation was a good first step towards that desirable *euthanasia* of the Mission."[31] Venn's vision of a self-supporting, self-governing, and self-propagating church in Sierra Leone was only partially fulfilled, and only during the first two decades of the experiment. Venn overestimated the financial capability of the Sierra Leone church. Self-support was not entirely achieved, although the majority of funds—70 percent by the 1880s—were raised by local Christians. Grants from the CMS and the Sierra Leone colonial government were needed to balance the budget of the Native Church Fund. Self-governance was also only realized in part. After 1877, all of the churches of Sierra Leone had African pastors or curates and were part of the Native Pastorate. As we have seen, Venn's policy regarding supervision of African staff by European missionaries changed over time. However, the policy remained ambivalent enough to allow intransigent missionaries to deny African clergy the respect they deserved as equal partners. Furthermore, an African bishop was not appointed until seventy-five years

29. Andrew Barnes, "Samuel Ajayi Crowther: African and Yoruba Missionary Bishop," Oxford Research Encyclopedias, February 26, 2018, https://oxfordre.com/africanhistory/view /10.1093/acrefore/9780190277734.001.0001/acrefore-9780190277734-e-278; Williams, *Ideal of the Self-Governing Church*, 29–31.

30. Hanciles, *Euthanasia of a Mission*, 256–57.

31. Eugene Stock, *The History of the Church Missionary Society* (London: CMS, 1899), 2:446.

after the launch of the Native Pastorate. Self-propagation by Sierra Leone Christians serving in the Yoruba and Niger Missions raised the expectation that similar evangelistic zeal would be exhibited within Sierra Leone. That proved not to be the case. The truth was the "CMS could have done more to develop the native church's missionary capacity." According to Venn, it was "the feebleness of our attempts to cultivate the native languages, . . . to provide versions of God's blessed volume, and to send forth native evange- lists to speak the great things of God in the vernacular languages" that led to this distressing outcome.[32]

In summation, Venn's implementation of three-self principles in the Sierra Leone Native Pastorate was only partially successful, but not because the principles themselves were misguided. The failure lay more in CMS mis- sionaries' lack of wholehearted support for the experiment, in persistent paternalism and racialism, in difficult financial realities on the ground, and in the shortcomings of some African pastors.[33]

The China Inland Mission and Three-Self Principles

By the last quarter of the nineteenth century, most Protestant missionary societies had adopted the three-self principles promoted by Henry Venn and Rufus Anderson—in theory, though often not in practice. Representative statements of missionaries at the 1877 General Conference of the Protestant Missionaries of China held in Shanghai bear witness to this fact. American Methodist Episcopal missionary S. L. Baldwin acknowledged, "That the na- tive church ought to become self-supporting at the earliest possible moment, and that it is our duty to do all in our power to bring about this result, are *propositions that none will dispute*." Similarly, Rev. Hunter Corbett of the American Presbyterian Mission noted, "It will probably be conceded that the chief work of the Missionary is to plant and establish self-governing and self-sustaining churches."[34] The question in late-nineteenth-century mission circles was not whether a self-supporting, self-governing, and self-propagating national church was the appropriate goal but how soon and in what order three-self principles should be initiated.

In this section, we will examine to what extent the China Inland Mission (CIM) embraced and implemented three-self principles. I chose the CIM as a

32. Hanciles, *Euthanasia of a Mission*, 249.

33. Hanciles, "Anatomy of an Experiment," 70, 75.

34. *Records of the General Conference of the Protestant Missionaries of China* (Shanghai: Presbyterian Mission Press, 1878), 283, 299.

case study for two reasons. First, the CIM was founded by J. Hudson Taylor in 1865, just as three-self principles were coming into vogue. This new and innovative faith mission was highly influential in the late nineteenth and early twentieth centuries. Furthermore, in the decade after Taylor's death in 1905, it achieved the notable distinction of becoming the largest Protestant mission agency in China, and later in the world. Second, the CIM is representative of the ambiguous approach toward three-self principles found in many evangelical missions of that era. The CIM also serves as a foil to the rigorous implementation of three-self principles in Korea, which will be discussed in the following section.

J. Hudson Taylor (1832–1905) was born in the town of Barnsley in Yorkshire, England. As a young man, Taylor sensed that God was calling him to serve in China. Therefore, in 1853 the then twenty-one-year-old Taylor set sail for China as a missionary with the Chinese Evangelization Society (CES), a short-lived mission organization founded by Karl Gützlaff (1803–51). Taylor settled in Shanghai, one of five treaty port cities opened to Westerners after the 1842 Opium War. From his base there, he set forth on eighteen itinerant evangelistic preaching tours in the vicinity. Also in this period, Taylor put aside his Western clothes, as Gützlaff had done previously, and donned Chinese apparel, including the traditional queue (pigtail) and shaved forehead. Four years later, Taylor and his CES colleague, Dr. William Parker, resigned from the CES to form the independent Ningpo Mission in Ningpo, a quiet treaty port 150 miles south of Shanghai. Central to Taylor's decision to leave the CES was its nonfulfillment of financial obligations to him; thereafter he resolved to "live by faith." Due to health problems, Taylor was forced to return to England for a lengthy and highly productive furlough (1860–66). During that time, he received a medical diploma from the Royal London Hospital, promoted missionary work in China in churches throughout the British Isles, and wrote the book *China's Spiritual Needs and Claims*. Taylor's most significant accomplishment, however, was the founding of the CIM.[35]

Taylor's experience with the ineffective CES had increasingly convinced him of the need for a new mission society. On June 25, 1865, Taylor recorded in his Bible that he had "prayed for 24 willing skillful workers" at Brighton beach. The following morning, he deposited £10 into a bank account for the China Inland Mission, and the organization was launched.[36] The CIM served as an early model for a new type of missionary society: the faith mission. Faith

35. J. Herbert Kane, "Legacy of J. Hudson Taylor," *International Bulletin of Missionary Research* (April 1984): 74–75.
36. Alvyn Austin, *China's Millions: The China Inland Mission and Late Qing Society, 1832–1905* (Grand Rapids: Eerdmans, 2007), 80.

missions were, according to Jeffrey Cox, a "late Victorian mission innovation" that portrayed "themselves as the cutting edge of missionary endeavor." They reacted "against the bureaucratic structures" of mission societies and the costly maintenance of Christian institutions such as mission stations and schools. They believed "that God will provide." This motto "struck a chord with a late Victorian public eager for 'the evangelization of the world in [their] generation.'"[37] As a faith mission, the CIM declared that the organization would not go into debt, that the missionaries' salaries were not guaranteed, and that mission personnel could not solicit funds (although they could and did, of course, accept donations).

The CIM was founded not long after the Treaties of Tientsin opened up the inland provinces of China to Western merchants and missionary work. The goal of the new society was to evangelize those previously unreached inland provinces, where, to quote an early CIM slogan, "a million a month . . . are dying without God." CIM publications frequently employed the image of millions of Chinese poised on the brink of eternal damnation, an image drawn from the earlier CES publication, *The Gleaner*, to which Taylor had subscribed.[38] This evangelization of inland provinces would be accomplished in large part by spiritually qualified missionary "idealists," who fell "below the educational standard expected in denominational societies." The CIM welcomed devout working-class men and single women within the ranks of its mission.[39]

Ironically, the methods Taylor employed to reach the interior of China were copied from the playbook of Karl Gützlaff and the CES, a mission he chose to leave.

> The China Inland Mission under Taylor's personal leadership was, for all practical purposes, the successor to the Chinese Evangelization Society. The emphasis on evangelizing in interior China, the rejection of denominationalism, and the reliance on God's direct guidance and support carried over to the China Inland Mission.[40]

A key method that Taylor adopted from Gützlaff, and that became the cornerstone of CIM mission strategy, was itinerant ministry with gospel proclamation. Taylor outlined this approach in a paper titled "Itineration Far and

---

37. Jeffrey Cox, *The British Missionary Enterprise since 1700* (New York: Routledge, 2008), 184.

38. Austin, *China's Millions*, 80; Jessie Gregory Lutz, *Opening China: Karl F. A. Gützlaff and Sino-Western Relations, 1827–1852* (Grand Rapids: Eerdmans, 2008), 311.

39. Cox, *British Missionary Enterprise*, 207.

40. Lutz, *Opening China*, 311.

Near as an Evangelizing Agency," which he presented at the 1877 Shanghai Missionary Conference. In his address, Taylor made a distinction between itineration and "localized and pastoral missionary work." While both were indispensable, itineration was "preliminary, for it tends to open the way for localized work." Itineration was likewise the first-century apostolic method. "Only by spending a very short time in many places could they [the apostles] within the compass of a lifetime reach the vast and needy regions in which they were to plant the Gospel." To evangelize the millions of unreached Chinese before the imminent return of Christ, rapid itineration from place to place was likewise required.[41]

The strong emphasis on pioneer work and itineration meant that the CIM during Taylor's tenure gave much less attention to church planting, pastoral work, and the development of indigenous leadership—in other words, the promotion of self-governance. In August 1867, just two years after the founding of the CIM, Taylor expressed a desire for self-governance. "We wish to see churches and Christian Chinese presided over by pastors and officers of their own countrymen," he wrote.[42] The reality was that a *concrete plan* was not developed or implemented to achieve this desire; this stands in sharp contrast to the detailed plan in Venn's 1861 policy paper discussed above. D. E. Hoste, one of the Cambridge Seven missionaries (a group of seven Cambridge students who became CIM missionaries to China) and Taylor's successor as general director of the CIM (1902–35), frankly admitted the lack of self-governance at his first CIM Annual Meeting in London.

> You are probably all aware that in the earlier days the work of this Mission was almost entirely pioneering and itinerating in the various parts of inland China . . . but what we may call pastoral work . . . was not carried on. . . . Now, however . . . we find ourselves compelled to give attention to the instruction and training of converts. . . . Pray that we may have grace in developing the gift and capacity of our Chinese fellow Christians.[43]

Hoste pledged thereafter to work toward self-governance, and during his tenure considerable strides were made.

This is not to imply that self-governance (and self-propagation) was entirely lacking in the CIM in the nineteenth century. Self-governance and self-

---

41. *Records of the General Conference*, 101–7.
42. A. J. Broomhall, *Hudson Taylor and China's Open Century* (London: Hodder and Stoughton, 1983), 4:356.
43. Phyllis Thompson, *D. E. Hoste: A Prince with God* (London: CIM, 1947), 106.

propagation evolved in two notable instances, due in large part to the independent spirit and remarkable skills of a pair of Chinese pastors. Pastor Wang Laiquan (1835–1901) had been personally mentored by Taylor in Ningpo and had accompanied him to England, where he stayed from 1860 to 1864. In 1866, he became pastor of a new church in Hangzhou. By 1871, Wang had opened four country chapels. He served the northern part of Zhejiang province as a "superintending pastor" or bishop over two ordained Chinese pastors, two evangelists, two preachers, a number of colporteurs, and a growing network of churches. By 1883, these Chinese churches had not yet achieved self-support, although a considerable amount of local funds had been raised. Pastor Xi Shengmo (ca. 1830–96) in 1886 likewise became a bishop of three districts of southern Shanxi province, and not only for Chinese workers. He also supervised a large group of CIM missionaries, including two of the famous Cambridge Seven (Stanley Smith and D. E. Hoste). He itinerated extensively and founded Christian meetings in twenty-seven villages near Pingyang. Pastor Xi was a reformed opium addict, and his principal method of evangelism was at the forty opium refuges he founded as "beachheads for mission extension."[44] Pastor Xi was also a gifted hymn writer; a portion of one of his hymns opens this chapter. These two examples point to the occasional, but successful, implementation of two of the three selfs: self-governance and self-propagation.

Taylor adopted another method from Gützlaff's playbook: his "strategy of relying on Chinese evangelists under the guidance of Western missionaries as the best hope of evangelizing all of China." However, Taylor "modified" the indigenizing strategy Gützlaff employed in the Chinese Union to include "a more prominent role for the foreign missionary and hierarchical leadership under Taylor."[45] This meant that while Chinese evangelists affiliated with the CIM did effectively propagate the gospel in the inland provinces of China, it was often not self-initiated. Rather, the majority of Chinese evangelists were both directed and paid by the CIM. This was contrary to an 1858 statement by the CMS that evangelism in the present age should reflect New Testament practice, which took place "without apostolic command . . . but rather as a result of 'individual earnestness.'" Venn's 1861 policy paper explicitly called for the "*self-exertion* [of native converts] for the extension of the Gospel."[46] Thus, the CIM during Taylor's tenure failed to adopt self-propagation as ideally conceived by Venn.

44. Austin, *China's Millions*, 233–34, 280–83, 285.
45. Lutz, *Opening China*, 311.
46. Williams, *Ideal of the Self-Governing Church*, 16–17; Shenk, *Henry Venn*, 121.

Self-support likewise was not achieved by the CIM during Taylor's tenure. In Taylor's response to a paper on "The Native Pastorate" at the 1877 Shanghai conference, the CIM leader emphasized that a clear distinction must be made between Chinese pastors and Chinese evangelists.

> The distinction between native pastors and evangelists . . . is a very important distinction, for evangelists are missionaries and as such should be supported by the mission, or by those who send them. The pastor on the other hand should be supported by his flock, if they are able.[47]

Chinese evangelists, like other missionaries, were entitled to financial support from a Western mission, as were Chinese pastors if their congregations were too small or unable to support them. Taylor went on to state that none of the CIM churches in 1877 were self-supporting. Taylor endorsed the so-called employment system, in which Chinese Christian workers were paid by a foreign mission to assist Western missionaries in evangelistic, medical, and educational ministries. The CIM was not unusual in this regard. According to Chao, the employment of local Christians was "the predominant . . . mission method in the 19th and 20th centuries in China." In 1876, one out of every eight Chinese Christians was employed by a foreign mission as an assistant, evangelist, servant, or other type of employee.[48] In the CIM, the heavy use of paid Chinese assistants under the superintendence of Western missionaries and the dependency of the Chinese church on foreign funds were not in keeping with either the self-support or self-governance principles.

This section has demonstrated that the CIM (like many other evangelical missions) did not consistently adopt three-self principles. Taylor himself did not promote or implement the full triad of three selfs. Self-governance was viewed as a desirable outcome, but a concrete plan to achieve it was neither developed nor implemented during his tenure. Self-support was not achieved, nor was a large-scale *independent* self-propagation of the gospel by Chinese Christians. The balance sheet of the CIM is more positive when it comes to self-identification with the Chinese people. Despite ridicule and opposition from other China missionaries, most CIM personnel followed Taylor's example and adopted Chinese clothing in the nineteenth and early twentieth centuries, although some later returned to wearing Western clothes.[49]

47. *Records of the General Conference*, 322.
48. Samuel Hsiang-En Chao, "John Livingston Nevius (1829–1893): A Historical Study of His Life and Mission Methods" (PhD diss., Fuller Theological Seminary, 1991), 53, 59.
49. Austin, *China's Millions*, 1–2, 120–23.

John L. Nevius and the Nevius Plan for Korea

The most successful example of well-implemented three-self principles in this era took place in Korea, starting in 1890 when the American Presbyterian Mission (APM) enthusiastically adopted the Nevius Plan. John L. Nevius (1829–93) was an APM missionary to China. Upon his arrival in 1854, Nevius and his wife Helen were appointed to work in the treaty port of Ningpo, where they served until 1857. There they lived on a mission station and followed the traditional practice of employing Chinese assistants as evangelists, colporteurs, teachers, and Bible women (local women who assisted foreign female missionaries in evangelism and social work). Nevius quickly became frustrated by confinement to a mission station, and in 1855 he began an itinerant ministry in the Ningpo area, with considerable success. In 1857 at San-poh, an outstation north of Ningpo, a revival broke out entirely through local leadership. This did much to convince Nevius of the untapped potential of Chinese evangelists, many of whom lacked formal training.[50] To fill this education gap, the Neviuses opened their own home to between thirty and fifty Chinese evangelists for a three-month (June to August) systematic Bible instruction class. He produced instructional materials in Chinese, including commentaries on the Gospel of Mark and Acts and a *Manual for Native Evangelists* (1862). Through this training, Nevius "was able to produce a remarkable number of effective native evangelists."[51]

In 1861, due to political upheavals in Ningpo, the Neviuses moved to Shandong province, where they ministered for the majority of the next thirty years. Nevius had become convinced that the "employment system" hindered the development of local Christian leaders. As we have seen, this approach was commonly used by mission societies in China, and even by Nevius himself while in Ningpo. However, in his new location in Shandong, he was determined to prove that the self-support of Chinese church leaders was both possible and beneficial. Nevius succeeded in instituting self-support. Only a very small number of Chinese Christians were employed by the Shandong mission. He and his colleagues planted over sixty independent and self-supporting churches "without hiring Chinese preachers and without requiring them to go through long years of formal theological training."[52]

In 1885, Nevius published a series of articles in the missionary journal *Chinese Recorder*. The articles were published in book form first in 1886, then

50. Helen Coan Nevius, *The Life of John Livingston Nevius* (New York: Revell, 1895), 151–55.
51. Chao, "John Livingston Nevius," 109, 295.
52. Chao, "John Livingston Nevius," 5.

in 1899 with the title *The Planting and Development of Missionary Churches*. In this volume, Nevius outlines his method for achieving self-supporting, self-governing, and self-propagating Chinese churches (see sidebar 9.3).[53] Like Venn, Nevius was convinced that self-support in the Chinese context was an essential first step. In his view, "making a paid agent of a new convert" brought with it numerous ills: it stirred up envy and dissatisfaction in the church; it increased the number of mercenary or "rice Christians"; and it "tend[ed] to stop the voluntary work of unpaid agents," all of which were detrimental for the development of a healthy national church.[54] Instead, new Christians should follow the admonition of 1 Corinthians 7:20 and "remain in the situation they were in when God called them." This had the advantage of allowing new converts to be a witness for Christ to relatives and friends in their natural social networks. All converts were to be taught by a local Christian more advanced in the faith and were to teach someone less advanced. Part of this discipleship training included instruction on the duty of giving as well as practical experience in evangelistic outreach (distribution of tracts, street preaching, etc.).[55]

Nevius's approach was built on the premise that leaders would emerge gradually and naturally from the ranks of church members. Nevius did not require pastors of rural churches to have formal theological education to be ordained, although Bible instruction was necessary. Outstations and small churches would be led by unpaid volunteers until such time that the local congregations were willing and able to support their pastors themselves. This approach stood in stark contrast to the "employment system" common in the CIM and other China missions. In practice, the Nevius method meant that only large churches or small circuits of churches were led by (usually mature) pastors paid from local funds. Expenses were further reduced by locating the churches in rented rooms or a house-church setting.[56] Nevius was not the inventor of three-self principles, and he seldom used that term. His genius lay in developing practical and achievable principles for an independent, indigenous Chinese church. Nevius's method was accepted by most of his coworkers in the APM Shandong mission. But even in his lifetime, Nevius had some detractors. The greatest opposition came from Calvin Mateer, one of his Shandong colleagues, who repeatedly and publicly attacked his methods, particularly self-support for Chinese workers. Ultimately, after Nevius's death in 1893,

53. Nevius's developing mission methods "owed a substantial debt" to conversations with and the example of Welsh Baptist missionary Timothy Richard. Brian Stanley, *The History of the Baptist Missionary Society, 1792–1992* (Edinburgh: T&T Clark, 1992), 182–83.
54. John L. Nevius, *The Planting and Development of Missionary Churches* (New York: Foreign Mission Library, 1899), 12–18.
55. Nevius, *Planting and Development of Missionary Churches*, 32–35, 51.
56. Nevius, *Planting and Development of Missionary Churches*, 34–35, 43–44.

his principles were largely abandoned in China. It was in Korea that a full test of his method took place.

In June 1890, John and Helen Nevius were invited to a meeting of Presbyterian missionaries in Seoul, Korea, in order to share the mission principles

---

SIDEBAR 9.3

John Nevius, *The Planting and Development of Missionary Churches* (1899)

It is our aim that each man, woman and child shall both be a learner from someone more advanced, and a teacher of someone less advanced. Theoretically, the missionary does nothing which the helper can do for him. . . . In this way much time is saved [and] the gifts of all are utilized and developed. . . .

Leaders are sometimes formally selected by their [out]station. . . . In many cases the leader is the person who originated the station with which he is connected, the other members of the station having been brought into the Church by his instrumentality. The members look up to him as their natural head and teacher, and a strong feeling of gratitude, Christian sympathy and responsibility grows up spontaneously. . . .

The chapels, with the chapel furniture, are provided by the natives themselves. As a rule, they are not separate buildings, but form a part of the ordinary Chinese dwelling house. Often the chapel belongs to the leader. Sometimes it is rented by the Christians, and in a few places it is a new building specially erected for the purpose of worship. . . .

In my opinion . . . the introduction of paid teachers in each station, even if it were possible, would not at present be desirable. The [unpaid] leaders understand better than a [paid] person from a distance could, the individual peculiarities of the neighbors. . . . They are likely to be more interested in . . . them, most of whom may be called their own converts, than anyone else could be, and more disposed to give them the care and attention necessary. . . . [A] larger number of teachers is thus secured than could be obtained in any other way, and learning and teaching go on together . . . the teaching being an important part of the learning, perhaps quite as useful to the teacher as to the taught. Though the knowledge of the leaders may be elementary and incomplete, they are quite in advance of the other church members and inquirers, and what they do know is just what the others need first to learn.

Source: John L. Nevius, *The Planting and Development of Missionary Churches* (New York: Foreign Mission Library, 1899), 32–36.

they had employed in the Shandong mission. The Neviuses stayed in Korea for only two weeks, but that was long enough for the visit to become "the determining factor in the direction of the history of the Mission in Korea." After careful consideration, the seven missionaries present at the meeting fully adopted and put into practice the Nevius Plan, as it became known in Korea. A year later, in 1891, when the Presbyterian Mission in Korea adopted its rules and bylaws, "the influence of the Nevius Principles was obvious in almost every section" of the bylaws; in some cases they quoted directly from Nevius's book.[57]

The Nevius Plan in Korea focused on self-support and the Bible class movement. In January 1893, the Council of the Presbyterian Mission adopted a strong statement on self-support: "An aggressive church must be a self-supporting church, and we must aim to diminish the proportion of dependents among our membership and to increase that of self-supporting and contributing members."[58] Unlike in China, Korean Bible women, evangelists, and pastors were not paid by foreign funds. The Bible class movement laid the foundation for a biblically literate church membership. Large classes were offered every winter in central locations for all who desired to attend, lay Christians and church leaders alike. In the summer, theological classes provided intensive biblical and doctrinal instruction for church leaders. These classes grew into the Pyongyang Presbyterian Seminary founded in 1901.

Under the Nevius Plan, the church in Korea grew rapidly. It would be remiss, however, to discount the other factors that contributed to this rapid growth. Religious factors include the largely Korean-led 1907 Pyongyang revival, which swelled church membership among both Presbyterians and Methodists. The similarity between Protestant and Confucian ethics made the Christian faith feel less foreign and easier for Koreans to embrace, as did the use of an indigenous name for God (*Hananim*) in the Korean Bible translation. Secular factors also played a pivotal role. Korea was not connected with Western imperialism; rather, it first became a protectorate of (1905) and then was annexed by Japan (1910–1945). During this period, local Christians were at the forefront of both the Korean nationalist and patriotic movements against Japanese imperialism. Furthermore, Christian missions introduced Western medicine and education, both of which were viewed positively by many Koreans as promoting modernization.[59] This positive

57. Keun Whan Kang, "A Critical Study on the Early Mission Policies of the Council of Missions in Korea in Light of the Nevius Plan," *Jing Feng* 1, no. 2 (2000): 204.
58. Kang, "Critical Study on the Early Mission Policies," 205.
59. Jung Han Kim, "Christianity and Korean Culture: The Reasons for the Success of Christianity in Korea," *Exchange* 33, no. 2 (2004): 132–52.

view of Korean Christians and Christianity by their countrymen had an enormous impact on the growth of the church. Nevertheless, "it is undeniable that . . . the contribution of the Nevius Plan" played a key role in "the rapid growth of the Korean church."[60] In 1927 General Secretary Robert Speer of the APM Board of Foreign Missions inspected the APM's Asian fields. He found that there were only thirty-two self-supporting APM churches in China, while there were 547 in Korea, although the Presbyterian mission to Korea had been initiated forty-seven years later than that in China.[61] Those figures speak for themselves.

In conclusion, Henry Venn, during his tenure as honorary secretary of the CMS, introduced radically advanced principles for the formation of an independent, indigenous church: the three-self principles of self-support, self-governance, and self-propagation. The formulation of these principles by Venn (and Rufus Anderson) was a turning point in the development of missiological strategy and theory, and therefore in the expansion of Christianity. Venn discovered that the three-self principles proved more difficult to put into practice than he had anticipated. The Sierra Leone Native Pastorate launched in 1861 was a noble attempt that failed not because the three selfs were inherently flawed but because of complicating factors in the field, the most crucial being financial difficulties and resistance by CMS missionaries. By the 1870s, three-self principles had been accepted in theory as the long-term mission goal of most Protestant missionary societies. Nevertheless, the majority of those same societies, of which the China Inland Mission is representative, failed to fully implement the three selfs. The CIM in the nineteenth century focused so exclusively on rapid evangelistic itineration throughout the inland provinces of China that the training and development of Chinese Christian leaders was largely neglected, leading to a lack of self-governance. Furthermore, the "employment system" for Chinese assistants led to dependency on Western funds, the antithesis of self-support. Self-propagation was likewise not achieved on a large scale. Presbyterian missionary to China John Nevius, in the Shandong mission district, rejected the employment system and rigorously promoted self-support and widespread Bible instruction. It was not until the last decade of the nineteenth century, however, that a full and successful test of three-self principles was achieved when John Nevius's principles were consistently and effectively applied in Korea. The Nevius Plan proved to be one key factor in the rapid growth of the church in Korea.

60. Kang, "Early Mission Policies," 202.
61. G. Thompson Brown, "Why Has Christianity Grown Faster in Korea Than in China?," *Missiology* 22, no. 1 (January 1994): 82.

We end this chapter with a prayer by Henry Venn:

O Lord, knowing that there is none righteous, no not one, that all are corrupt, and wholly so in their nature, give us a heart to pity and pray for all men; to be kind, tender-hearted and full of bowels of mercy. May we be led, by what we observe in others, to turn our eyes inward, and lament our own manifold defects, since we are all of one blood, and all inherit the same evil nature. Finally, we commend to you, O God, who alone can show to men in error the light of your truth, all who deny their natural blindness and depravity. O hide pride from their eyes. Convince them by your spirit, and by setting their evil ways and days before them, that they ought to abhor themselves, to bow down before you . . . begging to be made partakers of the riches of your grace in Christ Jesus who came to seek and save that which was lost. Hear us for his sake, our only Mediator. Amen.[62]

---

62. Christopher L. Webber, ed., *Give Us Grace: An Anthology of Anglican Prayers* (Harrisburg, PA: Morehouse, 2004), 179 (modernized).

Converting the Lost in the Era of Imperialism

The Scramble for Africa (1880)

From Greenland's icy mountains, from India's coral strand;
Where Afric's sunny fountains roll down their golden sand:
From many an ancient river, from many a palmy plain,
They call us to deliver their land from error's chain.
What though the spicy breezes blow soft o'er Ceylon's isle;
Though every prospect pleases, and only man is vile?
In vain with lavish kindness the gifts of God are strown;
The heathen in his blindness bows down to wood and stone.
Shall we, whose souls are lighted with wisdom from on high,
Shall we to those benighted the lamp of life deny?
Salvation! O salvation! The joyful sound proclaim,
Till earth's remotest nation has learned Messiah's Name.[1]

A t the end of the eighteenth and in the early decades of the nineteenth century, the British abolitionist crusade spawned a new focus on the

---

1. Bishop Reginald Heber (1783–1826) penned "From Greenland's Icy Mountains" in 1819. The hymn soon became the most famous missionary hymn of the nineteenth century, despite its imperial and racial overtones. Jeffrey Richards, *Imperialism and Music: Britain 1876–1953* (Manchester: Manchester University Press, 2001), 386.

continent of Africa as a venue for the Protestant missionary enterprise, a theme discussed at length in chapter 8. Despite intense humanitarian and missionary attention to the African continent by evangelical Christians, as late as the 1860s the British government had only marginal political or imperial interest there. This was expressed clearly in 1865 by a committee of the House of Commons that recommended that Britain reduce its existing commitments in West Africa and avoid new entanglements there at all costs. According to the committee, "All further extension of territory or assumption of Government, or new treaties offering any protection to native tribes, would be inexpedient; and that the object of our policy should be . . . our ultimate withdrawal from all [territories] except, probably, Sierra Leone." This lack of interest in imperial commitments in Africa was exhibited by several other European nations, for example Portugal and France, whose concern—like that of Britain—was focused primarily on trading posts on the west coast of Africa and a limited number of colonies.[2] In 1880, European nations controlled only 10 percent of the African continent. But by the eve of World War I in 1914, Western control had extended to all of the continent except Liberia and Ethiopia.

What brought about this rapid expansion of imperialism in Africa after 1880? Both scholars today and nineteenth-century contemporaries note the "suddenness" and unexpectedness of this "novel development." Adu Boahen argues that "as late as 1880, there were no real signs or indications of this phenomenal and catastrophic event." In fact, in that very year, renowned Liberian intellectual Edward Blyden expressed his belief that Africa would soon be developed by Africans and African Americans, not rapidly subjected to Western imperial control.[3] The catalyst for this unexpected new development was the formation of a colony in the interior of Africa, the Congo Free State, by Belgium's King Leopold II. Leopold had long yearned to annex a foreign colony; his attention was first unsuccessfully directed toward Asia before turning toward Africa. His first step toward achieving an African colony occurred in 1876, when he established the International Association for the Exploration and Civilization of Central Africa. This was the first of three successive organizations founded by the Belgian king. It was ostensibly an international humanitarian and scientific organization to suppress the slave trade and open up the Congo to exploration. The Committee for the Study

2. M. E. Chamberlain, *The Scramble for Africa*, 3rd ed. (Harlow, UK: Longman, 2010), 44, 110–11, 132–35.

3. A. Adu Boahen, *African Perspectives on Colonialism* (Baltimore: Johns Hopkins University Press, 1987), 1; H. L. Wesseling, *Divide and Rule: The Partition of Africa, 1880–1914*, trans. Arnold J. Pomerans (Westport, CT: Praeger, 1996), 73; Nancy J. Jacobs, *African History through Sources*, vol. 1, *Colonial Contexts and Everyday Experiences* (Cambridge: Cambridge University Press, 2014), 15–16, 57–60.

of Upper Congo, founded by Leopold in November 1878 as his second organization, added the goal of developing markets for trade and industry.[4]

In August 1877, Leopold received word that explorer Henry Morton Stanley (of "Dr. Livingstone, I presume!" fame) had successfully completed his trans-Africa expedition (1874–77). This news reinvigorated Leopold's desire for an African colony. He frankly expressed this sentiment in a letter to the Belgian ambassador in London, Henry Solvyns: "We must be careful, skillful and ready to act . . . [to] get us a slice of this magnificent African cake."[5] Toward this end, the Belgian king promptly recruited Stanley to lead an expedition to the Upper Congo to explore the region, to set up trading stations, and to sign treaties with local African rulers. Stanley was given a stack of blank treaties to utilize for this purpose during the Congo expedition (1879–84). He and his associates secured between four hundred and five hundred treaties in the name of Leopold's third and last Belgian organization, the International Association of the Congo (IAC). The IAC was neither international, nor scientific, nor humanitarian; rather, it was "a holding company with Leopold as the chief shareholder," whose sole aim was to achieve control of the Congo Basin.[6] The African chiefs did not view signing the treaties as "ceding territory to the foreigners, but sealing a bond of friendship." By 1884, Leopold—and more importantly, the other European nations—accepted the treaties as a legitimate surrender of territory and sovereignty to Leopold's personal control, *not* to the Belgian state. Thus, the king of Belgium, one of Europe's smallest countries, personally "acquired one of the largest and richest colonies in Africa."[7]

Leopold II's claim to the Congo Basin did not go unchallenged by other European powers, who already had or desired to have economic or political influence in Africa. In 1880 French explorer Savorgnan de Brazza signed a treaty with chief Makoko of the Bateke people north of the Congo River. This admittedly questionable treaty was ratified as valid by the French government in November 1882, thereby creating Brazzaville, later French Congo. In response and to protect their own interests, Britain and Portugal moved from their minimalist positions with regard to imperial ambitions. They unilaterally signed the Anglo-Portuguese Treaty in 1884 without consideration of the other European players. This treaty recognized Portugal's historic claim to the mouth of the Congo River and gave Britain unrestricted navigation rights on the river. It angered all the other major European powers, particularly France.

4. Wesseling, *Divide and Rule*, 73, 78, 80, 86, 91, 93; Chamberlain, *Scramble for Africa*, 50.
5. Wesseling, *Divide and Rule*, 71, 89.
6. Jacobs, *African History through Sources*, 65.
7. Wesseling, *Divide and Rule*, 76, 95–97.

Leopold felt provoked, since the treaty would cut off access to his proposed Congo Free State.[8]

Thus, a chain of events was set off by Leopold II's incursions into the heart of Africa. It led directly to the Berlin Conference of 1884–85. This international conference of the major European nations was called by France and Germany to resolve the disputed Congo issue and to establish the ground rules for the imposition of imperialism in Africa. While the conference "was convened to sort out rival imperial claims over specific territories . . . in the end it provided motivation and mechanisms for massive expansion. In its wake, Europe claimed or conquered great swaths" of Africa. "Thus, the conference legitimatized imperialist aspirations and hastened imperial conquest by creating the impetus to claim territory before anyone else did."[9] The Berlin Conference culminated in and validated the "Scramble for Africa," the colloquial term used to describe the rapid political partition, conquest, and colonialization of the African continent by European powers during the high imperialist era, circa 1880 to 1914. The Scramble for Africa was a historical turning point in the expansion of Christianity. The Scramble typified the dramatic change from earlier forms of imperialism to a new and a more virulent form during the high imperialist era. This virulence was on full display in the Congo, where Leopold II, after 1884, acted as a private entrepreneur, free from Belgian governmental and parliamentary constraints. In his pursuit of wealth, he exploited the local Congolese and created "the greatest scandal of the whole colonial era in Africa."[10] The Congo atrocities thus became "the symbol of the purest imperialism and the most brutal exploitation."[11]

The high imperialist era, epitomized by the Scramble for Africa, was not only a historical turning point in the rapid advance of imperialism. It was also a turning point in the relationship between imperialism and mission. As direct political control became more prevalent in this era, it became more difficult for missionaries in Africa (and also in Asia) to ignore or operate independently of colonial agendas, as they often had in the past. In contrast to the anti-missionary policies of the East India Companies during the early Protestant mission movement, colonial governments in the high imperialist era frequently financially supported schools and other aspects of the mission program, making independence more challenging. Furthermore, the "late Victorian missionary boom" led to a vastly larger cadre of missionaries serving in colonial contexts. This meant, among other things, that missionaries

8. Wesseling, *Divide and Rule*, 98–100, 104; Chamberlain, *Scramble for Africa*, 49–52.
9. Jacobs, *African History through Sources*, 63, 65.
10. Chamberlain, *Scramble for Africa*, 50.
11. Wesseling, *Divide and Rule*, 130.

became more hesitant to surrender leadership and control of mission churches to local Christians. Paternalism and distrust of native agents became more widespread. Last, more missionaries adopted aspects of the imperial civilizing agenda, which in part was based on the ideological foundations of the hierarchy of cultures, racial theories, and the "white man's burden."[12] A paternalistic attitude and the concept of the "white man's burden" are both on full display in the vastly popular nineteenth-century missionary hymn that opens this chapter.

In this chapter, I will first discuss the characteristics of high imperialism after 1880. This is followed by an examination of the relationship between imperialism and mission. I will argue that a distinction should be made between the topic of imperialism per se and that of the relationship between imperialism and mission. While an evaluation of imperialism per se is rightly negative, the relationship between mission societies or missionaries and imperialism is much more varied. Missionary responses to imperialism ranged from active collaboration to active resistance—with multiple other stances in between. Then, in a second section, I will include a historical summary of the Berlin Conference and the ensuing Scramble for Africa, followed by a discussion of the wide range of responses to imperialism by mission societies and missionaries in Africa during this period.

Imperialism and Mission

The concept of imperialism is notoriously problematic. Ever since the origin of the term in the 1840s, there has been little consensus among scholars as to its exact meaning. Rather, since its inception, the word has gone through twelve distinct changes in meaning, in large part since the "facts of imperial history are too complex to allow any one monolithic interpretation to gain universal academic acceptance." That being said, the essence of imperialism may be defined as the domination by one country of the political, economic, or cultural life of another country. The control may be political and involve the conquest of territory and the formation of colonies. It may express itself in the dominated country being a protectorate whose autonomous territory is "protected" by a stronger state in return for economic advantages. Or it may take the form of a "sphere of influence," in which there is no military or political control but often extreme economic dependency.[13]

12. Brian Stanley, *The Bible and the Flag: Protestant Missions and British Imperialism in the Nineteenth and Twentieth Centuries* (Leicester: Apollos, 1990), 63–70, 80.
13. Stanley, *Bible and the Flag*, 34–35, 50.

In the high imperialist era, European nations largely, though not entirely, switched from commercial ventures (e.g., trading posts) to the active conquest of previously unclaimed territories (colonies). A new element was added—the competition for colonies. In this era of rising nationalism, countries such as Germany and France desired "a place in the sun" (colonies) not only for the economic advantage but also to enhance their national prestige on the European stage. High imperialism in the period from 1880 to 1914 was *more pervasive* than previous forms of imperialism—the majority of Africa and Asia were subjected to imperial control in this time frame. It was *more intrusive*—the formation of colonies, more prevalent in this era, had greater impact on local populations. And in many cases, it was *more exploitive* of the local populations. Nevertheless, some scholars question the newness of the high imperialist era. For example, Brian Stanley reminds us that "the continuities in the aims of the British imperial policy were more important than the discontinuities." In *both* the mid and late Victorian periods, British imperial aims remained largely constant: to achieve and protect their foreign interests at minimal expense to the taxpayer. What changed was the "conditions in which it [British expansion] operated."[14] These changed circumstances ultimately resulted in the rapid advance of imperialist control during those "years of hectic European territorial expansion" in Africa and Asia.[15]

To complicate the issue even further, scholars question whether it is accurate to view the period from 1500 (the Iberian conquest of the Americas) to the 1960s (decolonialization of Africa and Asia) as a clear imperial or colonial age. Western countries exhibited only sporadic enthusiasm for imperial conquests in this period, and the vast Soviet Empire lasted until 1989. Furthermore, imperialism is not just a Western phenomenon. The Mughals in India and the Chinese and Japanese empires in the twentieth century are prime examples of Asian imperialism. Finally, not all forms of imperialism were the same; each case must be examined individually. For example, in Angola, the Portuguese regime directly and indirectly supported the slave trade. Japan was guilty of egregious abuse and even war crimes in many of its occupied territories in Asia and the Pacific during the Sino-Japanese War and World War II. British-controlled areas, on the other hand, were at times less exploitive, in large part due to the strong missionary lobby in British Parliament, as well as Britain's commitment to humanitarian objectives. Therefore, "neither unequivocal moral censure nor unqualified praise

14. Stanley, *Bible and the Flag*, 41–42, 45–46.
15. Andrew Porter, introduction to *The Imperial Horizons of British Protestant Missions, 1880–1914*, ed. Andrew Porter (Grand Rapids: Eerdmans, 2003), 1.

can do justice to the tangled web of exploitation and service which was the British empire."[16]

The missionary movement has been and continues to be accused of close collaboration with imperialism, of "working hand in hand with colonial powers" as agents of imperialism.[17] This accusation is made by African and Asian Christians and many scholars. In fact, this viewpoint has become so widespread that it has become a largely unquestioned and persistent perception. Lamin Sanneh laments that "the forces pitted against a fair understanding of mission today are formidable."[18] Even the numerous historical monographs published by academic historians have not been able to substantially alter this unnuanced perception. "Thus, perhaps it is time for a reevaluation of the glib assertions popular in intellectual circles today about the close connection between missionaries and colonialism."[19] In this chapter, I will attempt to do just that.

It is my conviction that a distinction should be made between two topics that are often conflated: imperialism per se (in and of itself) and the *relationship* between mission and imperialism. It is often (falsely) assumed that the two topics are the same, due to the prevailing assumption that all missionaries were agents of imperialism. The history of imperialism per se deals with such topics as how imperialism arose in particular contexts, why it arose as it did, what forms it took, the relationship between the imperial powers and their native subjects, and the process of decolonialization. In most cases, a largely negative evaluation of the impact of imperialism is included. That negative evaluation is usually warranted. Nigerian scholar Tejumola Olaniyan correctly documents the negative impact of colonialism on the African continent as follows: (1) political—geographic boundaries are arbitrary, drawn by the colonizers with little regard for indigenous ethnic, linguistic, or cultural communities, resulting in unstable governments, boundary clashes, and civil wars; (2) ideological—Western racial ideology assigned a negative value to all things African, resulting in a sense of inferiority and a loss of pride in their culture; and (3) economic—underdevelopment of agriculture and industry resulted in dependence on cash crops and the global market.[20] It is undoubtedly true that imperialism in general was predominantly negative during the high imperialist era.

16. Stanley, *Bible and the Flag*, 50–52.
17. Stanley, *Bible and the Flag*, 11.
18. Lamin Sanneh, *Translating the Message: The Missionary Impact on Culture*, 2nd ed. (Maryknoll, NY: Orbis, 2009), 122.
19. Robert Woodberry, "Reclaiming the M-Word: The Legacy of Missions in Non-Western Societies," *International Journal of Frontier Missiology* 25, no. 1 (Spring 2008): 23.
20. Tejumola Olaniyan, "Africa: Varied Colonial Legacies," in *A Companion to Postcolonial Studies*, ed. Henry Schwartz and Sanreeta Ray (Malden, MA: Blackwell, 2000), 268–81.

Nevertheless, the relationship between imperialism and mission was much more varied. In fact, the historical record demonstrates that there was a wide variety of responses by missionaries and mission societies to imperialism in the nineteenth and twentieth centuries—responses ranging from active collaboration to active resistance, with many stances in between. The two most extreme positions, active collaboration and active resistance, occurred much less frequently than less extreme positions. Occasionally, some missionaries sought imperial control or paved the way for it. More missionaries welcomed the stability, safety, and infrastructure that a moderate colonial regime brought. Racism was found among missionaries, though usually less often than in the missionary's country of origin. Paternalism was quite widespread among mission personnel. A few missionaries encouraged locals to actively resist imperialism. Many missionaries had a more positive view of indigenous culture than did the colonial administrators. They helped to soften the cultural disruption caused by imperialism. A very common missionary response was to decry colonial abuses and the mistreatment of local populations. In general, evangelical missionaries in the high imperialist era were driven by two overriding concerns:

> They were concerned at almost any cost to see the progress of the gospel maintained; and most missionaries cast themselves into the role of defenders of native interests against the exploitive designs of European commercial or political forces. These overriding concerns resulted in widely differing political stances according to the precise configuration of the various imperial forces in any particular mission field.[21]

In other words, missionary responses to imperialism varied, dependent in large part on the degree to which the colonial situation was amenable to the higher goals of conversion and the protection of native rights.

Other factors also came into play. It was not at all uncommon for the colonizing power of a mission field to be different from a missionary's country of origin. As a result, the missionary might have felt less sense of loyalty and an increased willingness to criticize the colonial government. A missionary's background, denomination, and political stance were also a factor. Many high church Anglican missionaries were well-educated, upper class, and politically conservative. They tended to be supportive of the hierarchical status quo and *empire*. In contrast, the dissenting or nonconformist British missions, such as the London Missionary Society, often emphasized libertarian values of human freedom and individual opportunity for all peoples. These missionaries were

21. Stanley, *Bible and the Flag*, 110.

more likely to resist or critique empire.[22] This brief overview of the characteristics of imperialism in the high imperialist era and of the relationship between missionaries and imperialism has demonstrated that both topics are far more complicated than contemporary popular rhetoric might lead one to believe. The relationship between missionaries and imperialism during the Scramble for Africa was also convoluted, as will be shown in the following account.

The Scramble for Africa and Mission

The Scramble for Africa inaugurated a new era of imperialism and mission in Africa; it was enabled and legitimatized by the Berlin Conference. German chancellor Otto von Bismarck invited representatives of the European nations with a stake in the Congo (Germany, France, Great Britain, Portugal, Belgium) to the Berlin West Africa Conference, which took place from November 1884 to February 1885. Eight other European nations and the United States were also included "to ensure general agreement on the conference resolutions"—in other words, international approval of all decisions.[23] No African representatives were present at the conference, despite the fact that it was convened to resolve the Congo issue and lay down rules for the subsequent occupation of African territories. One underlying concern of the representatives was to prevent military conflict between European nations as a result of the imposition of imperialism in sub-Saharan Africa—a goal that was successfully achieved.

The Berlin Act of 1885 recorded the resolutions of the conference in thirty-eight articles. Article 1 declared that the Congo Basin was a free trade zone for merchants of every nation. Navigation on the Congo and Niger rivers was open to all (arts. 13 and 26). Two articles upheld humanitarian concerns. European powers were obligated to preserve and improve the "moral and material wellbeing . . . of the native tribes," to instruct them and bring "home to them the blessings of civilization," and to protect "religious missions belonging to all creeds" (art. 6; see sidebar 10.1). Furthermore, they were required to put an end to the slave trade in their territories (art. 9). Articles 34 and 35 outlined what constituted "effective occupation" of new territories. It was not adequate for a nation to simply raise its flag along the African coast and claim everything that lay behind it in the hinterland. A European colonial power had to physically occupy what it claimed with troops, missionaries,

---

22. Steven S. Maughan, *Mighty England Do Good: Culture, Faith, Empire and World in the Foreign Missions of the Church of England, 1850–1915* (Grand Rapids: Eerdmans, 2014), 36.
23. Wesseling, *Divide and Rule*, 114.

Berlin Act of 1885

Article 6

All the Powers . . . bind themselves to watch over the preservation of the native tribes, and to care for the improvement of the conditions of their moral and material wellbeing, and to help in suppressing slavery, and especially the Slave Trade.

They shall, without distinction of creed or nation, favor and protect all religious, scientific or charitable institutions and undertakings created and organized for the above ends, or which aim at instructing the natives and bringing home to them the blessings of civilization.

Christian missionaries, scientists and explorers, with their followers, property and collections shall likewise be the objects of special protection.

Freedom of conscience and religious toleration are expressly guaranteed to the natives and to subjects and foreigners.

The free and public exercise of all forms of Divine worship, and the right to build edifices for religious purposes, and to organize religious missions belonging to all creeds, shall not be limited in any way whatsoever.

Source: T. Walter Wallbank, *Documents on Modern Africa* (Princeton: Van Nostrand, 1964), 16.

merchants, and infrastructure.[24] Finally, Leopold II's IAC was recognized as a sovereign state during the Berlin Conference in signed treaties by its two main rivals, France and Portugal, as well as by the other leading powers before or shortly thereafter. In August 1885, Leopold announced that his possessions in central Africa would thenceforth be called the Congo Free State. The new nation was allegedly a "native confederation" of "free states" under temporary European control. In reality "the policies of the Free State, of which he [Leopold] became absolute ruler, proved more brutally oppressive than those of any other colonial regime."[25]

The Berlin Conference and the resultant Berlin Act did not carve up the African continent for Western colonial powers, as has often been asserted. Partition was not on the agenda of the conference and was in fact explicitly rejected. Nevertheless, the conference served as the symbol for partition. The

24. T. Walter Wallbank, *Documents on Modern Africa* (Princeton: Van Nostrand, 1964), 16–17.

25. John D. Hargreaves, "The Berlin West Africa Conference: A Timely Centenary," *History Today* (November 1984): 20.

topic "had been placed on the agenda of European diplomats and refused to go away." The Berlin Conference thus "greatly speeded up" the ensuing Scramble for Africa.[26] The partition of Africa took place in several stages. In the first two decades of the Scramble (roughly 1880–1895), the majority of the African continent was divided up into protectorates. Boundaries were drawn by Europeans to define their various territories, often along rivers or with straight lines that seldom considered the ethnic, geographic, or political realities on the ground. In this first stage, a proclamation of sovereignty over a territory was usually based on a previously signed treaty with an African ruler, who was accorded protection (hence a protectorate) in exchange for exclusive trading and other rights. During this period, both the British and the French signed treaties with many local rulers—the British in parts of Ghana, Nigeria, and Benin; the French in the Congo Basin with the king of Dahomey and King Tofa of Porto Nova, among others. Some of these African partners were either pressured or forced to accept a treaty. Such was the case for the treaties between the Imperial British East Africa Company (IBEAC) and Buganda in 1890 and 1892—treaties that the Church Missionary Society (CMS) supported and that will be discussed more fully below.[27] In a second stage of the Scramble, which chronologically overlapped with the first stage, a series of bilateral treaties was enacted between the various European powers. For example, the Anglo-German Treaty of 1890 ceded German East Africa (later Tanganyika) to Germany in exchange for the recognition of Britain's claim to Zanzibar, Kenya, and Uganda.

It would require several decades before the "effective occupation" of colonies mandated in the Berlin Act was actually achieved. This third stage of the Scramble occurred through invasion, occupation, or military conquest. France began its occupation of western Sudan in 1885, of Senegal in 1886, and of parts of Ghana in 1898. Britain used military power to impose colonial rule on western Nigeria in 1892, on Benin in 1897, and on the Sokoto Empire of northern Nigeria between 1900 and 1904. By 1910, with the exception of only a few areas, the Scramble for Africa had been concluded—the "European occupation of Africa had been completed, and the colonial system had been imposed."[28]

Missionary responses to imperialism in the wake of the Scramble for Africa were varied. Most missionaries collaborated with imperialism to some extent. Extreme collaboration with an imperial power, however, was much rarer. One such glaring example occurred in 1888, when LMS missionary Rev. Charles

26. Wesseling, *Divide and Rule*, 126.
27. Hargreaves, "Berlin Conference," 20; Boahen, *African Perspectives*, 32–34.
28. Boahen, *African Perspectives*, 34.

Helm intentionally mistranslated a document from a group of South African businessmen that cheated Lobengula, the Ndebele king, out of his land. Helm was apparently motivated by the belief that the spread of the gospel would have greater success under imperialist control than under an African king. While "episodes of such 'holy' treachery were few," they did occur on occasion.[29] A somewhat more common response was for a mission society to seek colonial intervention. The Church of Scotland mission at Blantyre in southern Malawi faced ongoing disruptive problems, such as theft, local warfare, and slave trading. The mission openly called for a British protectorate, which occurred in 1891, to oust the Portuguese slave traders and officials from the region. Andrew Walls notes, "When they [missionaries] actively agitated for imperial expansion . . . the grounds were almost invariably pragmatic, local and missionary."[30] According to Church of Scotland mission representative Horace Waller in 1887, "their sole desire was to save the settled tribes . . . from the vice of demoralization which must result if the Portuguese were to push on to the lake [Malawi]."[31] Such expressed intentions, however, did not always result in positive outcomes.

Missionaries of the CMS likewise sought colonial intervention in Buganda, the most powerful traditional kingdom in what is today Uganda. The CMS had begun its ministry at the court of Bugandan King Mutesa I in 1877, where, after a slow beginning, they gradually won a steady number of converts. After Mutesa's son Mwanga acceded to the throne in 1884, civil war broke out between adherents of the three religions in the region: Protestantism, Catholicism, and Islam. By 1888, "Christian missions [in Buganda] stood on the brink of extinction at the hands of a militant and resurgent Islam." To counteract this development, Captain Frederick Lugard (1858–1945) arrived in Buganda in December 1890 with a military force of the IBEAC, a private commercial company chartered in 1888 to claim and administer colonies on behalf of Britain in East Africa. The captain successfully foiled German colonial aspirations in the region by foisting a treaty of protection on the reluctant King Mwanga (see sidebar 10.2). When the IBEAC communicated to the British Foreign Office its decision to withdraw its forces from Buganda for financial reasons, the CMS worked to protect the Protestant mission there. It raised substantial funds to allow the IBEAC to remain in Uganda for another year.

29. Mark Shaw, *The Kingdom of God in Africa: A Short History of African Christianity* (Grand Rapids: Baker, 1996), 214.

30. Andrew Walls, "Evangelization and Civilization: Protestant Missionary Motivation in the Imperialist Era: The British," *International Bulletin of Missionary Research* 6, no. 2 (April 1982): 63.

31. Shaw, *Kingdom of God in Africa*, 214.

SIDEBAR 10.2

Diary of Lord Frederick Lugard on the Treaty with Buganda (December 1890)

24 December 1890

We returned with treaty, pens, ink, table etc. I read it thro' sentence by sentence, and turned it into simple English. . . . There were several questions asked, all shrewd and intelligent. These people are very clever nor is it easy to bamboozle them.

26 December 1890

I got the message that they [head chiefs] would come and sign here, and go to the king [Mwanga] afterwards. . . . They said they would sign provided they were allowed to write a Codicil. . . . This they wrote themselves; it was mainly that the treaty was to be null, and another made, if the messengers from the coast came with other news than mine. Also a compact which they would not show me made between themselves was still to be binding. Its main provision was religious toleration for both sides. This I signed. . . .

   Their Codicil was read to the King, and he at once asked if all the tributary states would still be compelled to pay tribute. I replied as before that . . . we would see. . . . It would considerably cripple my treaty to enter into such an obligation. So I got them to add "and its tributary states" . . . which of course . . . bound me to nothing. Then the King . . . and . . . several of the head chiefs also signed. . . . Need I say how delighted De W[inton] and I were at our success! . . . In spite of all the trouble and opposition [I] had got the Treaty made and signed. . . . Not a bad 8 weeks' work!

Source: Nancy J. Jacobs, *African History through Sources*, vol. 1, *Colonial Contexts and Everyday Experiences* (Cambridge: Cambridge University Press, 2014), 69–70.

Then, in autumn 1892, the CMS "fully supported" a "remarkable campaign of public pressure and agitation for the retention of Uganda." This "largely spontaneous outburst of Protestant, antislavery and pro-imperial sentiment" resulted in the April 1894 decision to retain Uganda as a full British protectorate, no longer administered by the IBEAC. The generally apolitical CMS sought colonial intervention because it "too readily accepted . . . the prevailing imperial ideology . . . [and] swallowed too easily calculated arguments for national advantage when they were cloaked in the moral vocabulary of evangelical humanitarianism."[32]

32. Stanley, *Bible and the Flag*, 127–32.

An even more common response than seeking colonial intervention was for missionaries to welcome the stability, protection, and security that a moderate form of colonialism brought with it. David Livingstone, a decade before the Scramble, was convinced that colonization would "further the expansion of Christianity" and provide a "more secure setting" and "greater authority" for missionaries on the ground. During the decades of partition, "issues of security . . . were frequently uppermost in missionary calculations."[33]

In the last third of the nineteenth century, scientific racism gained dominance in European thought. This view taught the racial basis of civilization—that the white Anglo-Saxon or Teutonic races were fully human and that all other races were at an earlier evolutionary stage. The superior race had the obligation to take upon itself the "trusteeship" (also called the "white man's burden") to "ensure that inferior peoples were governed fairly and justly." Though today this set of ideas is (rightly) viewed as a pseudo-science, in its heyday it was touted by leading scholars at universities such as Oxford, Harvard, and Columbia.[34] What were typical racial attitudes among Protestant missionaries to Africa in the high imperialist era? Steven Maughan argues that

> missionaries commonly used "civilization" as a standard of judgment . . . thereby developing a paternalist attitude toward race and national culture that differed from scientific racism, both in its emphasis on civilizational development and its refusal to accept the notion of inherent racial inferiority. . . . For some missionaries, theories of race did become vehicles for explaining cultural differences, but missionaries, more than any other imperial groups, consistently rejected deterministic racial theory.[35]

Maughan emphasizes that the "majority of missionaries rejected scientific racism . . . and thus theories of the genetic inferiority of non-Europeans" on the biblical-theological grounds of the unity of all humanity. There was a range of missionary attitudes toward race "shading from relatively soft to harder and outright racism."[36] Though racism was not the only factor, it was a key motivation behind the refusal of CMS missionaries to serve under African Bishop Samuel Ajayi Crowther, as Henry Venn had desired (see chap. 9).

While some racism was found among missionaries, paternalism was much more widespread. At the end of the nineteenth century, the number of mis-

33. Andrew Porter, *Religion versus Empire? British Protestant Missionaries and Overseas Expansion, 1700–1914* (Manchester: Manchester University Press, 2004), 187, 268.
34. Andrew C. Ross, "Christian Missions and Attitudes to Race," in Porter, *Imperial Horizons*, 88–92.
35. Maughan, *Mighty England Do Good*, 34.
36. Maughan, *Mighty England Do Good*, 34, 453.

sionaries exploded at the same time that a "dramatic change in missionary attitudes" occurred. The dramatic increase in mission personnel meant that there was less need for indigenous pastors. Rather than implementing three-self principles, missionaries often distrusted indigenous leaders and were more reluctant to turn over the leadership of churches to them, instead keeping them in more subservient roles.[37] These paternalistic trends dictated a change in UMCA policies beginning in the mid-1890s, the same period when effective German colonial rule (German East Africa) was established. John Hine, the Anglican missionary bishop of Nyasaland, determined that "there should be no more native priests for ten years . . . and an increasing number of permanent deacons. We are pushing the native too fast and it demoralizes him."[38] Concurrently, the mission publication *Central Africa* called repeatedly for more European missionaries to supervise African workers and "to keep an eye on the Africans when ordained."[39]

The range of missionary responses to imperialism in the wake of the Scramble for Africa occasionally included active opposition to colonial rule. This occurred infrequently, but when it did, it was in situations where colonialism was not yet inevitable. Franz Michael Zahn (1833–1900), superintendent of the Bremen Mission, vigorously protested the occupation of Togo (West Africa) by his native Germany. He launched a lengthy pamphlet war in which he argued that European powers had no right to establish legal authority over non-European peoples and that the imposition of German imperialism would be detrimental to the African population. Zahn was also concerned that imperialism would hinder the spread of Christianity, since "the people's confidence . . . can easily be lost, when the missionaries belong to the ruling nation."[40] Missionaries also occasionally encouraged nationalist movements among the local people. Walter Miller, an English CMS missionary, served in northern Nigeria from 1899 to 1935. He soon became disillusioned with the British colonial government. Miller sought to awaken a cultural and political identity among the Hausa people, which stimulated their incipient nationalism. Miller was also "directly responsible for the founding of a political organization, the Northern People's Congress, to advance political aims against British authorities."[41] Both Zahn and Miller actively opposed the colonial regimes of their home countries.

37. Shaw, *Kingdom of God in Africa*, 216.
38. Porter, *Religion versus Empire?*, 289.
39. William Porter, "Postbag," *Central Africa* 15 (1897): 171; and "Our Anniversary," *Central Africa* 26 (July 1908): 182.
40. Shaw, *Kingdom of God in Africa*, 215.
41. Sanneh, *Translating the Message*, 156–57.

Certainly, many missionaries in this era failed to appreciate indigenous cultures. They frequently assumed the superiority of Western Christian civilization, which they associated with literacy, Western styles of education, modern medicine, and representative government. Since these elements were often lacking in African countries in this era, it was not uncommon for all Westerners, not just missionaries, to describe non-Western cultures in derogatory terms as "primitive" or "heathen." Protestant missionaries (and usually their converts) normally viewed African traditional religions negatively. This evaluation, however, was not primarily cultural but based on their theological view that most aspects of traditional religion were demonic or satanic. Nevertheless, most missionaries had a higher view of indigenous culture than their fellow countrymen at home and colonial officials in Africa. In the process of learning the local language and culture to effectively communicate the gospel, late nineteenth-century missionaries often came to value aspects of African culture. Some missionaries were even trailblazers in the scientific study of vernacular languages and traditional cultures. Two examples must suffice. Johann G. Christaller (1827–95), a Basel missionary to the Gold Coast (Ghana), devoted most of his life to studying African languages, translating the Bible into the Twi language, and collecting, transcribing, and preserving oral stories, legends, and proverbs. In contrast to other nineteenth-century German philologists, who viewed African languages as evolutionarily inferior to "more developed" languages, Christaller had a high view of Africans and their languages. He ends his 1892 pamphlet *The Languages of Africa* with this exhortation: "Let us honor the human dignity in African people, and also in the languages which are part of their life."[42] Christaller's outstanding contribution is memorialized today in the Akrofi-Christaller Institute of Theology, Mission and Culture in Akropong, Ghana. John H. Weeks's thirty years of missionary work (1882–1912) with the BMS in the Congo enabled him to gain an in-depth and sensitive understanding of local culture and religion. His academic *Anthropological Notes on the Bangala People* was published by the Royal Anthropological Institute of Great Britain in 1909. In his 1914 volume on the "habits, customs, and religious beliefs" of the Bakongo people, Weeks states his goal explicitly: "In this statement of native beliefs I have tried to reflect the native mind," and not "my view of the religious beliefs of the native."[43] Both of these missionaries sought to understand the indigenous culture accurately and sympathetically, to gain an insider's perspective.

42. J. G. Christaller, *Die Sprachen Afrikas* (Stuttgart: Kohlhammer, 1892), 212.
43. John H. Weeks, *Among the Primitive Bakongo* (London: Seeley, Service, 1914), 288.

But the most common missionary response in the high imperialist era was humanitarian: they opposed colonial abuses in general and the mistreatment of indigenous peoples in particular. Missions saw "their social role as the conscience of empire, sounding warnings to government if some European agency overstepped its limits."[44] Even African scholars, largely critical of Western missions, often admit their humanitarian role.

> Much as the missionaries appreciated the ends which [colonial] administrators had in view, they often deplored the means by which they were pursued. They set themselves up as defenders and spokesmen of the people. Along with humanitarian pressure groups in Britain, they used their propaganda organs to make more widely known the inhumanity of the regime which the secular authorities were trying to set up.[45]

Nowhere is this more clearly seen than in the response of missionaries and other humanitarian groups to the Congo atrocities of Leopold II.

Since the formation of the Congo Free State, Leopold as a private entrepreneur had invested heavily in natural resources in his personal fiefdom: first in ivory, then, after the invention of the rubber tire in 1888 caused demand for rubber to soar, in rubber plantations. Conditions for the local Congolese in the Free State worsened dramatically. In the early 1890s, the Anglo-Belgian Rubber Company set monthly quotas for rubber for each village in the Upper Congo region. Then, in 1898, all British investment in the Belgian rubber company was withdrawn, and it was renamed the Abir Congo Company. But the rubber quotas continued, and soldiers were sent into the villages to enforce them. Penalties for failure to meet the quota were severe: the burning of villages, taking of women as hostages, imprisonment, the cutting off of hands, and death. Initially, Protestant missionaries in the Congo naively believed in Leopold's general benevolence and that reported cases of cruelty to Congolese were "isolated aberrations." However, as eyewitness accounts (see sidebar 10.3) and evidence of atrocities mounted, some Congo missionaries swung into action. African American Baptist minister George Washington Williams personally witnessed the abuses while he was in the Congo investigating the possibility of establishing mission work there. He published *An Open Letter to King Leopold II* and wrote a report for US President Benjamin Harrison in which he decries the "crimes against humanity."[46] William Sheppard, an

---

44. Walls, "Evangelization and Civilization," 63.

45. A. E. Afigbo, "Christian Missions and Secular Authorities," in *The History of Christianity in West Africa*, ed. O. U. Kalu (London: Longman, 1981), 187.

46. T. Jack Thompson, *Light on Darkness? Missionary Photography of Africa in the Nineteenth and Early Twentieth Centuries* (Grand Rapids: Eerdmans, 2012), 168–71.

SIDEBAR 10.3

Testimony of Eyewitnesses to the Congo Atrocities

Lieutenant Tilkens writes [in letters]: "Commandant Verstraeten visited my station and congratulated me warmly. He said his report would depend upon the quantity of rubber I was able to provide. The quantity increased from 360 kilograms in September to 1500 in October and, from January onwards it will amount to 4,000 per month, which will bring me in a monthly premium of 500 francs. Am I not a lucky fellow? If I go on like this, within two years I shall have earned premiums of 12,000 francs." . . .

Senator Picard traveled in the Congo Free State. Here are his impressions: "The inhabitants have disappeared. Their homes have been burned; huge heaps of ashes amid neglected palm hedges and devastated abandoned fields. Inhuman floggings, murders, plunderings, and carryings-off. . . . The people flee into the wild or seek protection in French or Portuguese territory." . . .

"Children have their brains dashed out; murders without ceasing . . . soldiers are flogged by the agents' orders if they have been slack in the work of murder; women mutilated because they are true to their husbands. The Commission spends many hours, many days, listening to such reports. . . . Behind each who complains, stands hundreds who do not dare to speak, or lie hundreds slain who will never speak again. The wailings from the Congo are slow and repressed, but irresistibly, the cry grows."

Source: T. Walter Wallbank, *Documents on Modern Africa*
(Princeton: Van Nostrand, 1964), 18–20.

African American Presbyterian missionary among the Kuba people, counted eighty-one severed hands in a village in Kasai province. His publicized findings and article in a Presbyterian magazine gained international attention.

The most influential of the missionary activists, however, was a British Baptist missionary with the Congo Balolo Mission, Alice Seeley Harris. Soon after her arrival in the Congo in 1898, Harris began opposing the atrocities in articles published in the *Regions Beyond* mission magazine, on speaking tours with her husband John in England (1902) and in the United States (1905), and as a member of the Congo Reform Association. Alice's unique contribution was scores of "atrocity photographs" that she took to publicize the horrific nature of the abuses to an international audience. "Many other missionaries . . . were involved in photography for the purpose of substantiating accounts of atrocities; but none had so wide or sustained an influence on the Congo reform movement as Alice Harris."[47] Missionaries such as Williams, Sheppard, and the Harrises were the boots on the ground. They were among the first to blow the whistle on Leopold II's nefarious activities in the Congo. They were joined by a broader network of humanitarian activists, including authors (Mark Twain, Sir Arthur Conan Doyle, Joseph Conrad), politicians (Roger Casement), and organizations (the Congo Reform Association, founded by Edward Dean Morel). This network changed world opinion and brought about the eventual transfer of the Congo from Leopold's personal control to the Belgian government in November 1908. This was a great victory for human rights, and Protestant Congo missionaries played a key role.

In conclusion, the Scramble for Africa was a turning point in the expansion of Christianity in two ways. First, the Scramble typified the dramatic change from earlier forms of imperialism to a new and more virulent form during the high imperialist era (1880–1914) when wide swaths of Africa and Asia were rapidly conquered and colonized. High imperialism was a more pervasive, more intrusive, and more exploitive form of imperialism, and the Scramble was perhaps the purest and most egregious example of such imperialism. Second, the Scramble represented a turning point in the relationship between imperialism and mission. During this period, it became more difficult for missionaries to ignore or operate independently of colonial agendas, as they often had in the past. Yet the topic of imperialism per se is not the same as the issue of missionary responses to imperialism. While evaluations of imperialism per se are rightly negative, missionary responses to imperialism were varied and therefore require a more nuanced evaluation. In general, these missionary responses were primarily motivated by two kinds of concerns: evangelistic, to spread the gospel unhindered; and humanitarian, to protect the indigenous population.

Missionary responses to imperialism at the time of the Scramble for Africa ranged from active collaboration to active resistance, with multiple stances in between. Most missionaries in colonial settings collaborated with imperialism to some extent. Egregious cases of active collaboration with imperialism were less common, but did occur (e.g., Rev. Helm). Some missionaries sought imperial control when it was viewed as more beneficial for evangelism or the protection of native rights. Many welcomed a moderate form of colonialism for the security and infrastructure it provided. Some missionaries to Africa had racist attitudes, although paternalism was more prevalent than outright racism. A few missionaries actively resisted imperialism by their home countries

47. Thompson, *Light on Darkness?*, 188.

(Franz Zahn and Walter Miller). Many grew in their appreciation for the indigenous culture; some were exemplary in this regard (Johann Christaller and John Weeks). The most common missionary response was humanitarian—to protect the well-being and human rights of the local population. Nowhere is this more clearly seen than in the opposition to the Congo atrocities and the reign of terror instigated by Belgium's King Leopold II by a network of humanitarian activists, including missionaries George Williams, William Sheppard, and Alice and John Harris.

We end this chapter with a prayer from a male Congolese teenager dated circa 1880, just before the beginning of the Scramble for Africa. In it, he asks God to send and equip Western missionaries to evangelize his own Fyot people well. This prayer reflects the complexity of local responses to missionaries in the high imperialist age.

> O Father, make the missionaries go to Congo and teach the people. . . . O Father, fill their hearts with your Spirit, and make the hearts of the people believe as they are taught. O Jesus, you shall come again to bring us to heaven. . . . Keep all those people here on this earth, both Fyot and white men. O Jesus, give your Spirit to us, and make us very good . . . then the white men will return to us again in Congo and teach our kindred. . . .
>
> O Jesus, keep those missionaries in Congo as they teach the Fyot people there. Help them to learn well the Fyot tongue, and to instruct the people with care. O help the people to understand as they are being taught by white men. Make the white men . . . send to Congo persons to teach the people. They do not know the commands of Jesus.[48]

---

48. Quoted in H. Grattan Guinness, *The New World of Central Africa* (London: Hodder and Stoughton, 1890), 263–64.

Debating the Meaning of Mission

The Edinburgh World Missionary Conference (1910)

Jesus shall reign where'er the sun
does its successive journeys run;
his kingdom spread from shore to shore,
till moons shall wax and wane no more. . . .

People and realms of every tongue
dwell on his love with sweetest song;
and infant voices shall proclaim
their early blessings on his name.[1]

From June 14 to 23, 1910, an impressive group of roughly twelve hundred mission delegates met in the Assembly Hall of the United Free Church of Scotland on Castle Mound in Edinburgh, Scotland, for the World Missionary Conference (WMC). The Edinburgh conference had a lofty goal.

1. The hymn "Jesus Shall Reign" was sung at the morning session of the first full day (June 15, 1910) of the Edinburgh World Missionary Conference. The popular hymn was published by Isaac Watts in 1719 under the title "Christ's Kingdom among the Gentiles." *World Missionary Conference, 1910: History and Records of the Conference* (New York: Fleming H. Revell, 1910), 76.

Unlike the earlier Centenary Missionary Conference in London in 1888 and the Ecumenical Missionary Conference in New York in 1900, whose objective "was to inform, educate, and impress," the WMC's "first aim" was "to make the Conference as far as possible a consultative assembly," tasked with "a more earnest study of the missionary enterprise."[2] It was convened in order to scientifically analyze the past achievements of Protestant missions and to promote the "cooperative study" of the remaining obstacles "with a view to helping (the representative societies and boards) to solve them, and achieve together the evangelization of the world."[3]

In preparation for the WMC, an International Committee was formed under the leadership of American Methodist layman John R. Mott and the United Free Church of Scotland's secretary for mission studies Joseph H. Oldham. The committee selected eight topics that it judged to be "of cardinal importance and special immediate urgency" for the task of world evangelization. Each of these topics was assigned to a commission, or "preparatory working group." Their task was "to gather up, and present in summary form, the results of the largest experience and best thoughts of missionaries in the field."[4] To gather this data, the International Committee drafted a questionnaire for each commission and sent them out to hundreds of missionaries throughout the world. Each commission report was four to five hundred pages long, formed from data drawn from about one thousand missionary responses.

John Mott's watchword, "the evangelization of the world in this generation," did not become the official motto of the conference, but it articulated the vision of many of the delegates to the WMC. Mott defined the watchword in his volume published in 1900 with that title:

> It means the giving to all men an adequate opportunity of knowing Jesus Christ as their Savior and of becoming His real disciples. This involves a distribution of missionary agencies as will make the knowledge of the Gospel accessible to all creatures. . . . The evangelization of the world in this generation, therefore, means the preaching of the Gospel to those who are now living . . . in their lifetime.[5]

Mott placed priority squarely on the oral proclamation of the gospel. All other forms of missionary ministry—whether educational, medical, or literary—

2. *World Missionary Conference, 1910*, 8.
3. David A. Kerr and Kenneth R. Ross, eds., *Edinburgh 2010: Mission Then and Now* (Eugene, OR: Wipf & Stock, 2009), 4.
4. Kerr and Ross, *Edinburgh 2010*, 8.
5. John R. Mott, *The Evangelization of the World in This Generation* (New York: SVM, 1900), 3, 6.

were evaluated by the degree "to which they prepare the way for the Gospel message, promote its acceptance, manifest its spirit and benefits, multiply points of contact with human souls, and increase the number and efficacy of those who preach Christ."[6] Mott's conviction concerning the primacy of evangelism in the missionary task was reflected in the WMC Commission I report on "Carrying the Gospel to All the Non-Christian World." It affirmed that "all existing [mission] methods are needed, and that all are equally to be desired, each in its proper place." Some mission methods were essential and indispensable: preaching and teaching the gospel, establishing and developing churches on the mission field, and Bible translation. Other specialized methods, including education, medicine, and literature, were nonessential and secondary. They had "high and undoubted value," but their "usefulness" was not universal—it varied across the mission fields.[7]

The majority of the delegates at the WMC were evangelicals who passionately believed on theological grounds that the missionary task extended to the *whole world*, not just to predominantly non-Christian countries. However, in order to assuage the scruples of the Anglo-Catholic wing of the Anglican Church on this point, and to ensure its participation in the WMC, a compromise was struck. The WMC would only deal with "Carrying the Gospel to all the *Non-Christian* World," the topic of Commission I, and not to Europe (except Turkey), Latin America, or areas where Eastern Orthodoxy held sway. Thus, "Edinburgh 1910 implicitly declared Protestant proselytism of Roman Catholics, and less clearly of Orthodox and Oriental Christians, to be no valid part of Christian mission." John Mott admitted that, in the name of ecumenical cooperation, "we have been led beyond where we intended to go."[8]

This compromise limited the conference delegates to Protestant foreign missionaries who propagated the gospel among non-Christian peoples, thus excluding a wide swath of missionaries. The missionary representation was also uneven in other ways. No Roman Catholic or Orthodox Christians were present. Of the 1,215 official delegates representing 170 mission boards, only eighteen were Christians from the "younger churches" of the Global South who had been converted through the missionary enterprise. One hundred seventy were from continental Europe, predominately Germany. A full one

---

6. William R. Hutchison, *Errand to the World: American Protestant Thought and Foreign Missions* (Chicago: University of Chicago Press, 1987), 120.

7. World Missionary Conference, *Report of Commission I* (New York: Fleming H. Revell, 1910), 299, 312–13.

8. Brian Stanley, *The World Missionary Conference, Edinburgh 1910* (Grand Rapids: Eerdmans, 2009), 71–72.

thousand delegates hailed either from Great Britain or North America, which gave a decidedly Anglo-American perspective to the conference. Among the American delegates, mainline and other denominational missions predominated. Women and African Americans were underrepresented, as were representatives from the Holiness, Pentecostal, and what would later be called fundamentalist missions.[9] Furthermore, the delegates at the WMC assumed that Western missionaries would be the primary agents in the evangelization of the world for the foreseeable future. Thus, for the most part, the WMC upheld a traditional, conservative approach to mission. Nevertheless, more progressive themes were introduced in the conference debates by delegates of a more liberal persuasion and were reflected in the commission reports.

The "World Missionary Conference . . . has been described as a turning point, a lens, a landmark, and a watershed."[10] The conference was a landmark event. It was recognized as a "decisive and historic moment" by contemporaries and is still seen as such today. The 1900 Ecumenical Missionary Conference in New York was considerably larger (2,500 delegates and up to 200,000 in attendance), yet its ongoing significance paled in comparison to the WMC. The WMC was also a lens. The themes examined by the eight commissions have had "enduring value" and "great relevance." "Edinburgh 1910 raised questions which remain seminal for any serious discussion of church and mission today."[11] Finally, the WMC was a watershed moment and a turning point in the expansion of Christianity in this sense: it was a culmination of the traditional, conservative mission approach of the nineteenth century and a harbinger of newer missional trends in the twentieth. First, the WMC as the culmination and climactic high point of the nineteenth-century mission movement looked back and both analyzed and celebrated the missionary successes of the previous century. The conference was characterized by much missionary enthusiasm and optimism that the rapid evangelization of the world was within reach. But second, the WMC was also a harbinger for newer trends that redefined the missionary task and the meaning of mission, in large part due to the increasing popularity of theological liberalism within Protestantism. Societal changes due to industrialization, the horrors of the two world wars, the rise of communism, and the end to imperial expansion also played a key role in the coming of these newer trends. These trends and events shattered the earlier optimism and replaced it with more chastened

9. Stanley, *World Missionary Conference*, 71–73, 91–97, 323; Hutchison, *Errand to the World*, 126–28.

10. William Richey Hogg, "Edinburgh 1910—Ecumenical Keystone," *Religion in Life* 29 (1959–1960): 339.

11. Kerr and Ross, *Edinburgh 2010*, 307–8, 313.

expectations. The WMC's role as both a culmination of older trends and a harbinger of newer ones justifies the broad time frame of this chapter, which focuses on the period from the mid-nineteenth to the mid-twentieth century.

The WMC is often studied for its role in launching the ecumenical movement. The focus of this chapter, however, is another topic—the complex development and debate over the meaning of mission by theological conservatives and liberals from roughly 1850 to 1950. In particular, the debate hinges on what constitutes legitimate mission work. Were secondary (or ancillary) mission methods such as education, vocational training, and medical ministries only legitimate missionary activities when they directly contributed to evangelistic goals, as John Mott contended? Or were they legitimate "mission" in and of themselves? Was mission exclusively evangelistic and individualistic (preaching to convert individuals), or should mission include promoting Christianity as a diffusive or leavening influence in non-Christian societies? The debate was often framed in the nineteenth century as "Christianization" versus "civilization"; in the twentieth century the debate frequently hinged on mission as "preaching" or "proclamation" versus "social ministry." This range of different mission theories and practices was reflected in the commission reports of the WMC. It is important to note, however, that these theories and practices were not strict polarities. Rather, both theological liberals and conservatives adopted civilizing goals and social ministries in varying degrees during the time frame in question. Evangelicals frequently gave greater priority to gospel proclamation than theological liberals and advocates of the Social Gospel. That did not mean, however, that the latter groups entirely denied the importance of preaching and conversion. However, it was true that they generally "lacked enthusiasm for direct evangelism" and characteristically aimed "to bring people and societies to Christ by environmental influences and a kind of spiritual osmosis."[12]

In this chapter, we will examine the mission theory used to support or limit the practice of two ancillary mission methods: educational ministry (including vocational training and the businesses it spawned) and medical missions. Each of these two sections will briefly outline the relevant WMC Commission Report's findings on the ancillary mission method in question. This is followed by a deeper look at the mission theory and practice of a representative mission society or mission field that employed that mission method. I will note changes in mission theory and practice along the way. The first section focuses on the educational ministry of the ABCFM from the 1830s to 1910 and beyond. I give special attention to the evolving educational mission theory

12. Hutchison, *Errand to the World*, 103.

of Rufus Anderson, from a focus on its civilizing value to a narrower focus on its conversionary and edificatory value (the training of native clergy). Anderson's later approach led to a backlash from women missionary teachers, which resulted in the founding of separate women's missionary societies to circumvent mission educational restrictions, not only by the ABCFM but by other denominations as well. I will discuss vocational training—a subset of educational ministry—and the subsequent business enterprises of the Basel Mission (EMSB) in India, since they provide further texture to the debate over the meaning of mission. The second section examines the developing understanding of the purposes of medical missions in general, and in Korea in particular, from a utilitarian approach to strategic, evangelistic, and humanitarian or imitative approaches.

Education and Mission

Commission III of the 1910 Edinburgh WMC tackled the topic "Education in Relation to the Christianization of National Life." The very title of the commission "defined the place of education in the missionary enterprise in a broad sense. . . . Its horizons were to extend to the permeation of the entire fabric of national life in the mission lands by Christian ideals." This broad understanding of the goal of mission education had been "a subject of lively debate in Protestant missionary circles . . . for some time" and continued to be so in the following decades.[13] On the one hand, the Commission III report made clear that education was not driven by merely a concern to convert individuals but aimed to influence the entirety of society. On the other hand, it insisted, "We of this Commission are concerned with education considered only as a means, direct or indirect, towards the end of making Christian disciples." This debate over the meaning of educational mission explains the range of goals that Commission III assigned to mission education. First, it was *evangelistic* and served as "an instrument of direct evangelism," usually in primary schools. Second, it was *edificatory*, concerned with "developing and training leaders for the indigenous church" through secondary or higher education. Finally, it included *leavening*—"diffusing Christian ideals and influence through society at large"—even if that did not result in conversions or growth of the church.[14]

Commission III, in its conclusions, stressed the priority of the evangelistic and edificatory purposes for education over the leavening goal. However, it

13. Stanley, *World Missionary Conference*, 167.
14. Stanley, *World Missionary Conference*, 176–77.

conceded that in those situations "where Christianity and civilization were judged to be at an early stage of development, the Commission tended to revert to a diffusionist [leavening] view that saw mission education as integral to the task of constructing a new Christian social and cultural fabric."[15] As noted above, the debate over the meaning of mission in the nineteenth century was often framed as "Christianization versus civilization." There were notable "swings of the pendulum . . . in missionary ideology . . . as each generation debated the relative importance of 'civilization versus Christianization.'"[16] In this section, the pendulum swings in the views of civilization and education represented by Rufus Anderson (1796–1880) and the ABCFM will be examined. Born into a pastor's family in Yarmouth, Maine, Anderson volunteered to serve overseas in India in 1822, but he complied with the ABCFM's request that he remain instead in an administrative capacity at mission headquarters. He is a worthy representative for educational mission for two reasons. First, he was the secretary and chief policy maker of the ABCFM from 1832 to 1866, as well as "the outstanding American organizer and theorist of foreign missions in the nineteenth century." Second, not only did Anderson's views on the issue of mission education change dramatically over time; he also "developed the most wide-ranging rationale for these revisions."[17]

The conventional wisdom of Protestant missions in the early nineteenth century was to put civilization ahead of Christianization or, to use the categories of Commission III, to put leavening or diffusionist goals ahead of evangelism. For example, Samuel Marsden, a CMS missionary to the Maori in New Zealand (1814–28), believed that "commerce and the arts of civilization" must be "planted first," which would then "open the way for the gospel."[18] This was likewise true for the ABCFM's early missions among Native Americans (beginning in 1816) and in Hawaii (see chap. 7). In 1819 the Prudential Committee of the ABCFM charged the first company of missionaries to Hawaii to "aim at nothing short of . . . raising up the whole people to an elevated state of Christian civilization; of bringing or preparing the means of bringing, thousands and millions . . . to the mansions of eternal blessedness."[19] The expectation was that an "elevated state of Christian civilization" would pave the way for the conversion of the local population.

15. Stanley, *World Missionary Conference*, 198.
16. Paul William Harris, *Nothing but Christ: Rufus Anderson and the Ideology of Protestant Foreign Missions* (Oxford: Oxford University Press, 1999), 162.
17. Hutchison, *Errand to the World*, 78.
18. Timothy Yates, *The Conversion of the Maori: Years of Religious and Social Change, 1814–1842* (Grand Rapids: Eerdmans, 2013), 14.
19. *Instructions of the Prudential Committee of the ABCFM* (Lahaina, HI: Mission Seminary Press, 1838), 27.

Anderson, as the newly appointed secretary of the ABCFM, defended a civilizing goal for mission education in an 1834 article titled "Importance of Teaching Science to the Heathen in Connection with Christianity." Anderson claimed that "the object of modern missions" was "to form . . . *enlightened Christian communities* in every part of the unevangelized world." He rejected on the basis of experience, however, the "maxim that we must civilize men before we can Christianize them." Anderson then listed four reasons for teaching the sciences in Christian schools and seminaries: (1) they awakened "the dormant mind"; (2) they rendered the school curriculum "more interesting and useful to the heathen"; (3) they were necessary for an adequate education of indigenous pastors; and (4) they helped make a community "intelligent and civilized."[20] The civilizing and edificatory goals were present, but not the evangelistic.

That changed in the following decade. "A growing emphasis on preaching for conversions [within the ABCFM] shifted the focus increasingly to the individual and away from Anderson's early emphasis on forming '*enlightened Christian communities*,'" a civilizing goal.[21] In his 1845 sermon "The Theory of Missions to the Heathen," Anderson argued that the introduction of Western civilization into mission contexts was "a formidable hindrance," since it mixed their "sublime spiritual object," the conversion of the people, "with the more dubious aim of 'reorganizing . . . the structure of that social system of which the converts form a part.'" It had been a mistake for the ABCFM to send farmers and craftsmen to the mission field. "A simpler, cheaper, more effectual means of civilizing the savage, was the gospel alone," communicated through oral preaching.[22]

This had consequences for ABCFM mission schools. Anderson was well aware by this time that most mission schools were ineffective at bringing about conversion; they were not fulfilling the evangelistic goal. In 1854–55, Rufus Anderson led a deputation to India, Ceylon, and the Near East to urge those missions to terminate all schooling that did not directly serve conversionary purposes. Henceforth, it was inadequate to view schooling as "preparatory to conversion," or in the language of the WMC's Commission III, as a leavening influence. All mission education must cease to use English as the primary language of instruction. Instead, the new priority for education was to use vernacular languages to achieve the edificatory goal—to train and develop indigenous pastors according to three-self principles (see chap. 9).[23] The revised

20. Rufus Anderson, "Importance of Teaching Science to the Heathen in Connection with Christianity," *American Quarterly Observer* 2 (January 1834): 26–27, 31–33.
21. Harris, *Nothing but Christ*, 57.
22. Hutchison, *Errand to the World*, 82, 85.
23. Hutchison, *Errand to the World*, 84–85.

SIDEBAR 11.1

Rufus Anderson, "Outline of Missionary Policy" (1856)

Missions are instituted *for the spread of a scriptural, self-propagating Christianity*. This is their only aim. Civilization, as an end, they never attempt; still they are the most successful of all civilizing agencies, because (1) a certain degree of general improvement is involved in a self-propagating Christianity, and must be fostered as a *means* thereto; and (2) a rapid change in the intellectual and social life is a sure outgrowth there-from. . . . If we resolve the end of missions into its simplest elements, we shall find that it embraces (1) the conversion of lost men, (2) organizing them into churches, (3) giving those churches a competent native ministry, and (4) conducting them to the stage of independence and (in most cases) of self-propagation. . . . We are brought now to the chief question of missions: "What place, *relatively*, shall we assign to the *preacher*, the *teacher*, and the *book-maker*?" The value of *oral preaching* none will dispute. It must ever stand in the foreground. It is *indispensable*. . . . The school and the press, then, are to be regarded as auxiliaries. . . . Education as an end can never be promoted; as a means it is invaluable. . . . Speaking with greater precision we may say, that oral preaching is *absolutely* indispensable; the school and the press are relatively indispensable. There is no conceivable way that the ultimate end of missions can be attained without the living preacher; but it is possible, *hypothetically*, to reach this end without schools or books.

Source: *Report of the American Board of Commissioners for Foreign Missions* (Boston: T. R. Marvin, 1856), 51–53.

educational policy of Rufus Anderson and the ABCFM was summarized in the "Outline of Missionary Policy" included in the 1856 Annual Report (see sidebar 11.1). This policy reflected Anderson's "growing emphasis" on preaching, conversion, and the development of an independent, indigenous church. These were "indispensable" elements of the missionary task; the "school and the press," however, were merely "auxiliary" elements and therefore dispensable. This priority resulted in "increased suspicion of expensive press and educational operations."[24]

Anderson's change in educational policy was accepted by many, though not all, ABCFM missionaries. Dr. Crosby H. Wheeler (1823–96), a strong

24. *Report of the American Board of Commissioners for Foreign Missions* (Boston: T. R. Marvin, 1856), 51–53; Harris, *Nothing but Christ*, 75.

supporter of Anderson's new policy, was an ABCFM missionary among the Armenians in Harput in Ottoman Turkey. Wheeler's strict insistence that "missions should not open schools until they have converts prepared to support them" made self-support the "cornerstone of the Three-Self Formula" and "represented not only the ascendency but also the hardening of Anderson's [educational] policies."[25] In contrast, Royal G. Wilder (1816–87), who had supervised an ABCFM boarding school and developed a number of elementary schools in Ahmednagar, India, and its environs (1846–52), rejected Anderson's new policy. Due to his inability to get along with his missionary colleagues there, he was transferred to Kolhapur in 1852. Wilder's desire to continue educational ministry was denied by Anderson. A heated public controversy ensued. Wilder gathered evidence from other missions to support his contention that educational ministry and *not* preaching was the only effective method for missions in India. He touted the "civil and social benefits" of mission education (a civilizing or leavening goal) in articles and in his four-hundred-page volume, *Mission Schools in India*, published in 1861. His writings kept the debate over the purpose of mission education alive.[26]

Another group felt alienated by Rufus Anderson's revised educational policies—female missionary teachers. The education of indigenous girls and women had provided a special niche that single and married women missionaries could fill on the mission field. Anderson's 1854–55 deputation to India and Ceylon insisted that all education must directly serve evangelistic and three-self goals. As a result, the number of girls' primary schools in those countries was reduced, the goal of higher education was limited to training wives for indigenous pastors, and education in English was excluded from boarding schools. The "end result of making education subservient to evangelism was to frustrate the major way that female missionaries were able to minister in the Indian context. The implications were especially negative for single women who were most responsible for female higher education." Some ABCFM female missionaries agreed with the new policy (e.g., Fidelia Fiske). But the majority of Congregationalist women "quietly worked to reverse Anderson's strictures against educational mission."[27] One way that this was accomplished was through the formation of separate women's missionary societies.

In 1868, a group of Congregationalist women formed the Women's Foreign Missionary Society of New England as an auxiliary of the ABCFM. This

---

25. Harris, *Nothing but Christ*, 160.
26. Harris, *Nothing but Christ*, 151, 155–56.
27. Dana L. Robert, *American Women in Mission: A Social History of Their Thought and Practice* (Macon, GA: Mercer University Press, 1997), 121–22, 124, 131–32.

occurred just seven years after the founding of the first women's society by Sarah Doremus in 1861, the interdenominational Women's Union Missionary Society. Rufus Anderson had retired as foreign secretary of the ABCFM in 1866, and it was no accident that the new Congregationalist society was established during the tenure of his successor, Nathanial Clark, who was considerably more sympathetic to the women's cause. Ironically, Eliza Anderson, Rufus's wife, was on the women's board. Shortly thereafter, the Women's Foreign Missionary Society of the Methodist Episcopal Church was founded, and the women's missionary movement was launched. By 1900, forty-one women's missionary societies had been established. They were staffed, directed, and funded by women, and they supported twelve hundred missionaries. The rise of the women's foreign mission movement led to the temporary demise of Anderson's educational priorities, which ranked education as subservient to evangelism and the development of three-self churches. The burgeoning number of single women missionaries in the late nineteenth century coincided with and fueled a resurgence of mission schools.[28] In fact, by the early twentieth century, the number of mission-founded schools was greater than the total number of missionaries or churches on the mission field.[29] This trend continued even after 1910 as most of the women's missionary societies were gradually merged into their denominational boards due to an increased emphasis on ecumenical unity.

The reevaluation of the goal of missionary education and the resurgence in mission schools in the last decades of the nineteenth century reflected a broader trend within Western Christianity. The rapid growth and popularity of liberal Protestant theology within mainline denominations in North America by the 1920s meant that the legitimacy of evangelism and conversion as missionary goals was questioned. This lack of urgency for mission and evangelism was related to an increasingly positive view of the salvific potential of non-Christian religions by theological liberals. Their general lack of belief in the exclusive claims of Christianity eroded the viability of evangelism. In addition, adherents of the Social Gospel viewed otherworldly salvation as inadequate to address the social ills of modern society. If mission was pursued at all, it should aim to further the goal of social justice. These liberal trends resulted in a renewed commitment to civilizing mission goals, with "Christian service and example [viewed] as valid modes of evangelization."[30]

In response to these trends, theological conservatives (fundamentalists and evangelicals) after 1920 once again advocated that education, as well as

28. Harris, *Nothing but Christ*, 161–62.
29. Hutchison, *Errand to the World*, 100.
30. Hutchison, *Errand to the World*, 103, 105, 111.

medicine and social service, be subordinated to oral preaching—an emphasis reminiscent of Rufus Anderson's mid-nineteenth-century priorities. Education and medical missions were not valid as a form of leavening society; rather, the evangelistic goal must remain primary—at least in theory, though often not in practice. Northern Baptist Augustus Strong expressed it thus: "The preaching of the old doctrines of sin and salvation" must never "give place to 'another gospel' of cooperative Christian work. . . . To lay greater emphasis upon the fruits of Christianity than upon its roots, is to insult Christ and ultimately to make Christianity only one of many earth-born religions."[31] Protestant theological conservatives from the 1920s onward rejected the maxims espoused by liberal theologians and adherents to the Social Gospel. Mission meant, first and foremost, preaching the gospel of sin and grace. It was not until the 1970s and the Lausanne Congress on World Evangelization (see chap. 12) that a sizable group of evangelicals (re)affirmed holistic mission and the integral connection between the Great Commission and the Great Commandment. By then, the debate over the meaning of mission had, like a pendulum, swung back and forth several times.

Commission III of the 1910 Edinburgh WMC analyzed and evaluated not only traditional mission education but also industrial education, or vocational training as we call it today, and the mission businesses that such training spawned. From its foundation in 1815, the Evangelical Missionary Society of Basel (EMSB), like the ABCFM, supported the civilizing goal. Unlike the latter, it also had a positive view of the integration of Christian trade and industry with evangelistic mission work. It was by no means the only missionary society to promote vocational education and industrial and commercial enterprises, but it was the "largest and best known," with the most "extensive and developed economic activity" of any society.[32] On its South Indian field (from 1834 on), the need for vocational training and employment opportunities was acute for Christian converts, who were often ostracized from their caste and, therefore, from their occupation. For this reason, the EMSB founded vocational training schools and factories for weaving cloth, printing, and tile manufacture, which by 1913 employed 3,600 workers.

The EMSB evolved in its understanding of the goal of its industrial education and businesses. After a visit to the Indian field in 1851–52, Mission Inspector Josef Josenhans (tenure 1850–79) declared in the 1853 Annual Report of the EMSB's Industrial Commission that business activities were not merely an aid to mission but *"may be called a mission work in itself*; evange-

---

31. Hutchison, *Errand to the World*, 140–41.
32. William J. Danker, *Profit for the Lord: Economic Activities in Moravian Missions and the Basel Mission Trading Company* (Eugene, OR: Wipf & Stock, 1971), 80, 113–14.

lization, not by preaching or direct promulgation of the Gospel, but by the power of example."[33] Thus, during Josenhans's tenure, the EMSB defined vocational training and commercial enterprises not as ancillary activities supporting the primary goal of evangelization but as mission in and of itself. That changed during the tenure of his successor, Mission Inspector Otto Schott (tenure 1879–84). Like Rufus Anderson, Schott was a firm advocate of three-self principles. He believed that the EMSB's business activities hindered the development of an independent Indian church by focusing attention on those already converted rather than on the non-Christian population and by creating an unhealthy dependence on the mission. The mission industries, he wrote, "are hindering the progress of the congregations toward independence. . . . They [the converts] will not reach their pedagogical aim, because the missionaries control everything, even the smallest details, and distrust the people. . . . As long as we continue in this way, we cannot develop any spiritual life." The Basel "Mission Committee was not willing to accept Schott's understanding of mission."[34] Therefore, in June 1884, Schott submitted his resignation. Inspector Schott was a casualty in the debate over the meaning of mission within the EMSB. Interestingly, the WMC's Commission III report came to the same conclusions Schott had thirty years earlier. It concluded that industrial undertakings in India fostered dependency among the converts, which was inimical to the development of an independent, indigenous church on three-self principles. "Paid employment" of Christian converts creates a "body of hangers-on," it wrote, who "fail to form habits of independence and self-reliance."[35]

In summary, Rufus Anderson's educational mission theory evolved over time. Early in his tenure as ABCFM secretary, Anderson espoused a civilizing goal for mission education. His adoption of three-self principles in the middle decades of the nineteenth century led to a seismic shift in his educational mission theory. Thenceforth, he espoused that education had to serve conversionary and three-self goals. Anderson's new priorities were praised by some ABCFM missionaries (e.g., Crosby Wheeler) but resulted in a backlash from others (e.g., Royal Wilder). The pushback from female missionary teachers was even more pronounced; it resulted in the formation of separate women's missionary societies. In the last decades of the nineteenth

33. Henry S. Wilson, "Basel Mission's Industrial Enterprise in South Kanara and Its Impact between 1834 and 1914," *Indian Church History Review* 14, no. 2 (December 1980): 98.

34. Karl Rennstich, "The Understanding of Mission, Civilization and Colonialism in the Basel Mission," in *Missionary Ideologies in the Imperialist Era: 1880–1920*, ed. Torben Christensen and William R. Hutchison (Arhus, Denmark: Aros, 1982), 97–98.

35. World Missionary Conference, *Report of Commission III* (New York: Fleming H. Revell, 1910), 302.

century, a resurgence in the number and scope of mission schools occurred. The fundamentalist-modernist controversy of the 1920s led to bifurcation of the purpose of mission education between theological liberals and conservatives: the former espoused largely diffusionist or leavening goals; the latter placed priority on conversionary and edificatory goals, even as they, in many cases, continued to found and promote mission schools. Finally, a similar debate over the meaning of educational mission took place in the EMSB in India. Vocational training and business enterprises were deemed by Mission Inspector Josenhans as evangelization and mission in and of themselves. His successor, Otto Schott, vehemently disagreed, in large part due to his three-self convictions. Thirty years later, the WMC Commission III report agreed with much of Schott's assessment.

Medicine and Mission

Commission I of the WMC outlined the "agencies of evangelization" used in each mission field. Although medical missions were relegated to the non-essential, ancillary mission methods, they were nevertheless, according to the Commission I report, one of the "specialties of the mission propaganda" that had "high and undoubted value." Their "usefulness in various fields" varied. In Africa, for example, medical ministry was "extremely useful. . . . It is an offset to the evils of witchcraft, and directs sufferers to the true source of healing." In contrast, the role of medical missions in Japan was "waning" and played a "subordinate role" due to the advanced state of "excellent government hospital facilities." In China, the "greatest need" was for "direct evangelistic work." Nevertheless, female missionary doctors were still greatly needed; they were culturally "essential" to treat the "suffering womanhood" in China.[36]

Four key purposes for medical missions were presented in the Commission I report: three of them were included in the findings of the Sectional Conference on Medical Missions (see sidebar 11.2), which convened during the WMC, and one (the strategic purpose) was found elsewhere in the report. The first purpose was a *utilitarian* one, to maintain missionary health on the mission field. "Medical missionaries should be sent to every district where missionaries are located" to provide professional medical assistance if it is otherwise unavailable. A second purpose was a *strategic* one, to "break down barriers" and to "attract reluctant and suspicious populations" in unresponsive fields.

36. World Missionary Conference, *Report of Commission I*, 2, 305, 310, 313.

SIDEBAR 11.2

Sectional Conference on Medical Missions in *Report of Commission I*, WMC (1910)

This Sectional Meeting of Medical Delegates, Medical Missionaries and other Medical Practitioners interested in the Medical Aspects of Missionary Work desire to represent to the Commission on "carrying the Gospel to all the world" their unanimous opinion—

(1) That Medical Missions should be recognized as an integral and essential part of the Missionary Work of the Christian Church—

    a. Because we are led by the example and command of Christ to make use of the ministry of healing as a means of revealing God to man; and

    b. Because the efficacy and necessity of such work as an evangelistic agency has been proved in many lands again and again, and such work has been sealed by the blessing of God.

(2) That Medical Missions should be continued and extended, and that they should be under the charge of fully-qualified Medical Missionaries. . . .

(3) That all Societies should send fully-qualified Medical Missionaries to every district where Missionaries are located when other qualified medical assistance is not available.

Source: World Missionary Conference, *Report of Commission I* (New York: Fleming H. Revell, 1910), 317.

A third purpose was an *evangelistic* one, to lead people to Christ. Medical ministry was necessary since its efficacy as an "evangelistic agency" had been "proved in many lands again and again." The fourth and last purpose was a *humanitarian* and *imitative* purpose, to follow and obey Christ's example to heal the sick and relieve suffering. Due to the importance of these purposes, the medical mission delegates at the WMC unanimously believed that "Medical Missions should be recognized as an integral and essential part of the Missionary Work of the Christian Church."[37] The four purposes above are listed in roughly the order in which they developed in mission history.

37. World Missionary Conference, *Report of Commission I*, 313–14, 317; Andrew F. Walls, "'The Heavy Artillery of the Missionary Army': The Domestic Importance of the Nineteenth Century Medical Missionary," in *The Church and Healing*, ed. W. J. Sheils (Oxford: Blackwell, 1982), 288.

The following overview of the development of medical missions is structured around these four purposes.

In the early decades of the Protestant missionary movement, medical doctors were seldom sought or accepted by missionary societies. In 1852 it is estimated there were only thirteen European medical missionaries; in contrast, by 1900 there were 650. James Henderson, a well-trained physician, could find no mission board that would accept his services in 1858. If he had been accepted by a board, his role as a missionary physician would most likely have been limited to the *utilitarian* purpose—to provide medical care for mission personnel in order to decrease mortality and increase effectiveness, particularly in those regions where health hazards were rife. There were two main reasons why mission societies were hesitant to accept medical candidates. The clergymen, who controlled most mission boards, were convinced that "medical work was likely to distract from the true missionary object of conversion to Christ." Also, the medical profession only began to gain respectability in the late 1850s, due to groundbreaking medical advances in anesthetics, hygiene, epidemiology, and bacteriology. Those advances led to a "substantial re-evaluation" and a broadening of purposes for the medical missionary in the last three decades of the century. Nevertheless, the Sectional Conference on Medical Missions at the WMC still recommended the utilitarian purpose in those locations lacking adequate medical care for mission staff.[38]

The reevaluation of the role of medical professionals in the missionary enterprise broadened their scope of usefulness. The conviction arose that medical missionaries could build effective bridges to peoples resistant to Christianity. According to the Commission I report, this *strategic* purpose was especially relevant in locations such as India and in Muslim countries. There, medical missions helped destroy "barriers of intolerance . . . and serious misunderstandings of our faith" and effectively modified "the attitude of both Government and people toward missionary work."[39] Nowhere was the strategic purpose of medical missions seen more clearly than in its role in opening up Korea to Protestant missionary work. Dr. Horace Allen, an American Presbyterian medical missionary, was the first Protestant missionary to the Hermit Kingdom. In September 1884, he was appointed physician to the American diplomatic legation in Seoul. Although Korean king

38. C. Peter Williams, "Healing and Evangelism: The Place of Medicine in Late Victorian Protestant Missionary Thinking," in Sheils, *Church and Healing*, 271–73; Christoffer H. Grundmann, *Sent to Heal: Emergence and Development of Medical Missions* (Lanham, MD: University Press of America, 2005), 45–51; World Missionary Conference, *Report of Commission I*, 317.
39. World Missionary Conference, *Report of Commission I*, 307, 311, 313–14.

Kojong (1852–1919) was reform-minded, Korea's antiforeign laws were still in force, and early Presbyterian and Methodist missionaries were limited to educational and medical ministry. Dr. Allen gained favor with the royal family when he saved the life of Queen Myeongseong's nephew by Western medical procedures after the young man had been seriously wounded in a coup d'état in December 1884. In gratitude, the king provided a plot of ground in Seoul and helped furnish and maintain a Western-style government hospital there, staffed by missionaries. The cordial relationship with the royal family meant that, increasingly after 1895, Protestant missionaries could pursue direct evangelism.[40] The strategic purpose of medical missions had opened the door and ultimately aided evangelism. Between 1903 and 1908, the Great Korean Revival brought thousands into the church. By the time of the 1910 WMC, Commission I reported that, in Korea, direct evangelism by Western missionaries and Korean evangelists was "one of the characteristic features of mission work in that country" and that "medical work as a method" was no longer "very prominent or extensively used."[41] Korea was no longer a country resistant to the gospel; therefore, the strategic purpose of medical missions was no longer essential.

The third purpose of medical missions was *evangelistic*, to bring individuals to faith in Christ. Not surprisingly, both Rufus Anderson of the ABCFM and Otto Schott of the EMSB emphasized that medical missions must serve conversionary goals. The ABCFM first defined the role of the missionary physician in its 1845 "Manual for Missionary Candidates."

> A *missionary physician* should have . . . a competent medical education; and he should be prepared to make his professional knowledge and skill all directly subservient to the furtherance of the Gospel. It is important that he should be well acquainted with the natural sciences, and specially that he should be well read on the great topics of Christian theology.

For the ABCFM in the mid-nineteenth century, medical work must be "directly subservient" to evangelization. Although a missionary doctor must be "well-read" in Christian theology and must evangelize, he was not a full missionary like his clerical colleagues but only an assistant missionary, until 1897. The EMSB under Inspector Schott defined its position on medical missions in 1880 in a similar fashion to the ABCFM: "The purposes of medical missions are never simply limited to healing the body. Rather, the intention is always

40. L. George Paik, *The History of Protestant Missions in Korea, 1832–1910* (Seoul: Yonsei University Press, 1970), 84–86, 97–107, 134–38.
41. World Missionary Conference, *Report of Commission I*, 302–3.

to lead the heathen closer to the gospel. . . . Its purpose is thus not scientific or philanthropic, but rather religious."[42] Schott, in emphasizing that medical missions were not a "philanthropic" but an evangelistic endeavor, bucked the growing trend in mission circles.

In the last two decades of the nineteenth century, many evangelical missionary societies continued to stress that spiritual goals (saving the soul) had priority over healing the body. Public sympathy, however—even among evangelicals—had shifted to the benevolent aspect of missionary work. In an era when Christianity was losing intellectual credibility, "the simplistic belief in the eternal punishment of the heathen declined" among theological liberals. As a result, "there was less concentration on saving men from a fearful eternity [and] more on creating a meaningful present" through altruistic medical service and other good deeds. The benevolent, *humanitarian* purpose of medical missions was stressed. A corollary to the humanitarian purpose was the *imitative* one, which called medical professionals to imitate Christ's compassion for the sick and his healing ministry. John Lowe, the secretary of the Edinburgh Medical Missionary Society Training Institute, was an early voice (1871) for the imitative purpose of medical missions. Although the conversion of locals remained an important goal, for Lowe "medical missions were . . . more than a useful auxiliary to evangelism." It was necessary to heal the sick in order to "fulfill our Lord's Commission in all its breadth and fullness" and to "preach the Gospel by word and deed." "To hold forth the Word of Life, along with a practical manifestation of the spirit of the Gospel, is therefore the true meaning of 'Preaching the Gospel,' and this is the aim and object of Medical Missions."[43] The WMC's Sectional Conference on Medical Missions states this conviction even stronger. Medical missions were an essential part of missionary work, "because . . . the example and command of Christ" leads us "to make use of the ministry of healing as a means of revealing God to man." The WMC medical delegates were saying, in effect, that healing the sick was not an aid to evangelism but was evangelism itself, since healing revealed God to people. This more radical reinterpretation of the relationship between evangelism and healing affirmed that "ministering to the ills of the body was the Christian's task as much as the saving of the soul."[44] This view was widely accepted in theologically liberal circles in the first half of the twentieth century. Although most evangelical mission societies continued to view spiritual ministry as primary, the philanthropic trends

42. Grundmann, *Sent to Heal*, 3–4, 7.
43. Williams, "Healing and Evangelism," 278, 280–82.
44. Williams, "Healing and Evangelism," 280; World Missionary Conference, *Report of Commission I*, 317.

within society led some theological conservatives to argue that medical mission was a part of evangelism.

Medical missions was an ancillary mission method that only came into its own in the 1870s, considerably later than education and vocational training. In the early decades, medical missionaries served a utilitarian function—to protect the health of mission personnel on the foreign field. Later, as the medical profession gained respectability in the broader culture, the scope of medical missions broadened to include the strategic purpose of breaking down resistance to Christianity through medicine in unresponsive locations. An evangelistic purpose for medical missions was the ultimate goal for most evangelical missions throughout the time frame in question. In contrast, many theological liberals and some evangelicals espoused a primarily humanitarian and imitative purpose for medical missions. They aimed to follow the example of Christ's healing ministry and to meet the bodily needs of the sick and suffering.

In conclusion, the 1910 Edinburgh WMC was a turning point in the expansion of Christianity. It marked the culmination of older, traditional mission trends from the nineteenth century and was a harbinger of newer missional emphases in the twentieth century. Nowhere was this seen more clearly than in the range of mission goals, theory, and practice for two ancillary mission methods: education, including vocational training and business enterprises, and medicine. The importance of civilizing mission goals waxed and waned during the nineteenth and twentieth centuries. Evangelical missions in the first decades of the Protestant mission movement affirmed civilizing goals for mission education. This changed by the mid-nineteenth century. The recognition that civilization did not generally lead to conversion, as well as the new emphasis on three-self principles, led to a stricter focus on conversionary goals and the development of indigenous leaders. This affected evangelical mission theory regarding mission education and medicine. In the same time frame, those of a more liberal persuasion continued to uphold civilizing goals, even when they did not result in converts and the growth of the Christian church. In their view, it was a legitimate mission goal for Christian civilization to serve as a leavening or diffusive factor in non-Christian societies. The rise in popularity of liberal Protestant theology and the Social Gospel, as well as the fundamentalist-modernist controversy in the 1920s, resulted in a more stringent bifurcation of mission goals for theological liberals and conservatives: liberals generally continued to stress social ministries rather than direct evangelism; conservatives placed priority on preaching while maintaining some social ministry. The debate over the meaning of mission from 1850 to 1950 was complex and characterized by multiple and changing viewpoints for most groups involved.

We end this chapter with the prayer of John R. Mott at the closing session of the WMC:

> God grant that all of us may in these next moments resolve henceforth so to plan and so to act, so to live and so to sacrifice, that our spirit of reality may become contagious among those to whom we go; and it may be that . . . before many of us taste death we shall see the Kingdom of God come in power.[45]

45. John R. Mott, "Closing Address," in *World Missionary Conference, 1910*, 351.

Reaching Missional Maturity

Lausanne '74 and Majority World Missions (1974)

To God be the glory, great things he hath done:
so loved he the world that he gave us his Son,
who yielded his life an atonement for sin,
and opened the life-gate that all may go in.
Praise the Lord, praise the Lord,
Let the earth hear His voice!
Praise the Lord, praise the Lord,
Let the people rejoice!
O come to the Father, through Jesus the Son,
And give Him the glory, great things He hath done.[1]

From July 16 to 25, 1974, the first International Congress on World Evangelization (LCWE) convened at the Palais de Beaulieu in the historic city

1. "To God Be the Glory," written by Fanny Crosby (1875), was popular in Great Britain early after its release. It was reintroduced to an American audience at Billy Graham's 1954 Nashville evangelistic crusade and so well received that it became a staple at subsequent Graham crusades. William J. Reynolds, *Companion to Baptist Hymnal* (Nashville: Broadman, 1976), 228–29.

of Lausanne, Switzerland. The 1974 Lausanne Congress was the brainchild of Billy Graham (1918–2018), prominent American evangelist and Christian statesman. The LCWE was a successor congress to the 1910 Edinburgh World Missionary Conference (WMC) and to the 1966 Berlin World Congress on Evangelism. The 1966 Berlin Congress was cosponsored by two institutions founded by Billy Graham. It refocused evangelical attention on the task of world evangelization.

By the early 1970s, however, Billy Graham had become convinced that another larger congress, the LCWE, was needed for several reasons. First, in the years since the Berlin Congress, it had become increasingly apparent that evangelical Christianity was burgeoning in the Global South, where the "younger churches" were rapidly becoming mission-sending forces. A congress was needed that reflected these new realities by including more representation from the non-Western world. The LCWE made significant strides toward broader representation. Nearly 2,500 official delegates from over 150 different countries and 135 different Protestant denominations participated in the LCWE. At Graham's insistence, eleven out of the thirty-one members of the planning committee and over a thousand of the delegates were from the southern hemisphere.[2]

The goal of the LCWE was "to unite all evangelicals in the common task of total evangelization of the world."[3] In reality, among the evangelicals in attendance, there were divergent and at times discordant voices, particularly from delegates from the Global South. Latin American representatives René Padilla and Orlando Costas issued strident calls for "holistic" or integral mission to address the endemic structural injustices within society. The Kenyan general secretary of the Presbyterian Church of East Africa, John Gatu, called for a moratorium of foreign missions to Africa in order to "facilitate the national church's growth in self-reliance and to release resources for unevangelized areas." Each of these concerns was reflected in the language of the Lausanne Covenant (LC), which was signed by roughly 2,000 out of the 2,500 delegates at the end of the congress—Gatu's in LC §9, and that of the Latin American delegation in §5 on Christian Social Responsibility. Lausanne '74 revealed both the unity and the divisions within global evangelicalism.[4]

2. Brian Stanley, "Lausanne 1974: The Challenge from the Majority World to Northern-Hemisphere Evangelicalism," *Journal of Ecclesiastical History* 64, no. 3 (July 2013): 534–37, 540.
3. J. D. Douglas, ed., *Let the Earth Hear His Voice: International Congress on World Evangelization* (Minneapolis: World Wide Publications, 1975), 156.
4. John Stott, ed., *Making Christ Known: Historic Mission Documents from the Lausanne Movement, 1974–1989* (Grand Rapids: Eerdmans, 1996), 24; Stanley, "Lausanne 1974," 541–47; Robert A. Hunt, "The History of the Lausanne Movement, 1974–2010," *International Bulletin of Missionary Research* 35, no. 2 (April 2011): 83.

The second reason Graham thought the LCWE was needed was that he believed it was imperative to address the theological foundation for an evangelical understanding of mission and evangelism in contradistinction to ecumenical formulations. In his opening speech, titled "Why Lausanne?" the evangelist declared that the congress had been convened "to re-emphasize those biblical concepts which are essential to evangelism." These included the authority of Scripture, the lostness of humanity outside of Christ, and "the necessity of evangelism for the salvation of souls."[5] Evangelical missional convictions were addressed in the LC. Paragraph 3 affirms that "there is only one Savior," Jesus Christ, and that it is "derogatory to Christ and the Gospel" to imply that "Christ speaks equally through all religions and ideologies." The covenant defines "evangelism . . . [as] the proclamation of the historical, biblical Christ as Savior and Lord, with a view to persuading people to come to him personally and so be reconciled to God" (§4). The evangelistic task was an urgent one, as both the motto of the congress, "Let the Earth Hear His Voice," and LC §9 make clear (see sidebar 12.1). Although "social action" and "socio-political involvement" were *not* evangelism, the two were not "mutually exclusive"; rather "both [were] part of our Christian duty" (§5).[6]

Third, the LCWE was convened to "consider honestly and carefully both the unevangelized world and the church's resources to evangelize the world." Therefore, a key goal of the congress was to develop appropriate contemporary strategies for world evangelization. Not only did delegates at the LCWE attend plenary sessions and evening presentations, but some participated in one of the thirty-two evangelistic strategy groups, which developed summary reports presented to the whole congress. Reports strategized, for example, on the evangelization of children, students, the handicapped, the poor, racial minorities, and hippies, as well as atheists, animists, occultists, and adherents of major world religions. In addition, national strategy groups for fifty-two countries or regions evaluated their present evangelistic and mission capabilities and set goals and outlined strategies to reach the unevangelized within their purview. One other evangelistic strategy was broadly promoted at the congress by delegates Peter Wagner and Ralph Winter: a focus on "unreached people groups," distinct ethnocultural units lacking an indigenous church capable of evangelizing their own nation. This evangelization strategy enthused some but was rejected by others as smacking too much of social-scientific emphases and American pragmatism.[7]

5. Stott, *Making Christ Known*, xiv.
6. Stott, *Making Christ Known*, 16–24, 33.
7. Stott, *Making Christ Known*, xiv; Douglas, *Let the Earth Hear His Voice*, 483–982, 1318–1461; Hunt, "History of the Lausanne Movement," 83.

SIDEBAR 12.1

Lausanne Covenant §9, "The Urgency of the Evangelistic Task" (1974)

More than 2,700 million people, which is more than two-thirds of mankind, have yet to be evangelized. We are ashamed that so many have been neglected; it is a standing rebuke to us and to the whole church. There is now, however, in many parts of the world an unprecedented receptivity to the Lord Jesus Christ. We are convinced that this is the time for churches and parachurch agencies to pray earnestly for the salvation of the unreached and to launch new efforts to achieve world evangelization. A reduction of foreign missionaries and money in an evangelized country may sometimes be necessary to facilitate the national church's growth in self-reliance and to release resources for unevangelized areas. Missionaries should flow ever more freely from and to all six continents in a spirit of humble service. The goal should be, by all available means and at the earliest possible time, that every person will have the opportunity to hear, understand, and receive the good news. We cannot hope to attain this goal without sacrifice. All of us are shocked by the poverty of millions and disturbed by the injustices which cause it. Those of us who live in affluent circumstances accept our duty to develop a simple life-style in order to contribute more generously to both relief and evangelism.

Source: John Stott, ed., *Making Christ Known: Historic Mission Documents from the Lausanne Movement, 1974–1989* (Grand Rapids, Eerdmans, 1996), 33.

The LCWE was a significant turning point in the expansion of world Christianity. Prior to the LCWE, it *may* have been possible to view evangelicalism as a largely Western phenomenon; not so after the LCWE. The congress plainly demonstrated that evangelicalism had become a "multicultural global community." The priorities of evangelicals from the Global South, most notably on issues of social and economic justice, could no longer be ignored. Nevertheless, it is important to note that in the West such issues often remained in the realm of ethics and failed to impact "the evangelical understanding of the mission of the church, which still tended to be expressed in terms of the saving of souls."[8] Despite this caveat, the LCWE heralded the reality that evangelicalism had become a global phenomenon.

8. Brian Stanley, *The Global Diffusion of Evangelicalism: The Age of Billy Graham and John Stott* (Downers Grove, IL: IVP Academic, 2013), 155.

One of the most pivotal changes promoted by the LCWE, and the subject of this chapter, was the idea that mission could no longer be viewed as a "one-way enterprise," from "the West to the rest" (Africa, Asia, Latin America). Rather, by the 1970s, the former mission fields in the Global South had developed vibrant and mature Christian movements that were rapidly becoming mission-sending forces. "The beginning of a new day" had dawned "for the one mission of the church." The former mission churches not only received missionaries but sent missionaries to other countries, including to the secularized West. Mission was now "from everywhere to everywhere."[9] The Lausanne Covenant echoed this concern for mission from everywhere to everywhere in LC §9: "Missionaries should flow ever more freely *from and to all six continents* in a spirit of humble service." In the immediate aftermath of the LCWE and in part due to its influence, this trend increasingly became reality. Today vibrant churches in the Global South have reached missional maturity. They are sending ever more missionaries outside their national borders—so much so that "today it is unthinkable that the evangelization of the world is even possible without the full collaboration of the 'Whole Church bringing the Whole Gospel to the Whole World.'"[10]

In the remainder of this chapter, we will first briefly examine the historical context for the LCWE. Then our focus turns to Majority World missions from three countries with vibrant mission movements today on three continents in the Global South: Nigeria, Brazil, and Korea. In each of these locations, mission activity by local Christians occurred by the early twentieth century. However, before the 1970s and 1980s, outreach was primarily focused on evangelism (at times cross-cultural) within their own or neighboring countries—that is, in the language of Acts 1:8, outreach was to their Jerusalem, Judea, and Samaria. The LCWE, however, brought mission to the ends of the world more sharply into focus, and in the immediate post–Lausanne '74 era, significant strides were made to realize that goal. Evangelical cooperative alliances were formed at the regional, national, and continental levels. Majority World mission movements were launched and reached maturity. For each of the three countries listed above, I will first discuss twentieth-century mission efforts. Then I will show the impact of the LCWE on the formation of national mission movements, followed by ongoing and more recent trends. Along the way, I will highlight representative Majority World missionaries for each country.

9. Anderson, "American Protestants in Pursuit of Mission," 109.
10. Timothy Tennent, "Lausanne and Global Evangelicalism: Theological Distinctions and Missiological Impact," in *The Lausanne Movement: A Range of Perspectives*, ed. Lars Dahle (Oxford: Regnum Books, 2014), 58.

Historical Context for the Lausanne Congress on World Evangelization

The LCWE was a successor congress not only to the 1966 Berlin World Congress on Evangelism but also to the 1910 Edinburgh WMC. The LCWE and the WMC had several distinct similarities. To varying degrees, both conferences focused on traditional evangelism, on the important role of local Christians, and on the urgency of the missionary task. We noted in chapter 11 that the WMC espoused a traditional, conservative, and largely evangelical understanding of mission. Although there were some more liberal, dissenting voices at the WMC, among mission methods, pride of place belonged squarely on the proclamation of the gospel. However, as part of the compromise to ensure Anglican participation at the WMC, all theological and doctrinal debate was excluded from the conference. In contrast, Billy Graham made sure at the 1966 Berlin Congress and the LCWE that the biblical and theological underpinnings for world evangelization were asserted and affirmed. Despite this difference, both the WMC and the LCWE proposed a traditional evangelical understanding of mission. Paragraph 9 of the LC emphasizes that the ultimate "goal" of mission is "that every person will have the opportunity to hear, understand, and receive the good news" (see sidebar 12.1).[11] Most participants at the WMC would have echoed that sentiment.

The legacy of the Edinburgh WMC represented a breadth of viewpoints regarding the agents of evangelization. On the one hand, the delegates at the WMC assumed that Western churches, mission societies, and missionaries would assume "the initiative and the authority in Christianity's expansion [throughout the world] . . . for generations to come." On the other hand, the Commission I report expressed the aspirational goal that the younger

> church[es] on the mission field must be the chief evangelistic agency if the Gospel is to be preached to all men in our day. The evangelization of the non-Christian world is not alone a European, an American, an Australasian enterprise; it is equally an Asiatic and African enterprise.[12]

This aspirational goal had made great strides toward becoming a reality by the time of Lausanne '74. Paragraph 9 of the LC, in a second similarity with the WMC, echoed the same concern and added its voice to a broadened call for mission from everywhere to everywhere.

11. Stott, *Making Christ Known*, 33.
12. David A. Kerr and Kenneth R. Ross, eds., *Edinburgh 2010: Mission Then and Now* (Eugene, OR: Wipf & Stock, 2009), 311; World Missionary Conference, *Report of Commission I* (New York: Fleming H. Revell, 1910), 368.

A third similarity between the WMC and the LCWE is that both conferences stressed the urgency of the task of world evangelization. One goal of the WMC was to galvanize support for the "evangelization of the world in this generation." Paragraph 9 of the LC likewise addresses the "Urgency of the Evangelistic Task." It notes that "more than two-thirds of mankind have yet to be evangelized," which is a "standing rebuke" to the church. "This is the time . . . to pray earnestly for the salvation of the unreached and to launch new efforts to achieve world evangelization." The urgency of the missionary task was also a theme at the 1966 Berlin World Congress on Evangelism. Like the LCWE, this congress also had Graham's fingerprints on it, since it had been cosponsored by the Billy Graham Evangelistic Association and *Christianity Today*, the magazine Graham had founded ten years earlier. Graham's opening speech at the Berlin Congress made explicit reference to the 1910 Edinburgh WMC. The evangelist called for "greater unity" and a "fresh and larger bestowal of supernatural power" to accomplish the worldwide "task of evangelizing our generation."[13] Graham's reference to the unofficial watchword of the 1910 Edinburgh WMC placed the Berlin Congress, and therefore the LCWE, as a direct heir of one of the two branches that developed out of the 1910 conference—the evangelical branch. The other, ecumenical branch was represented by the World Council of Churches' Division of World Mission and Evangelism, which was formed from the 1961 merger of the World Council of Churches (WCC) and the International Missionary Council (IMC).

The bifurcation of the legacy of the 1910 WMC into an evangelical and an ecumenical stream was first fueled by the debate over the theology of mission that arose during the fundamentalist-modernist controversy of the 1920s and 1930s. Fundamentalists in the pre–World War II era, and conservative evangelical networks associated with Billy Graham in the United States and J. I. Packer and John Stott in the United Kingdom in the postwar period, expressed deep concern over the understanding of mission common within ecumenical circles linked to the WCC. The 1932 Hocking Report expressed one ecumenical mission theme: Christianity could no longer claim to be uniquely or exclusively salvific since the "common search for truth" was found in all religions. Other common emphases were that social and political action should take priority over preaching and evangelism and that the leavening influence of Christianity on society, rather than individual salvation, was the goal of mission.[14] More recently, the 1968 Uppsala Assembly of the WCC had defined

13. "Lausanne Movement Pays Tribute to Founder Billy Graham," Lausanne Movement, February 21, 2018, https://www.lausanne.org/news-releases/billy-graham-tribute.

14. Gerald H. Anderson, "American Protestants in Pursuit of Mission: 1886–1986," *International Bulletin of Missionary Research* 12 (July 1988): 105–6.

the church's mission as humanization and political liberation. As a result of these trends, conservatives felt that "mission became marginalized by being largely reinterpreted in socio-political terms. Thus the vision of Edinburgh 1910 suffered an almost total eclipse."[15]

As liberal Protestantism increasingly focused its overseas agenda on relief and development work, it abandoned the task of world evangelization to fundamentalists and evangelicals. Conservative Protestants in the mid-twentieth century renewed their mission efforts for the worldwide advance of the gospel. A number of new faith missions (e.g., Orinoco River Mission, Latin American Mission) and evangelical parachurch organizations (InterVarsity Christian Fellowship, Campus Crusade for Christ) were established to help achieve that goal. These developments culminated with the 1966 Berlin Congress, where John Stott directly addressed evangelical missional concerns. He proclaimed that the Great Commission of Matthew 28 was given "not to reform society, but to preach the Gospel. . . . The primary task of the members of Christ's church is to be Gospel heralds, not social reformers."[16] The historical stage was now set for the LCWE, where evangelicals from across the globe reaffirmed and redefined the worldwide mission of the church. Delegates from the Global South at the LCWE were inspired to turn their previous mission efforts into mission movements. This was true for the delegates from the Evangelical Church of West Africa (ECWA) in Nigeria.

Mission of SIM/ECWA in and from Nigeria

In 1893, three young men—Rowland Bingham, Walter Gowans, and Thomas Kent—left North America to serve as independent missionaries in the interior of "the Soudan," which in this era referred to a wide swath of central West Africa. "For many missionary recruits in the 1880s and 1890s," such as Bingham, Gowans, and Kent, the "western Sudan . . . was 'undoubtedly the opportunity of the hour.'" This region of Hausaland in northern Nigeria was entirely unreached with the gospel. Furthermore, it was not only located on the frontier of Islam's southward expansion into areas where traditional African religions had previously held sway, but until 1900 it was likewise a region free of colonial control and secular Western influence. Thus, for personnel of the new African faith missions, it was the "perfect arena" to contain the downward spread of Islam through timely and effective evangelization.[17] The beginnings

---

15. Stott, *Making Christ Known*, xii.
16. Stanley, *Global Diffusion of Evangelicalism*, 64, 155.
17. Andrew Porter, *Religion versus Empire? British Protestant Missionaries and Overseas Expansion, 1700–1914* (Manchester: Manchester University Press, 2004), 223–24.

SIDEBAR 12.2

Stephen Panya Baba, "Preparing Church and Mission Agencies" (2012)

The attitude of the pioneering missionaries of SIM, which was passed on to the established church . . . [is seen in] a letter by Mr. Gowans to his mother in which he said: "Our success in this enterprise means nothing less than the opening of the country for the gospel. . . . Even death is not a failure. His purposes are accomplished. He uses deaths as well as lives in the furtherance of his cause." . . . In less than a year, two of the three pioneer missionaries died in what later became today's Nigeria. God, however, providentially spared Roland Bingham, who pressed on with the work against all odds, and which eventually resulted in the establishment of the then SIM churches, now Evangelical Church Winning All (ECWA) churches. . . . The Evangelical Missionary Society (EMS) of ECWA's missionaries have continued to minister in disease-infested remote areas and in the fanatically volatile Islamic core north of Nigeria. This is a legacy that was inherited from the pioneer missionaries and which has continued to be passed on to subsequent generations. Recently, during the April 2011 Muslim uprising among Christians in Northern Nigeria, one of our EMS missionaries, Isma Dogari, was abducted, forced into the mosque, and compelled to renounce Christ and accept Islam. When he refused, they gouged his eyes out and then killed him. . . . There is definitely a need to consciously reawaken and prepare the church and mission agencies to face the challenges of missions in the twenty-first century . . . suffering, persecution, and martyrdom.

Source: William D. Taylor, Antonia van der Meer, and Reg Reimer, eds., *Sorrow and Blood: Christian Mission in Contexts of Suffering, Persecution and Martyrdom* (Pasadena, CA: William Carey, 2012), 342–43.

of what would become the Sudan Interior Mission (SIM) were challenging. Gowans and Kent died of malaria shortly after their arrival in 1894, forcing Bingham to return home to Canada, which he did again after his second failed attempt to form an African base in 1900. The third attempt to establish a mission station succeeded in 1902 at Patigi in west-central Nigeria. Suffering marked the beginnings of the SIM; it is also characteristic of contemporary mission in northern Nigeria, as the text from Stephen Panya Baba, the current president of ECWA, indicates (see sidebar 12.2). The ECWA denomination, over which Baba presides, was renamed in 2011 from the Evangelical Church of West Africa to the Evangelical Church Winning All to reflect its mission emphasis and broader expansion across Africa and beyond.

From the beginning, SIM missionaries "developed a lifestyle of evangelism" among their African converts, who soon "assumed the burden and responsibility to take this gospel of the kingdom to others."[18] One early evangelist connected with the SIM was Inusa Samaila (1890–1972). Inusa was a Muslim Hausa-speaker of Zabarma ethnicity, born in French Niger. He converted to Christianity after contact with SIM missionaries in Patigi in 1909; at his baptism, Inusa received the name Samaila (Samuel). In 1910, just a year after his conversion, Inusa began working as an evangelist alongside SIM missionaries, first briefly in Kwoi and then in Karu (1911), where Inusa had a longer, more significant and independent ministry. He not only preached in Hausa, but in time he also mastered the local language of the Gbagyi, a mixed Muslim and traditional-religionist ethnic group. He became an effective cross-cultural missionary, aided by his own Muslim background and Qur'anic studies.[19] Inusa spent the remainder of his long career working as an evangelist/missionary and, after 1955, as an ordained pastor among the Gbagyi in Abuja and Wushishi, as well as in other locations.

Inusa's experience in northern Nigeria was replicated by other SIM African evangelists. The mission among the Tangale people was launched in 1917 in Kaltungo in the largely Muslim state of Gombe in northeastern Nigeria; by 1919 the SIM had won its first converts. Teachers and evangelists were regularly recruited from converts who had graduated from literacy classes. By 1930, these evangelists had reached every major Tangale village with the gospel. Then, in 1932, SIM missionary John Hall challenged the Tangale Christians to become volunteer missionaries as part of a concerted outreach to the region far north of Tangaleland. Further appeals for missionary service were issued by SIM personnel in 1936, 1938, 1942, and 1945. Tangale Christians responded to these calls and served as apprentices assigned to SIM missionaries for varying periods of time. Their living was financed either through self-support (farming or trade) or through contributions from local congregations. Those volunteers who proved gifted in evangelism were sent to a Bible school for further training.[20]

18. Panya Baba, *A Vision Received, a Vision Passed On: The History of the EMS of ECWA, 1948–1998* (Jos, Nigeria: Africa Christian Textbooks, 2009), 11.

19. Baba, *Vision Received*, 30–31; Shobana Shankar, *Who Shall Enter Paradise? Christian Origins in Northern Nigeria, ca. 1890–1975* (Athens: Ohio University Press, 2014), 10–17; Gwamna Dogara, "SIM and the Neglected Gbagyi Story," in *Transforming Africa's Religious Landscapes: The Sudan Interior Mission (SIM) Past and Present*, ed. Barbara M. Cooper et al. (Trenton, NJ: Africa World Press, 2018), 423.

20. Reuben Goje Maiture, "SIM and the Tangale Factor in the Christianization of the Hausa of Northern Nigeria, 1915–1976," in Cooper et al., *Transforming Africa's Religious Landscapes*, 454, 456–57, 462–67; Baba, *Vision Received*, 35.

During this period, Muslim rulers in the Gombe emirate as well as British colonial officers restricted Christian missionary activity in some territories of far northern Nigeria. Although Western missionaries were strictly prohibited access, in some cases Tangale evangelists gained entry through slow and winsome ministry. Karau Pane (d. 1976) was one of twelve Tangale evangelists deployed as an evangelist in 1932 in response to Hall's appeal. He earned his living selling fruit at the market in Gombe town and used that opportunity to witness to his customers. In 1935 Pane received permission to settle in Gombe to teach literacy. In time, he came to be regarded as a "great teacher who knew everything about Isa (Jesus)." Pane's debates with Muslim teachers convinced some locals of the truthfulness of the Christian faith. His ministry opened up several locations in the Gombe emirate, where other Tangale evangelists completed the task of pioneer church planting. Later he served as an itinerant evangelist in Tera and Bolewa lands, as well as in Borno, Niger, and Chad. By 1940 the Tangale church had one hundred self-supporting Tangale Christian workers as well as twenty cross-cultural missionaries among Muslims and traditional religionists in other parts of Nigeria.[21]

In the late 1940s, there was a revival among the SIM-affiliated Nigerian congregations. African itinerant evangelists challenged the churches to increase their witnessing and outreach both locally and in neighboring Benin. At the same time, Dr. Douglas Percy, principal of the Billiri Bible school, suggested that an African Missionary Society (AMS) be established to coordinate and "train evangelists . . . [to] reach the unreached peoples of Northern Nigeria." The AMS was founded in November 1948 as a joint African and SIM venture. From the start, the AMS was entirely supported by local funds. Nevertheless, in the first five years, the new organization was not self-governing. Rather, AMS missionaries worked in cooperation with or under SIM staff. At roughly the same time as ECWA was founded as an independent, indigenous denomination in 1954, the AMS requested self-governance from SIM. The mission agreed and by 1962 its role in the AMS was entirely discontinued. The name of the organization was changed to the Evangelical Missionary Society (EMS) in 1964. The EMS was the first independent, indigenous mission society in Nigeria. At the founding of the EMS, Tangale missionaries made up more than one-third of its personnel.[22]

Three hundred seventy delegates from Africa participated at the 1974 LCWE. Dr. Byang Kato, the former general secretary of ECWA (1967–73)

21. Maiture, "SIM and the Tangale Factor," 457–59; 464–71.
22. Yusufu Turaki, *Theory and Practice of Christian Missions in Africa: A Century of SIM/ECWA History and Legacy in Nigeria, 1893–1993* (Nairobi: International Bible Society, 1999), 491, 494, 498, 503–4.

and the then-current secretary of the Association of Evangelicals of Africa and Madagascar (1973–76), gave a plenary address on "Evangelism Opportunities and Obstacles in Africa." According to Kato, one opportunity was that African traditional religions were "losing their grip" on the "younger generation," who were faced with the choice of adopting either Islam or Christianity. Another was that the "extended family system in Africa provides a great opportunity for reaching many people with the Gospel." Obstacles to evangelism included liberal ecumenism, which reduced salvation to "political and economic liberation," and the lack of cooperative evangelical mission organizations. The "East Africa Geographical Report" concurred with Kato's assessment that evangelism was "marred by the spirit of competition and lack of coordination." It likewise noted, "Lausanne '74 has challenged us to take a greater part in the task of worldwide evangelization . . . not only to the neighboring countries but also to the other parts of the earth."[23]

These concerns (cooperative efforts and mission to the ends of the earth) were addressed to varying degrees in the following years. In August 1975, delegates of the LCWE gathered for the first Nigerian National Congress on Evangelization. It was convened as a "platform for . . . implementing an evangelization strategy to reach the then unreached people groups in Nigeria." In 1982 Panya Baba, the director of the EMS from 1970 to 1988 and the father of Stephen Panya Baba, founded the Nigeria Evangelical Mission Association (NEMA) with six mission agencies, including the EMS. Their goal was to cooperate on research and training projects. NEMA established the Nigeria Evangelical Missionary Institute to train young men and women for cross-cultural missions. The NEMA Searchlight Project identified and researched unreached people groups in Nigeria.[24] Each of these endeavors was an emphasis identified (cooperative efforts) or promoted (unreached people groups) at the LCWE.

One such unreached people group was the Maguzawa, a non-Muslim subgroup of the Hausa. In 1975, the Nigerian government's universal primary education policy required pupils to attend either Muslim or Christian religious education classes. This situation led many Maguzawa to request Christian teachers to come to their villages to instruct pupils and their family groups. The EMS and ECWA responded by recruiting teachers to provide the mandated Christian religious education in the schools and by sending a survey team to the Maguzawa in the Katsina district in July 1975. One member of

23. Douglas, *Let the Earth Hear His Voice*, 156–58, 1353.
24. Tesilimi A. Lawanson, "Calvary Ministries (CAPRO): A Case Study on a Model of Majority World Initiatives in Christian Mission," in *Missions from the Majority World: Progress, Challenges, and Case Studies*, ed. Enoch Wan and Michael Pocock (Pasadena, CA: William Carey, 2009), 343; Baba, *Vision Received*, 166–67, 178–80.

the survey team, Rev. Tambaya Hassan, convinced the EMS to adopt the Maguzawa ethnic group as a new focus for their mission work. The 1970s were "years of wonderful response to the gospel [for the EMS]. . . . Among the Maguzawa [the response] was almost overwhelming."[25]

Tambaya Hassan's chief contribution to the evangelization of the Maguzawa was in training new missionary recruits to present a culturally appropriate gospel. Hassan had been raised and converted in Malumfashi, the main town of Katsina district, in the early years of SIM ministry there. Since he was well acquainted with Maguzawa culture, Hassan and his wife taught a two-week course on Hausa culture for all non-Hausa EMS missionaries to the Maguzawa. He encouraged the new missionary recruits to aim to win whole households to Christ (a theme Kato had stressed at the LCWE), since decisions to change religion were familial, not individual, affairs. Hassan also stressed that Christian substitutes for important Maguzawa ceremonies should be adopted. For the Maguzawa, it was unthinkable and a sign of ingratitude to God to fail to have a "naming ceremony" at the birth of a child; therefore, Hassan introduced a Christian ceremony. Furthermore, it was customary to have a conversion ceremony when a Maguzawa converted to Islam. Therefore, drawing on Luke 15:7, Hassan introduced a repentance feast, to which not just the Christian community but also non-Christians were invited to rejoice with the new converts to Christ.[26]

The second concern identified at the LCWE was the need for mission to the ends of the earth, a goal that has been more challenging to achieve. From the beginning, the EMS was engaged in cross-cultural ministry within Nigeria and in neighboring African countries. It was only in the late 1980s and 1990s that ministry outside of Africa was launched. In 1989, veteran missionaries James and Hannatu Gabis were sent to East London to plant a church among Africans and other immigrants. Similarly, in 1995 Rev. Sunday Bwanhot planted a largely African church in Chicago. This reflects an important Majority World mission trend—former mission churches evangelizing the secular West—in North America, but especially in Europe. Although the ministry of these immigrant churches was primarily directed to Africans (diaspora ministry), evangelism of the local population was an "important" but "incidental by-product." Today the EMS of ECWA is the largest mission organization of any African denomination. It supports 1,830 missionary couples in Nigeria and in seventeen other countries.[27]

25. Baba, *Vision Received*, 104–6.

26. Baba, *Vision Received*, 105–7.

27. Baba, *Vision Received*, 204–6; Philip Jenkins, *The Next Christendom: The Coming of Global Christianity*, 3rd ed. (Oxford: Oxford University Press, 2011), 122; "History," ECWA, accessed June 14, 2021, https://www.ecwausa.org/history-of-ecwa-church; "About Us," EMS of ECWA, accessed September 1, 2021, https://emsofecwa.org/about.

Mission in and from Brazil

Brazil is not only the largest country in South America; it also is the most populous, with over 210 million people, representing a diverse mix of races, ethnicities, religions, countries of origin, and cultures. It is unique as the only Portuguese-speaking country on the continent. It is also unique as the first and largest missionary-sending country in Latin America. It was not until the post–Lausanne '74 era that a full-blown Brazilian mission movement was launched. Nevertheless, already in the early decades of the twentieth century, evangelical Protestantism there was vibrant and growing "through active and intentional sharing of its message . . . by converts." In a country where Roman Catholicism dominated the religious scene, "evangelism and missionary activity were central to their [Protestant evangelical] identity."[28]

There were two main arenas of missionary work for Brazilian evangelicals in the early twentieth century, both of which continue to this day: among the indigenous Amazonian ethnic groups and in Portugal or Portuguese-speaking (Lusophone) countries. By 1923, the key Brazilian Protestant denominations had each initiated mission work or appointed national missionaries among Amazonian ethnic groups: the Baptists appointed a Brazilian to work in Bahia; the Presbyterians appointed one in Mato Grosso; and the Episcopal Church organized a missionary society for ministry among indigenous groups in Rio Grande do Sul. In April 1925, this commitment to ministry among indigenous ethnic groups was evidenced at the Congress on Christian Work in South America, held in Montevideo, Uruguay, which was attended by representatives of mission boards and the national churches. The Commission Report on the "Indians of Brazil" under the chairmanship of Odilon de Moraes noted the "widespread desire" of the Brazilian churches to work among remote and unevangelized indigenous groups. It stated that although the Amazonian peoples, numbering at that time 1.5 million in three hundred to four hundred ethnic groups, were nominally Roman Catholic, many continued to secretly practice animistic cults and visit witch doctors. The report indicated that a multipronged mission approach that included educational and medical ministry was necessary. Furthermore, vocational and agricultural training should be provided to save the "Indians from exploitation . . . by shrewd merchants and rubber extractors."[29]

28. Todd Hartch, *The Rebirth of Latin American Christianity* (Oxford: Oxford University Press, 2014), 19–20.
29. Robert E. Speer and Samuel G. Inman, eds., *Christian Work in South America: Official Report of the Congress on Christian Work in South America* (New York: Fleming H. Revell, 1925), 1:10–11, 179, 184, 189–92.

Erasmo Braga (1877–1932), a leading Brazilian Presbyterian minister, chaired the Brazilian Commissions for three of the twelve topics discussed at the Montevideo Congress and was also a member of four other commissions, including that on the "Indians of Brazil." Braga was influential in the founding of the Caiua Indian Mission for ministry among the Guarani-Caiua people living in the Mato Grosso region of Brazil. He was also involved in supporting missions to Portugal. In 1920 the first Brazilian Presbyterian missionary to that country was sent, João Marques de Mota. Four years later (1924), when the Brazilian Presbyterians decided to close their Portuguese mission, Erasmo Braga and his father Rev. Carvalho Braga, a first-generation immigrant from Portugal, started the first Brazilian missionary agency, the Brazilian Missionary Society for the Evangelization of Portugal. Due to the massive need for evangelization within Brazil, Portugal remained the only Brazilian foreign mission field until the post–World War II period, when mission work was inaugurated in several neighboring Spanish-speaking countries.[30]

Latin America was represented by 219 delegates at the 1974 LCWE, but their influence on the inclusion of social issues in the Lausanne Covenant far outstripped their numbers. The impact of the LCWE on the Latin American delegates was likewise great. The congress "gave a further impetus to cross-cultural missions" and "provided an incentive to deepen a sense of responsibility for worldwide evangelization."[31] The trends noted above of mission among indigenous ethnic groups and Portuguese-speakers were reflected at the 1974 LCWE. The Brazil Geographical Report asserted that the "greatest opportunity and responsibility . . . of Brazilian missionary work is . . . to those people with whom we have racial and linguistic affinity"—in other words, with the "Portuguese and Spanish-speaking people of Latin America, Africa, Europe, and Asia." Other areas of concern were the unreached indigenous groups and the Asian and European ethnic minorities living within Brazil. Finally, the report noted that "new forms of collaboration" with "other denominations and groups" and an "intensification of the missionary work beyond the national borders of Brazil" were needed.[32]

30. Speer and Inman, *Christian Work in South America*, 1:11–20, 194–95; Alderi Souza de Matos, "Braga, Erasmo (1877–1932)," Boston University School of Theology, History of Missiology, accessed January 19, 2021, http://www.bu.edu/missiology/missionary-biography/a-c/braga-erasmo-1877-1932; J. Daniel Salinas, "The Great Commission and Latin America," in *The Great Commission: Evangelicals and the History of World Missions*, ed. Martin Klauber and Scott M. Manetsch (Nashville: B&H, 2008), 138; Edward L. Smither, *Brazilian Evangelical Missions in the Arab World: History, Culture, Practice, and Theology* (Eugene, OR: Wipf & Stock, 2012), 55.

31. Guillermo Cook, "Protestant Mission and Evangelization in Latin America," in *New Face of the Church in Latin America*, ed. Guillermo Cook (Maryknoll, NY: Orbis, 1994), 48.

32. Douglas, *Let the Earth Hear His Voice*, 1344–46.

The Brazilian mission movement developed significantly in the post–Lausanne '74 years. In 1975 Brazil's first interdenominational national mission was founded, the Missão Antioquia (Antioch Mission), with Presbyterian pastor Décio de Azevedo as its first president. Two years later, the mission opened a seminary and missionary training center, now located in São Paulo. By 2012, the Antioch Mission had one hundred Brazilian missionaries serving in nineteen countries in Latin America, the Middle East, Asia, and Africa. Shortly after the founding of the Antioch Mission, in 1976, the Association of Brazilian Transcultural Missions was established to promote cooperation, research, and missionary training for member missions. Initially it comprised only a handful of member organizations; today there are more than ninety. Collaboration with other denominations and groups was a key concern expressed by the Brazilian delegation at the LCWE. Also, in 1976 the first Latin American mission conference convened on the campus of the University of Paraná in Curitiba, Brazil, with 450 Brazilian and fifty other Hispanic university students and graduates as delegates. The Declaration of Curitiba reflected concerns expressed in the Lausanne Covenant. It lamented the "lack of missionary vision in the Latin American church" and asserted that the "church that is not missionary is not the church." It challenged the delegates to heed the call of Jesus Christ and to cross not only "geographical frontiers" but also "frontiers of inequality, injustice and ideological idolatry." The Curitiba conference "started a boom in Latin American missions" that resulted in over one thousand missionaries being sent throughout the world by 1982. The first Ibero-American Missionary Congress (COMIBAM), convened in 1987, added further momentum. It aimed to "heighten awareness," "share information," and create the "missionary structures" necessary to enable Latin America to take its place among Christian nations as a "mission-sending force."[33]

Antonia (Tonica) van der Meer, a Brazilian of Dutch descent, felt her call into Christian service when she was a student delegate at the 1976 Curitiba conference. The conference had been organized by the Brazilian Student Movement, in which Tonica was an active member. Her conviction that God had called her into cross-cultural student work was confirmed in 1979. She attended All Nations Christian College in Ware, England, to gain the requisite biblical and missiological training. Then, in 1983, Tonica accepted a call to develop the new International Fellowship of Evangelical Students student ministry in Portuguese-speaking Angola. Her ten-year ministry in Angola

33. Smither, *Brazilian Evangelical Missions*, 55–57, 60–61; Cook, "Protestant Mission," 50; Samuel Escobar, "Latin America," in *Towards the Twenty-First Century in Christian Mission*, ed. James M. Phillips and Robert T. Coote (Grand Rapids: Eerdmans, 1993), 131; Hartch, *Rebirth of Latin American Christianity*, 186.

SIDEBAR 12.3

Antonia Van der Meer, "Angola: A Missionary Experience" (2012)

I served in Angola from 1984–95 with the Angola Evangelical Alliance to help establish a student movement. . . . I helped to establish contacts between ministries in Angola and Christian organizations abroad. My student work involved visits to four provinces. In 1986 ministry started smoothly, but pressure began to build [due to the Angolan civil war]. . . . A faithful remnant of eight students in the ministry were called before authorities three times and asked to choose between their studies or their faith. They said, "We want to serve our country, but we cannot deny our Savior." So, they were expelled from the university. They were forced into the army. . . . In Benguela/Lobito I had about one hundred young people ready to learn as much as I could teach them. . . . Only a few pastors had any training, and at school their faith was questioned. I started to take them some books, which I bought with my salary. . . . With some friends I visited a hospital and fell in love with this ministry of encouragement, evangelism and practical service. . . . They [the patients] were lonely and helpless. They loved receiving visits. Some wanted to become Christians in our very first visit. Many knew too little about God, Jesus of the Bible, and it took them several months to understand the gospel message. Others were Marxists, but their barriers were lowered through friendship and many came to believe.

Source: William D. Taylor, Antonia van der Meer, and Reg Reimer, eds., *Sorrow and Blood: Christian Mission in Contexts of Suffering, Persecution and Martyrdom* (Pasadena, CA: William Carey, 2012), 229–31.

included student work; Bible teaching in churches, in Bible schools, and with the Angolan Evangelical Alliance; and hospital visitation to victims of the Angolan civil war (1975–2002) (see sidebar 12.3). While still in Angola, Tonica became convinced that the Brazilian mission movement suffered from a lack of robust missionary training and member care. Therefore, in 1996 she accepted a position at the Evangelical Missions Center in Viçosa, Brazil, where she has served as development coordinator, dean, teacher, and mentor. She earned a master's degree from the Baptist Brazilian Theological Faculty in São Paulo and a doctorate in missiology from Asia Graduate School of Theology and is recognized today as a leading Brazilian missiologist.[34]

34. Tonica van der Meer, "My Journey," in *Global Mission Handbook: A Guide for Crosscultural Service*, ed. Steve Hoke and Bill Taylor (Downers Grove, IL: InterVarsity, 2009), 76; "Antonia

Tonica's journey highlights the growing maturity of the Brazilian mission movement, as well as the ongoing inclination to serve in ministries in Lusophone regions and among indigenous ethnic groups. These trends are likewise seen in our next representative Brazilian missionary. Rogério Rosa da Silva had served the Portuguese-speaking congregation of the Roding Lane Free Church near London for a number of years. During a visit to Brazil in May 2010, he accepted the invitation of two Wycliffe Bible translators associated with the Summer Institute of Linguistics, Shirley Chapman and Meinke Salzer, to visit the Paumari, an indigenous ethnic group living on the middle Purus River in Amazonas state. Chapman (since 1963) and Salzer (since 1976) had first analyzed the Paumari language and culture—and by 1996, they had completed the translation of the New Testament and four Old Testament books. The Bible translations enabled the formation of the Evangelical Indigenous Paumari Church in 1982. During Rogério Rosa's 2010 visit, Paumari Christians voiced their desire to have the remainder of the Old Testament translated into their mother tongue. This persuaded Rogério to leave his ministry in England and accept responsibility for the Bible translation project, as well as the training of Paumari Christian leaders—a role he has held since January 2012.[35]

By far the "most successful Latin American Protestant export to the rest of the world" is "Brazilian Pentecostalism." The Igreja Universal do Reino Deus (IURD), or the Universal Church of the Kingdom of God, has witnessed the "most impressive . . . rapid expansion outside of Brazil" of any Pentecostal group. In 1985 the IURD launched its first international church plant in Paraguay. Then, from 1989 to 1994, it opened more than fifty churches in Portugal among Brazilians, lower-class Portuguese, and Lusophone Angolan and Mozambican immigrants. Its preference for Lusophone ministry meant that Portuguese-speaking countries in Africa, such as Angola and Mozambique, and Lusophone communities in South Africa were targeted. In each of these locations, IURD missionaries focused on the poor and marginalized in society. Their health-and-wealth message and their direct confrontation of spiritual powers resonated well with the disenfranchised. By 2014 the IURD had planted more than one thousand churches in over eighty countries.[36] These examples demonstrate that, since the LCWE, the Brazilian mission movement has made significant strides toward becoming a "mission-sending force." In

---

van der Meer," William Carey Publishing, accessed June 3, 2021, https://missionbooks.org /collections/author-antonia-van-der-meer.

35. "Welcome to paumariBible," paumariBible, accessed June 3, 2021, http://www.paumari bible.org.

36. Hartch, *Rebirth of Latin American Christianity*, 102–3, 187–93.

2010 Brazil had thirty-four thousand cross-cultural Protestant missionaries, a number second only to the United States.

Mission in and from Korea

From its beginnings in the 1880s, the Korean Protestant church was characterized by evangelistic zeal. The majority of converts were won not by Western missionaries but through the efforts of ordinary Korean Christians and Bible women, who enthusiastically witnessed to friends and neighbors, preached in towns and villages, and distributed and sold Scripture portions and tracts. Evangelism by locals was a key factor in the remarkable influx of new converts into the Korean Presbyterian and Methodist churches during the Great Revival movement of 1903–8. Following the revival, a new evangelistic initiative emerged. Korean pastors and missionaries encouraged local Christians to pledge a certain number of days for personal evangelism and the distribution of tracts, and a total of one hundred thousand days was pledged in 1909. This endeavor resulted in an evangelistic harvest.[37]

In 1907 the independent Presbyterian Church of Korea (PCK) was launched. That same year, the first seven graduates of the Presbyterian Theological Seminary in Pyongyang were ordained as pastors. One of the seven, Lee Ki-Pung (1868–1942), became the first cross-cultural missionary of the PCK. During his two periods of ministry on Cheju (today Jeju) Island (1908–15; 1926–31), the Lee family planted churches in nine locations and thereby laid the foundation for the Cheju church. Lee, a Korean nationalist, was executed in 1942 by Japanese officials for refusing to bow to the portrait of the Japanese emperor.[38] During the decades of Japanese colonial rule (1910–45), the PCK also sent eighty Korean pastors to Siberia, Japan, the United States, Mexico, Manchuria, China, and Mongolia to minister to Korean immigrants and to plant Korean churches, although they often sought to convert the local people as well.

This diaspora mission approach (among Korean immigrants and in the Korean language) stood in sharp contrast to the most significant and sustained (1913–57) early mission of the PCK—in Shandong, China. According to a contemporary mission journal, *Korea Mission Field*, the Shandong mission was the Korean "church's greatest pride," since it was "real unquestioned 'Foreign Mission Work' carried on in the Chinese language, wholly for the

37. Sebastian Kim and Kirsteen Kim, *A History of Korean Christianity* (Cambridge: Cambridge University Press, 2015), 166–69.
38. Sa-Rye Yi, *Missionary and Martyr: The Life and Faith of Rev. Yi Gi-Pung*, trans. John S. Park (Seoul: KIATS, 2008), Kindle.

Chinese," and not for Korean immigrants. Furthermore, "no white man has anything to do with the work. . . . [It] is wholly in the hands of the Koreans as to policy and fulfillment."[39] In 1912, when the General Assembly of the PCK organized a Board of Foreign Mission, it resolved, "Today . . . let us start foreign evangelism and send missionaries to China." The idea of a China mission had long appealed to the Korean church, since, according to Shandong missionary Rev. Bang Ji-il (1937–57), "we have received the Confucian culture from China in the past. And now we pay it back with the gospel of life."[40] The American Presbyterian Mission (APM) North had developed the Shandong presbytery, but in 1913 it turned over the area around Laiyang to three Korean missionary couples of the PCK as their mission territory. The success of the mission was hindered due to anti-Korean and anti-Christian sentiment and illness among the missionaries.

In 1917 the mission was relaunched with two new missionaries, Rev. Bang Hyo-won and Rev. Hong Seung-han. To prevent potential anti-Korean sentiments, the new missionaries learned the Chinese language well and adopted the local culture as much as possible. Bang (1886–1953) noted, "You have to be a Chinese, if you want to win a Chinese. . . . You have to wear their clothes . . . eat their food . . . learn their morals and courtesy. . . . [Otherwise] you will have difficulty in preaching the gospel to the Chinese people." According to Bang, the implementation of this approach meant that their "mission work has developed very progressively." Even those in the anti-Christian movement "protected the Korean missionaries" and viewed them as "genuine Christian evangelists." It was also beneficial that the Korean missionaries were *not* associated with Western cultural and economic imperialism in China. Unlike the APM North, which paid the salaries of Chinese Christian workers, the Korean missionaries, who had been raised on the Nevius Plan (see chap. 9), instilled the self-support principle from the outset in the churches they planted. In 1922 a Bible school was opened in Laiyang to train local leaders, and the first graduates in 1929 became pastors of self-supporting churches. From the beginning, local and itinerant evangelistic initiatives included Chinese Christians as team members, thus furthering the self-propagating principle. The Shandong mission continued until 1957, when the last missionary, Rev. Bang Ji-il, was forced by the Chinese Communist Party to leave China.[41] The

39. "Foreign Mission Work of the Korean Presbyterian Church," in *Korea Mission Field* 18 (1923): 81.

40. Kim and Kim, *History of Korean Christianity*, 300–304, 306; Choi Young-Woong, "The Mission of the Presbyterian Church of Korea in Shandong, North China, 1913–1957," in *Transcontinental Links in the History of Non-Western Christianity*, ed. Klaus Koschorke (Wiesbaden: Harrassowitz, 2002), 118–20.

41. Choi, "Mission of PCK in Shandong," 122–27.

successful contextualization methods of the Shandong mission were exemplary and rare among Korean missions in this era.

The Korea National Strategy Report at the LCWE was the work of a diverse group of sixty-five Korean delegates. The report recognized that the "lack of cooperation" between the various denominations and Christian organizations had "hindered evangelization." "Near-neighbor evangelism" was taking place and was fruitful, but "cross-cultural evangelism" was their "weakest area," despite the fact that the "urgency . . . and the necessity of this kind of evangelization" was widely accepted. Since God had richly blessed the Korean church, the delegation viewed it as their "responsibility to play an important role in the evangelization of our own country, of Asia, and of the world." To achieve this goal, a "stronger program" of cross-cultural missionary training needed to be implemented. The report's final sentence confirmed the impact the LCWE had on the delegates and ultimately on the Korean mission movement. It read: "This Congress has increased our awareness of needs, helped us to consider ways to meet them, and strengthened our dedication and determination to do, under God, all we can to 'let the earth hear his voice.'"[42]

Unlike in Nigeria and Brazil, where their mission movements developed or accelerated rapidly shortly after and in part due to the LCWE, another decade was needed for that to occur in Korea. It was not until the late 1980s that enthusiasm for cross-cultural missions became widespread, the number of foreign missionaries accelerated quickly, and large cooperative mission organizations such as the Korean World Missions Association (KWMA) and the Korea Research Institute for Mission (KRIM) were founded. In 1979 there were just ninety-three Korean cross-cultural missionaries. That number grew to more than a thousand by 1990. In 2015 there were more than twenty-six thousand Korean missionaries ministering in over 170 countries. There were several reasons for this explosive development beginning in the late 1980s. First, the Korean church grew exponentially in the 1960s and 1970s, and by the 1980s this growth was channeled into overseas missions. Furthermore, government restrictions were relaxed on overseas travel and foreign residence. As part of its economic policy, the South Korean government encouraged the emigration of its citizens in the 1960s. By 2009 seven million Koreans, many of them Protestants, lived abroad in 176 countries, where they frequently sought to evangelize their fellow Koreans and the locals as well—a diaspora mission approach. At the same time, there was a surplus of Christian workers in South Korea, making ministry overseas more popular. Finally, Korean Christians embraced the concept of "unreached people groups" promoted by Ralph Winter and Peter

42. Douglas, *Let the Earth Hear His Voice*, 1398–99.

Wagner at the LCWE. Their focus was particularly on unreached people groups within Asia, where the cultural distance was narrower, enabling them to be more effective evangelistically. Today more than half of all Korean missionaries serve within Asia, the largest numbers in China, Japan, and the Philippines.[43]

One ongoing weakness of the Korean Protestant mission movement first identified at the LCWE was that it evidenced "little self-conscious reflection on mission" and would not "until the twenty-first century." Missionaries frequently received little or no missionary training. Mission organizations often lacked clear policies regarding missionary qualifications and accountability, among other things.[44] One missionary educator recognized these shortcomings and suggested solutions to them. Chun Chae-Ok (1938–2016) converted to Christianity during her first year at the renowned Ewha Women's University in Seoul. Ever since its founding in 1886 by a female Methodist missionary, Ewha had been engaged in mission outreach. That trend was deepened during the tenure of Dr. Kim Hwal-lan (Helen) as dean (1931–39) and then president (1939–61) of Ewha.[45] Kim was not only Chun's mentor, but her 1959 challenge to the Ewha student body to consider educational ministry in Pakistan resulted in Chun's own call to mission. In October 1961, after a missionary internship in rural Korea, Chun and two fellow Ewha graduates became the first female Korean missionaries to a Muslim country. From 1962 to 1966 Chun served as a missionary teacher at the predominantly Muslim Pigott Girls High School in Hyderabad, Pakistan. Then, after a study leave from 1966 to 1969 at All Nations Christian College and the London Bible College, Chun transitioned in her next term (1970–74) to theological education at the United Bible Training Center in Gujranwala in Punjab and at a Bible institute she founded in connection with the Sindh diocese of the Church of Pakistan in Karachi. After earning her master's degree and doctorate of missiology at Fuller Theological Seminary, Chun returned to Ewha University in 1977, where she became the first full-time professor of missiology at a Korean university. She served as the executive director of the World Evangelical Alliance (1974–79), founder (1992) and executive director of the Institute of Islamic Studies in Korea, president of the Korean Society of Missiology (1994–96), and president of the International Association for Mission Studies (1996–2000). She was also a member of the Lausanne Committee for World Evangelization.[46]

43. Kim and Kim, *History of Korean Christianity*, 300–307, 311–12.
44. Kim and Kim, *History of Korean Christianity*, 311.
45. Chun Chae-ok, "Rediscovering Ewha Mission and Its Contribution to Education," in *Christian Mission and Education in Modern China, Japan, and Korea*, ed. Jan A. B. Jongeneel, Peter Tze Ming Ng, Chong Ku Paek, and Scott W. Sunquist (Frankfurt: Peter Lang, 2009), 115–29.
46. Hansung Kim, "Chae Ok Chun: The First Female Korean Missiologist," *Journal of Asian Mission* 21, no. 1 (2020): 53–56, 59–62.

Chun's missiological emphases defied neat classification as evangelical or ecumenical. Her mission experience in Pakistan had convinced her that ministry to Muslims should aim to promote mutual understanding through friendship, love, and dialogue. Chun advocated for more Korean female missionaries and promoted a woman's missiology of emptiness, suffering, comfort, and community. Chun's third key concern was for the development and maturation of Korean cross-cultural missions, a topic she addresses in several articles in Korean journals. One early article from 1986 remains largely "fact-based and general," but later articles (1996, 2001) became "more prescriptive and directive."[47] This prescriptive element is reflected in an undated archival manuscript titled "Priorities for [Korean] Cross-Cultural Missions." In this document, Chun notes that the "regular study of Korean missions and missionaries" was taking place at Korean research centers. Despite these efforts, missionary training, mission funding, and cooperative national and international mission relationships were still inadequate. She believed that the key to solving these issues lay primarily with Korean pastors and secondarily with local churches. The "attitude pastors have toward cross-cultural missions" is "crucial," she wrote, since they "are rightly respected and obeyed by local church members in Korea." Only when pastors promote cross-cultural missionary training, robust mission funding, and interdenominational cooperation in mission will the task of cross-cultural Korean mission reach its full potential.[48] Korean mission leaders such as Chun sought solutions to missional weaknesses. Despite the growing maturity of the Korean mission movement in the twenty-first century, more work remains to be done, particularly with regard to cross-cultural competency, contextualization, and indigenous church principles.

In conclusion, this chapter has examined the exciting growth and maturity of cross-cultural missions from the former mission churches in the Global South as well as the considerable impact of the 1974 Lausanne Congress on those developments. The evangelical Protestant mission movements in Nigeria (ECWA/EMS), Brazil, and Korea had a number of similarities as well as some differences from one another. Already by the early twentieth century, evangelical Christians in all three countries were motivated to engage in local and cross-cultural evangelism within the boundaries of their own countries and in neighboring ones. This was seen in the ministries of Inusa Samaila and Karau Pane in Nigeria and beyond, of Erasmo Braga in Brazil, and of Lee Ki-Pung

47. Kim, "Chae Ok Chun," 65–68, 70–74. Chun Chae-Ok, "Integrity of Mission in the Light of the Gospel: Bearing the Witness of the Spirit, An Asian Perspective," *Mission Studies* 24, no. 2 (January 2007): 247–59.
48. "Korean Missions Compendium Chun" (Wheaton: Billy Graham Center Archive, n.d.), col. 338–101–27.

in Cheju and PCK missionaries in Shandong. The LCWE played a significant role in stimulating interest in cross-cultural mission beyond national boundaries and in developing cooperative mission organizations to further the goal of world evangelization. Within a few years after the LCWE, cooperative organizations were developed, and major conferences and congresses were held in Nigeria and Brazil. The Antioch Mission was founded in Brazil, and a new outreach was launched by the EMS among the Maguzawa, an unreached people group at the time.

Due to unique historical circumstances, Korea, in contrast to the other two countries, needed until the late 1980s to launch a mission movement and to develop cooperative mission organizations (KWMA) and a mission research institute (KRIM). Another difference is that Korea had an earlier (ca. 1910 on) and more sustained focus on diaspora mission to Korean immigrants around the world. In contrast, diaspora ministry first developed among the EMS in Nigeria in the 1980s–1990s, when the first missionaries to North America and Europe were sent to work among African and other immigrant populations. From the early twentieth century on, Brazilian missions had their own unique emphases: ministry among the Amazonian indigenous groups and in Portugal and Portuguese-speaking countries in Africa. Brazilian missionaries Tonica van der Meer and Rogério Rosa da Silva are examples of these trends. The historical overviews of the mission movements in Nigeria, Brazil, and Korea underscore an important turning point in the history of the expansion of Christianity. There has been a "shifting balance in missionary activity. . . . The once-fixed notions of 'sending countries' and 'receiving countries' have been tossed into the air."[49] Churches in the Global South not only receive mission partners from other parts of the world but also have reached missional maturity and become mission-sending forces. Mission is now from everywhere to everywhere!

We end this chapter with the concluding words of the 1974 Lausanne Covenant:

> Therefore, in the light of this our faith and our resolve, we enter into a solemn covenant with God and with each other, to pray, to plan and to work together for the evangelization of the whole world. We call upon others to join us. May God help us by his grace and for his glory to be faithful to this our covenant! Amen, Alleluia![50]

---

49. Mark Noll, *The New Shape of World Christianity: How American Experience Reflects Global Faith* (Downers Grove, IL: IVP Academic, 2009), 10.

50. Douglas, *Let the Earth Hear His Voice*, 9.

Conclusion

In the unfolding narrative of the history of the expansion of Christianity, a number of significant themes have emerged during different historical periods. The very fact that certain themes repeatedly appear is noteworthy and an indication of their dynamic importance, whether positive or negative, for the spread of the Christian faith. In my concluding remarks, I will briefly discuss what I view as the most important recurrent themes, which are organized under the following rubrics: mission theology, mission agents and structures, mission and culture, mission and the state, and mission motivation and lifestyle.

Mission Theology

Theology matters. The degree to which the various branches of the church in a particular time and place put into practice the universal mission mandate was in part dependent on their theology of mission. In the fourth and fifth centuries, the New Testament apostolic commissions motivated key representatives of both the Western (Patrick) and East Syrian churches (Narsai) to engage in or promote a robust, cross-cultural mission. At the time of the Protestant Reformation, however, the magisterial Reformers advocated a narrower understanding of those commissions. The apostolic office was a temporary one for the early church (Calvin) or had an unstoppable dynamic that continued on its own accord (Luther). In the next generation, Lutheran Orthodox theologian Johann Gerhard stated it more strongly. He argued that Matthew 28:16–20 had been intended for the apostles alone. Therefore, it was no longer compulsory for contemporary Christians to spread the gospel globally. Not surprisingly, the latter theological views were demotivating for mission and were one factor for the minimal mission outreach.

Another theological conviction that discouraged mission was held by New England Puritan John Cotton. He believed that the present era was not the correct eschatological time for an influx of Gentiles into the church. This Jews-then-Gentiles eschatological scheme cut the nerve of mission in New England until John Eliot (temporarily) reidentified Native Americans as part of the ten lost tribes of Israel and therefore as Jews and not Gentiles. Interestingly, Zinzendorf also maintained a Jews-then-Gentiles theology; he expected only a sprinkling of Gentile conversions in the present era, whom he called the "first fruits." Despite this demotivating theology, the Moravian leader pioneered a global mission motivated by love for Christ to win (some) souls for the Savior. Later Moravians rejected Zinzendorf's first-fruits theology, since thousands had been won for the Lamb and not just a few.

In order for the Protestant mission movement to be launched, it was necessary for those theologies that discouraged mission to be addressed. In his seminal volume, the *Enquiry*, William Carey did just that. He argued that the apostolic commissions were still applicable for present-day Christians and that the multitude of Gentile conversions in recent decades proved that now was the correct salvation-historical era to propagate the gospel worldwide. Furthermore, Carey and his colleague Andrew Fuller rejected the anti-missionary implications of hyper-Calvinism, which believed that it was inconsistent to uphold God's election to salvation and at the same time call the lost to accept Christ. Instead, Carey and Fuller espoused a moderate, mission-friendly form of Calvinism, and the Protestant mission movement grew rapidly. In the early twentieth century, liberal Protestants rejected the evangelical tenet that lost sinners outside of Christ face God's eternal punishment. Rather, they affirmed the salvific potential within all religions. Mission was redefined in ecumenical circles, and social and political action often replaced preaching and evangelism. In general, this approach was less motivating for mission, and the number of mainline missionaries plummeted in the twentieth century. Theology does indeed affect mission practice.

Mission Agents and Structures

In the first decades of the Christian movement, the gospel was spread both by church-appointed missionaries and by the spontaneous evangelistic ministry of individual Christians. Paul, his coworkers, and other apostles were designated missionaries who, along with hundreds of unnamed Jewish believers, evangelized the Mediterranean basin with remarkable results. By the mid-second century, however, the church-appointed missionary or evangelist all but disappeared from the historical record. Mission did occur, but it was unplanned and unorganized. It came about for the most part incidentally through individual initiative. Christian immigrants, merchants, soldiers, and slaves shared their faith when they voluntarily or involuntarily changed location. Lay Christians became the primary agents of evangelization within the Roman Empire, and also beyond its frontiers, as the East Syrian evidence shows. The important role of nonclerical Christians in the expansion of Christianity continued in the succeeding centuries, even as a new group of mission agents arose—the monastics.

Monasticism developed in the early fourth century. Already in late antiquity and the early Middle Ages, East Syrian, Celtic, and Anglo-Saxon monks and clerics had embraced the mission mandate and had become a driving force in the evangelization of Asia and Europe. Later, in the thirteenth to fifteenth centuries, a new type of religious order, the mendicants (Franciscans and Dominicans), provided the primary missionary impulse for the Roman Catholic Church. Then, beginning in the mid-sixteenth century, the newly founded Jesuit order energetically pursued foreign mission. Until the (temporary) dissolution of the order in 1773, the Society of Jesus was the premier mission order and converted hundreds of thousands to the Catholic faith. Between 400 and 1700, monastic orders not only supplied the missionary personnel for the Roman Catholic mission movement, but they also provided the organizational structure for mission—something that had been lacking since the postapostolic era.

Protestants in the sixteenth century were slow to embrace world mission for various reasons—some legitimate, some less so. One further disadvantage for early Protestants was that they lacked an organizational structure for mission such as monasticism provided for Roman Catholicism. Therefore it is not surprising that one factor in the rise of the Protestant mission movement was the successful adaptation of the earlier voluntary religious society for the specific needs and cause of mission. In his *Enquiry* (1792), William Carey proposed that a Protestant missionary society be established, and that same year the Baptist Missionary Society (BMS) was founded. With the founding of the BMS, the organizational structure of the Protestant missionary movement was born. Within the following two decades, a dozen new and prominent Protestant missionary societies were founded, enabling the task of global mission to accelerate rapidly.

In the first decades of the Protestant mission movement (ca. 1790–1850), Western missionaries played an important pioneering role in opening up large swaths of Africa and Asia to the gospel. In the mid-nineteenth century, however, two key Protestant mission theorists, Henry Venn and Rufus Anderson, recognized that the role of the foreign missionary must change in order to produce the goal of mission—an independent, indigenous church. Western missionaries should no longer pastor indigenous congregations; that was the role of local teachers and preachers. Rather, the missionaries' tasks consisted of training and empowering local leaders for the work of ministry and evangelistic preaching to the unconverted in regions beyond. Only then would a self-supporting, self-governing, and self-propagating indigenous church be produced. Most Protestant missionaries in the late nineteenth century accepted the validity of three-self principles, at least in theory. Some missionaries, such as John Nevius in Shandong, China, and the American Presbyterian Mission in Korea consistently and successfully applied indigenous principles. Other missionaries and mission societies pushed the goal of an independent, indigenous church further into the future.

Despite this trend, there were many nineteenth- and twentieth-century examples of indigenous missionaries and, somewhat later, independent, indigenous mission societies. In 1857, Henry Venn entrusted the leadership of the Niger Mission to Samuel Ajayi Crowther. Although the mission was initiated by the Church Missionary Society, it was staffed entirely with Sierra Leone Christians, who served as cross-cultural missionaries in the predominately Muslim territory of northern Nigeria. Also in northern Nigeria, lay Tangale evangelists affiliated with the Sudan Interior Mission evangelized every major village in Tangaleland in the 1930s and responded to calls for cross-cultural ministry further north. In 1948 the Evangelical Missionary Society of ECWA, the largest Nigerian mission organization, was founded. Today it supports 1,830 missionary couples in Nigeria and in seventeen other countries.

Similarly, both lay Korean Christians and ordained pastors and missionaries actively evangelized both within Korea and beyond. The witness of lay Christians was a key factor in the remarkable growth of the Korean Presbyterian and Methodist churches during the Great Revival movement of 1903–8. In 1907, the same year that the independent Presbyterian Church of Korea (PCK) was established, that body sent its first missionary to Cheju Island. Five years later, in 1912, it dispatched missionaries to Shandong, China. It was not until after the 1974 Lausanne Congress that Christian leaders in the Global South formed cooperative mission structures and launched their own full-orbed cross-cultural mission movements. History shows that appropriate mission structures—whether they be religious orders, missionary societies, or contemporary church-based models—are needed for an effective global mission outreach. Also needed is the missional engagement of all segments of the church, both lay and clerical.

Mission and Culture

Christian missionaries throughout the centuries have carried the gospel message across geographic, religious, ethnic, and cultural frontiers. By its very nature, Christian expansion involves cultural encounters, interreligious dialogue, and communication across ethnocultural divides, all of which can be challenging. Some missionaries immersed themselves in the receptor culture and achieved a high level of cultural and linguistic proficiency. Most foreign missionaries reached moderate levels of cross-cultural competency, but they were effective if they won the trust of the local people. Some, however, adopted a tabula rasa (or blank slate) approach to culture, which was common in the sixteenth- and seventeenth-century missions in the Americas under the Portuguese and Spanish patronage systems. Missionary adherents to this viewpoint insisted that potential converts had to adopt European language and culture in order to become Christians. They believed the indigenous culture had to be virtually eliminated—erased clean like a blank slate prior to conversion.

Throughout history, the best cross-cultural missionaries aimed to gain the requisite cultural competency to faithfully communicate the gospel in a manner understandable to the target population. They accomplished this in a number of ways. First, they learned the local language well. In late antiquity and the early Middle Ages, both Patrick and Boniface acquired the local language and used it in their respective ministries in Ireland and present-day Germany. Some of the best Protestant missionaries in the nineteenth century (Ziegenbalg, Carey, and Judson) mastered the local language(s) with two goals in minds: to effectively communicate the gospel and to provide the nascent church with a translated Bible—a high priority for evangelical Protestants.

Second, the best missionaries sought to gain an in-depth understanding of the local culture and religion. Two in-depth examples of cultural adaptation to the Chinese context were discussed in this book: that of the East Syrian mission (635) and that of the Jesuit missionary Matteo Ricci and his compatriots nearly a millennium later (1582–1610). The East Syrian mission in the seventh century expressed Christian ethics in Confucian categories and used Taoist and Buddhist terms for God yet retained orthodox Christian theology. By the eighth century, however, Taoist and Buddhist religious beliefs overshadowed or replaced aspects of Christian doctrine. Sixteenth-century China missionary

Matteo Ricci adopted an innovative approach to cultural accommodation. He was convinced that original Confucianism was not idolatrous but essentially monotheistic and that ancestor veneration was a legitimate expression of filial piety for Chinese Christians. Despite the controversies the Riccian approach spawned, it has influenced contemporary understandings of inculturation/contextualization.

Protestants were also committed to cultural understanding and adaptation. In the Serampore Covenant, William Carey and his colleagues pledged to read Hindu literature, to note Hindu manners and rituals, and to engage in conversations with Hindus in order to better understand their worldview, their customs, and their religious doctrines and practices. Their goal was to gain a hearing for the gospel and to avoid being "barbarians" to the Hindus. Similarly, Bartholomäus Ziegenbalg sought to understand the Tamil Hindu culture through sensitive conversations with Tamil partners. He collected and studied their written classics. On the basis of this research, Ziegenbalg wrote two lengthy ethnological works: *Malabarian Heathendom* (1711) and *Genealogy of the Malabarian Gods* (1713).

Third, the best missionaries took societal and political norms into account. In the fifth century, Patrick followed the common cultural practice of seeking permission from the local kings or chiefs before entering their territory to evangelize. He paid the requisite tribute or gave the customary gifts and recruited their younger sons to accompany him on his travels to add credibility to his mission. Similarly, Karau Pane (d. 1976) sought and received permission to teach literacy, and ultimately to share his Christian faith, in the Muslim Gombe emirate of northern Nigeria through slow, sensitive, and respectful ministry.

Finally, when appropriate, the best missionaries created functional substitutes for religious and cultural rituals. Pope Gregory the Great in 601 instructed Abbot Mellitus, the leader of the mission to Anglo-Saxon England, to preserve well-built pagan shrines, which should be cleansed of idols and reconsecrated for Christian worship. Furthermore, a joyous Christian festival should be substituted for idolatrous sacrificial feasts. Gregory maintained that the *outward* adaptation to Anglo-Saxon religious culture was legitimate and even conducive to conversion as long as the *inward* content remained Christian. Similarly, in the 1970s, Tambaya Hassan introduced two Christian rituals among the Maguzawa people of Nigeria to serve as substitutes for indigenous ceremonies: a naming ceremony at the birth of a child and a repentance feast for new Christian converts. These historical examples of the nexus between mission and culture reveal both the necessity and the complexity of cross-cultural adaptation and communication.

Mission and State

At a number of important junctures, the Christian church and its mission became entangled with the state, either to the detriment or to the benefit of mission. The first juncture occurred when Emperor Constantine gave direct support for the Christian religion after the Edict of Milan in 313. This inaugurated the period of Christendom, in which the boundaries of Western Christianity were increasingly viewed as identical to those of the Roman Empire. The result of this for mission *outside* the Roman Empire was detrimental and devastating. Very few Christians in the three centuries after Constantine viewed mission outside the borders of the empire as part of the church's responsibility or mandate. Two notable exceptions were Patrick, who evangelized Ireland (ca. 450), and the mission to Anglo-Saxon England sent by Pope Gregory the Great (597).

A second important nexus between Christian mission and the state occurred in the seventh and eighth centuries, both in the East and in the West. The East Syrian mission to China profited from the support of the early Tang dynasty emperors. Taizong (638) officially recognized the Christian religion as beneficial for the Chinese. He allowed its propagation and even financed the first Chinese church in Xi'an. His successor Gaozong promoted the founding of Christian monasteries. These actions helped advance the spread of Christianity. When this official support was replaced with anti-Christian policies by later Tang rulers, Empress Wu Hou (691) and Emperor Wuzong (845), Christianity in China declined and then disappeared by 907. In the West, the Frankish rulers Pippin II and Charles Martell of the rising Carolingian dynasty were well aware that the Christianization of recently conquered areas effectively destroyed resistance to their rule. This was one reason that they supported mission work in such territories. Pippin II assigned parts of newly conquered Frisia to Anglo-Saxon missionary Willibrord as his mission territory. He bestowed property on the mission and in 695 even played a key role in Willibrord's consecration as archbishop. Similarly, Charles Martell provided powerful secular support and protection for Boniface's mission. This mutual cooperation between church and state was embraced by the papacy *and* the Anglo-Saxon missionaries as both beneficial and a key to their mission success. Political support benefited Christian mission in Frankish territories; it was both a benefit and a detriment in Tang China.

In the early Protestant missions, the relationship between church and state was convoluted. The business objectives of the East India trading companies in the eighteenth century were often sharply at odds with missionary goals. This meant that individual missionaries were at times imprisoned, as Bartholomäus

Ziegenbalg was by the Danish governor of Tranquebar in 1708. Until 1813, missionaries of the BMS and other societies in India were regularly denied residence in territory controlled by the British East India Company (BEIC). In time, however, a closer relationship developed between missionaries and both trading companies and colonial governments. For example, by the 1790s, the Danish-Halle mission had become more closely affiliated with the political goals of the BEIC, in part due to its cooperation with the English SPCK. The colonial government of Sierra Leone established and financed most village chapels and schools in the colony, leading to closer ties between the CMS and the state.

That trend was intensified in the high imperialist era (ca. 1880–1914). As direct political control became more prevalent, it became more difficult for missionaries in Africa and Asia to ignore or operate independently of colonial agendas as they often had in the past. Missionaries had two overriding concerns in this era: to propagate the gospel unhindered and to protect the native populations from imperial abuses. These priorities and the colonial situations in which missionaries operated helped determine the wide range of individual responses to imperialism. These missionary responses ranged from blatant, active collaboration to clear resistance to imperialism, with multiple other stances in between. Most missionaries desired a moderate form of colonialism that provided infrastructure and protection for their mission, as well as safety and well-being for the local population. Though missionaries often aimed to remain apolitical, the relationship between Christian mission and the state took center stage at several important junctures in history.

Mission Motivation and Lifestyle

Several theological motivations for mission were already noted in the section on mission and theology above: the universal mission mandate (Patrick, Narsai), the love of Christ (Zinzendorf), and the evangelical tenet that lost sinners outside of Christ face God's eternal punishment. The humanitarian motive for mission became more prominent in the eighteenth century and continues to this day. It often took the form of protesting or abolishing religious or cultural practices deemed cruel or inhumane. For example, William Carey in India decried the practice of widow burning (*sati*), female infanticide, exposure of the sick and elderly, and hook-swinging. Evangelical British abolitionists sought to abolish the slave trade, to root out all remaining vestiges of slavery in Africa, and to spread the gospel to victims of the slave trade. They were animated by both a humanitarian motive and the need to make restitution for Britain's complicity in the slave trade. From the 1870s to the 1880s, a new humanitarian focus arose—medical missions. Medical work served a number of missional purposes, including a utilitarian, a strategic, and an evangelistic purpose. By the end of the nineteenth century, medical missions also increasingly touted the humanitarian and imitative purposes of demonstrating Christ's compassion for the sick through a healing ministry.

Although a self-sacrificing lifestyle is mandated for all Christians (Rom. 12:1–2; Eph. 5:1–2), James Scherer reminds us that mission by its very nature is costly and requires self-sacrifice. He writes, "The heart of mission is always making the Gospel known where it would not be known without a *special and costly act* of boundary-crossing witness."[1] The costly nature of sharing the gospel is seen throughout Christian history. The first Christian martyr, Stephen, was stoned to death while preaching the gospel (Acts 7). Patrick went to Ireland, knowing that his mission there might involve insults, persecution, imprisonment, and even death. Ziegenbalg and Plütschau faced opposition from the Danish East India Company in India and were even imprisoned by them. Moravian Leonhard Dober responded to slave Anton Ulrich's call to become a slave for the sake of the gospel on the Caribbean island of St. Thomas. In 1732 he became one of the first two Moravian missionaries among the slave population there. Nineteenth-century missionaries to West Africa were well aware that their likelihood of death from tropical diseases was quite high. In the first twenty years of the CMS ministry in Sierra Leone, fifty men and women died, most of them from disease. Nevertheless, missionaries continued to pour into Africa, at times using coffins as packing crates for their belongings. The cost of cross-cultural mission continues to this day, as the execution in April 2011 of a Nigerian EMS missionary, Isma Dogari, proves. These examples are admittedly more extreme than what the average missionary experiences. Nevertheless, all missionaries who intentionally transverse cultural boundaries with the gospel and who aim to "become all things to all people so that . . . [they] might save some" (1 Cor. 9:22) must adopt a self-sacrificing lifestyle and lay aside aspects of their own culture and language to be effective.

The church of Christ has expanded throughout the globe despite the failings of missionaries, the shortsightedness of mission societies, and the dearth of prayer and support from home churches. Looking back on this history allows us on the one hand to learn from the grievous mistakes and wrongs that were perpetrated alongside the proclamation of the Christian faith. But

1. James A. Scherer, *Gospel, Church, and Kingdom: Comparative Studies in World Mission Theology* (Minneapolis: Augsburg, 1987), 37.

the balance sheet for Christian expansion includes on the other hand glorious moments of sacrifice for the sake of the gospel, languages learned and cultures understood, Scriptures translated and literacy taught, new and creative methods employed, physical and social wrongs resolved, and the gospel of Christ's redemption preached and believed among all peoples and nations. That gives us confidence to look to the future, resting in the promises of Jesus Christ: "I will be with you always unto the end of the age" (Matt. 28:20), and "I will build my church and the gates of hell shall not prevail against it" (Matt. 16:18).

Select Bibliography

Primary Sources

Anderson, Rufus. *Memorial Volume of the First Fifty Years of the American Board of Commissioners for Foreign Missions*. 5th ed. Boston: ABCFM, 1862.

Bettenson, Henry, and Chris Maunder, eds. *Documents of the Christian Church*. 4th ed. Oxford: Oxford University Press, 2011.

Bieler, Ludwig. *The Works of St. Patrick, St. Secundinus, Hymn of St. Patrick*. New York: Newman, 1953.

Buxton, Thomas Fowell. *The African Slave Trade and Its Remedy*. London: John Murray, 1840.

Carey, Eustace. *Memoir of William Carey*. London: Jackson and Walford, 1836.

Carey, William. *An Enquiry into the Obligations of Christians to Use Means for the Conversion of the Heathens*. London: Hodder and Stoughton, 1891.

Carey, William, Joshua Marshman, William Ward, John Chamberlain, Richard Mardon, John Biss, William Moore, Joshua Rowe, and Felix Carey. "The Serampore Form of Agreement." *Baptist Quarterly* 12, no. 5 (1947): 125–38.

Carter, Terry G., ed. *The Journal and Selected Letters of William Carey*. Macon, GA: Smyth & Helwys, 2000.

Cureton, William. *Spicilegium Syriacum: Bardesan, Meliton, Ambrose, and Mara Bar Serapion*. London: Riverton, 1855.

Douglas, J. D., ed. *Let the Earth Hear His Voice: International Congress on World Evangelization*. Minneapolis: World Wide Publications, 1975.

DuBose, Francis M., ed. *Classics of Christian Missions*. Nashville: Broadman, 1979.

Emerton, Ephraim, trans. *The Letters of Saint Boniface*. New York: Columbia University Press, 1940.

Eusebius. *Ecclesiastical History*. Translated by C. F. Cruse. London: Bagster and Sons, 1842.

Gregory the Great. Letter 76. In vol. 13 of *A Select Library of Nicene and Post-Nicene Fathers of the Christian Church*, 2nd series, edited by Philip Schaff and Henry Wace. New York: Christian Literature, 1890–1900; repr., Peabody, MA: Hendrickson, 1994.

Heanley, R. M. *A Memoir of Edward Steere*. London: George Bell, 1888.

Hillgarth, J. N., ed., *Christianity and Paganism, 350–750: The Conversion of Western Europe*. Rev. ed. Philadelphia: University of Pennsylvania Press, 1986.

History and Records of the [World Missionary] Conference. New York: Fleming H. Revell, 1910.

Hitchcock, F. R. Montgomery, trans. *The Treatise of Saint Irenaeus of Lugdunum Against the Heresies*. Vol. 1. London: SPCK, 1916.

Hsia, R. Po-chia. *Matteo Ricci and the Catholic Mission to China: A Short History with Documents*. Indianapolis: Hackett, 2016.

Hussey, Joseph. *God's Operations of Grace but Not Offers of His Grace*. Scotts Valley, CA: CreateSpace, 2017.

Instructions of the Prudential Committee of the ABCFM. Lahaina, HI: Mission Seminary Press, 1838.

Jacobs, Nancy J. *African History through Sources*. Vol. 1, *Colonial Contexts and Everyday Experiences*. Cambridge: Cambridge University Press, 2014.

Knight, William. *Memoir of the Rev. H. Venn*. London: Longmans, Green, 1880.

Koschorke, Klaus, Frieder Ludwig, and Mariano Delgado, eds. *A History of Christianity in Asia, Africa, and Latin America, 1450–1990: A Documentary Sourcebook*. Grand Rapids: Eerdmans, 2007.

Maas, Michael. *Readings in Late Antiquity: A Sourcebook*. New York: Routledge, 2003.

Maurice, Matthias. *A Modern Question Modestly Answered*. London: James Buckland, 1737.

McLeod, Frederick G., trans. *Narsai's Metrical Homilies on the Nativity, Epiphany and Ascension: English Translation*. Turnhout, Belgium: Brepols, 1979.

Mott, John R. *The Evangelization of the World in This Generation*. New York: SVM, 1900.

Nevius, Helen Coan. *The Life of John Livingston Nevius*. New York: Fleming H. Revell, 1895.

Nevius, John L. *The Planting and Development of Missionary Churches*. New York: Foreign Mission Library, 1899.

Nobili, Roberto de. *Adaptation*. Edited by S. Rajamanickam, SJ. Palayamkottal: De Nobili Research Institute, 1971.

Noble, Thomas F. X., and Thomas Head, eds. *Soldiers of Christ: Saints and Saints' Lives from Late Antiquity and the Early Middle Ages*. University Park: Pennsylvania State University Press, 1995.

Phillips, George, ed. and trans. *The Doctrine of Addai the Apostle*. London: Trübner, 1876.

Prosper of Aquitaine. *The Call of All Nations*. Translated by P. De Letter. Mahwah, NJ: Paulist Press, 1978.

Records of the General Conference of the Protestant Missionaries of China. Shanghai: Presbyterian Mission Press, 1878.

Reichel, William C., ed. *Memorials of the Moravian Church*. Vol. 1. Philadelphia: Lippincott, 1870.

Report of the American Board of Commissioners for Foreign Missions. Boston: T. R. Marvin, 1856.

Saeki, P. Y. *The Nestorian Documents and Relics in China*. 2nd ed. Tokyo: Tokyo Institute, 1951.

————. *The Nestorian Monument in China*. London: SPCK, 1928.

Speer, Robert E., and Samuel G. Inman, eds. *Christian Work in South America: Official Report of the Congress on Christian Work in South America*. Vol. 1. New York: Fleming H. Revell, 1925.

Steere, Edward. *Central African Mission: Its Present State and Prospects*. London: Rivington, 1873.

Stott, John, ed. *Making Christ Known: Historic Mission Documents from the Lausanne Movement, 1974–1989*. Grand Rapids: Eerdmans, 1996.

Talbot, C. H., trans. and ed. *The Anglo-Saxon Missionaries in Germany*. New York: Sheed and Ward, 1954.

Tozer, William G. *Letters of Bishop Tozer*. Edited by Gertrude Ward and Helen Tozer. London: UMCA, 1902.

Vööbus, Arthur. *The Statutes of the School of Nisibis*. Stockholm: Este, 1961.

Wallbank, T. Walter. *Documents on Modern Africa*. Princeton: Van Nostrand, 1964.

World Missionary Conference. *Report of Commissions I and III*. New York: Fleming H. Revell, 1910.

World Missionary Conference, 1910: History and Records of the Conference. New York: Fleming H. Revell, 1910.

Secondary Sources

Ådna, Jostein, and Hans Kvalbein, eds. *The Mission of the Early Church to Jews and Gentiles*. Tübingen: Mohr Siebeck, 2000.

Atkins, Gareth. *Converting Britannia: Evangelicals and British Public Life, 1770–1840*. Woodbridge, UK: Boydell, 2019.

Austin, Alvyn. *China's Millions: The China Inland Mission and Late Qing Society, 1832–1905*. Grand Rapids: Eerdmans, 2007.

Baba, Panya. *A Vision Received, a Vision Passed On: The History of the EMS of ECWA, 1948–1998*. Jos, Nigeria: Africa Christian Textbooks, 2009.

Baum, Wilhelm, and Dietmar W. Winkler. *The Church of the East: A Concise History*. New York: Routledge Curzon, 2003.

Bays, Daniel H. *A New History of Christianity in China*. Malden, MA: Wiley-Blackwell, 2012.

Bevans, Stephen B., and Roger P. Schroeder. *Constants in Context: A Theology of Mission for Today*. Maryknoll, NY: Orbis, 2004.

Boahen, A. Adu. *African Perspectives on Colonialism*. Baltimore: Johns Hopkins University Press, 1987.

Brockey, Liam Matthew. *Journey to the East: The Jesuit Mission to China, 1579–1724*. Cambridge, MA: Harvard University Press, 2007.

———. *The Visitor: Andre Palmeiro and the Jesuits in Asia*. Cambridge, MA: Harvard University Press, 2014.

Brown, Peter. *The Rise of Western Christendom*. 2nd ed. Malden, MA: Blackwell, 2003.

Burkitt, Francis C. *Early Eastern Christianity*. Eugene, OR: Wipf & Stock, 2005.

Carson, Penelope. *The East India Company and Religion, 1698–1858*. Woodbridge, UK: Boydell, 2012.

Chamberlain, M. E. *The Scramble for Africa*. 3rd ed. Harlow, UK: Longman, 2010.

Chao, Samuel Hsiang-En. "John Livingston Nevius (1829–1893): A Historical Study of His Life and Mission Methods." PhD diss., Fuller Theological Seminary, 1991.

Charles-Edwards, T. M. *Early Christian Ireland*. Cambridge: Cambridge University Press, 2000.

Clay, John-Henry. *In the Shadow of Death: Saint Boniface and the Conversion of Hessia, 721–754*. Turnhout, Belgium: Brepols, 2010.

Cogley, Richard. *John Eliot's Mission to the Indians before King Philip's War*. Cambridge, MA: Harvard University Press, 1999.

Cook, Guillermo, ed. *New Face of the Church in Latin America*. Maryknoll, NY: Orbis, 1994.

Cooper, Barbara M., Gary R. Corwin, Tibebe Eshete, Musa A. B. Gaiya, Tim Geysbeek, and Shobana Shankar, eds. *Transforming Africa's Religious Landscapes: The Sudan Interior Mission (SIM), Past and Present*. Trenton, NJ: Africa World Press, 2018.

Cox, Jeffrey. *The British Missionary Enterprise since 1700*. New York: Routledge, 2008.

Cummins, J. S. *A Question of Rites: Friar Domingo Navarette and the Jesuits in China*. Brookfield, VT: Ashgate, 1993.

Dahle, Lars, ed. *The Lausanne Movement: A Range of Perspectives*. Oxford: Regnum Books, 2014.

Danker, William J. *Profit for the Lord: Economic Activities in Moravian Missions and the Basel Mission Trading Company*. Eugene, OR: Wipf & Stock, 1971.

Duesing, Jason G., ed. *Adoniram Judson: A Bicentennial Appreciation of the Pioneer American Missionary*. Nashville: B&H Academic, 2012.

Dunne, George H. *Generation of Giants: The Story of the Jesuits in China in the Last Decades of the Ming Dynasty*. Notre Dame, IN: University of Notre Dame Press, 1962.

Evans, G. R. *The Thought of Gregory the Great*. Cambridge: Cambridge University Press, 1988.

Fletcher, Richard. *The Barbarian Conversion: From Paganism to Christianity*. Berkeley: University of California Press, 1997.

Forrester, Duncan B. *Caste and Christianity: Attitudes and Policies on Caste of Anglo-Saxon Protestant Missions in India*. New York: Routledge, 2017.

Freeman, Philip. *St. Patrick of Ireland: A Biography*. New York: Simon & Schuster, 2004.

Frykenberg, Robert Eric. *Christians and Missionaries in India: Cross-Cultural Communication since 1500*. Grand Rapids: Eerdmans, 2003.

Gameson, Richard, ed. *St. Augustine and the Conversion of England*. Stroud, UK: Sutton, 2000.

Gehring, Roger W. *House Church and Mission: The Importance of Household Structures in Early Christianity*. Peabody, MA: Hendrickson, 2004.

George, Timothy. *Faithful Witness: The Life and Mission of William Carey*. Worcester, PA: Christian History Institute, 1998.

Godfrey, John. *The Church in Anglo-Saxon England*. Cambridge: Cambridge University Press, 1962.

González, Justo, and Ondina González. *Christianity in Latin America: A History*. Cambridge: Cambridge University Press, 2008.

Green, Michael. *Evangelism in the Early Church*. Grand Rapids: Eerdmans, 1970.

Gross, Andreas, Y. Vincent Kumaradoss, and Heike Liebau, eds. *Halle and the Beginning of Protestant Christianity in India*. Vol. 1, *The Danish-Halle and the English-Halle Mission*. Halle: Franckesche Stiftungen, 2006.

Grundmann, Christoffer H. *Sent to Heal: Emergence and Development of Medical Missions*. Lanham, MD: University Press of America, 2005.

Hanciles, Jehu. *Euthanasia of a Mission: African Church Autonomy in a Colonial Context*. Westport, CT: Praeger, 2002.

———. *Migration and the Making of Global Christianity*. Grand Rapids: Eerdmans, 2021.

Harris, Paul William. *Nothing but Christ: Rufus Anderson and the Ideology of Protestant Foreign Missions*. Oxford: Oxford University Press, 1999.

Hartch, Todd. *The Rebirth of Latin American Christianity*. Oxford: Oxford University Press, 2014.

Heartfield, James. *The British and Foreign Anti-slavery Society, 1838–1956: A History*. Oxford: Oxford University Press, 2016.

Hempton, David. *The Church in the Long Eighteenth Century*. London: I. B. Tauris, 2011.

Hendrix, Scott H. *Recultivating the Vineyard: The Reformation Agendas of Christianization*. Louisville: Westminster John Knox, 2004.

Hennell, Michael. *John Venn and the Clapham Sect*. London: Lutterworth, 1958.

Hudson, Dennis. *Protestant Origins in India: Tamil Evangelical Christians, 1706–1835*. Grand Rapids: Eerdmans, 2000.

Hutchison, William R. *Errand to the World: American Protestant Thought and Foreign Missions*. Chicago: University of Chicago Press, 1987.

Hylson-Smith, Kenneth. *Evangelicals in the Church of England, 1734–1984*. Edinburgh: T&T Clark, 1988.

Jakobsson, Stiv. *Am I Not a Man and a Brother? British Missions and the Abolition of the Slave Trade and Slavery in West Africa and the West Indies, 1786–1838*. Uppsala: Almquist & Wiksells, 1972.

Jenkins, Philip. *The Next Christendom: The Coming of Global Christianity*. 3rd ed. Oxford: Oxford University Press, 2011.

Jeyaraj, Daniel. *Bartholomäus Ziegenbalg: The Father of Modern Protestant Mission*. New Delhi: Indian SPCK, 2006.

Jongeneel, Jan A. B., Peter Tze Ming Ng, Chong Ku Paek, and Scott W. Sunquist, eds. *Christian Mission and Education in Modern China, Japan, and Korea*. Frankfurt: Peter Lang, 2009.

Kalu, O. U., ed. *The History of Christianity in West Africa*. London: Longman, 1981.

Kerr, David A., and Kenneth R. Ross, eds. *Edinburgh 2010: Mission Then and Now*. Eugene, OR: Wipf & Stock, 2009.

Kim, Sebastian, and Kirsteen Kim. *A History of Korean Christianity*. Cambridge: Cambridge University Press, 2015.

Klauber, Martin I., and Scott M. Manetsch, eds. *The Great Commission: Evangelicals and the History of World Missions*. Nashville: B&H, 2008.

Koschorke, Klaus, ed. *Transcontinental Links in the History of Non-Western Christianity*. Wiesbaden, Germany: Harrassowitz, 2002.

Laven, Mary. *Mission to China: Matteo Ricci and the Jesuit Encounter with the East*. London: Faber and Faber, 2011.

Lewis, A. J. *Zinzendorf, the Ecumenical Pioneer: A Study in the Moravian Contribution to Christian Mission and Unity*. Philadelphia: Westminster, 1962.

Lewis, Mark Edward, and Timothy Brook. *China's Cosmopolitan Empire: The Tang Dynasty*. Cambridge, MA: Belknap, 2009.

Leyser, Conrad, and Hannah Williams, eds. *Mission and Monasticism*. Rome: Pontificio Ateneo S. Anselmo, 2013.

Lutz, Jessie Gregory. *Opening China: Karl F. A. Gützlaff and Sino-Western Relations, 1827–1852*. Grand Rapids: Eerdmans, 2008.

Mackintosh, Robin. *Augustine of Canterbury: Leadership, Mission and Legacy*. Norwich: Canterbury, 2013.

MacMullen, Ramsey. *Christianizing the Roman Empire AD 100–400*. New Haven: Yale University Press, 1984.

Malek, Roman, ed. *The Chinese Face of Jesus Christ*. Vol. 1. New York: Routledge, 2017.

Markus, R. A. *Gregory the Great and His World*. Cambridge: Cambridge University Press, 1997.

Mason, J. C. S. *The Moravian Church and the Missionary Awakening in England, 1760–1800*. Rochester: Boydell, 2001.

Maughan, Steven S. *Mighty England Do Good: Culture, Faith, Empire and World in the Foreign Missions of the Church of England, 1850–1915*. Grand Rapids: Eerdmans, 2014.

Minamiki, George. *Chinese Rites Controversy: From Its Beginning to Modern Times*. Chicago: Loyola University Press, 1985.

Moffett, Samuel. *A History of Christianity in Asia*. 2 vols. San Francisco: Harper, 1992–2005.

Mungello, D. E., ed. *The Chinese Rites Controversy: Its History and Meaning*. Nettetal, Germany: Steyler Verlag, 1994.

Neill, Stephen. *A History of Christian Missions*. 2nd ed. New York: Penguin, 1991.

Noll, Mark. *The New Shape of World Christianity: How American Experience Reflects Global Faith*. Downers Grove, IL: IVP Academic, 2009.

Öberg, Ingemar. *Luther and World Mission: A Historical and Systematic Study*. Translated by Dean Apel. St. Louis: Concordia, 2007.

O'Loughlin, Thomas. *Discovering Saint Patrick*. Mahwah, NJ: Paulist Press, 2005.

Paik, L. George. *The History of Protestant Missions in Korea, 1832–1910*. Seoul: Yonsei University Press, 1970.

Palmer, James T. *Anglo-Saxons in a Frankish World, 690–900*. Turnhout, Belgium: Brepols, 2009.

———. "Defining Paganism in the Carolingian World." *Early Medieval Europe* 15, no. 4 (November 2007): 402–25.

Phillips, James M., and Robert T. Coote, eds. *Towards the Twenty-First Century in Christian Mission*. Grand Rapids: Eerdmans, 1993.

Porter, Andrew, ed. *The Imperial Horizons of British Protestant Missions, 1880–1914*. Grand Rapids: Eerdmans, 2003.

———. *Religion versus Empire? British Protestant Missionaries and Overseas Expansion, 1700–1914*. Manchester: Manchester University Press, 2004.

Robert, Dana L. *American Women in Mission: A Social History of Their Thought and Practice*. Macon, GA: Mercer University Press, 1997.

Ross, Andrew. *A Vision Betrayed: The Jesuits in Japan and China, 1542–1742.* Maryknoll, NY: Orbis, 1994.

Sanneh, Lamin. *Abolitionists Abroad: American Blacks and the Making of Modern West Africa.* Cambridge, MA: Harvard University Press, 1999.

———. *Translating the Message: The Missionary Impact on Culture.* 2nd ed. Maryknoll, NY: Orbis, 2009.

Schnabel, Eckhard J. *Early Christian Mission.* 2 vols. Downers Grove, IL: InterVarsity, 2004.

Shankar, Shobana. *Who Shall Enter Paradise? Christian Origins in Northern Nigeria, ca. 1890–1975.* Athens: Ohio University Press, 2014.

Shantz, Douglas H. *An Introduction to German Pietism: Protestant Renewal at the Dawn of Modern Europe.* Baltimore: Johns Hopkins University Press, 2013.

Shaw, Mark. *The Kingdom of God in Africa: A Short History of African Christianity.* Grand Rapids: Baker, 1996.

Sheils, W. J., ed. *The Church and Healing.* Oxford: Blackwell, 1982.

Shenk, Wilbert R. *Henry Venn: Missionary Statesman.* Eugene, OR: Wipf & Stock, 2006.

Smither, Edward L. *Brazilian Evangelical Missions in the Arab World: History, Culture, Practice, and Theology.* Eugene, OR: Wipf & Stock, 2012.

Standaert, Nicolas, ed. *Handbook of Christianity in China.* Vol. 1, 635–1800. Leiden: Brill, 2001.

Stanley, Brian. *The Bible and the Flag: Protestant Mission and British Imperialism in the Nineteenth and Twentieth Centuries.* Leicester: Apollos, 1990.

———, ed. *Christian Missions and the Enlightenment.* Grand Rapids: Eerdmans, 2001.

———. *The Global Diffusion of Evangelicalism: The Age of Billy Graham and John Stott.* Downers Grove, IL: IVP Academic, 2013.

———. *The History of the Baptist Missionary Society, 1792–1992.* Edinburgh: T&T Clark, 1992.

———. *The World Missionary Conference, Edinburgh 1910.* Grand Rapids: Eerdmans, 2009.

Stark, Rodney. *The Rise of Christianity.* San Francisco: HarperCollins, 1997.

Stoner-Eby, Anne Marie. "African Leaders Engage Mission Christianity: Anglicans in Tanzania, 1876–1926." PhD diss., University of Pennsylvania, 2003.

Tabbernee, William, ed. *Early Christianity in Contexts: An Exploration across Cultures and Continents.* Grand Rapids: Baker, 2014.

Tang, Li. *A Study of the History of Nestorian Christianity in China and Its Literature in Chinese.* 2nd ed. New York: Peter Lang, 2004.

Taylor, William D., Antonia van der Meer, and Reg Reimer, eds. *Sorrow and Blood: Christian Mission in Contexts of Suffering, Persecution and Martyrdom.* Pasadena, CA: William Carey, 2012.

Thompson, E. A. *Who Was Saint Patrick?* New York: St. Martin's Press, 1986.

Thompson, T. Jack. *Light on Darkness? Missionary Photography of Africa in the Nineteenth and Early Twentieth Centuries.* Grand Rapids: Eerdmans, 2012.

Turaki, Yusufu. *Theory and Practice of Christian Missions in Africa: A Century of SIM/ECWA History and Legacy in Nigeria, 1893–1993.* Nairobi: International Bible Society, 1999.

Walls, Andrew F. *The Missionary Movement in Christian History.* Maryknoll, NY: Orbis, 1996.

Walton, Steve, Paul Trebilco, and David Gill, eds. *The Urban World and the First Christians.* Grand Rapids: Eerdmans, 2017.

Ward, Kevin, and Brian Stanley, eds. *The Church Mission Society and World Christianity, 1799–1999.* Grand Rapids: Eerdmans, 2000.

Wesseling, H. L. *Divide and Rule: The Partition of Africa, 1880–1914.* Translated by Arnold J. Pomerans. Westport, CT: Praeger, 1996.

Wheeler, Rachel. *To Live upon Hope: Mohicans and Missionaries in the Eighteenth-Century Northeast.* Ithaca, NY: Cornell University Press, 2008.

Williams, C. Peter. *The Ideal of the Self-Governing Church: A Study in Victorian Missionary Strategy.* Leiden: Brill, 1990.

Winkler, Dietmar W., and Li Tang, eds. *Hidden Treasures and Intercultural Encounters: Studies on East Syriac Christianity in China and Central Asia.* Vienna: LIT Verlag, 2014.

Worcester, Thomas, ed. *The Cambridge Companion to the Jesuits.* Cambridge: Cambridge University Press, 2008.

Yates, Timothy. *The Conversion of the Maori: Years of Religious and Social Change, 1814–1842.* Grand Rapids: Eerdmans, 2013.

Zwiep, Mary. *Pilgrim Path: The First Company of Women Missionaries to Hawaii.* Madison: University of Wisconsin Press, 1991.

Index